Learning the Art of Helping

Building Blocks and Techniques

Third Edition

Mark E. Young
University of Central Florida

PEARSON

Merrill
Prentice Hall

Upper Saddle River, New Jersey
Columbus, Ohio

Library of Congress Cataloging-in-Publication Data

Young, Mark E.
   Learning the art of helping: building blocks and techniques / Mark E. Young. — 3rd ed.
     p. cm.
   Includes bibliographical references and index.
   ISBN 0-13-111753-X
    1. Counseling. 2. Psychotherapy. I. Title.

   BF637.C6Y583 2005
   158'.3–dc22
                                                             2004049233

Vice President and Executive Publisher: Jeffery W. Johnston
Publisher: Kevin M. Davis
Development Editor: Autumn Crisp Benson
Editorial Assistant: Amanda J. King
Production Editor: Mary Harlan
Production Coordinator: Lea Baranowski, Carlisle Publishers Services
Design Coordinator: Diane C. Lorenzo
Text Design and Illustrations: Carlisle Publishers Services
Cover Design: Jason Moore
Cover Image: Corbis
Production Manager: Laura Messerly
Director of Marketing: Ann Castel Davis
Marketing Manager: Autumn Purdy
Marketing Coordinator: Tyra Poole

This book was set in ITC Century by Carlisle Communications, Ltd. It was printed and bound by
R. R. Donnelley & Sons Company. The cover was printed by Coral Graphics Services, Inc.

Pearson Prentice Hall™ is a trademark of Pearson Education, Inc.
Pearson® is a registered trademark of Pearson plc
Prentice Hall® is a registered trademark of Pearson Education, Inc.
Merrill® is a registered trademark of Pearson Education, Inc.

Pearson Education Ltd.   Pearson Education Australia Pty. Limited
Pearson Education Singapore Pte. Ltd.   Pearson Education North Asia Ltd.
Pearson Education Canada, Ltd.   Pearson Education de Mexico, S.A. de C.V.
Pearson Education—Japan   Pearson Education Malaysia Pte. Ltd.

10 9 8 7 6 5 4 3 2
ISBN: 0-13-111753-X

To Joe, Claire, and Olivia Begalla and to Isabelle Young
My riches

About the Author

Mark Young is a Professor at the University of Central Florida. He received his doctorate from Ohio University in 1985. He has trained helpers for more than 17 years and worked in community mental health, private practice, college counseling centers, and corrections for more than 20 years. His professional writing has focused mainly on therapeutic methods and techniques and couples counseling. If you have comments or suggestions on what you have read, please send e-mail to *meyoung@mail.ucf.edu*.

Preface

An overarching metaphor is used in this book: that learning the art of helping is a journey with a beginning but no real end point. Those who embark on this quest find it to be a lifelong process of discovery rather than a destination. There is always more to learn about human behavior and the process of change.

Let us take the metaphor one step further. Let us suppose that two people are traveling to a foreign country to learn more about it. One is an engineer and the other is a historian. As they travel together, the engineer will notice and respond to the bridges and buildings, while the historian looks for monuments and clues to the great events of the past. If you were the tour guide for these two people, you would want to know something about each person's interests to accommodate them on the trip. Learning words and phrases that incorporate engineering feats or historical situations might increase interest and make each learner feel that his or her field is important. Similarly, in your journey to become a helper, you bring along your life experience, family history, and cultural background, as well as your biases and prejudices, likes and dislikes. At every stage, you will test your new learning against what you already know. You will accept most readily those things that fit within your present way of looking at the world.

Not every learning environment can achieve this kind of tailor-made curriculum. Your teachers will probably not have the time to really think about the background you bring to this new experience. But you can be responsible for your own learning and integrate new thoughts with what you already know by the process of reflection. In every chapter, there are opportunities to stop and reflect and to engage in additional learning activities. The decision to present the material in this way is based on the philosophy that, as an individual, you carry with you a set of assumptions about the world that affects what you learn and how you assimilate new learning. New material becomes connected to the storehouse of information you have already collected and the skills you presently possess. Reflecting on new material helps you integrate it with what you already know, but it also lays bare your prejudices and untested assumptions. For this reason, the process of reflection is not as benign as it may first appear. If you really become involved in reflecting and make it a habit, you will have made a giant step on your journey. You will have made a commitment to understanding yourself as well as those you are trying to help.

Reflection means thinking about new learning through writing, contemplation, or discussion with others. It is particularly important to reflect on issues that cause you emotional distress, that clash with what you already know, and that you have trouble grasping. Learning to reflect is a skill that will serve you well in difficult situations on the journey to become a professional helper. Helping is filled with difficult diagnostic, ethical, and practical problems. By incorporating a reflective process early in your journey, you will avoid many of the pitfalls caused by making snap judgments.

There are several effective methods for reflecting. They include discussing your thoughts with a small group, bouncing your ideas off another person, or e-mailing your views to fellow learners and teachers. One of the best ways to learn to reflect is through the use of a journal. A journal is not just a collection of emotional reactions. It should include your feelings about the material, but it should also contain a serious consideration of alternative viewpoints or competing voices. In other words, use reflection when you find yourself at a crossroads between two points of view. Learn to state your current thinking on a particular topic and then write down an alternative viewpoint as well. For example, you may have learned that advice giving is a very helpful technique in dealing with friends and families. In this book, it is rather strongly stated that you should consider retiring this skill for now because it is not very effective and can, at times, be dangerous. Before deciding on this dilemma, perhaps you could write a bit on the virtues of each argument instead of blindly accepting my premise or rigidly sticking to your own point of view. See if there is a way to integrate these divergent positions.

There is a Japanese exercise called "the pillow technique" that illustrates good reflective thinking. Each corner of the pillow represents an area to ponder when a controversy arises. The exercise begins when you can identify two contrasting viewpoints on a topic; A is true or B is true. For example, A = giving advice is extremely helpful, and B = giving advice is not helpful. In reflecting on the issue, move methodically from one corner of the pillow to the next, giving each point of view due consideration. In the first corner, think of all the reasons you believe that giving advice is extremely helpful. In the second corner, think of all the reasons why advice is *not* helpful. At the third corner, think of all the reasons why neither A nor B is true, and finally in the fourth corner, list all the ways that A and B might both be true.

Of course, it is not necessary to go through this entire process when you reflect on the material in this book. But it should be a conscious process for which you set aside time. That is why Journal Starters have been included in each chapter. If you wish, you can choose one of the starters and write a new journal entry for each chapter as you go along. Alternatively, you can choose to write in your journal when you experience a conflict or wish to test out a new idea. Try to write about those things that interest, excite, or trouble you. Share your writings with others and reflect together.

Organization of the Book

This book contains 15 chapters and teaches 21 basic building block skills and several more advanced skills as well. Chapters 1 and 2 introduce you to the book, its organization, and its approach. Chapter 3 delves deeply into the therapeutic relationship, perhaps the most important ingredient for producing change. Chapter 4, new to this edition, introduces the topic of differences between helper and client that create challenges and barriers. Chapters 5, 6, 7, and 8 teach the basic helping skills, including non-verbal skills, opening skills, reflecting, and advanced reflecting. Chapter 9, entitled "Challenging Skills," teaches how to give feedback and how to confront inconsistencies in a client's story. Chapter 10 is an overview of basic assessment techniques to collect data and gain a clearer picture of the client and the client's problems. Chapter 11 adds goal-setting skills so that you can narrow down the list of client issues and focus on the most important. Chapter 12 is called "Solution Skills." Solution skills are techniques to assist clients in creatively solving problems. Chapter 13, "Outcome Evaluation and Termination Skills," explains how to set and measure outcomes and how to deal with the final phase of the helping relationship. The final two chapters of the book, Chapters 14 and 15, are organized around curative, or "therapeutic," factors. These are the "megaskills" that helpers from different persuasions commonly use to enhance client growth. In this book, we describe six factors. The first is the therapeutic relationship, which is covered in Chapter 3. It is so important that I decided to address this early in the book. The remaining curative factors are enhancing efficacy and self-esteem (Chapter 14), practicing new behaviors (Chapter 14), lowering and raising emotional arousal (Chapter 15), activating client expectations, motivation, and hope (Chapter 15), and providing new learning experiences (Chapter 15). Under each of these therapeutic factors, you will learn standard helping techniques such as role-playing, relaxation, and reframing. Although these techniques are more advanced, once you have established the foundation with the building blocks, you will be ready to construct these more elaborate methods.

Acknowledgments

In my own journey, there have been many who have taught and inspired me to be a better person and a better helper. I must acknowledge my teachers Rajinder Singh, J. Melvin Witmer, Harry Dewire, and James Pinnell. I must also mention my friends who have encouraged me in my writing, Sam Gladding, Gerald Corey, Jeffrey Kottler, Adam Blatner, John Norcross, and Jerome Frank. I appreciate the feedback from my colleagues at Ohio State University, Darcy and Paul Granello, and I recognize the helpful comments of those who reviewed the previous edition and suggested improvements for the third edition: David Duys, Southern Illinois University at Carbondale; Anne Medill, Northern Arizona University; Ken Miller, San Francisco State University; and Zarus E. P. Watson, University of New Orleans.

I would like to thank my editor, Kevin Davis, for his confidence and his high expectations that helped to make this book so much better. I am also grateful for the work of Mary Harlan and Autumn Benson at Merrill/Prentice Hall and of Lea Baranowski at Carlisle Communications, who helped to edit this manuscript and manage its production. Finally, I recognize the contribution of my wife, Jora, who is both my most demanding critic and my staunchest supporter.

Discover the Companion Website Accompanying This Book

The Prentice Hall Companion Website: A Virtual Learning Environment

Technology is a constantly growing and changing aspect of our field that is creating a need for content and resources. To address this emerging need, Prentice Hall has developed an online learning environment for students and professors alike—Companion Websites—to support our textbooks.

In creating a Companion Website, our goal is to build on and enhance what the textbook already offers. For this reason, the content for each user-friendly website is organized by topic and provides the professor and student with a variety of meaningful resources. Common features of a Companion Website include:

For the Professor—

Every Companion Website integrates **Syllabus Manager™,** an online syllabus creation and management utility.

- **Syllabus Manager™** provides you, the instructor, with an easy, step-by-step process to create and revise syllabi, with direct links into Companion Website and other online content without having to learn HTML.
- Students may logon to your syllabus during any study session. All they need to know is the web address for the Companion Website and the password you've assigned to your syllabus.
- After you have created a syllabus using **Syllabus Manager™** students may enter the syllabus for their course section from any point in the Companion Website.
- Clicking on a date, the student is shown the list of activities for the assignment. The activities for each assignment are linked directly to actual content, saving time for students.
- Adding assignments consists of clicking on the desired due date, then filling in the details of the assignment—name of the assignment, instructions, and whether it is a one-time or repeating assignment.

- In addition, links to other activities can be created easily. If the activity is online, a URL can be entered in the space provided, and it will be linked automatically in the final syllabus.
- Your completed syllabus is hosted on our servers, allowing convenient updates from any computer on the Internet. Changes you make to your syllabus are immediately available to your students at their next logon.

For the Student—

- **Counseling Topics**—17 core counseling topics represent the diversity and scope of today's counseling field.
- **Annotated Bibliography**—includes seminal foundational works and key current works.
- **Web Destinations**—lists significant and up-to-date practitioner and client sites.
- **Professional Development**—provides helpful information regarding professional organizations and codes of ethics.
- **Electronic Bluebook**—send homework or essays directly to your instructor's email with this paperless form.
- **Message Board**—serves as a virtual bulletin board to post—or respond to—questions or comments to/from a national audience.
- **Chat**—real-time chat with anyone who is using the text anywhere in the country—ideal for discussion and study groups, class projects, etc.

To take advantage of these and other resources, please visit the *Learning the Art of Helping: Building Blocks and Techniques*, Third Edition, Companion Website at

www.prenhall.com/young

Research Navigator: Research Made Simple!

www.ResearchNavigator.com

Merrill Education is pleased to introduce Research Navigator—a one-stop research solution for students that simplifies and streamlines the entire research process. At *www.researchnavigator.com,* students will find extensive resources to enhance their understanding of the research process so they can effectively complete research assignments. In addition, Research Navigator has three exclusive databases of credible and reliable source content to help students focus their research efforts and begin the research process.

How Will Research Navigator Enhance Your Course?

- Extensive content helps students understand the research process, including writing, doing research on the Internet, and citing sources.
- Step-by-step tutorial guides students through the entire research process from selecting a topic to revising a rough draft.
- Research Writing in the Disciplines section details the differences in research across disciplines.
- Three exclusive databases—EBSCO's ContentSelect Academic Journal Database, the *New York Times* Search by Subject Archive, and "Best of the Web" Link Library—allow students to easily find journal articles and sources.

What's the Cost?

A subscription to Research Navigator is $7.50 but is **free** when ordered in conjunction with this textbook. To obtain free passcodes for your students, simply contact your local Merrill/Prentice Hall sales representative, and your representative will send you the Evaluating Online Resource Guide, which contains the code to access Research Navigator as well as tips on how to use Research Navigator and how to evaluate research. To preview the value of this website to your students, please go to *www.educatorlearningcenter.com* and use the login name "Research" and the password "Demo."

Brief Contents

Contents

9   Challenging Skills   174

10   Assessment and the Initial Interview   196

14 Curative Factors and Advanced Skills: Part I   282

Note: Every effort has been made to provide accurate and current Internet information in this book. However, the Internet and information posted on it are constantly changing, so it is inevitable that some of the Internet addresses listed in this textbook will change.

Helping as a Personal Journey

1

L earning to be a professional helper is a journey that takes years. It is a personal journey because you must be committed to understanding yourself as well as your clients. In this book you will learn the essential counseling skills, but it is not enough to be skilled; at every turn, you face self-doubt, personal prejudices, and feelings of attraction, repulsion, and frustration. Helpers typically experience self-doubt when clients encounter complex and unfamiliar problems; they typically experience attraction and repulsion because of the helpers' needs and prejudices based on cultural conditioning. All helpers become frustrated at times when clients fail to reach the goals expected of them. These reactions can be roadblocks on our journey if they interfere with our ability to form a solid client/helper relationship or when we see the client as a reflection of ourselves rather than as a unique human being. This journey requires that we simultaneously try to focus on the client while keeping a strict eye on our own tendencies to judge, to boost our egos, or to force our viewpoint on others.

Becoming a Reflective Practitioner

Because of the challenges caused by our personal reactions and unique client characteristics, we believe that helpers need a method of integrating new learning and coping with moments of indecision and doubt. In this book, we teach one method of dealing with the dilemma of understanding the client and monitoring the self. This is an approach called the *reflective practitioner*. Being a reflective practitioner means that you make a commitment to personal awareness of your automatic reactions and prejudices by taking time to think back on them and perhaps record them in a journal or discuss them with a supervisor or colleague. In other words, the helper consciously reviews what has happened and decides on a plan of action. Jeffrey Kottler (2004) considers reflection to be not only a necessary characteristic of an effective helper but also a benefit. It trains one to be open to contemplation, to become resourceful and inquisitive in one's lifestyle as well as in one's work.

You may find that your teachers ask you to use reflective methods in class and on your own. For example, your teacher might use Socratic questioning, ask you to do journal writing, have you watch and reflect on video segments, or divide the class into small groups to react to case studies or reflecting teams (Griffith & Frieden, 2000). Just as every client will not respond to the same technique or skill in exactly the same way, you as a student will react to different learning situations based on your history and favored learning styles. Some students learn best by listening and then reflecting; others need to write down what they are learning; some do best when they can have hands on experience and then talk about the theory. Thus, you will respond differently to different assignments throughout your program of study based on your individual preferences. Still, reflection can help you even when a teacher's method does not suit your learning style. You can record what is said and then write your reaction and rebuttals in the margins. You can come to class with questions and concerns based on last week's lesson.

Using Reflection to Help You Overcome Challenging Helping Situations and Enhance Your Learning

If you are engaged in a course of study to become a professional helper, you will be confronted with many new learning experiences both when you are in the classroom and when you actually meet your clients. For example, a client may be hostile and uncooperative. Your training tells you to help the client to articulate his or her concerns more fully. But this seems to make the client even madder. The process of reflection can help at such times. Let me give an example from my own experience. When I was first learning group counseling, I read in several textbooks that clients should never receive both group and individual therapy at the same time. As I began to practice group counseling, I found support for this rule in the fact that when clients received both treatments, they did not contribute to the group, saving their most personal issues for their individual sessions. One day I received a new client for my group who had undergone a number of very traumatic events and was still in individual counseling with another therapist. She performed beautifully in group, and she felt that individual counseling was a vital support in her life. I went to my supervisor with my dilemma. Normally, I would insist on the client dropping out of individual counseling while she attended my group, but now my rule of thumb was in jeopardy because it did not seem to be limiting her progress or the group. In fact, she was applying the insights of individual counseling to her interpersonal world! I revealed my dilemma to my supervisor, and she helped me try to put my old rule and my new experience together. With her help, I constructed a revised rule: "Most of the time, clients will not benefit from both forms of treatment; however, there are times, especially when the client is in need of a great deal of support, that both modalities might be beneficial." I have found that the process of reflection allows me to better accommodate new information rather than rejecting it out of hand. You will undoubtedly experience similar moments as you study the skills of helping. You may be shocked when you discover that the methods you have always used to help your friends are not recommended in a counseling relationship. At times like these, reflection can help you meld old and new information.

Using Reflection When Helping Clients with Backgrounds Different from Your Own

An important and frequent challenge occurs when you encounter people who are completely different from you in one or several ways: culture or ethnicity, socioeconomics, education, race, and family rules and relationships. For example, you will encounter family situations where people openly express their thoughts and feelings and others where they rarely if ever reveal their inner lives to each other. Because of your own upbringing, you might be shocked or you might disapprove. If you undertake the challenge of becoming a reflective practitioner, allow yourself to register surprise and all the other emotions as you encounter these novel situations. Later, take time to think back on what you know and what you have learned and compare it with your new experience. Through reflecting, you will be better able to separate your personal prejudices about what seems normal and perhaps look at the situation from an alternate viewpoint. The ability to see another perspective is enhanced when you have the opportunity to reflect with teachers, fellow students, and supervisors. Growth means that we expand and are able to see multiple viewpoints. That is why we think of helpers as "expanders," not "shrinks."

Using Reflection to Accommodate New Information About Yourself

Perhaps more than any other profession, helping requires helpers to become aware of their own personalities, preferences, values, and feelings. Reflection can help you integrate new discoveries that you make about yourself. It allows you to carefully consider the feedback you are getting from supervisors, teachers, fellow students, and even your clients. In the course of your training, others will comment on your interpersonal style (the typical way you interact with others), your words, and even your gestures and posture. You will frequently become defensive, rationalizing your mistakes, discounting the person who gives the feedback, or blaming the client for a lack of progress. These are natural reflexes to the threat of feeling uncertain, impotent, or incompetent. The reflective practitioner is one who examines and reflects upon critical incidents and strong personal feelings in the course of supervision, rather than making excuses or blaming others. So being a reflective practitioner also means having the courage to ask for feedback from others and then to reflect on how you can work more effectively in a particularly difficult situation (Schön, 1983). The following discussion describes some ways that you can be proactive in reflecting on your practice, including asking for supervision, developing a support group of fellow learners, becoming a client yourself, keeping a personal journal, and completing the exercises in this book.

Ask for Supervision

Supervision is the practice of a helper and a supervisor sitting down to review the helper's problems and successes with clients. In supervision, you will reflect on possible courses of action, ethical issues, and personal reactions. Everyone in the helping field needs periodic supervision whether he or she is a student or a long-time practitioner. Professional helpers are required to be under supervision while they are students and during their postdegree internships. Lawrence LeShan (1996) reported that his own mentor still sought supervision for herself, even when she was in her 80s, indicating that the reflective process is necessary at all stages of the journey. As a student, you may have the opportunity to ask supervisors and faculty members to look at your tapes and discuss cases with you. Make use of this valuable opportunity to reflect on your work.

Develop a Support Group of Fellow Learners

Another golden opportunity for reflecting on your new learning is to develop a supportive group of colearners with whom you can discuss your personal reactions. Many therapists in private practice are members of such groups. In some training programs, students are part of a cohort or group that goes through every class together. If you are not part of a cohort, you can still develop a supportive group that meets regularly, shares information, and studies together.

Become a Client

Another way of building in a reflective component is to enter a counseling relationship as a client. More than half of therapists enter therapy after their advanced training, and about 90 percent consider it to be very beneficial (Norcross, 1990). Many universities offer free counseling to students, and this may be a way to experience what it is like to sit in the other chair. You should be aware that some schools restrict their counseling centers to people who are in critical need.

Keep a Personal Journal

One of the most popular methods for reflecting is to keep a personal journal. Journaling about one's problems, feelings, relationships, and dreams has dramatically increased in recent years. Some helpers even use journals as a therapeutic technique (Stone, 1998). They write their reflections to clients in letters, or client and counselor journal together and compare notes. There is also a boom in online Internet journals. For example, the American Association of Retired Persons (AARP) has an online journal for those experiencing grief and loss which can be downloaded from the AARP web site. There is even a magazine called *Personal Journaling*.

Learning to Reflect Through Exercises in This Book

As you read this book, there will be several opportunities to develop this reflective habit. In every chapter, we have included "Stop and Reflect" sections that ask you to consider your reaction to real cases or situations. You will also have the opportunity to receive feedback from your fellow students and to reflect on your own progress when you practice new skills. Finally, we have included suggested journal questions at the end of each chapter. These questions are meant to kindle your thinking, but do not feel that answering these questions is your only journaling option. If you do not find the stimulus question to be relevant, design your own, or record your reaction to practice sessions each week.

Reflecting on Your Attitudes About Helping

Now, let us practice reflecting by responding to an inventory of your attitudes about helping. The key step is to record your answers and then think back on what they might reveal about you. Rather than writing what might impress your teacher or fellow students in this self-assessment, respond as honestly as possible. Toward the middle of this course and again at the end, you may wish to review this inventory, change your answers, reflect on the inventory in writing, and determine if your attitudes have shifted. For the time being, answer the questions and then write down a reflection or two about what you notice in your answers. Remember, the "Stop and Reflect" sections in this book have no right or wrong answers. They ask for personal reactions and, the hope is, will stimulate your thinking. They can make your learning more interactive if you take the time to respond as authentically as you can. When you are asked to agree or disagree, try to be as honest as possible and be aware of any internal censoring that occurs. You may or may not wish to share your answers with others during a class discussion, but by putting your answers on paper, you can take a step back and look at your thoughts from a more objective viewpoint. You may find that your implicit viewpoints about human nature, your attitudes about helping, and your personal values come into sharper focus. Let us begin this experiment in reflecting by becoming aware of the basic attitudes you bring to the helping relationship.

Stop and Reflect

1. Write A or D next to each of the following statements indicating whether you agree or disagree. Put down any thoughts that may clarify or qualify your responses.

D - clients are kids who are sent / dont seek me

    a. In most cases, clients come to me for help because they are in a crisis. They need leadership. In order to help, I should generally be active and directive, providing guidance and advice.

A b. Clients may have different values about families, religious principles, and what is important in life. It is not up to me to change clients' values or even talk about such personal issues.

but many def's of good dep on clients needs

A c. The relationship between helper and client must be a good one. Without "good chemistry," the counseling process will be difficult, if not impossible.

though I'm not sure I'm good at it.

A d. I must remain at a professional distance. Caring too much about a client makes me lose my objectivity.

    e. People are responsible for their own problems. I must get clients to work on themselves, rather than blaming others.

D f. If I have not been through an experience personally, I cannot help another person deal with it.

if a little disclosure helps rapport. fables?

D g. I should never disclose anything personal to a client; the client's issues should be paramount.

2. Answer the following questions:

    As a helper, which do you think you are most likely to focus on in helping a client to change? (You may circle more than one.)

    a. A client's feelings
    b. A client's thoughts and perceptions
    c. A client's behaviors

Why? _____

_____

    When talking with a client about a problem, which do you think are most likely to interest you?

    a. The history of the problem
    b. The present difficulties caused by the problem
    c. The client's future goals

Why? _____

_____

    Do you think a helper is more responsible for helping a client adjust to the difficulties in the world or for changing the society that breeds these problems?

Why? *both but more helping the client - thats your resp*

and you have to be realistic about possibilities
for social change

3. Describe briefly a specific circumstance in which you actually displayed each of the following helper characteristics:

Empathy (the ability to put yourself in the shoes of another, to understand the other person's subjective reality):

_____

_____

Positive regard (the ability to respect another person even though you may not like what he or she has done):

_____

_____

Genuineness (the ability to be honest and open with another person even though what you have to say might be difficult to express):

_____

_____

Courage to confront (the ability to bring up inconsistent thoughts, feelings, and behaviors displayed by the client and the willingness to address "touchy subjects"):

_____

_____

4. The following are some difficult situations helpers face. Rank-order them from 1 to 5, depending on how uncomfortable you might feel in each case. In this ranking system, 5 denotes the most difficult for you and 1 is the least difficult.
   5 • A client is considering suicide.
   1 • A client is suffering from the death of a loved one.
   2 • A client is struggling over whether to get an abortion.
   4 • A client has religious beliefs that you feel are wrong.
   1 • An adolescent client is trying to decide whether he is gay or straight.
   4 • A married client is having an affair.
5. Stop and Reflect: As you look back on your answers, what life experiences have probably shaped your answers? Which issues are most likely to elicit conflict and personal challenges for you during your training? Which answers were the most difficult for you to answer? Where were you stumped? Where were you most confident?

How a Helper Develops: Perry's Stages

Susan has known for a long time that she wants to work with people. During her teenage years, a school counselor helped her cope during her parents' divorce. She worked as a camp counselor and really enjoyed helping kids. Since then, she has always hoped to work in a helping profession. She is finally taking her first course, a techniques class where she will begin her formal training. Suddenly, she is filled with a combination of excitement and apprehension. What if she can't do it? What if she says the wrong thing in front of the class or to a fragile client? She is confident in her abilities to memorize facts from the textbook and to select the best answers in multiple-choice exams, but can she really learn and demonstrate her skills? Is she in the wrong place? Three weeks into the class, Susan is still nervous. When her professor calls on her to practice a role play, her stomach is in knots. She feels light-headed as she makes her way to the front of the classroom. She fears that she will forget the skills she has just learned, that she will make a mistake, that her mind will go blank, and that she will appear foolish to her classmates and professor. After a few weeks of practice, Susan has some moments of accomplishment as she gets feedback from her teacher and fellow students. She still struggles, but there are moments when she feels more comfortable and confident.

Beginning a new course of study can be simultaneously exciting, overwhelming, and intimidating. Maybe you have even watched an experienced professional at work and thought, "How does he or she know what to say? How will I ever know the right answers?" Perhaps you also feel apprehensive as you read this, wondering whether you will ever learn to help with words. The desire to learn the "right" answers and to make the "right" interventions, and the nervousness that accompanies it, is a natural part of the process of becoming a helper. It may be helpful to know that students often progress through a series of developmental stages and that this tendency to want answers immediately is normal. Let us begin with an overview of the developmental stages that you can expect to experience during your training. The stages of cognitive development presented here are based on the work of Perry (1970), who studied undergraduate students during a 20-year period. Later research found that Perry's stages are also applicable to graduate students learning a new profession (Simpson, Dalgaard, & O'Brien, 1986) and also to counseling students (Fong, Borders, Ethington, & Pitts, 1998; Granello, 2002).

By recognizing these stages as they arise, you may be able to avoid some of the discouragement that may accompany learning new skills when you realize that you are on the expected path. You may also be able to identify some ways to get beyond the thinking patterns that are holding you back. The three stages are the dualistic stage, the multiplistic stage, and the relativistic stage.

The Dualistic, or "Right/Wrong," Stage

The first stage is a dualistic or absolutist position that can also be called the "right/wrong" stage. It is characterized by the belief that a helper's responses to a client are either right or wrong. In the beginning, trainees often believe that there is only one right way to respond to a client's statement or situation. This black/white, success/failure way of thinking increases the internal pressure and makes helpers overly concerned with their own performance. Moreover, they may fail to listen fully to their clients because they are thinking about what they are going to say next. They may feel that by planning their next statement, they will be able to construct a better response. Actually, they are losing the train of the interview. Students in this stage often ask for direct feedback with questions such as "Was that right?" "How long should I wait before giving advice?" and "What should I have told the client when she asked me that question?"

The Multiplistic Stage

As you learn the therapeutic building blocks presented in the early chapters of this book, you will recognize that there are actually many possible responses to each statement a client makes. Eventually, you will become comfortable with the knowledge that there is no one right answer at any moment in the helping process. Because of the diversity in clients' backgrounds, experiences, and worldviews, what is "right" for one client is not helpful at all to another.

For example, a client considering leaving her boyfriend might say something like this: "I think that I should get out of the relationship, and then other times I think that I should stay. Everyone is giving me advice. What do you suggest?"

You might react in several different ways.

You could respond with a question: "What aspects of the relationship make you question whether you should continue it?"

You could respond with a reflection of feeling: "You feel overwhelmed and confused, and you would like someone to guide you."

You could respond with a confrontation: "On the one hand, you are saying that you are confused by all the advice; on the other hand, you want me to give my viewpoint. How will another viewpoint help?"

Each of these responses could be helpful, depending on the client's situation. When you discover that there are several right answers to the same client statement, you will have moved into a multiplistic way of thinking. In fact, at the multiplistic stage, all interventions and techniques may seem equally appropriate. You may find yourself feeling overwhelmed by so many possibilities and wonder what differentiates a good response from a great one.

Students at this stage often report being frustrated and defensive with supervisors who "correct" them because they do not yet know how to select the most helpful course of action. All roads seem to be equally valid. For example, a student may pose a series of probing questions to a client. The supervisor might point out, in turn, that the questions made the client feel interrogated and that the best idea would have been to identify and reflect the client's feelings. The student at the multiplistic stage knows that questioning can be a valid approach, but he or she does not yet understand when this approach is most appropriate and therefore concludes that a mistake has been made. Students at this stage may feel that because there are many possible "right" responses to a given situation, there is no organized system in helping. In fact, the students' ideas may seem just as valid as the instructor's. Here are some common statements students make at this phase of development, indicating their confusion when confronted with several helpful responses:

"I watched Albert Ellis on film. He was very effective, and he didn't do any of the things you taught us."

"I can't see why you told me not to ask so many closed questions when you told Ximena that it was all right with her client."

"I thought you said that we weren't supposed to give advice, and now you're saying that I should have given this client more direction."

The Relativistic Stage

When you have gained some experience through study and practice, you will move into a relativistic stage. At this stage, you will recognize that although many types of responses may be appropriate, depending on circumstances, some are relatively better than others. You will become more skilled at choosing from the many possibilities based on the available information and on the goals for the session.

Let us reconsider the client we discussed earlier who was asking for help with a relationship problem. The client said, "I think that I should get out of the relationship, and then other times I think that I should stay. Everyone is giving me advice. What do you suggest?" We identified three different possible helper responses, each of which leads in a different direction. The interventions and possible client reactions are as follows:

Question: "What aspects of the relationship make you question whether you should continue it?"
Response: The client will probably discuss the good and bad points of the relationship.
Reflection of feeling: "You feel overwhelmed and confused, and you would like someone to guide you."
Response: The client will talk about feelings and may indicate why she feels so helpless.
Confrontation: "On the one hand, you are saying that you are confused by all the advice; on the other hand, you want me to give my viewpoint. How will another viewpoint help?"
Response: The client may respond with anger at the helper's perception that she is maintaining her confusion by asking people for advice. The client may also begin to explore her lack of confidence in her own decisions.

Obviously, none of these responses is glaringly wrong, but each will take the session in a different direction. When you reach the relativistic stage, you will judge a response as good or bad depending on whether it takes the session in the direction you want to go. You will have moved past a belief in right or wrong answers and toward an understanding that your choice of responses will have particular repercussions. This will happen when you have the knowledge and self-confidence to make effective choices among a wide variety of interventions and techniques. As contrasted with the dualistic stage, you will probably not be so concerned with your own performance, and you will be better able to think about the effects of certain responses on the client and the effectiveness of the responses in reaching the desired goals. Achieving the relativistic stage takes time. By becoming a reflective practitioner, you can speed this process along; however, it has been my experience that you may not become a comfortable resident of the relativistic stage until long after this course is over.

Do Counselors Develop?

Darcy Granello's (2002) article entitled "Assessing the Cognitive Development of Counseling Students: Changes and Epistemological Assumptions" deserves special attention. In her research, Dr. Granello studied counselors as they progressed through their training (longitudinal study), and she also compared groups of students who were at different stages in their training (cross-sectional study). In general, she found that counselors do change in their thinking along the lines Perry suggests (though perhaps not so neatly). The students in her study showed most growth during the later stages of their training—when they are most involved with clients. Experience in human services, age, and grade point average seemed to have no effect on how quickly students developed. What we can take away from this study are that (1) time may be a necessary factor in training even for those who are older and wiser and have previous experience and (2) contact with clients may accelerate our growth when it is in combination with ongoing training.

The main value of thinking about stages of development is that it can help you recognize that your struggles are part of a normal progression. In the beginning, try to focus less on grades and right answers. Instead, keep your focus on the effects your interventions are having on your clients. Listening to feedback and reflecting on it and making changes based on the feedback will be the most helpful tools to spur your development as a helper.

The Development of Expertise

Another way of thinking about helper development is that it is a matter of developing expertise or mastery. This definition is more skills-oriented than Perry's cognitive system. The concept of levels of expertise is a commonsense approach that has been around for centuries, especially in the skilled trades. For example, we often hear of a master carpenter, master plumber, or master electrician. The terms *master counselor* and *master therapist* have also been used among helpers. For instance, the American Association of Marriage and Family Therapists has, for a long time, invited and videotaped master therapists working with real clients. It has long been known that expertise in helping does not come solely from university degrees or from years of experience. Becoming a master is probably the result of training, experience, mentoring, and a passion and zeal for the profession that keeps one a lifetime learner.

Robert Hoffman and his associates (1995) have studied the concept of expertise and concluded that mastery comes after a long period of hands-on experience, perhaps even 10 years, during which one gains at least 50,000 bits of information (Hoffman, Shadboldt, Burton, & Klein, 1995). Thus, it is understandable that expertise in helping also takes a lengthy apprenticeship because of the vast differences among clients and the immense amount of knowledge needed to assess, diagnose, and treat various disorders and problems. Hoffman and his colleagues use traditional "guild" terminology from the trades to divide expertise into seven stages. In Table 1.1, you will see this concept applied to the development of expertise in helping (Young, 1998).

Implications of the Concept of Expertise to Training Helpers

The first piece of disappointing news is that one cannot master the art of helping in 1 semester or even 2 years of training. Sometimes it is overwhelming when you realize

Table 1.1

"Guild" Terminology for Helper Development (Based on Hoffman et al., 1995)

Naivette	One who knows nothing about the practice or counseling of psychotherapy—a layperson. This term was coined by Hoffman to identify a person who is completely naive to the trade.
Novice	The word novice means one who is new. The novice is a new trainee who is on probation, for example, someone beginning the first class in basic counseling skills but not yet accepted into the program.
Initiate	A person who has been selected for a program and has begun introductory training—a new student in his or her first semester.
Apprentice	A student still undergoing instruction but who is beyond the introductory level. The apprentice is fully immersed in the practice of counseling and works as an assistant. Students in practicum and internship experiences are apprentices. In the trades, apprenticeship lasts from 1 to 12 years.
Journeyman	Journeyman means one who can do a day's work unsupervised. A journeyman works on orders from his or her supervisor. In the counseling field, this period may last 2 to 3 years after graduation before the supervisor or the licensing state allows the person to work independently.
Expert	An expert is an exceptional journeyman who is highly thought of by his or her peers, whose diagnostic and counseling skills are exceptionally accurate, and who can quickly and effectively deal with normal counseling situations. In addition, the expert is one who can handle "tough cases" and may have some particular area of expertise based on considerable experience with a particular type of problem—for example, substance abuse, crisis intervention, domestic violence, and so on. Expert status is by no means inevitable. Some helpers stay at the journeyman stage for life.
Master	A master therapist is one of a select group of experts who are qualified to teach others. A master is one whose judgments and practices become standards for others to follow. One way to identify a master is that he or she is regarded as an expert by other experts. Frequently, this is because the master is thought of as "the expert" in a particular area within the field.

Source: Young, M. E. (1998). Skills-based training for counselors: Microskills or mega-skills? *Counseling and Human Development, 31,* 2. Reprinted with permission of Love Publishing.

how much there is to know. Although becoming a master in the helping arts is a lifetime journey, we sometimes expect to have some measure of competence quickly. Those feelings may elude you for quite some time. Take comfort in the small victories when your instructor or fellow students notice your progress—even if it is hard for you to see.

A second implication is that, despite what state legislatures allow, a new helper is probably not able to handle all the day-to-day decisions independent of supervision after 2 years of education and 2 more years of supervised experience. A journeyman still needs ongoing contact with an expert or master counselor. Supervision is a vital part of the journey because it provides a forum for you to reflect.

Third, people enter this training with varying levels of expertise. A significant number are already journeymen when they register for basic counseling skills training (McLennan, 1994). If you are in this situation, you may feel that your time is being wasted going back over the basic skills. I have frequently taught basic skills to students who have been working as helpers for several years. Invariably, the more experienced students eventually feel that the course has been extremely valuable. They report that it was beneficial to reexamine their basic positions on important questions such as "Under what circumstances should I give advice?" If you already have some helping experience, you may find that on-the-job training has not been systematic and that this course can help fill in the gaps. You may also discover that your experience allows you to make connections not available to you the first time you learned these skills. If you feel that this course is repetitious, ask your instructor for more challenging assignments. Also, with your instructor's permission, find ways to help other members of your training group by giving them detailed feedback. Encourage them to reflect on their learning. You will be learning supervision skills as you do so.

This suggestion is consistent with the findings of Skovholt, Ronnestad, and Jennings (1997), who state that expertise is not merely a cognitive phenomenon. We cannot become an expert merely by cramming our heads with knowledge. Part of what spurs people to the next level of development is learning to reflect on their experiences. Recently I told one of my colleagues that a certain individual should know what he is doing. After all, I said, "he has 15 years experience." "Yes," said my colleague, "but it is the same year over and over again." I believe he was making this same point, albeit in a more cynical way. The process of becoming a master counselor or master therapist takes experience, but it also needs the catalyst of reflection that you must call upon every day.

The Challenge of Development

Although the major shifts in your thinking may follow some of the predictable stages of development described by Perry or noted in the discussion of expertise, there are a number of other challenges that arise. During the initial period of instruction, you will encounter frustration and feelings of incompetence that accompany helping skills training, so much so that many students feel like throwing in the towel. By thinking about these issues now, you may be able to recognize them when they arise and you will deal with them more effectively.

Taking Responsibility for Your Own Learning

Helping skills training requires you to perform skills in front of other people in practice situations. To receive the maximum benefit from practice sessions, you must open yourself up to feedback and suggestions. There is a strong tendency to compare oneself with others and to view training as a competition. Although that may have been a good strategy in some classes, it can be a detriment in learning helping skills because it may keep you from practicing in front of others and receiving the information you need. For example, you may appear to be ahead or behind your classmates as you learn a particular skill in this book. If the class moves ahead, you may need to continue to work on that skill by practicing with fellow students, watching videotapes of your performance, reading, or getting special help from the instructor. You must take responsibility for educating yourself and request the training that you need, rather than seeing the process of learning as a "mug and jug" phenomenon, in which the teacher pours from the jug of knowledge into the student's mug. You must move from teacher-directed learning to student-directed learning (Caffarella, 1993). In your training, this may mean that you face embarrassment if you are honest about what you do not know or cannot do. Although you may be able to keep your difficulties hidden for a little while, eventually you will be alone with a client and you will need these skills to really be of help.

Finding a Mentor

One of the best ways to learn the helping skills is to watch effective models and to receive feedback from teachers. It is a challenge, however, to find experienced helpers who have the time to act as mentors. Once I watched one of my own teachers in a session with a client. I remember saying to myself, "He acts like being with that person is the most important thing in the world." Although I had read about "eye contact," "empathy," and "unconditional positive regard," when I saw the quality of his presence, I grasped, for the first time, how powerful such attention can be. How few are the times when someone really stops to listen.

Teachers and supervisors are vital guides throughout the journey, especially in the beginning, and you must seek them out. As time goes on, it is true that one learns to have more faith and confidence in one's own judgment and abilities (Skovholt & Ronnestad, 1992). Even then, supervision and mentoring are essential for self-assessment and reflection.

Finding the Perfect Technique

Beginning helpers are extremely anxious about learning specific techniques and interventions. They gather techniques and tricks of the trade at workshops, hoping that one will be the magic pill that cures all clients. When you feel anxious or ineffective, it is normal to experience a desire to learn every technique available and assume a sort of "cookbook" approach to helping. There is nothing wrong with learning all you can. It is unlikely, however, that you will find a perfect technique that will work for every client. The pursuit of a perfect technique or silver bullet is characteristic of dualistic, or right/wrong, thinking. In the relativistic stage, you will evaluate a technique to see if it is best for a specific client, with a particular problem, in a particular situation.

In Limbo

As you begin the process of learning to help, you may find that you abandon your "pretraining" natural helping style. Although beginning helpers are often naturally therapeutic, they typically find that they must temporarily set aside their old ways of helping. You may find that the new techniques and interventions feel artificial or "not like me" at first. Do not be surprised to hear yourself say, "I used to know what to do when a friend was upset. Now that I've begun to study helping, I no longer know what to say." Even your attempts to regain your old self seem awkward and artificial. It is a little like the centipede that was asked how she could coordinate those hundred legs and walk. Once she started thinking about it, she couldn't do it. As you consciously learn the helping process, it may be difficult to be natural.

Arnold Lazarus (1990), the founder of multimodal therapy, cautions us that training can sometimes undermine our natural talents. He tells the story of his friend, a dentist, who was a natural listener and was very therapeutic with his patients. But the dentist went back to school to become a therapist. Lazarus felt that the result was a rather phony person who resorted to jargon instead of listening. Perhaps Lazarus's friend was experiencing a stage characterized by overzealousness and insecurity that most new initiates go through. But the story is there to remind us that we have much to lose. If we abandon our genuineness, personal warmth, and all the other qualities that make people feel we are listening and caring, our training will be something to overcome rather than to rely on. It is hoped that as you give up old habits and learn new skills, you will find a way to integrate the old "therapeutic friend" with the new "therapeutic helper."

Accepting Feedback and Being Perfect

Your willingness to accept feedback will be another indicator of developmental change. As noted earlier, students in the dualistic stage accept feedback but feel discouraged when they "do it wrong." In the multiplistic stage, they may be defensive in the face of feedback and attempt to justify their actions, rather than listening to critiques and suggestions. As you gain confidence and see how different responses take clients in different directions, it is easier not to take such criticism personally because you feel confident in your basic skills. The risk in the relativistic stage is that you may be too hard on yourself, demanding perfection when you are just beginning. Try to focus on your strengths, build on what you are doing well, and learn from feedback.

I experienced a similar crisis when I turned from full-time therapist to textbook writer. Although I was confident in my approach to clients, I was sensitive about how my writing would be seen by others. I also know writers who are afraid to show their work to others. Writing and engaging in a therapeutic relationship are both very personal forms of self-expression, and so we are tempted to hide our work and avoid any damage to self-esteem. It turns out that showing our work to others is the fastest road to growth.

Following Ethical Guidelines

We are all familiar with errors in medical treatment. However, we may fail to recognize that clients in a helping relationship can also be harmed by inappropriate advice, emotionally arousing techniques, and subtle messages of contempt when we cannot understand their cultures, religions, families, or beliefs. The Hippocratic challenge to all practitioners of the healing arts is *primum non nocere*, first do no harm. Ethical guidelines help us avoid harm to clients by asking us to adhere to some general rules.

Ethical guidelines have been proposed by virtually every professional organization in the helping professions. These standards can be found in recent publications, and updated versions are available online. Ethical guidelines and codes largely deal with the work environment; however, ethical dilemmas are also likely to arise in your training group. The following are some guidelines you may wish to adopt as a group during your class. Optimally, you should discuss these thoroughly, so that everyone is in agreement. On the other hand, rules are inadequate to deal with every problem that arises. In many cases, it will be necessary to talk with your instructor about how to handle these conflicts.

Guideline 1: Do not reveal what other training group members say about themselves during role-playing and practice sessions.

This means that you should not tell your best friend, your father, or your spouse. Although there may not seem to be any serious harm, forming these boundaries will set up an atmosphere of trust and allow for more freedom for all participants. It may be your first experience in keeping professional secrets. Try thinking of it as a sacred trust, similar to the seal of the confessional taken by Catholic priests.

Guideline 2: Avoid giving advice.

This is a practical suggestion as well as an ethical guideline. From the practical standpoint, you may find that giving advice, especially early on, can damage the relationship and slow down client progress. From the ethical perspective, are you really competent and knowledgeable enough to give advice? Could your advice be dangerous to a person's relationships or his or her academic or professional life? Could it undermine the client's self-confidence? These concerns suggest that you might wish to resist giving advice during this part of your training and develop some alternative skills.

Guideline 3: Do not impose your values on others.

Avoid making value judgments on a person's lifestyle, life experiences, or philosophy of life. Similar to giving advice, your judgments may be based on inadequate knowledge, may reflect your own limited experiences, or may communicate contempt or lack of acceptance of the other person. Learning to be sensitive to the cultural differences and unique experiences of clients helps us to avoid the trap of subtly communicating that a person's values and worldview are unacceptable.

Guideline 4: Be careful with feedback to clients and to fellow students.

Give feedback only when asked, and package it in a way that the other person can accept. Give only specific and constructive feedback. Giving vague and very negative feedback can be damaging. Give feedback on areas where the person wants more information. Sometimes when you are frustrated by a client's lack of movement, you might be tempted to become too confrontational. Before confronting one of your clients, consider whether you are doing this to help the client or to reduce your own feelings of powerlessness. In other words, consider whose needs the confrontation and feedback are meeting.

Guideline 5: Stay mainly with the techniques described in the book or those taught by your instructor.

Using an unfamiliar and potentially harmful method should only be attempted with the guidance and permission of your teacher or supervisor. A powerful technique may have an equally powerful negative effect when misapplied. Generally speaking, reading about a technique or seeing it demonstrated at a workshop is not sufficient training.

Guideline 6: Notify your instructor or supervisor at once if a member of your training group or a client is contemplating suicide or is considering harming others.

Even if you are relatively sure that the probability of violence is low, it is vital that you discuss any suggestion of violence with someone in authority. This is good training for your later work when you must learn to consult when an ethical or clinical problem arises. Although many of the issues described in these guidelines will not surface in your training group, you should still be prepared. Talk with your group about how you might handle specific situations. Make sure everyone is in agreement to abide by the ethical guidelines.

Other Challenges

The Work Environment for Helpers at the Turn of the Century

The work settings of helpers at this point in history are dramatically different from those of 50 years ago. These environments dictate, to some extent, which helping skills will be most utilized. Specifically, at the mid-century mark, psychoanalysis was the accepted paradigm. At that time, clients might have been seen over a period of several years, with sessions two or three times per week. Today, the typical client in a private practice, college counseling center, drug treatment center, hospital, or community counseling setting is seen for only 6 to 10 sessions. Compared with the 1950s, today the sessions are aimed more at achieving specific goals, rather than focusing on the past. Much of this emphasis has been due to the managed care revolution in health care, but there has also been a general disillusionment among helpers about the efficacy of long-term work.

In the 1950s, school counselors focused almost entirely on career testing and career counseling as well as scheduling. Today, school counselors are much more concerned with handling the psychological problems of students and dealing with disruptive and violent behavior. School counselors require keen diagnostic and crisis management skills and work more with parents and families and on a short-term basis. In summary, whether you work in a community, university, private practice, hospital, or school, you will more than likely be challenged to become a brief, present-oriented, and goal-directed helper.

Individual Differences

If you are a member of a minority group or a female, have a disability, are one of the first in your family to attain higher education, or are going through a particularly stressful life stage (e.g., getting married or divorced, leaving home, having children), this can add an additional challenge to the process of becoming a helper. Students facing outside stressors may also have difficulty maintaining the flexible schedule that is required (Gaff & Gaff, 1981). Specifically, consider how the following differences may have an impact:

Minority students may lack same-race peer interactions and minority role models (Cheatham & Berg-Cross, 1992). Female students raised in traditional families may have difficulty trusting in an internal authority (Bernard, 1981; Marx, 1990). Some male students may not be as attuned to relationships and feelings as their female counterparts. Hypermasculine upbringing may cause male trainees to seek solutions quickly before understanding the client. They may fail to recognize such feelings as fear and helplessness in themselves and may therefore have difficulty recognizing them in others.

Such considerations should serve to illustrate that development is not the same for each person, rather than discouraging those with special situations. An individual's progress cannot be confined to a timetable (Barrow, 1987), nor is it necessarily a linear, step-by-step process. Sometimes you may feel that you are taking two steps forward and one step back. Allow yourself time to develop and move at your own pace. Development is not a competition with your classmates; it is a personal journey.

The Perfect Helper, or When Do I Quit Developing?

Your development as a professional helper does not end with graduation; it is a lifelong process toward mastery. Academic training will give you the skills, but practice, supervision, networking, and experience will make you a helper. Neither a Ph.D. nor a certificate from a training institute will mean that you have become the perfect helper. Students develop during their training, and this does not stop when they finish their formal education. In fact, interviews with professionals possessing more than 20 years of experience revealed that these helpers believed most of their development occurred after graduation (Skovholt & Ronnestad, 1992). Equipped with diplomas, but not a lot of work experience, new professionals may feel the effects of the "impostor phenomenon." Beginning helpers also tend to see themselves as frauds who are vulnerable to being found out (Harvey & Katz, 1985). Those professionals who have been out of school more than 10 years speak of a deeper authenticity in their work, the reassurance of accumulated wisdom, and the ability to make individual and personalized interventions with their clients. Do you have to wait 10 years until you can be a good helper? No—you can be the best helper you can be at your particular stage. Keep learning, keep receiving supervision, and do not pretend you know more than you do. One of the best books on this topic is *Finding Your Way as a Counselor* (Kottler, 1996). It is a collection of stories by practicing counselors about the issues they face as they develop. Besides making us feel that we are not alone, the writers give us help in thinking about how to get over these hurdles we continue to face.

To address ongoing developmental needs, the concept of lifelong learning is essential for helpers. Our knowledge of new techniques, advances in research in the field, new client populations, and emerging social issues can be updated through workshops, professional journals, classes, study groups, and conventions. The foundation you receive in your formal training is crucial. But it is not enough. You will need to learn about the newest treatments and programs developed by other helpers rather than reinvent the wheel each time a new client problem confronts you.

Who Can Be an Effective Helper?

Questioning whether you are really cut out for a job is to be expected when you enter a new field. Are you similar to the professionals you know? What must you know and what abilities must you possess going in? Although there is no one personality configuration that defines the perfect helper, various writers have looked at specific traits that lead to effective helping. They have also looked at the beliefs and attitudes most conducive to learning and working in the profession. Knowing more about these may help you because many of these qualities can be acquired.

The Legacy of Rogers

The writings of Carl Rogers (1967) have provided much of the framework for the core facilitative conditions that many see as the necessary ingredients for change and growth. More than anyone else, Rogers talked about therapeutic attitudes. Rogers believed that clients would move toward growth and positive outcomes if the helper provided the right environment. This environment, he felt, was more a reflection of the helper than an outcome of prescribed techniques or interventions. He considered three personal characteristics to be essential for a helper: congruence, positive regard, and empathy.

Congruence

Congruence is the ability to be completely genuine with another person. Congruency means that there is consistency between what a person feels and says and how he or she acts. When we are congruent, we are not afraid to take risks and to spontaneously share reactions and thoughts with clients. If we are congruent, we react to clients in the here and now and do not hide behind the facade of the professional role. A simple example of incongruence is when our verbal and nonverbal messages conflict. Suppose you tell a client that you will provide support on the phone during a period of crisis, but then you do not regularly return phone calls. The nonverbal action comes across more clearly than the verbal message. A helper who is incongruent is not trusted by the client.

Positive Regard

Positive regard does not mean that helpers must approve of every client behavior. Rather, the helper must respect the personhood of each client and believe that all persons have inherent worth. Hazler (1988) wrote about finding unconditional positive regard while working with a prison population. He described the insight that occurred when he was able to differentiate the prisoners (as real, valuable persons who had hopes and dreams and goals) from their crimes (which were brutal). A helper who works from unconditional positive regard never rejects a person, although he or she may reject that person's actions.

Empathy

Empathy, or empathic understanding, is the ability to understand another person's feelings or worldview. Responding to another's feelings can be called emotional empathy, whereas taking the time to reflect an understanding of a person's motives, intentions, values, and thinking might be called cognitive empathy. Helpers suspend their own judgment as they learn the subjective worldview of their clients. Rather than evaluating the content of client statements, the purpose is to simply understand the client's feelings, beliefs, experiences, and goals. Rogers believed that through empathy, clients feel understood and are empowered to solve their own problems.

Again, the habit of reflecting is an activity we can employ to monitor our tendency to judge rather than to empathize.

Courage to Confront

The effective helper has the supportive qualities that Rogers mentions, but he or she is also able to "go for the jugular." Clients come to a helper for more than support. Sometimes the job of a helper is to make the client aware of painful realities. Helpers may be forced to show the client their annoying interpersonal behaviors and be willing to risk the client's anger when delicate issues need to be addressed. Effective helpers are not so dependent on the client's approval that they will fail to bring up touchy subjects. As one moves from dualistic to relativistic thinking, it is easier to think about the client's best interests and not be so focused on oneself.

Other Research on Effective Helping

In the writings of 15 different authors, we found 55 characteristics, attitudes, and beliefs of effective helpers. We have tried to consolidate these into five key elements (Combs, Avila, & Purkey, 1971; Corey, Corey, & Callanan, 2003; Gladding, 2000; Kottler, 2004; McConnaughy, 1987; Patterson & Eisenberg, 1983; Spurling & Dryden, 1989; Truax & Carkhuff, 1967).

First and foremost, an effective helper has a positive, accepting view of other people. He or she accepts people who are different and is not judgmental about other people's lifestyles, values, cultures, and religions. He or she wants to help others and believes that people have the desire to change. The helper must be able to communicate his or her nonjudgmental attitude as well as warmth and caring.

Second, the effective helper has good self-esteem and is a secure and mentally healthy person. He or she is not attracted to helping in order to experience power over others or to feel superior to those with more serious problems. He or she seeks cooperation rather than control. Effective helpers appreciate themselves but know their limitations, too. They are able to examine themselves critically. They have the courage to look at themselves under a microscope. They make personal growth integral to their lifestyles.

Most writers agree that the effective helper has good self-care skills. Many who are attracted to this profession want to help others, but soon find that in order to do so they must make certain that they have something to give. It is easy to become emotionally bankrupt and burned out if one does not develop techniques for stress management, time management, relaxation, leisure, and personal self-renewal. The effective helper has a stable and fulfilling personal life with close family and friends to provide support as a buffer to the stress of helping.

The effective helper is both creative and intellectually competent, a renaissance person, who appreciates both the science and the art of helping. The effective helper has specialized knowledge of human relationships, human motivation, and human development and understands how to create change. Those who remain vital in the profession have "insatiable curiosity" to learn and grow in their skills and knowledge (Spurling & Dryden, 1989). Creativity and flexibility are equally vital. Helping requires one to devise innovative ideas with different clients in different situations. A helper must be able to deal flexibly with ambivalence, unfinished business, and moral dilemmas. He or she has to allow clients to work through difficult situations without moving them to premature decisions.

When Moreno, the founder of psychodrama, was once asked what the most necessary quality was for a group leader, his unexpected response was "courage." This fifth characteristic of an effective helper has two facets: First, the helper must be able to listen unflinchingly to stories of great pain. Like a physician who sets a broken arm, he or she must be able to look with a detached eye at human destruction and see where the healing can be started. Second, the helper's job requires risk taking and action without the security offered by other sciences. Individuals who believe that they can control every circumstance and that there is a procedure and a solution for every crisis have a difficult time as helpers. For example, there are no psychological tests that accurately predict a person's tendency to be violent. Helpers' decisions must be based on experience, training, and even intuition. Because human behavior is relatively unpredictable, effective helpers must be able to live with that uncertainty.

What Can You Bring to a Client?

There is no one set of personal qualities that makes an effective helper. There is room in the profession for many types of individuals, each of whom brings significant strengths and simultaneously must be aware of the limitations of his or her own personality style. The example of a former student may help to illustrate this. Maria, a graduate student, got under my skin sometimes because she had little patience for long theoretical discussions and did not like studying anything that did not have immediate application. She seemed to roll her eyes when the discussion became too intellectual. She was practical and concrete and liked people who were "down-to-earth." She wanted to solve problems and make a difference in the lives of children. It seemed to me that sometimes she tended to be too quick to come to closure with adult clients when they became stuck or were indecisive. Sometimes she pushed them to make decisions and seemed insensitive to their turmoil.

However, Maria now works effectively as a school counselor. Her particular strength is that she knows how to manage crises. She instantly grasps what has to be done and takes bold and concrete steps to accomplish it. She has excellent judgment and is indispensable to her school because she knows how to take quick action and exudes calm and poise in times of confusion. Maria's case illustrates that each of us brings strengths to the helping role. Much depends on knowing our own abilities and finding an environment where they can be put to good use.

As you consider the characteristics of effective helpers that we have identified, remember two things. First, many of the characteristics can be developed. They are not necessarily inborn. Second, each person brings unique characteristics to the helping profession, and as in Maria's case, the challenge is to find a place where these gifts will help others. Do not look at the characteristics of effective helpers in order to identify those you do not have. Helpers should not be clones. A client will have a relationship with you, not a set of skills. By focusing on your strengths, you will have much to bring to a client.

Stop and Reflect

The characteristics of effective helpers identified by the experts are listed in brief form in the following statements. Answer the accompanying questions as truthfully as possible, because your answers may point out areas you may wish to address later in your training. Which of these qualities do you presently possess and on which do you want to improve? For those skills you need to develop, think for a moment about what you might do to challenge yourself. What extracurricular activities might help you to grow?

Positive View of Humankind
You believe that most people are basically good and are striving for self-improvement. You enjoy people and believe that people can change.

    How true is this for you?
    How can you grow?

Stable and Mentally Healthy
You have good self-esteem and are basically a secure, mentally healthy person. You may not be able to make a completely unbiased self-assessment, but friends and family can give you feedback on your coping ability.

    How true is this for you?
    How can you grow?

Good Self-Care Skills
You do not become overly involved with those you are helping. You know your limits and are able to set boundaries to protect yourself from burnout.

    How true is this for you?
    How can you grow?

Intelligent and Psychologically Minded
You are an intellectually curious person who is interested in the psychological world of other people. You can appreciate both a scientific and an artistic approach to learning about helping.

    How true is this for you?
    How can you grow?

Creative
You are a creative person in some aspect of your life. You are not rigid or inflexible in your attitudes. You are not bothered by many prejudices about people, cultures, religions, and family customs that differ from your own.

    How true is this for you?
    How can you grow?

Courageous
You have enough courage to examine your own personal problems and to seek help and guidance for yourself when you need it. You are willing to admit that you need to

change and grow. You are able, for the most part, to deal with the cruelties that other people inflict on each other without being so disturbed that it disrupts your own life or your ability to help.

> How true is this for you?
> How can you grow?

Summary and Suggestions

Entering a new field of knowledge brings about uncertainty and challenges us to remain open and nondefensive. One central point of the chapter is that learning the art of helping follows some predictable stages. Knowing this should allow us to be less self-critical when we face the normal developmental hurdles. We need to be patient considering the time and knowledge that we must gain is significant. Reflection is the process of thinking about what we are learning. Even more, it means identifying discrepancies and problems that do not fit our normal solutions and taking stock of our own reactions. We also need to develop the habit of reflection so that we can separate our clients' goals from our own personal wishes.

Learning the art of helping is a long journey, and everyone travels at a different rate, bringing unique traits and differing gifts. Although experts have identified characteristics of effective helpers, including self-acceptance, cooperation, and the ability to reach out to others, there is not just one kind of person who can practice the helping arts. The core conditions of Carl Rogers remain a legacy to beginning helpers. They remind us that our job is to be personally honest, to have a positive regard for our clients, and to convey empathy.

You might find it helpful to consider some methods for reflection, self-assessment, and self-improvement that other students have found conducive to their own learning and development.

- Many have found it helpful to keep a journal of their thoughts and feelings during this course. Identify your fears and moments of success and then look back from start to finish seeing how far you have come. Take the opportunity to journal when you are stuck or have trouble progressing. Write down your frustrations and then talk them over with your instructor or use your journal as a basis for your questions in class.
- Consider getting together on a regular basis with other students to practice new skills and to provide support for each other.
- You may want to keep a record of unrealistic thoughts, self-criticisms, and exaggerated expectations that you may be holding for yourself. Are you focusing enough on what you do well, or is self-criticism becoming a barrier to growth?
- Think about recording your practice sessions and writing down all your responses. Identify each of your responses and think about how it affected the client.

By now you might be thinking that learning to help is a long journey requiring much of the learner. It is that, but it is also a voyage of personal discovery and an opportunity to encounter and appreciate other people at a level of intimacy that few professions allow. As you begin, remember the advice of the mountain climber: Don't look at the summit; keep your attention on your next step. One day you'll get to the top, but right now appreciate where you are.

Exercises

1. In groups of three, discuss your reasons for wanting to become a professional helper. What are your expectations and concerns?
2. Think of a time when you learned a new skill (e.g., playing tennis or learning to sew). What stages did you go through? How did you improve? Were you self-critical at first?

If so, what effect did your negative thinking have? Can you identify any particular thoughts that you had during that time? Discuss them with classmates and see if you can relate your previous experience to what you might encounter as you learn helping skills.

Homework

Homework 1

Make an appointment with a professional who has been working for only a few years (say, 1–5). Ask him or her the following questions and react briefly in writing to each one of them. (Be sure to add a couple of questions of particular interest to you.)

1. Does another helper supervise you? If so, what do you value about these sessions?
2. Thinking about the therapists you have known or observed, what qualities do they possess that you admire?
3. When do you feel least confident in your job?
4. To what theoretical orientation do you subscribe?
5. What kinds of professional reading do you do?

6. Do you benefit from conferences?
7. Did you notice any big "jumps" or stages in your ability to help?
8. Other questions . . .

Homework 2

Review your résumé or your past work history, whether paid or volunteer. Include jobs you held in organizations in high school or college if your work history is short. List your jobs and, under each, write significant learnings you gained about working with other people, both clients and coworkers. Even if your job was not in a helping capacity, did you find ways to help others? Has helping been a regular part of your work life or is it a new development? Summarize your learnings in a final paragraph.

Journal Starters

Think about starting a personal journal that chronicles your experiences on the journey to becoming a helper. Development of expertise is sometimes described as gaining knowledge, skills, and attitudes in a particular domain. Through this book, lectures you attend, and other courses, you are definitely gaining knowledge and skills. The journal, on the other hand, allows you to reflect on your own attitudes about helping and to react personally to what you are learning. Such reflection is the basis for modern approaches to assessment such as the portfolio. By looking back over your work, you can gauge your own development and think about future goals. A journal is not just a record; it should be reread and thought about.

You can use a computer, purchase a blank book, or develop a three-ring binder to construct a journal that allows you to add other information such as articles, poems, and pictures. Bring your reflections to class or share them privately with your instructor. Because this class invites so much personal growth, your instructor may ask you to complete journal entries several times during the semester. Try to be as honest as you can; think about what you share, too, not only in a journal but with your classmates. Is it possible to share too much about a particular topic that might overwhelm others? Whether you are asked to share some of your journal or not, approach it with complete honesty and edit it later. Sometimes I suggest that students write everything down and then remove or black out those portions they want to keep private before they hand in their assignment.

The following are two stimulus sentences you can use to provide a warm-up for your journaling. Each chapter contains several of these starters. Because these are warm-ups, continue writing even if you feel that you have

departed from the original stimulus sentences. After writing for a while, reflect on what you are learning in class and focus on the challenges you face. Feel free to modify these journal starters or create your own.

1. Thinking about my previous relationships with significant others in my life, what are the best and worst parts of my personality? How might these show up in my relationships with clients? What fears do I have about my abilities?
2. Reviewing times in my life when I have not been as successful as I wanted to be, how did I react? What helped me to overcome the problem? How can I best deal with setbacks in my basic skills training? What feelings do I have as I start this process?

For more journal ideas and activities, refer to Chapter 1 in *Exercises in the Art of Helping*.

References

Barrow, J. C. (1987). Is student development "dissonance roulette"? *Journal of College Student Personnel, 28*, 12–13.

Bernard, J. (1981). Women's educational needs. In A. W. Chickering (Ed.), *The modern American college* (pp. 256–278). New York: Jossey-Bass.

Caffarella, R. S. (1993). Self-directed learning. *New Directions for Adult and Continuing Education, 57*, 25–35.

Cheatham, H. E., & Berg-Cross, L. (1992). College student development: African Americans reconsidered. *College Student Development, 6*, 167–191.

Combs, A. W., Avila, D. L., & Purkey, W. W. (1971). *Helping relationships: Basic concepts for helping professions*. Boston: Allyn & Bacon.

Corey, G., Corey, M. S., & Callanan, P. (2003). *Issues and ethics in the helping professions* (6th ed.). Monterey, CA: Brooks/Cole.

Fong, M. L., Borders, L. D., Ethington, C. A., & Pitts, J. H. (1998). Becoming a counselor: A longitudinal study of student cognitive development. *Counselor Education & Supervision, 38*, 100–114.

Gaff, J. G., & Gaff, S. S. (1981). Student-faculty relationships. In A. W. Chickering (Ed.), *The modern American college* (pp. 642–657). New York: Jossey-Bass.

Gladding, S. (2000). *Counseling: A comprehensive profession* (4th ed.). Upper Saddle River, NJ: Merrill/Prentice Hall.

Granello, D. H. (2002). Assessing the cognitive development of counseling students: Changes and epistemological assumptions. *Counselor Education & Supervision, 41*, 279–292.

Griffith, B. A., & Frieden, G. (2000). Facilitating reflective thinking in counselor education. *Counselor Education & Supervision, 40*, 82–93.

Harvey, C., & Katz, C. (1985). *If I'm so successful, why do I feel like a fake? The imposter phenomenon*. New York: St. Martin's Press.

Hazler, R. J. (1988). Stumbling into unconditional positive regard. *Journal of Counseling and Development, 67*, 130.

Hoffman, R. R., Shadboldt, N. R., Burton, A. M., & Klein, G. (1995). Eliciting knowledge from experts: A methodological analysis. *Organizational Behavior and Human Decision Processes, 62*, 129–158.

Kottler, J. A. (2004). On being a therapist (3rd ed.). San Francisco: Jossey-Bass.

Kottler, J. A. (Ed.) (1996). *Finding your way as a counselor*. Alexandria, VA: American Counseling Association.

Lazarus, Arnold A. (1990). Can psychotherapists transcend the shackles of their training and superstitions? *Journal of Clinical Psychology, 46*(3), 351–358.

LeShan, L. (1996). *Beyond technique: Psychotherapy for the 21st century*. Northvale, NJ: Jason Aronson.

Marx, S. D. (1990). Phase I: On the transition from student to professional. *Psychotherapy in Private Practice, 8*(2), 57–67.

McConnaughy, E. A. (1987). The person of the therapist in psychotherapeutic practice. *Psychotherapy, 24*, 303–314.

McLennan, J. (1994). The skills-based model of counseling training: A review of the evidence. *Australian Psychologist, 29*, 79–88.

Norcross, J. C. (1990). Personal therapy for therapists: One solution. *Psychotherapy in Private Practice 8*(1), 45–59.

Patterson, L. E., & Eisenberg, S. (1983). *The counseling process* (3rd ed.). Boston: Houghton Mifflin.

Perry, W. G., Jr. (1970). *Forms of intellectual and ethical development in the college years*. New York: Holt, Rinehart, & Winston.

Rogers, C. R. (1967). *Person to person: The problem of being human*. Moab, UT: Real People Press.

Schön, D. A. (1983). *The reflective practitioner: How professionals think in action*. New York: Basic Books.

Simpson, D. E., Dalgaard, K. A., & O'Brien, D. K. (1986). Student and faculty assumptions about the nature of uncertainty in medicine and medical education. *Journal of Family Practice, 23*(5), 468–472.

Skovholt, T. M., & Ronnestad, M. H. (1992). Themes in therapist and counselor development. *Journal of Counseling and Development, 70*, 505–515.

Skovholt, T. M., Ronnestad, M. H., & Jennings, L. (1997). Searching for expertise in psychotherapy, professional psychology, and counseling. *Educational Psychology Review, 9*, 361–369.

Spurling, L., & Dryden, W. (1989). The self and the therapeutic domain. In W. Dryden & L. Spurling (Eds.), *On becoming a psychotherapist*. London: Tavistock/Routledge.

Stone, M. (1998). Journaling with clients. *Journal of Individual Psychology, 54*, 535–545.

Truax, C. B., & Carkhuff, R. R. (1967). *Toward effective counseling and psychotherapy: Training and practice*. Chicago: Aldine.

Young, M. E. (1998). Skills-based training for counselors: Microskills or mega-skills? *Counseling and Human Development, 31*, 2.

The Nuts and Bolts of Helping

2

The purpose of this chapter is to orient you to this book and the teaching methodology. You will learn some important definitions. In addition, you will be introduced to the basic skills, or "building blocks," that are the basis for later chapters. These building blocks are the basic elements that make up more complicated counseling techniques that you also will be learning. Because beginning helpers often question how basic skills fit into the larger picture, you will study the theoretical concept of "common curative factors." We end the chapter by taking you through the process of a basic helping session. After reading and completing the exercises in this chapter, you should have a framework that will help you organize your learning.

Defining Some Important Terms

What Is Helping?

Helping is a broad term that encompasses all the activities we use to assist another person, whether we have a therapeutic relationship or not. For example, a school administrator who takes time to listen to a crying first grader can utilize helping skills. A foster parent can learn to listen to the child and to the biological parents. A teacher's aide in a sixth-grade classroom can take a nonjudgmental stance when a child talks about why homework is late. Marital partners can help each other deal with disappointments and frustrations. Helping does not require a contract or a professional, confidential relationship. Helping only requires a person desiring help (a client), someone willing and able to give help (a helper), and a conducive setting (Hackney & Cormier, 1988). You can learn helping skills and use them whether you are on the way to becoming a professional or you simply want to help those with whom you live and work.

While *helping* is the overarching term, different settings and different contracts between helper and client mean that there are a variety of ways that the helping can be defined (see Figure 2.1). To the newcomer, this can be confusing. In the next sections, we will clarify some of the most common terms, including *interviewing*, *counseling*, and *psychotherapy*.

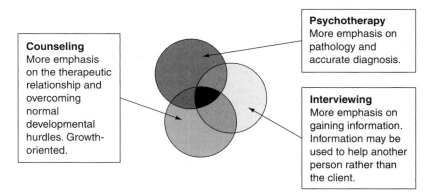

Figure 2.1
Different Emphases Among Psychotherapy, Counseling, and Interviewing
Despite these differences, there are many common theoretical underpinnings as well as common skills. The area overlapped by all three circles represents this shared base.

Interviewing

According to the simplest definition, *interviewing* is a conversation between an interviewer and an interviewee. During the conversation, the interviewer gathers and records information about the interviewee. In essence, during an interview, the interviewer is eliciting data, not trying to improve the situation of the interviewee. Thus, interviewing is one method of assessment, like giving a client a paper-and-pencil test. Both can ask simple and direct questions or use a fill-in-the-blank approach. Interviews can be *structured* with a series of predetermined questions or *unstructured* with the helper fitting questions in during the flow of the session. There are published structured interviews for a variety of psychological conditions and problems, from eating disorders to depression. If you utilize an intake or history form during the first session with a client and fill in all the spaces, you are conducting an interview. Interviewing is part of the assessment process that we discuss in more detail later. But it is important to talk about the relationship between assessment and helping early on, so that you can begin to distinguish their separate but complementary roles.

The purpose of an interview may be to help an interviewee or to make a decision about that person. For example, many counseling centers hire intake interviewers who talk with clients and then assign them to the appropriate counselor or refer them to another service or treatment facility. Employers interview applicants for jobs, promotions, or entrance into a special training program. An interview may also be used to test the interviewee's skills, poise, or ability to think in a "live" setting. This is called a *situational* interview. For example, some companies use a stress interview (a type of situational interview) to determine which of their employees can operate best under pressure. The interviewee is "grilled" and even treated disrespectfully to gauge his or her reaction. Many people think that this kind of interview is unethical, but the point is that an interview can provide an opportunity to observe the reaction of a student or employee in a contrived situation similar to actual situations that he or she may encounter.

Helpers interview to determine the appropriateness of counseling for an individual, to assess some skill, or to confirm a diagnosis. In contrast to business settings, these interviews are designed to ultimately benefit the client. In clinical settings, interviewing and counseling are rarely separate processes. For example, I was recently seeing a couple for counseling. During the first session, they both wanted to talk about their anger and frustration related to financial difficulties. It seemed clear that they blamed each other for the problem, and each wanted to unload. While I felt that it was important that they be allowed to express some of these feelings, I had other items on my agenda. I needed to know if financial problems were the only issues. In my experience, couples most frequently complain about the following issues: their inability to communicate, children and in-laws, sex, and finances. I wanted to make sure that I covered each of these areas and that I was not missing something important. It is also essential to know if there has been violence in the relationship, if substance abuse is involved, or if either party suffers from a mental disorder. So I frequently stopped their argument about finances to insert a question about these other areas. In the middle of the session, the wife revealed that she was concerned about her husband's drinking. I immediately took time to ask the husband several questions about his drinking and looked back at the OQ–45, a short test we give to all our clients during the first session. He had marked several of the questions that indicate substance abuse problems. I used the data from the test, from his spouse, and from the client himself to determine the extent of his problem. By the end of the session it was clear that his drinking was a serious problem that needed treatment before we could solve any of the other issues, even their finances, the reason for their coming.

This case demonstrates several important issues. First, helping and interviewing frequently occur during the same therapeutic session. Second, interviewing, as part of the assessment process, can make your helping more effective because it is a way of making sure you are going in the right direction and treating the right problems. Finally, interviewing can be disruptive of the relationship. Clients want to tell you their version of the story, and interviewing is experienced as an intrusion. A helper must go back and forth between helping and interviewing in almost every session because clients bring up new issues as the relationship deepens. It is up to the helper to repair the relationship that the clients are upset or confused by being disrupted and to explain the reasons for the interview so the clients still feel that their concerns are being heard.

In summary, interviewing is utilized in a variety of settings, not all of which are designed to help the interviewee. There are intake interviews, job interviews, diagnostic interviews, and situational interviews. Sometimes interviews are conducted to help a company or some other institution to determine if the individual meets their standards or possesses certain skills. Interviewing is an art whose medium is the relationship; it is not merely a mechanical process of filling in the spaces. A skilled interviewer knows how to quickly develop a working relationship with an interviewee in order to obtain the most relevant information for the decision-making process. The interviewer creates a climate where the interviewee will feel like talking and asks relevant questions to gain vital information. The basic helping skills you learn in this text will help you create this climate of openness, warmth, and acceptance needed for an effective interview. This atmosphere increases the quantity and quality of information obtained. In the assessment chapter (Chapter 10), you will have an opportunity to utilize your helping relationship skills and also learn to interview for key data.

What Are Counseling and Psychotherapy?

Counseling and *psychotherapy* are professional helping services provided by trained individuals who have contracts with their clients to assist them in attaining their goals. Counselors and psychotherapists use specific techniques to persuade, inform, arouse, motivate, and encourage their clients and to thoroughly assess their issues and backgrounds. Sessions with a counselor or psychotherapist take place on a regularly scheduled basis, usually weekly, and last about 1 hour. A therapeutic relationship will last several months or even several years. Although counselors and psychotherapists may help clients deal with emergencies, they also try to empower clients to address persistent problems in living and make changes in their lives that will lead to overall improvement rather than momentary relief. In most states, counselors, social workers, psychologists, marriage and family therapists, and psychiatrists can all practice counseling and psychotherapy.

In the literature and in practice, the words *counseling* and *psychotherapy* are now used interchangeably. Historically, however, different professional groups have tended to prefer one or the other, creating confusion for professionals and clients. Between 1920 and 1950, *psychotherapy* was used to describe the process of helping clients who were troubled by mental disorders. *Mental disorders* are defined as severe disturbances of mood, thought, and behavior for which there are specific diagnostic criteria. Examples include major depressive disorder, schizophrenia, and panic disorder. For each disorder, there is a list of criteria that the client must meet to possess the diagnosis. The criteria for more than 300 mental disorders are outlined in *DSM-IV-TR*, the American Psychiatric Association's (2000) manual, which is the bible of mental disorders. Even today, these are the only problems that most health insurance companies recognize as reimbursable. From the beginning, the processes of assessment, diagnosis, and treatment planning have been integral aspects of psychotherapy.

Counseling was invented as psychotherapy for "normal people," beginning in the early 1960s. Medical terminology was shunned by counselors, along with words such as *treatment* and *diagnosis*. Counselors believed in seeing each individual as a unique person, rather than a diagnostic label. For that reason, personality tests and other assessment activities were minimized, and identifying areas of growth rather than dysfunction was emphasized. Counseling was focused more on the counselor/ client relationship as the medium for change rather than on the tools and techniques. Although these values are still common among counselors today, the distinctions between counseling and psychotherapy have blurred. Now, counseling includes helping people with mental disorders as well as those experiencing normal developmental problems. Modern counselors routinely use assessment tools, learn diagnostic methods, and engage in treatment planning. By the same token, professionals such as psychologists and marriage and family therapists who prefer the term *psychotherapy* or *therapy* also help clients with difficulties such as adolescent adjustment, marital issues, and the transition to college or work—what we might call "normal problems." Although some may still feel there are good reasons to make distinctions between the terms *counseling* and *psychotherapy*, they will be used interchangeably in this book. Both will refer to the contractual and professional relationship between a trained helper and a client.

How Is Professional Helping Different from Friendship?

As you learn the art of helping, you will be able to provide friends with a listening ear, a caring attitude, and emotional support, enhancing your relationships and aiding those you care about. There is, however, a difference between friendship and a professional helping relationship; each is built on a distinct contract. A friendship is based on the assumption that we are there for each other—a two-way street. In a professional helping relationship, it is the client's issues that are discussed and the client's welfare that is paramount. In exchange, the helper receives compensation for professional services rendered. Consider this analogy: You mention to your friend, who is a dentist, that you have a toothache. She may suggest that you take some aspirin and that you make an appointment with a dentist as soon as possible. Despite her professional capabilities, she probably won't pull out her dental equipment and start drilling in the living room. Although the analogy does not hold completely, helping can also be a painful process best accomplished in a more professional setting.

For example, a professional helper is required to identify and articulate issues not normally broached in a friendship, such as painful childhood memories. Moreover, the professional helper is committed to hours of listening, confidentiality, responsibility for the outcome, and disregard for whether the client ultimately likes him or her. The helper's concern, as a professional, is to do a good job, not to maintain a relationship for its own sake.

One reason for drawing the distinction between a professional helping relationship and a friendship is that it is easy to make mistakes in both settings when you begin learning helping skills. You might be tempted to use elaborate techniques on your friends when all they are asking for is support. On the other hand, you might find yourself treating a client as a friend. Remember that with friends you have no agreement or contract for change, but instead you have an opportunity to care, to show concern, and to provide support. In the professional helping relationship, you have a contract to help the client make specific changes in his or her life, not to make a new friend, enjoy each other's company, or discuss the weather, your family, or your favorite hobby. What makes this difficult is that we have learned our natural helping skills in the context of our friendships and family relationships. It is easy to find ourselves being sociable and sympathetic, rather than thinking about how to help the client. It is also easy to act like a therapist with our friends, who may find this behavior intrusive and phony.

Before leaving this topic, let us take a moment to emphasize the importance of a contract in relationships. Eric Berne (1961), the founder of transactional analysis, felt that this was a vital aspect of the helping relationship but was often ignored. Clients must know what they are agreeing to and must participate in the changes that they are about to make. Berne believed that problems in relationships frequently occur because the parties have made assumptions but not outlined their expectations of each other. For example, clients may assume that everything that they say to their counselor is confidential, but it is not. There are several instances where counselors must release information—for example, to prevent harm to others. Some counselors outline the parameters of the helping relationship in a handout that they discuss with their clients. As you become a professional helper, you will recognize how important it is to identify the contract early in the relationship so that people you meet on an airplane and clients you see in your office know if you are a friend or a professional helper.

What Can You Expect from a Helping Relationship?

Beginners' hopes about what can be achieved in a professional helping relationship are often very grand. When, inevitably, the hopes are dashed, naturally there is disappointment. In this section, we will identify some common unrealistic beliefs about the helping process that many struggle with, and we will examine the corresponding more reasonable expectations.

Unrealistic Belief: I must help clients solve all their problems.
Reasonable Expectation: If all goes well, I may make a good-sized dent in a problem or two and the client will continue to progress when the relationship ends.

Most agencies and private practitioners find that, on average, helpers and clients see each other for 6 to 10 sessions. Most clients do not expect long-term relationships, and they come to a helper to deal with specific problems. Indeed, contrary to our expectations, clients who have even just a session or two with a helper are often very satisfied with the results. Helpers must not become disappointed when they want more changes than the client wants.

> **Unrealistic Belief:** If the client is not motivated, it is my fault.
> **Reasonable Expectation:** Although I can stimulate clients to consider making changes, I cannot force them.

It is estimated that nearly a third of helpers' clients today are involuntary referrals by courts, government agencies, or others. Although clients can be forced to attend sessions, helping is a voluntary relationship. Ethically, we cannot attempt to coerce clients to change. We can supply the opportunities for change, but the client must meet us halfway. In the real world, some clients are genuinely opposed to changing their lifestyles, even self-destructive ones. Others know that they need to change but require encouragement. The art of helping involves getting clients to envisage and consider a different kind of life and persuading them to change. For example, when an alcoholic client is sent by the court for treatment, the helper's job is twofold. First, the helper must intensify the client's awareness of the negative consequences of drinking; second, the helper must help the client to see the advantages of sobriety. However, even with detoxification and Alcoholics Anonymous, the odds are less than even that the client will stop drinking.

> **Unrealistic Belief:** If I care about my clients or have good practical experience, that is enough.
> **Reasonable Expectation:** Besides caring and practical experience in the helping field, I must learn all the skills I can.

No matter how good our intentions are, caring about another person is not a substitute for professional knowledge of how to help him or her. A caring physician is, of course, better than one who is indifferent, but the physician must also be well trained and kept fully abreast of his or her specialty through continuing education. Similarly, caring will enhance your helping skills, but it cannot replace them.

Some helpers believe that they are already fully trained. They have practical skills gained in the helping field, and they go on for formal education merely to "have their tickets punched." This is a potentially dangerous attitude. When we see the wide variety and severity of client problems and the new treatments that are cropping up everywhere, it is unreasonable to believe that we can ignore skills training in our formal education or that we can ever really be finished learning.

> **Unrealistic Belief:** If I am a good helper, my client will never need help again.
> **Reasonable Expectation:** If I am successful, the client may consult me again when a similar problem arises.

It is unrealistic to expect that clients will be "cured" in a single encounter with a helper. A family doctor model is a better analogy for the helping relationship. Such a relationship can be revived if the client needs help at a later developmental stage.

Unrealistic Belief: If I am effective with one client, I will be effective with every client.
Reasonable Expectation: I will not be the best match for every client.

Even famous therapists have found that they are not effective with every person who consults them. There are many reasons why a helping relationship may not succeed; some are not under the helper's control. The client may perceive a mismatch because the helper is not of his or her gender, race, or social class. The client may instantly dislike the helper because the helper reminds him or her of someone in the past. It is easy to feel rejected and disappointed if a client does not wish to continue the helping relationship, especially if you feel positive about it.

Unrealistic Belief: It is unacceptable to make a mistake.
Reasonable Expectation: I am a fallible human being who can learn from my mistakes.

If you attend workshops and seminars, you will see well-known counselors and psychotherapists showing videos of their amazing successes. In *The Imperfect Therapist* (1989), Jeffrey Kottler and Diane Blau have suggested that we can learn just as much from our failures, but we rarely talk about them. It is both ego protection and a fear that we are incompetent that keep us from discussing our mistakes with colleagues, supervisors, and teachers. However, if we do not examine these missteps, we are likely to repeat them.

Unrealistic Belief: Sometimes I feel incompetent; therefore, I am not competent.
Reasonable Expectation: There will be many times in my training and work as a helper when I will feel incompetent. It goes with the territory.

No matter how long you have worked as a helper, clients will surprise you. They have problems you have never heard of and problems your supervisor has never encountered. This can be either an assault on your self-esteem or a reminder that you need to keep learning. Although you need to keep abreast of changes in the field and reach the highest level of training that you can, neither a Ph.D. nor a certificate from a training institute will prepare you for everything. Feeling incompetent should motivate you to learn more about a client and his or her problems, but it should not paralyze you. You can seek supervision or possibly refer your client if an honest appraisal of the situation suggests that this would be in the client's best interest.

Stop and Reflect

Learning the art of helping is a personal journey that asks you to examine your own ideas and reflect about what you are reading. Try to use the "Stop and Reflect" sections, such as this one, to jot down your thoughts and reactions and to share them with another classmate or small group. You will certainly find other points in the book where your own ideas are challenged. Learn to pause at those moments and contrast the two positions. If you can begin this habit now, you are well on your way to becoming a reflective practitioner.

Start by considering each of the following questions about friendship and helping:

- Have you ever given a friend help that was not well received or that changed the friendship? Discuss with a small group.
- Some people think that our mobile, stressful society has led to a lack of community and has separated us from our extended family. If friendships and family relationships were closer, do you think that professional helping would be needed?
- What would you do if a friend told you that he or she was contemplating suicide? Think about your answer and then discuss it with the class. In what other situations do you think that a professional helper might have an advantage?
- Have you noticed that in group situations, you become interested when someone mentions something you agree with or when you have similar backgrounds? This "similar-to-me effect" has a powerful influence on our connections with people. In a job interview, you may be more apt to hire someone who joined the same sorority, came from your home state, or reminds you of yourself at a younger age. When you look for friends, do you look for someone who is similar to you? Does this search for similarity mean that it is harder to make contact with someone who is quite different? How could one's preference for similar people be a handicap in a helping profession?

Learning Basic Skills and Common Curative Factors

Basic helping skills are normally taught as small units called *microskills* (Ivey, 1971). This makes learning easier, but it also creates problems. Individual skills often seem so elementary that students may be confused about why they are important. Students have trouble seeing the big picture because they learn first one piece and then another. One conceptual framework that may help to put these small pieces into the bigger puzzle is understanding that these fundamentals are effective because they evoke common curative factors, or "megaskills" (Young, 1998).

It is estimated that there are between 100 and 500 different theoretical orientations, from cognitive behavioral to psychodrama (Corsini, 2001; Herink, 1980; Parloff, 1979). Common curative factors are thought to be the basic healing properties that underlie all effective counseling theories and techniques. The lifetime work of Jerome Frank (1971, 1981) showed how different theories rely on these factors for their effectiveness. Although helpers seem to be utilizing different techniques, they are actually drawing on similar methods. Frank described six common therapeutic factors that seem to cut across theoretical persuasions (Frank & Frank, 1991):

1. Maintaining a strong helper/client relationship
2. Increasing the client's motivation and expectations of help
3. Enhancing the client's sense of mastery or self-efficacy
4. Providing new learning experiences
5. Raising emotional arousal and promoting emotional expression (Later, we make a rationale to include techniques in this category that lower emotional arousal such as relaxation training.)
6. Providing opportunities to practice new behaviors

Most therapies utilize these curative factors to produce change. One of the best researched and most potent factors is the helper/client relationship. Because it is so crucial, we will examine it in more detail in the next chapter. The therapeutic building block skills you will learn are mainly aimed at helping you maximize this curative factor. By learning to create a climate of openness and listening, you will have the foundation to develop more advanced skills and to implement the other curative factors.

Therapeutic Building Blocks

Therapeutic building blocks is the phrase we use to describe the basic helping skills discussed in the last section. These are the most fundamental components of the helping interview, such as asking open-ended questions or maintaining eye contact. These building blocks are like the elements of the periodic table we all learned in high school chemistry (I apologize if this brings back traumatic memories). There are both simple elements like carbon and more elaborate elements like uranium. The therapeutic building blocks represent the foundational behaviors used to create change, but they can be combined into more complex techniques. In this book, we identify 21 therapeutic building blocks. They represent the combined wisdom of many theorists and helpers over time. Although 21 may seem to be an overwhelming number, 9 of the building blocks are quite simple (we call them invitational skills) and very easy to master. The building block skills are divided into six categories (see Table 2.1). Each category represents an important helping activity as follows:

Invitational Skills (9 Skills—Chapter 5)
Invitational skills are the basic means by which the helper invites the client into a therapeutic relationship. These skills encompass all the subtle verbal and nonverbal messages that helpers send to encourage a client to open up without applying pressure. For example, imagine how you would feel if the helper constantly checked her watch or looked out the window. You may think that paying attention is only polite, but it is also a skill. Eye contact and body posture are two of the invitational behaviors you will learn and practice in Chapter 5.

Reflecting Skills (2 Skills—Chapters 6 and 7)
Whereas invitational skills invite clients to tell their stories, reflecting skills let them know that you have heard their stories. Reflections are condensed versions of the facts and emotions the client has conveyed. The helper shares these "snapshots" of the client's story to let the client know that he or she is being understood both in terms of content and at the affective level. When clients feel understood, they disclose more deeply and the important issues begin to surface. These skills take some time to develop. Recognizing and reflecting the gist of the client's story and underlying emotions is something you will practice throughout your training.

Advanced Reflecting Skills (2 Skills—Chapter 8)
Advanced reflecting skills help a client move even deeper than the reflecting skills do. They include *reflecting meaning* and *summarizing*. Advanced reflecting skills are hunches that helpers make and repeat to their clients to see whether they understand the unique impact of their clients' problems beyond the basic facts and

Table 2.1
The Building Block Skills

Skill Category	Building Blocks
Invitational skills	
Nonverbal skills	Eye contact
	Body position
	Attentive silence
	Voice tone
	Gestures and facial expressions
	Physical distance
	Touching
Opening skills	Encouragers
	Door openers
	Minimal encouragers
	Questions
	Open questions
	Closed questions
Reflecting skills	Paraphrasing
	Reflecting feelings
Advanced reflecting skills	Reflecting meaning
	Summarizing
Challenging skills	Giving feedback
	Confrontation
Goal-setting skills	Focusing on the client
	Boiling down the problem
Solution skills	Giving advice
	Giving information
	Alternative interpretation/reframing
	Brainstorming

feelings. For example, the loss of a job is not just the change in economic status and feelings of loss. Depending on the person, losing a job may also be seen as a sign of failure or evidence of incompetence. Understanding the unique meanings that people assign to events and helping them identify their beliefs about themselves, others, and the world are advanced skills that move clients to deeper self-understanding.

Challenging Skills (2 Skills—Chapter 9)

Whereas invitational skills, reflecting skills, and advanced reflecting skills encourage deeper self-examination, challenging skills push clients to recognize discrepancies in their statements. Challenging skills identify incongruities in a client's story and may give information on client strengths and weaknesses. For example, a client who says that he wishes to stop smoking but does not follow any of the suggestions made by the helper might be challenged about the discrepancy between words and behavior. Challenging skills can strain the relationship, but they may also remind clients that the helping relationship is a work project, not a social encounter. *Giving feedback* and *confrontation* are fundamental challenging skills.

Goal-Setting Skills (2 Skills—Chapter 11)

Up to this point, the aim of the skills has been to encourage the client to disclose in as much depth and breadth as possible. Goal-setting skills, however, begin to narrow the focus. The first key goal-setting skill is to keep the client focused on his or her own issues and ask the client to identify the most crucial areas of concern. For example, helpers encourage clients to talk about how they themselves can change, rather than focusing on how to change others. The second key helping skill in this area is to "boil down" the problem, which involves shaping a client's vague or unrealistic goals into specific and achievable targets. These building block skills of *focusing on the client* and *boiling down the problem* are needed to help clients develop short- and long-term goals.

Solution Skills (4 Skills—Chapter 12)

Once tentative goals have been collaboratively established, solution skills are employed to help clients achieve those goals. Solution skills outline alternatives for action and press the client to consider new possibilities. *Giving advice* is a commonly misused solution skill, the advantages of which are usually outweighed by the drawbacks. Other solution skills include *giving information*, using *alternate interpretation*, and *brainstorming*.

The Importance of the Building Block Skills

We have said that one of the problems confronting most beginning helpers is that they learn elementary skills in isolation and cannot see how the skills fit into a grand scheme. They do not understand how flashy theory-based techniques such as Gestalt's "empty chair" relate to the baby steps they are learning in class. They begin making fun of their own tendencies to say "Um Hmm . . ." and "What I hear you saying is . . . ." They secretly yearn to do what famous therapists do in training films: have a tremendous impact on clients. Just as in basketball or baseball, every helper needs to practice the fundamentals. In sports, when fundamentals are mastered, they are linked into more complex movements, or plays. Without solid fundamentals, the plays are less effective. An example of this principle is shown in the 1980s film *The Karate Kid*. When he begins to study karate, the student, Daniel, is put to work sanding wood, painting, and waxing cars. At one point, he rebels and angrily confronts his teacher for having wasted his time. Daniel wants to be Bruce Lee. In a moving scene, the teacher shows him how each of the seemingly unrelated tasks is a fundamental move in the art of karate. Through repetition, the movements become second nature; when combined in a combat situation, they form an impenetrable defense. Your training in the helping skills will be very similar. You will learn basic helping movements, many of which will seem awkward and repetitive. However, when they are properly learned and put in the appropriate sequence, they form more elaborate and elegant techniques. The art of helping develops when the basics have become second nature.

Consider another example. When you first began to drive a car, you probably learned about the functions of various parts of the car, for example, the brake pedal, the gas pedal, the steering wheel, and the gearshift lever. You might have learned to accelerate, brake, and steer as separate activities before you put them all together in your first attempt at driving. The more you drove, the more automatic some functions became. You probably don't even remember pressing the gas pedal down during your last outing. If you learn to accelerate smoothly early in your driver training, that skill may stay with you, even when you are attempting more complex maneuvers. In the same way, practicing the basic building blocks until they become automatic will provide a foundation for the more complicated techniques you learn later.

Stages of the Helping Process: A Road Map

Figure 2.2 presents the stages of the helping process over time. The diagram shows five helper tasks that occur more or less sequentially from the first session to the last. This five-part structure is based on the work of several different writers (Dimond & Havens, 1975; Dimond, Havens, & Jones, 1978; Ivey & Mathews, 1986). The arrows indicate the typical progression of a client problem and the activities of helper and client through the process. In each stage, for the helping process to progress, something is required from both the helper and the client. For example, in the first stage, *relationship building*, the helper engages in nonverbal activities to build a trusting relationship. The helper does this primarily by using invitational, reflecting, and advanced reflecting skills. As a result, the client opens up and discloses more fully. Most helpers find that they use a session or two in the beginning just for building the therapeutic relationship and allowing time for the client to open up. As its central position suggests, relationship building interacts with all the other stages because the strength of the relationship helps to move the helping process forward and empowers the methods and techniques used later on. For example, a strong therapeutic relationship allows a client to disclose more easily in the assessment stage.

In the second stage, *assessment*, the helper collects information and the client provides it through answers to questions or data from intake forms or tests. In this book, assessment skills are covered in Chapter 10, although we have not included them in the therapeutic building blocks. The reason for not saying more about assessment in this book is that these skills, while important, tend to sidetrack us from our central purpose, which is to learn the fundamentals of a helping relationship. Normally, your

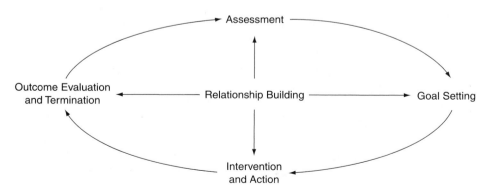

Figure 2.2
Stages of the Helping Process

course of study will include an entire course on assessment. Many helpers might spend an entire session collecting background data, and some might spend a session or two conducting more in-depth evaluations using tests. However, assessment actually occurs throughout the helping process when a new problem emerges and the helper takes some time from the session to collect needed information

The third stage in the helping process is *goal setting*. In goal setting, the client must participate by thinking about and agreeing to the goals that are mutually determined. The helper must use his or her expertise to shape these goals into clear statements and accept only those goals that will lead to real improvement in the client's life.

For the client, goal setting can help bring structure when things seem out of control. Goals bring hope and encourage the client to imagine a different future. Still, not all helpers like to set clear identifiable goals for the helping relationship. Some prefer to let each session unfold and to deal with the issues that arise week to week. Nevertheless, goal setting has become a necessity today because most agencies, hospitals, insurance companies, and managed care companies require detailed lists of goals (called *treatment plans*) for each client. Treatment plans often have specific behaviors that clients must produce in order to accomplish the goal in the expected time frame.

Next, in the *intervention and action* stage, the helper identifies and implements helping techniques to accomplish each of the treatment goals. The helper does this based on his or her theoretical background and training. The client is expected to take action to aid in this process. The degree to which this is successful depends largely on three things: the strength of the client/helper bond, the extent to which the goals are really important to the client, and the acceptability of the helper's methods.

If the helper implements a technique that is repugnant to the client, is mysterious, or seems to miss the mark, progress will be slowed. Again, the helper must return to the therapeutic relationship to see if client and helper are on the same page or whether the client feels that the helper is imposing treatment on him or her.

In the *outcome evaluation and termination* stage, the helper invites the client to think about the progress being made, and together they decide whether to continue the helping relationship. As the client reflects on changes made, the helper also shares his or her evaluation of progress and may utilize standardized outcome measures to give the client feedback.

Evaluation also is the last stop in the stages of the helping process depicted in Figure 2.2. Once a problem has been resolved, the cycle either begins again with a new problem or leads to termination of the relationship. The stages of the helping process will become clearer in the case example below. The case is described in the words of Jane, a counselor, whose client, Barbara, was referred by her daughter because of depression.

Relationship Building: The Heart of Helping

Jane: "Barbara is 68 years old with gray hair; she is somewhat slim but apparently in good physical condition. Barbara's husband died 6 months ago, and although she felt that she had handled the first 3 months well, recently she had become depressed and apathetic about life. She reminded me a lot of my grandmother, and I felt an urgency to help her when I realized how much her depression was interfering with her life. She had recently started taking antidepressant medication, but her doctor had insisted that she also receive counseling. Barbara had never seen a counselor before, so I took some time to explain the process to her. She was skeptical—believing nothing could help her—so I spent about half of the first session listening, reflecting, and getting to know her better. I told her a little bit about myself because I sensed that we would not be successful unless she trusted me. Near the end of the session, I told her that we would be working on the feelings of depression that she was experiencing, and I told her about the techniques we might use. We also discussed the issue of confidentiality, and I explained that I could not even discuss our sessions with her daughter without her permission. This seemed to alleviate some of her tension because Barbara saw asking for help as a weakness and was afraid that others would judge her for being depressed. We signed an agreement for treatment that outlined the limits to confidentiality and the fees. By the end of the session, Barbara seemed more hopeful about progress, but the work of dealing with her depression was still before us."

At the center of the helping process is the therapeutic relationship, which provides the core conditions or supports for the other activities of the helper. The relationship is the glue or the center of the helping process. The relationship has a special place in Figure 2.2 to emphasize its central role in the helping process. In relationship building, the helper uses invitational skills to convey understanding, to allow the client to open up, and to create a safe environment. This is exactly what Jane did with Barbara during their first session. Jane tried initially to allay any misgivings that Barbara might have had by developing a personal relationship and by dealing with Barbara's real concern that entering a helping relationship was a sign of weakness. It is obvious in this case that if the relationship were not firmly established, getting needed information in the assessment stage would be extremely difficult.

Assessment Stage

Jane: "When I first saw Barbara, I was a little bit surprised to see that she was well groomed, alert, and talkative. Her depression seemed to have started about 3 months after the death of her second husband, Carl. I took a complete history of Barbara's life and noted a number of losses. Barbara's mother died when Barbara was 20 years old. She had her only daughter at age 28. The next year, she lost a baby through a miscarriage, the complications of which left her unable to have more children. Barbara's first husband subsequently died during military training. In addition to the death of her second husband, Barbara was now coping with financial problems. Carl's will had named her as the sole beneficiary, but his children were contesting the will. The family problems and the lack of money were both sources of worry.

"One of the things I did in the very first session was to assess her suicide risk. Barbara denied any suicidal thoughts. She said, 'Sometimes I wish I were dead, but I would never kill myself.' Barbara had strong religious beliefs against suicide, she did not own a gun, and her depression was not so severe that I was worried about her taking her own life. I did call the family physician and asked him to limit the number of antidepressant pills that were issued to Barbara each week to reduce the possibility of an overdose. I diagnosed Barbara's problems as mild

depression stemming from grief and associated stress, with only a small risk of
suicide. I also gave her the Beck Depression Inventory and found that she was
moderately depressed, which fit with my personal assessment.

"One of the things that I noticed was that any time Barbara identified something
she was doing well, she discounted it and seemed to exaggerate the minor defi-
ciencies in her performance. For example, she still went to church twice a week,
but she was very discouraged over the fact that it often took her 15 minutes to
decide what clothes to wear in the morning. Barbara agreed to keep a journal of
her 'negative thoughts' so that we could deal with them in future sessions."

Assessment is the second stage of the helping process. As is apparent in
Barbara's case, much of the assessment stage is inseparable from the relationship-
building stage because helpers are observing their clients and collecting information
from the moment that they first meet. This process continues throughout the helping relationship, but most of the background data pour in during the first few
sessions. Some agencies ask that intake forms (sometimes called *psychosocial
histories*) be completed and a preliminary diagnosis be made during the first session.
The drawback is that a thorough assessment takes several hours, and if the entire
first session is spent in gathering information, the client may not return because he
or she has not made a real connection with the helper. Clearly, when the relationship
is well established, assessment is more complete and easier to accomplish because
clients are much better able to freely disclose information about the problem and
about themselves.

Assessment includes formal and informal ways that helpers collect information
about clients, among them paper-and-pencil tests, client reports, and helper observations. Collecting background data helps us determine whether the services available
are appropriate for a particular client and ensures that we are not missing a serious
mental disorder such as schizophrenia, a substance abuse problem, or suicidal or
violent behavior. Beyond this, assessment is the organizing of data on the client's
problem, providing baseline data (the intensity, frequency, and duration of the problem at the beginning), and relevant history.

Goal-Setting Stage

Jane: "In the second session, I started off by giving Barbara a summary of what
I had learned so far. She had three major problems as I saw it: feelings of depression that interfered with her life, financial problems, and disruption of family
relationships caused by the fight over the will. We both agreed that there was little
she could do at the present time to work on the money issues or deal with the legal
challenge, as these were longer-term problems. Instead, we decided to focus
efforts on reducing her feelings of depression. If she could deal with the depression, she would be better able to move the legal process along. In order to do this,
I asked Barbara to think about what she would be doing if the depression lifted
and what she would be feeling and thinking. This was easy for her. Barbara said,
'I would be able to play golf again. I would get dressed early every morning, and
I would not have these negative thoughts going around in my head.' Using Barbara's
ideas, we hammered out some goals for the next few sessions. First, we agreed that
we would reduce the negative self-talk by using cognitive therapy techniques.

Second, Barbara would become more physically active to overcome her lethargy and help her get back to her old routine. This was more of a challenge than I first expected. Barbara resisted playing golf because she was afraid that friends would notice her depression, and she wanted to appear normal. I encouraged her to accept the fact that being depressed was a normal reaction to the loss of a spouse and that she did not have to expect so much of herself right now. I suggested that by acting 'normal,' Barbara would start to feel 'normal.'"

Once a helper has gained an understanding of the client's problem and the important background issues, it is time to identify the helping goals. Here, Barbara and Jane identified one goal: to reduce Barbara's depression. Two interventions were selected because Jane, the helper, had been trained in these methods. The first intervention was to reduce Barbara's negative self-talk, and the second was to increase her physical activity. In this book, we advance the theory that goals, such as the one set by Barbara and Jane, are a collaborative construction of helper and client. Although goals do not necessarily have to be defined behaviorally, if the desired outcomes are observable, it is easier to know when they have been achieved. For example, if Barbara plays golf three times a week and goes for an evening walk two times a week, we are on target. In the goal-setting phase, professionals draw up treatment plans that state agreed-upon goals and the interventions that will be used to achieve them. This plan instills hope in the client and invites his or her participation as a team player.

Intervention and Action Stage

Jane: "The third session was spent in going over the negative thoughts that Barbara had recorded. When summarized, they seemed to have two persistent themes: 'I should not be depressed,' and 'I am a burden on everyone by being depressed.' These seemed to reflect Barbara's beliefs that she should appear perfect to everyone and that she should not rely on others for help. We discussed the fact that Barbara even felt that she was a burden to me. During the session, we identified some ways of countering her negative thinking by examining the flaws in her negative conclusions. She readily admitted that the thoughts were not logical, but she did not know how to stop them. We suggested that she combat these thoughts in a two-step process. First, stop the thought when she noticed it; second, replace the thought with one that was more constructive. For example, when the thought came up, 'I am a weakling for being depressed,' she was to argue back, 'Feeling this way is a natural part of grieving. I am not perfect; no one is.' We decided to check on how effective these replacement thoughts were at the next meeting. She was to practice 'stopping and inserting' over the next week. During the previous session, I had encouraged Barbara to begin playing golf one time a week as an experiment. I explained that she might not feel 'normal,' but that the exercise would help to reduce the depression. She reluctantly agreed to try it, but at this session Barbara admitted that she had not done so yet."

During the intervention and action stage, professional helpers utilize more advanced skills and ask clients to take active steps to reach their goals. For example, Jane advised Barbara to get some exercise. In this stage, the client is invited to do something to begin solving the problem. As is typical, Jane met with mixed success in getting Barbara to take action. Note again in Figure 2.2 that relationship building occupies a central position and is connected to the intervention and action stage. In the case of Barbara and Jane, you might see how important a trusting, confiding, therapeutic relationship is to the implementation of techniques. At this stage, if Barbara does not have confidence and trust, she will not wholeheartedly engage in the activities suggested by Jane. Barbara is also more likely to complete homework assignments because Jane is expecting her to do so.

Outcome Evaluation and Termination Stage

Jane: "We spent about five sessions working on Barbara's negative thinking and increasing her physical exercise. Although her physician decided to discontinue the antidepressant medication because of severe dizziness, Barbara's depression gradually lifted over this time. Every three or four sessions, I gave Barbara the Beck Depression Inventory and her depression showed a slow but steady decline.

"I asked Barbara to evaluate her progress after about 2 months of counseling. She said, 'Well, I am back to doing most of the things I used to do. I am still very sad sometimes when I think about Carl, and I still have trouble making decisions. That is not totally over. I guess I won't be happy until that is resolved. I am still afraid to be around people too much because I don't want them to see how I feel.' "

"I noticed that Barbara's statement still focused on what was missing in her life and underrated the gains she had made. I asked her to give herself a pat on the back for having reduced her depression and increasing her physical activity. She was reluctant to do this but admitted that things were substantially improved. We also discussed the most recent score on the Beck Depression Inventory, which showed a substantial positive change since her first session."

"I continued to see Barbara for 3 more months. The last month was mainly to monitor her progress and to make certain that changes were lasting. I also referred her to a grief support group at the local hospice, but she declined to attend. At the last session, we set an appointment for 6 months to see how things are going."

Helpers regularly ask their clients to evaluate their progress on goals by reflecting verbally or in writing or by using self-report tests. Also, some time in each session is devoted to gauging the effectiveness of specific techniques and homework. Outcome evaluation also occurs during the final sessions when the helper and client—like Jane and Barbara—review and celebrate the resolution of problems and look at the change from first to last sessions. When client and helper agree that the goals have been reached, either new goals are established (completing the circle in Figure 2.2) or the relationship is terminated.

Stop and Reflect

Let us think back for a moment to the case of Jane and Barbara. Jot down your answers to the following questions and discuss them with classmates or your training group.

Relationship Building
Jane was reminded of her grandmother when she first saw Barbara. Because Jane seemed to care about her own grandmother, this created a motive to help Barbara.

Can you think of some situations that might arise between Barbara ∤ Jane's feelings might not have been productive? In your own experi ent age groups, think about whether you feel more comfortable working adults, or older people. Which group will create the biggest challenge for you? Disc some past experiences that might account for this.

Assessment

One of the first issues Jane assessed was Barbara's suicide potential. All helpers have to make judgments about this in the first few sessions, even those who work with young children. Because assessing suicide and violent behavior is not an exact science, how do you think you might handle a situation in which you are not certain about a particular client's suicidal intentions? If you were a client, how do you think you would feel about taking tests like the Beck Depression Inventory?

Goal Setting

In the case of Jane, the helper, and Barbara, the client, they both agreed that Barbara needed to deal with her depression, but it was Jane who suggested the goal of increasing physical exercise. Some feel that the helper's job is only to accomplish the client's agenda. Others feel that the helper's expertise and a diagnosis should be the basis of the goals. For example, some would say that because Barbara was depressed, she needed medication and a certain kind of therapy, whether Barbara wished to deal with her depression or not. Who do you think should set the goals in the helping relationship: the helper, the client, or both?

Intervention and Action

In thinking about which techniques to use, Jane mainly focused on cognitive techniques: identifying and replacing negative thoughts. Barbara only reluctantly agreed to the procedure. How do you think you might deal with a client's lack of motivation to work on a problem, do homework assignments, or participate in a particular technique during a session? What might you say?

Evaluating Outcomes and Termination

In this stage, Jane highlighted Barbara's successes, but Barbara focused on the fact that she was not 100 percent back to normal. Why do you think Barbara made this statement? Could she be fearing the termination of the helping relationship? What other issues might be behind her unwillingness to recognize success? How do you think you might deal with her fears about termination or other reasons for her reluctance to celebrate success?

Summary

Helping, interviewing, counseling, and *psychotherapy* are all terms that have been used to describe the relationship that identifies problem issues and brings about positive change. Helping skills are best used within a professional relationship that includes a trained helper and a client seeking help. A therapeutic relationship has special characteristics that differentiate it from other relationships. Among these are a contractual relationship between helper and client. There are limits to how much one can employ helping skills with personal friends and family.

In this book, you will be learning 21 basic helping skills, or building blocks. When combined and elaborated, these building blocks form more complex techniques. It is important to take the time to practice the fundamental skills and gain mastery of them, even if they seem overly simple or awkward.

In the case of Jane and Barbara, we emphasized how crucial this relationship is in accomplishing the goals of the helping relationship. Each of the other stages of helping—assessment, goal setting, intervention and action, and outcome evaluation and termination—is dependent on the quality of the client/helper bond.

Exercises

Group Exercise: 20 Questions

Dividing into Groups and Constructing Questions

Earlier we made the statement that interviewing is enhanced by developing an atmosphere that allows the client to feel comfortable and relaxed. In this exercise students divide into groups of four or five. Each group develops a list of 20 questions it would like to ask someone about his or her life if the group members wanted to get important information or know the person better.

Structured Interview

When the list is compiled, one member of the group, an interviewer, asks these questions of another person in the group, the interviewee. The interviewee should answer honestly but may pass on any question if it is too personal.

Unstructured Interview

In the second part of the exercise, two new individuals participate in an interview. This time, the interviewer does not use the list. Instead he or she tries to get the interviewee to talk about personal issues in a normal conversational way. The interviewer may want to ask general "open questions" such as "Can you tell me a little bit about your family?" It should be more informal, but the emphasis should be on helping the client feel comfortable and relaxed.

Discussion and Analysis

Finally, the group discusses the two contrasting interviews. What was the effect of each interview style on the interviewees? What are the advantages and disadvantages of each style? In the second unstructured interview, did you obtain the answers to all the questions on the list? What did you get that was new or unexpected in the unstructured situation?

Additional Exercise

To get a better idea of the helping process, let us examine the five stages shown in Figure 2.2. Think about a problem that you are experiencing. It can be a small problem you are now facing or an issue from the past that you can pretend is an issue today. Jot down your answers to the following questions about each stage of the helping process.

a. Relationship building:
   How important would it be for a helper to be warm and inviting; or would you prefer a more businesslike atmosphere?

   _____

   _____

How much would you like the helper to say about himself or herself?

_____

_____

How long do you think it would take before you trusted a helper enough to disclose something extremely personal?

_____

_____

What sort of personal characteristics would you want in a helper?

_____

_____

b. Assessment:
What important issues would a helper have to find out about you, your family, your environment, your goals, your cultural and religious background, and your history before he or she could help you?

_____

_____

How would you feel about spending the first session answering questions about your problem?

_____

_____

How might you respond to the helper's request that you take complete tests or inventories?

_____

_____

c. Goal setting:
Imagine yourself without the problem. What would you be doing, thinking, or feeling that you are not experiencing now?

_____

_____

Can you turn your problem into a goal? For example, rather than stating the problem,

"I bite my fingernails," transform it into a future scenario, such as "I would like to have attractive nails that I would not be ashamed of in public."

_____

_____

d. Intervention and action:
What kind of approach by a helper would you object to? Is there anything that immediately comes to mind that you might want the helper to do? React to each of the interventions below as to whether you would want the helper to use this specific technique. If the problem you have selected does not really fit with a particular technique, just leave it blank.

_____

_____

With my chosen problem, I would most like to:

Listen to advice about how to solve my problem _____

Write in a journal to express my feelings

_____

Just have someone to listen (no advice)

_____

Keep a record of specific behaviors _____

Role-play my problem _____

Enter group therapy and hear the reactions of others _____

Bring a family member with me to a session

_____

Complete an assignment to say no to others more often _____

Hear a story by the helper about how he or she handled a similar problem _____

Other (anything here that you think would help) _____

e. Outcome evaluation and termination: How would you know that you had definitely completed your goal?

_____

_____

How would you be thinking, feeling, and acting when you had accomplished it?

_____

_____

Homework

Homework 1

Go over the list of unrealistic beliefs about helping and the corresponding reasonable expectations given in this chapter. Identify two or three that you think might create difficulties for you in the helping relationship. Write a paragraph about each belief giving your reactions and indicate how you might deal with that thought if it should arise in your interaction with a client. Alternatively, identify some of the beliefs you have about helping that you think are realistic.

Homework 2

You will sometimes hear helpers talk about being "over involved" with clients, and they may sometimes suggest that you "keep a professional distance." What kinds of behaviors do you think would indicate that a helper was too involved in a client's life? What limits should the helper set in the relationship? Does this necessarily mean that the helper should not care about a client? What ethical guidelines do professional helpers rely on to determine whether the professional relationship has become too close? Write down your reaction to these questions in a page or two.

Journal Starters

1. In this chapter, you read about the case of Jane and Barbara. What do you imagine it would be like to work with someone much older than yourself? How would you feel if you were much younger, say 30 years younger, than your client? Do you have friends who are older than you? Why do you think age makes such a difference in relationships—or does it?
2. Think about some key friendships in your life. What is it that has made them so important for you? Compare your feelings of closeness in your friendship with your feelings about favorite teachers you have known. What is the qualitative difference? Can you gain something from relationships in which you are not emotionally close to someone?
3. *Rescuing* is sometimes defined as doing more than 50 percent of the work in a helping relationship. Have you ever tried to help someone who did not put forth much effort to help himself or herself? How did you end up feeling? As you think about that, how do you think this affected your relationship with that person? Is it difficult to imagine working with someone who may not really want to be helped?

For more journal ideas, as well as more practice with the nuts and bolts of helping, refer to Chapter 2 in *Exercises in the Art of Helping*.

References

American Psychiatric Association. (2000). *Diagnostic and statistical manual of mental disorders: Text revision* (4th ed.). Washington, DC: Author.

Berne, E. (1961). *Transactional analysis in psychotherapy*. New York: Grove Press.

Corsini, R. J. (Ed.). (2001). *Handbook of innovative psychotherapy* (2nd ed.). New York: Wiley.

Dimond, R. E., & Havens, R. A. (1975). Restructuring psychotherapy: Toward a prescriptive eclecticism. *Professional Psychology, 6,* 193–200.

Dimond, R. E., Havens, R. A., & Jones, A. C. (1978). A conceptual framework for the practice of prescriptive eclecticism in psychotherapy. *American Psychologist, 33,* 239–248.

Frank, J. D. (1971). Psychotherapists need theories. *International Journal of Psychiatry, 9,* 146–149.

Frank J. D. (1981). Therapeutic components shared by all psychotherapies. In J. H. Harvey & M. M. Parks (Eds.), *Psychotherapy research and behavior change* (pp. 175–182). Washington, DC: American Psychological Association.

Frank, J. D., & Frank, J. B. (1991). *Persuasion and healing* (3rd ed.). Baltimore: Johns Hopkins University Press.

Hackney, H., & Cormier, L. S. (1988). *Counseling strategies and interventions* (3rd ed.). Upper Saddle River, NJ: Prentice Hall.

Herink, R. (1980). *The psychotherapy handbook: The A to Z guide to more than 250 different therapies in use today.* New York: New American Library.

Ivey, A. E. (1971). *Microcounseling: Innovations in interviewing training.* Springfield, IL: Thomas.

Ivey, A. E., & Mathews, J. W. (1986). A metamodel for structuring the clinical interview. In W. P. Anderson (Ed.), *Innovative counseling: A handbook of readings* (pp. 77–83). Alexandria, VA: American Counseling Association.

Kottler, J., & Blau, D. (1989). *The imperfect therapist.* San Francisco: Jossey-Bass.

Parloff, M. B. (1979, February). Shopping for the right therapy. *Saturday Review,* 135–142.

Young, M. E. (1998). Skills-based training for counselors: Microskills or Mega-skills. *Counseling & Human Development, 31*(3), 1–12.

The Therapeutic Relationship

3

In the beginning was the relationship.
Martin Buber

In the last chapter, we talked about the high expectations we have for ourselves in the helping relationship. We also highlighted the differences between a therapeutic relationship and a friendship. But what is so special about this helping relationship? In this chapter, we will dig a little bit deeper into the mystery of the interaction between client and helper, discussing briefly why helpers and researchers place so much emphasis on it. More practically, we will also talk about how you can build such a relationship with another person. Finally, we turn to the issue of mistakes that can be made that strain or weaken the helping relationship and the knotty problems of transference and countertransference. Before addressing these important issues, though, let us take a look at a real client's recollection of the helping relationship in her own words:

> I came to counseling because my husband was having an affair, and I was devastated over the impending breakup of my marriage. I was anxious, depressed, and having trouble eating and sleeping. I was like a zombie at work. I don't want to give the impression that I am a weak person. I had always been the kind of person others leaned on. This was the first time I had ever been so needy. I felt like the rug had been pulled out from under my life.
>
> I heard that Jim was the best therapist in the area so I called to make an appointment. Jim was a minister who also had a degree in counseling. Although I am not a Christian, I am very spiritually oriented, and I wanted someone who could understand that side of me. In many ways, Jim fit perfectly my ideas of what a helper should be. He was older than me by 25 years, had gray hair, and I had heard that he had been happily married for many years to another therapist in the area. I had also heard that he studied with some famous teachers. My expectations were high, and I was desperate.
>
> At our first meeting, Jim got up to greet me at the door, shook my hand warmly with both of his, ushering me into his crowded office. Then, I had one of the most powerful experiences of my life. He listened to me for the next half hour as though nothing else in the world was more important. I had talked to a few friends about the situation, but he seemed to make me feel that there was all the time in the world, and I sensed that all my problems were no burden to him. Although I cried through much of the first session, Jim remained calm and at the end offered some hope. First, he asked me the question, "What holds you together?" I then talked about my spiritual beliefs. It made me realize that I could rely on that to help me through this crisis. Later, he commented, "I don't think it is time to give up on this yet." Having that light at the end of the tunnel made a lot of difference. I was able to hold on for a few weeks while things sorted themselves out. I continued to see Jim over the next few months.
>
> Once, I came to a session and found that there was a mix-up in communication and only a half hour of my session remained. I was upset because I really needed to talk to someone. I was bursting with sadness and anger. That night I dreamt that I was sitting in Jim's waiting room and everybody else was allowed to go in except me. Even though it wasn't his fault, I felt displaced. When we talked about it in the counseling session, Jim said, "I guess it was hard for you to face another rejection." This really helped me become aware of how discarded and unwanted I felt in my relationship with my husband. I also felt sick to my stomach when I realized how dependent I had become on my therapist. As time went on, I became stronger and was able to handle my problems much better. Knowing Jim was there was a great comfort sometimes. At other times, I was frustrated that when I needed to talk to him, it was still 3 or 4 days until our session. For some irrational reason, it made me mad that he was not available when I called.
>
> After 4 or 5 months, Jim told me one day that he thought I had become too dependent on the relationship and that we needed to reduce our sessions to once

per month. I agreed that things were better and silently assented to this new arrangement. After that session, I met a friend for lunch, and as we went through the buffet line, I took three knives, three forks, three spoons, and four napkins. I was so disoriented by powerful feelings, I could hardly concentrate. Part of me saw Jim's reducing our sessions as a form of confidence in me. But I also felt suddenly adrift. It took 6 months or so before I was able to really get back on solid ground and feel a sense of confidence.

I feel that I owe Jim a debt that I can never adequately repay. He helped me survive during the lowest period of my life. I don't idealize him any longer, but I recognize his caring and his undivided attention as one of the things that pulled me through."

                                                                                              Alicia B.

The Importance of the Therapeutic Relationship in Creating Change

One of the ongoing dilemmas for a helper is the tension between relationship and technique. How much emphasis should be placed on making sure that the helper/client relationship has been established? Is it better to make certain you understand how to utilize a particular method of treatment? Of course, you want to be on the cutting edge by knowing the newest and the most effective techniques available to help your client. Many treatments have now been standardized and recorded in manuals.

For example, there are manualized treatments for various kinds of depression, anxiety, sexual abuse, etc. This standardization has led to a better ability to evaluate treatments and to devise better ways to teach these techniques to clients. Some argue that too much emphasis has been made on the technique of helping and too little on the therapeutic relationship, the heart of helping (Erskine, 1998; Kelly, 1994).

The research of Lambert (1986) and others indicates that utilizing effective techniques accounts for some of the success in helping but that the *therapeutic relationship* accounts for about twice as much as technique. Therapists and researchers have long recognized the importance of a strong working alliance in potentiating change (Bachelor & Horvath, 1999; Belkin, 1980; Fiedler, 1950). From behaviorists (Kanfer & Goldstein, 1986) to Carl Rogers (1957), helpers have indicated that achieving client goals is much more likely in a good relationship. In fact, the quality of the therapeutic relationship appears to be more predictive of success than the theoretical approach of the helper (Nuttall, 2002). It is truly a common curative factor among all theoretical approaches (Hubble, Duncan, & Miller, 1999).

The helper/client relationship is also an important factor in understanding why clients drop out of counseling in the first few sessions. Often, it is due to feeling uncomfortable with the helper, not liking the helper, or deciding that the helper is not capable of helping. So the power of the therapeutic relationship is not only key to creating improvement; it is also vital that this environment be created immediately to prevent attrition. Think about how you might feel if you went to a physician and although you recognized that he or she probably has a lot of technical skill, the physician showed no warmth or concern and did not seem to listen. You might complain, but more likely, you would "vote with your feet" by not returning. As in any professional relationship, if the helper does not instill confidence and communicate warmth and acceptance in the first few sessions, the client's fragile hopes may be dashed, and he or she will give up on the helper or even give up on seeking professional help altogether.

The central importance of the relationship in the helping process is portrayed in Figure 3.1, which shows the six therapeutic factors introduced in Chapter 2. The therapeutic relationship is shown at the center of the diagram to suggest that the other factors depend, to a large extent, on the power of the relationship for their effectiveness. It is also true that the stages of the helping process—relationship building, assessment, goal setting, intervention and action, and evaluation and termination—all require the presence of a strong, cooperative relationship between helper and client in order to move through these steps (see Figure 2.2). Obtaining a full and accurate assessment, for example, requires that the client feel safe enough to disclose the good, the bad, and the ugly. In this chapter, you will learn skills to enhance the relationship, so as to maximize the effectiveness of the other therapeutic factors and to identify and reduce impediments to the relationship that can lead to client dropout and slower progress.

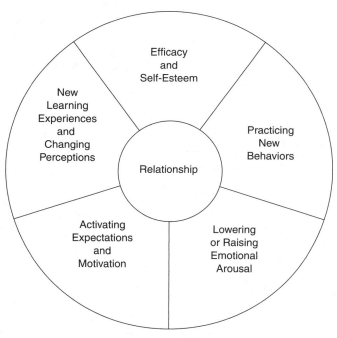

Figure 3.1
Six Common Therapeutic Factors

The Unique Characteristics of a Therapeutic Relationship

Professional helping relies on a special therapeutic relationship involving a trained helper and a client wanting help. The most effective helping relationships have the following attributes, which differentiate them from other relationships. In the previous chapter, we talked about the difference between friendship and a helping relationship. Keep this difference in mind as you look over this list:

There is a mutual liking—or at least respect. A therapeutic relationship has at its base respect. Does the therapeutic relationship have to be one where client and helper have mutual fondness? Perhaps not, but at least the helper conveys respect for the client's autonomy, and the client respects the helper's expertise. Without this, a real alliance may not be possible. This does not mean that the client cannot be helped; it means that one of the therapeutic factors is not being used to its potential and that any change will probably be the result of other curative factors.
The purpose of the relationship is the resolution of the client's issues. Compared with other relationships, the helper/client dyad is unbalanced in favor of the client. Even if the client invites it, the helper does not ask for or receive support from the client. It is a one-way street where the helper is the giver. The helper's own issues are dealt with outside of the client's hour.
There is a sense of teamwork as both helper and client work toward a mutually agreed-upon goal. The client can draw strength from the fact that the helper is there to provide support for change in the mutually decided direction. Just as a friend might become your ally in quitting smoking or maintaining an exercise program, the client feels the helper's presence as a constant nudge to grow.
There is a contract specifying what will be disclosed to others outside of the relationship. Safety and trust are established, allowing honest disclosure by the client and feedback from the helper. Unlike a friendship at work, confidences with a family member, or feelings shared with a neighbor, the client begins to realize that secrets will not circulate. As the client experiences this safety, he or she begins to discuss deeper and deeper issues. At times, the helping relationship requires the helper to give the client honest feedback or nonjudgmental information about the client's behavior.
There is an agreement about compensation for the helper. Although some helpers may be volunteers, most receive credit or money for each client hour. Even the volunteer may benefit by listing the work experience on his or her résumé. At the beginning of the relationship, helper and client discuss compensation. Help from a professional is usually not a gift but a fee-for-services relationship.
There is an understanding that the relationship is confined to the counseling sessions and does not overlap into the participants' personal lives. As a general rule, helpers try to devote regularly scheduled times to a client. Crises are exceptions to the rule, but nearly all helpers have a system for dealing with emergent problems. Most helpers give out a 24-hour crisis hotline number rather than their home phone number. They do not interact socially with clients when it can be avoided so that objectivity is not strained by other considerations.
As a contractual relationship, the relationship can be terminated at any time. A unique aspect of the helping relationship is that once the client has reached the identified goals, the helping relationship is put on hold until some

future help is needed. The relationship can be ended by either party at any time. Sometimes agencies specify how many sessions a client may be seen, and frequently insurance companies limit their payments to a certain time frame. Generally, the helper terminates the relationship when sufficient progress has been made or if the client is not making progress at all. Sometimes the relationship is ended by referral to another helper. Referral may be necessary when special needs are detected such as a need for sex therapy or substance abuse treatment.

How Can a Helper Create a Therapeutic Relationship?

So far, we have examined the therapeutic relationship from the perspective of a client and heard about its importance and special characteristics. But how can a helper create this special experience? Before looking at our suggestions, remember that you probably already know some of the ways to make a relationship work. You may have found that people naturally seek you out for help already. It is important to recognize your natural abilities and not discount them as you eliminate some behaviors and try out new ones.

Relationship Enhancers

Frederick Kanfer and Arnold Goldstein (1986, p. 21) identified key _relationship enhancers_ or helper behaviors that improve the quality of the therapeutic relationship. They include some nonverbal skills such as posture, as well as empathy, expertness and credibility, and self-disclosure. These helper behaviors lead to the emotional qualities or _relationship components_: liking, respect, and trust. In other words, the relationship enhancers create a favorable emotional climate for helping. Naturally, the presence of liking respect and trust have _relationship consequences_. They are communication, openness, and persuasibility. If we like, respect, and trust someone, there is a free flow of information—no holding back, and that person's suggestions hold more weight. Furthermore, when there is communication, openness, and persuasibility, there is the possibility of change. Thus, the very small helper behaviors called relationship enhancers cannot be ignored because they lead ultimately to the kind of safe and open relationship that gives the client the courage to change. Because our focus in this part of the chapter is on creating and enhancing the therapeutic relationship, let us look at four relationship enhancers (empathy, expertness, credibility, and self-disclosure) in a little more detail. We will leave non-verbal behaviors such as posture for a later, more in-depth discussion.

Physical Closeness, Posture, and Warmth

In the next chapter, you will learn the basic skills associated with physical distance, the creation of a warm atmosphere for helping, posture, and other body language skills. These nonverbals invite the client into a safe relationship and lead to greater openness. Although these may seem like small things, the ability to create an inviting relationship can have a powerful effect on others in all kinds of situations (Purkey, 1987). Let us assume that you are going for two different job interviews.

In the first case, the interviewer greets you by shaking your hand. Her voice is friendly and informal. When you arrive at her office, she smiles and welcomes you. Then she sits down in a chair next to you, turning it around so she can face you directly. Contrast this scenario with another office in which a secretary ushers you into the interviewer. The interviewer greets you from behind her desk. She spends much of the session staring at a file and making notes as she asks direct questions about your history. Under which circumstances are you likely to feel the most comfortable and to open up about your past? In which situation are you most able to get across the information you would like the potential employer to know? If one of these interviewers were to ask you to say something very personal about yourself, to whom would you be most likely to disclose? Although interviewing is not necessarily a helping relationship, even in this circumstance it is easy to see how powerful the small nonverbal enhancers can be in eliciting greater communication, openness, and persuasibility.

Empathy

The word *empathy* is derived from the German word *Einfhlung*, which means "feeling oneself into" another person's experience. Empathy means that you grasp the facts, the feelings, and the significance of another person's story; more important, empathy involves the ability to *convey* your accurate perceptions to the other person. There is a vast literature on the importance of empathy. Although much of it focuses on the helping relationship, empathy has proved to be a vital aspect of other interpersonal situations. Empathy training has been found to be an essential in good leadership and parenting (Gordon, 1986). Stephen Covey, in *The Seven Habits of Highly Effective People* (1990), recommends seeking "first to understand then to be understood" as one of the ingredients of personal job success regardless of your profession.

Recent news events have focused on alienated adults and teenagers who seem to lack any recognition of the feelings and needs of others. The book *Emotional Intelligence*, by Daniel Goleman (1995), suggests training in emotional awareness as the long-term cure for this condition in our society. Goleman's research shows that awareness of one's own emotions and those of others is among the most important predictors of success, mental health, happy families, and friendships. In summary, beyond its uses in helping, the skills of empathy can have a positive spillover into other areas of a person's life.

Helper empathy   The special thing about empathy in the helping relationship is that here the term encompasses the experiences of both client and helper. Empathy does not occur in this situation if the helper has not communicated understanding to the client. If the helper hears the story only superficially or appears judgmental, even if he or she is accurate about the facts, the client does not experience the helper's empathy. Empathy occurs when the client feels and may even say, "That's it! That's how I feel!" If we further analyze this statement, it could be said that a client experiences empathy when the helper communicates that he or she understands the facts, the emotions, and the special meanings of the client's story.

Empathy and differences   Empathy is a crucial skill in overcoming cultural, gender, and other differences between client and helper. Empathy means taking a "tutorial stance" rather than an authoritarian position when we are confronted with a person's life experience that clashes with our own. A *tutorial stance* means the helper becomes a learner, seeking to understand the client—recognizing that the helper must learn from the client what it is like to be that person.

Racism and prejudices about various cultural groups can be seen as a form of narcissism or self-absorption. We become so attached to our own perspective that we have no tolerance for those who do not share it. Of course, we all come to an interpersonal situation with cultural "baggage" and a worldview that contains prejudices of one kind or another. These will show up in our verbal and nonverbal messages. Clients recognize our attitudes not only from the things we say, but also by body language that may signal subtle disapproval. In the next chapter, we take up the issue of how to deal with these kinds of differences.

Empathy is a first step in getting us off our ethnocentric narcissism and signals to clients that we are trying to "feel ourselves into" their world, rather than attempting to convert them to our perspective. Although empathy provides a doorway to the inner life of another person, is it really ever possible to enter the world of another completely, leaving behind the vestiges of our own beliefs? We may not be able to completely grasp another person's reality; however, it is important that our clients recognize that we are struggling to understand, that we care enough to try. In the next chapter, we focus specifically on how to help someone who is different.

What empathy isn't *Empathy is not merely supporting or agreeing with the client.* Consider the following story related by a school counselor:

Last week, I saw 17-year-old Monique, a young woman who has been accepted to college with a full scholarship. She has a keen intellect and is especially good in math. She has always preferred older men, and now she has become pregnant by a man, David, who is 15 years older than she is. Recently, she found out that he was lying to her about his relationships with other women and that he had even lied to her about his job, saying that he was an architect when, in fact, he is a paraprofessional in an architect's office. Her parents have told her she cannot remain in their home because they do not wish to raise another child. Although David will support her, she is afraid of him because she has heard he can become violent. Monique is also afraid to stay with him and feels that if she has a child with him, they will be bonded forever. She is considering an abortion because she feels that she misjudged him and cannot see a good future for herself or the child.

This situation presented a dilemma for the helper because, although she could empathize with the client's situation, she felt that by empathizing she was supporting the client's decision to obtain an abortion. Many helpers are afraid to empathize with a client for fear of taking sides. In fact, though, empathy can help clients examine their feelings at a deeper level and make decisions that are more consistent with their own feelings and values. You can communicate understanding about the circumstances that spawned the problem without supporting or agreeing with the client's subsequent action.

Empathy is not pretending to understand. In the next chapters, you will learn some techniques to help you communicate empathy to clients. You will discover, however, that empathy is not effective if it is not sincere. Clients pick up on the nonverbals as well as on what you say. Merely saying the prescribed formula will not help the client if you truly do not understand the situation. The best advice for the beginning helper is to be patient. Spend as much time as you need to hear the story before you tell the client that you understand.

Empathy is not taking on your client's problems.   For the most part, helper fears about being overwhelmed by the client's problems are unfounded. Empathic people try to understand another person's pain in order to relieve it (Johnson, 1990). Consequently, it may be natural to fear that problems are "catching" and that by entering another person's world too deeply, we may become depressed ourselves. Although it is impossible not to be affected in some way by great pain, you learn over time to deal with it within the session and not let it hamper your time with the next person or carry over into your personal life. The great therapist Frieda Fromm-Reichmann (1960) claimed that we must learn to be like skin divers able to go to the depth of a client's problems but also able to surface when we need to.

Empathy is not a one-time behavior.   Although empathy is especially important in the relationship-building stage of the helping process, empathy is crucial throughout. As the relationship develops, the client may disclose more and more deeply. For example, as marriage counseling progresses, instead of talking about the problems the kids are having at school, a couple might begin to examine their attitudes about child rearing and their disagreements about how to discipline. These very personal topics might require the helper to empathize at a deeper level, trying to understand their perspectives and how these were shaped by their own families.

Expertness and Credibility

For the relationship to gel, the helper must first qualify for the job (Ritter, Bowden, Murray, Ross, Greeley, & Pead, 2002; Yalom, 1985). In other words, it is important for the client to perceive the helper as a competent professional, an expert. Writers have called this client perception *credibility* (Sue & Zane, 1987) or *expertness* (Barak, Patkin, & Dell, 1982; Heppner & Dixon, 1986; Ritter et al., 2002; Strong, 1968). Client expectations of competence are increased by objective evidence of competency: the helper's office, therapeutic rituals, reputation, and even the certificates and diplomas hanging on the walls (Frank, 1961; Loesch, 1984). Larry Bloom (Bloom, Schroeder, & Babineau, 1981; Bloom, Weigel & Trautt, 1978; Schroeder & Bloom, 1979) has researched the notion of credibility in the therapeutic relationship. One of his findings is that helpers who are seen in a traditional professional office are perceived as significantly more credible than those seen in a more informal setting.

If a client perceives the helper as credible, the client is also more likely to be attracted to and respect the helper. Ultimately, experts are more persuasive (Corrigan, Dell, Lewis, & Schmidt, 1980; Strong, 1968). In a review of the literature, Heppner and Dixon (1986) indicated that objective evidence of training, as well as certain helper behaviors and "prestigious cues," affects ratings of helper expertness by the clients. These behaviors and cues include (1) appearing confident, organized, and interested and (2) exhibiting nonverbal behaviors associated with attentiveness. Using interpretive statements and psychological jargon was also found to increase ratings of expertness. Although the latter may seem phony, they are consistent with Frank's (1961) idea that one of the ways that helpers influence clients is to induct them into a therapeutic ritual and set of procedures. According to Frank, the office setting, the ritual, and the therapeutic procedures all help to reassure the client, overcome the client's fears, and combat the demoralization that has caused the client to seek help. How would you feel, for example, if you were facing a serious lawsuit and you found that your attorney's office was a disorganized room behind a convenience store? In the next chapter, we will look at how differences such as gender and culture affect this issue of credibility.

The issue of competence does have a dark side. The client may overestimate and idealize the helper's powers. He or she may attribute success to the helper, rather than to his or her own efforts. Although helpers are uncomfortable with the admiration of clients, it may be difficult and perhaps counterproductive to discourage the client's perception that the helper is an expert, at least in the beginning. Sheldon Kopp (1978) uses a metaphor to explain this. Kopp compares the client to Dorothy in *The Wizard of Oz*, who sees the helper as a powerful sorcerer (Oz) hidden behind a screen. Because of the client's confidence in the sorcerer's power, he or she is empowered to go out and kill the wicked witch. Here, killing the wicked witch symbolizes the client's efforts to achieve goals and make necessary changes in his or her life. It is only at a later stage that the client is ready to see the helper as just a person behind the curtain. A client may have to go through the process of therapy before realizing that the source of strength, like Dorothy's, has been there, within himself or herself, all the time. If the client does not eventually abandon this magical view of the helper, the client will not be able to take responsibility for the change process and will instead wait for the wave of the helper's wand. As Alicia B.'s story in the beginning of the chapter suggests, however, faith in the helper is useful, especially when the client has lost faith in his or her own ability to cope.

Some helpers find this kind of talk disturbing because it implies that the helper should try to present a powerful but possibly phony image. This certainly could have harmful effects for both client and helper. Helpers are not sorcerers and should not try to feed their egos in the helping process. On the other hand, some helpers have the mistaken impression that they should do nothing to communicate credibility and expertness to clients. Dressing informally and being overly casual may make the helper, but not the client, feel more comfortable. Perceptions of expertness lead to positive outcomes, including faith and trust in the process of helping, and faith is powerful medicine (Ritter et al., 2002).

Self-Disclosure and the Therapeutic Relationship

> In the first place, it is hypothesized that personal growth is facilitated when the psychotherapist is what he is, when in the relationship with his client, he is genuine and "without" front or facade, openly being the feelings and attitudes which at the moment are flowing in him. We have coined the term "congruence" to try and describe this condition. By this we mean that the feelings the therapist is experiencing are available to him, available to his awareness, that he is able to live these feelings, be them, and able to communicate them if appropriate. (Rogers, 1972, p. 129)

The quote from Carl Rogers emphasizes one very positive effect of self-disclosure by the helper, namely, that the client begins to see the helper as an honest and open person. Rogers's quote also contains a caution. Self-disclosure by the helper must be "appropriate." In other words, the helper must consider what kinds of disclosure will be helpful to the client. Self-disclosure is not initiated to develop a social relationship or to allow the helper to ventilate feelings (Weiner, 1979). Still, helper self-disclosure has been shown to increase trust in the relationship (Johnson & Matross, 1977; Jourard, 1971), make the helper more attractive (Goodyear & Schumate, 1996), deepen client self-disclosure, and encourage expression of feelings (McCarthy, 2001; Nilsson, Strassberg, & Bannon, 1979; Sermat & Smythe, 1973). It appears that moderate levels of self-disclosure are better than highly personal or only mildly personal disclosures (Bannikotes, Kubinski, & Purcell, 1981; Edwards & Murdock, 1994).

The research on self-disclosure has come to differentiate between self-disclosing and self-involving statements by the helper (Cashwell, Shcherbakova, & Cashwell, 2003; McCarthy, 1979, 1982). Helper self-disclosure occurs when the helper relates facts about himself or herself. Self-involving statements occur when the helper shares his or her thoughts and emotions about the client. To show this distinction, take a look at the two helper statements below:

> "You said you wanted to know a little bit about me. I have been practicing for the last 7 years in this area, but I grew up in New England where most of my family still lives. I'm married and have three children. My practice here centers on individuals going through divorce. I also run couples groups, which I really like." (self-disclosing statement)
>
> "I've noticed in the past few weeks that you seem to be irritated whenever I bring up the fact that you have not been looking for work. I am wondering if it is just too stressful a topic, and I find myself being reluctant to mention this even though it is one of the main problems we agreed to work on." (self-involving statement)

In general, research has supported self-involving statements but has not always endorsed self-disclosure (Cashwell et al., 2003; Knox, Hess, Petersen, & Hill, 1997; Watkins, 1990). One reason is that much seems to depend on the client's preference for self-disclosure (Cashwell et al., 2003). In other words, clients vary in how much disclosure they can handle without feeling that the helper is too self-focused or unprofessional. Second, it appears that timing is important. Self-disclosing statements (facts about the helper) are more useful early in treatment, while self-involving statements may be more effective later on (McCarthy, 2001). Finally, there are all kinds of disclosures, ranging from the superficial "I have a master's degree" to the very personal "I once had a drinking problem."

Too much self-disclosure can be a serious mistake. One of the best discussions of this is contained in Kottler and Blau's book, *The Imperfect Therapist* (1989). According to the authors, "Whether the therapist's ignorance, insensitivity, or narcissism are at fault, more than a few clients have been chased out of treatment because they felt negated by the repeated focus on the therapist's life" (p. 137). Kottler and Blau go on to say that clients are "frightened away" because helpers who talk about themselves make the client feel less important. Clients with low self-esteem do not want to hear about the successes of others. Helpers may lose their authority as transference figures and might be less able to influence the client through modeling. Finally, the client becomes bored with the repetition of therapist stories and anecdotes. The mistake here is that the helper simply spends too much time in self-disclosure. Taking too much time for helper self-disclosure may put more stress on a client who already feels overburdened. Kottler and Blau contend that the saddest aspect of this situation is that the helper is usually unaware of the problem. To give a concrete example, a couple recently came to me for premarital counseling. They had been dissatisfied with a previous therapist because "She didn't seem interested in us. Instead, she spent the whole hour talking about her relationship with her husband and how they handled their differences. It seemed like they had the perfect marriage. It was a waste of time and money." Later, I found out that this therapist and her husband were getting a divorce because of serious problems. Although one might be tempted to explain the lack of therapeutic connection as a feeling that the couple could not measure up, it is just as likely they felt ignored and bored.

Common mistakes in helper self-disclosure   The following are some examples of other common errors in self-disclosure made by helpers. The purpose of self-disclosure is to enhance the relationship, help the client realize that he or she is not alone, help the client see another viewpoint, or convey that the client's experience is normal. However, if the helper's story clashes with the client's, self-disclosure may have the opposite effect. Many of the mistakes are due to the helper failing to realize that the client needs to focus on his or her own issues. Obviously, self-disclosure shifts the focus onto the helper. Once disclosure is made, it is imperative that the helper shift the focus back onto the client.

Mistake 1: The helper's self-disclosure is too deep. The client has to react to the helper, rather than focus on parallels between the two stories.

> **Situation:** The client expresses that she feels like a failure because she is going through a divorce.
> **Inappropriate Disclosure by the Helper:** "When I was going through my third divorce, I thought that there was something wrong with me. After all, I am supposed to help other people with their problems. So I went into therapy for over a year."
> **Appropriate Disclosure by the Helper:** "I have been through divorce myself and I can relate to those feelings. I guess they are pretty common."

Mistake 2: Self-disclosure is poorly timed. When a person has gone through a traumatic event, it is a poor time to get him or her to focus on the helper's story. Rather, the client should be encouraged to disclose more.

> **Situation:** The client's mother died last week. (In this case, the client cannot really appreciate or focus on another person's story.)
> **Inappropriate Disclosure by the Helper:** "I know just how you feel because my mother died about 5 years ago after a long illness. It was a long time before I got over it."
> **Appropriate Disclosure by the Helper:** "I don't know exactly what you are going through, but I know a little bit about what it means to lose someone that close. I can guess that this whole thing has been very painful for you."

Mistake 3: The helper's self-disclosure does not match the client's experience.

> **Situation:** The client has received a basketball scholarship to go to college. No one in her family has ever gone to a university. She is having trouble achieving satisfactory college board scores for admission.
> **Inappropriate Disclosure by the Helper:** "Once I wanted to go to a prep school that cost $20,000 per year. But I had to go to one that cost a lot less because my family couldn't afford it."
> **Appropriate Disclosure by the Helper:** "I can relate to your story in that I have had some goals in my life that I wanted that badly. It must be frustrating to be almost there and run into this new hurdle."

In summary, self-disclosure is a technique that must be used with caution and at the right time. For this reason, we discuss it here because it can affect the therapeutic relationship, but we will also reintroduce it as you learn building blocks skills. Self-disclosure can be used to bond with the client. Self-disclosure at this stage can help the client feel less alone. Self-involving statements can be used later in the counseling process to (1) inspire hope in the client and (2) provide feedback, confrontation, or an alternative viewpoint. We will learn more about self-disclosure in Chapter 5 when we look at invitational skills and self-involving statements and in Chapter 9 when we discuss challenging skills.

Other Factors That Help or Strain the Therapeutic Relationship

In the last section, we examined the effect of helper self-disclosure on the therapeutic relationship. Here, we will talk about some other commonly identified issues that may lead to a stronger or weaker therapeutic alliance. Among these are the environment where helping takes place, the therapeutic blunders that we can try to avoid, and the issues of transference and countertransference.

Facilitative Office Environment

The helper's office should be quiet, comfortable, orderly, and well lit. Most professionals and clients prefer soft lighting to bright fluorescence. Decorating that is comfortable rather than clinical is helpful, especially at the beginning of a therapeutic relationship (see Pressly & Heesacker, 2001). Sigmund Freud called his office a "consulting room." In other words, it should not be the therapist's living room, nor should it look like a laboratory (Bloom, Weigel, & Trautt, 1977). The office should not be merely an outgrowth of the helper's personality but a workplace. Generally, it is recommended that the helper face away from the desk so that there are no obstacles between client and helper (Pietrofesa, Hoffman, & Splete, 1984). Side tables are useful for a clock and the indispensable boxes of facial tissue. Although it is easy to depict the ideal, not all helpers today have the model facilitative environment. School counselors see students in the hallways and in the lunchroom in 5-minute snatches some times. Other helpers work in cubicles without soundproofing. Many work out of their cars, doing home visits and actually conducting sessions in their clients' homes. For them, the issues of distractions and privacy must be dealt with creatively. Many have traveling kits that can be unpacked to create a "therapeutic space," with clocks, tissues, and play equipment for working with children.

Distractions

Noise from outside can interfere with the session, disrupting a delicate moment or giving the client the feeling that he or she may be heard by persons outside. A "Quiet Please" sign or one that says "Session in Progress" should be placed on the outside of the door. In some cases, it may be necessary to purchase a mechanical white-noise or ocean-sound device that can act as a "sound blanket." Position office seating to provide the most freedom from glaring lights, noise, and the possibility of being overheard.

Other disturbances to be avoided during the session include knocking on the door and phone calls (Benjamin, 1969). Beier and Young (1998), in their classic book on therapeutic communication, *The Silent Language of Psychotherapy*, make the point that a helper communicates the importance he or she places on the relationship by the way in which these distractions are handled. If you were a client, how would you feel if I answered the phone during our sessions and ate a bag of potato chips? What would you conclude?

Schmoozing

Schmoozing is a Yiddish word that is nearly the equivalent of our English phrase "shooting the breeze." It refers to discussions between the client and the helper that are merely social and apparently unrelated to the client's problems. Schmoozing may have value at some points in the therapeutic relationship: It allows for a truly human encounter between client and helper. Sometimes the client is curious about the helper's personal life. Where this curiosity does not endanger the helper's safety and privacy, schmoozing (self-disclosure) can help client and helper develop a better relationship. At other times, useful information about the client's hobbies and special abilities comes to light in this way. Schmoozing is too easily abused to be encouraged wholesale. Like self-disclosure, it may place too much focus on the helper rather than on the client. Schmoozing puts helping on a social level and, if overused, may distract us from the major purpose of the session, which is to help the client find solutions.

Therapeutic Faux Pas

Faux pas is a French term meaning "false steps" or "wrong turns." It is better to think of faux pas not as mistakes, but as detours that can be corrected later. Thomas Gordon (1986) identified 12 such "wrong turns," known as the "dirty dozen," that may occur in the development of a helping relationship. These are listed—with examples—in Table 3.1.

Gordon feels that there are two general messages communicated by the 12 roadblocks. First, they communicate that the client is incapable of solving his or her own problems. Second, they communicate that the client needs another person to solve the problems for him or her. Both are disempowering messages that take the responsibility for change away from the client and place it in the hands of

Table 3.1
Roadblocks to Communication

1. **Ordering, Directing, Commanding**
   You must do this
   You cannot do this.
   I expect you to do this.
   Stop it.
   Go apologize to her.

2. **Warning, Admonishing, Threatening**
   You had better do this, or else . . .
   If you don't do this, then . . .
   You better not try that.
   I warn you, if you do that . . .

3. **Moralizing, Preaching, Imploring**
   You should do this.
   You ought to try it.
   It is your responsibility to do this.
   It is your duty to do this.
   I wish you would do this.
   I urge you to do this.

4. **Advising, Giving Suggestions or Solutions**
   What I think you should do is . . .
   Let me suggest . . .
   It would be best for you if . . .
   Why not take a different approach?
   The best solution is . . .

5. **Persuading with Logic, Lecturing, Arguing**
   Do you realize that . . .
   The facts are in favor of . . .
   Let me give you the facts.
   Here is the right way.
   Experience tells us that . . .

6. **Judging, Criticizing, Disagreeing, Blaming**
   You are acting foolishly.
   You are not thinking straight.
   You are out of line.
   You didn't do it right.
   You are wrong.
   That is a stupid thing to say.

7. **Praising, Agreeing, Evaluating Positively, Buttering Up**
   You usually have very good judgment.
   You are an intelligent person.

   You have so much potential.
   You've made quite a bit of progress.
   You have always made it in the past.

8. **Name-Calling, Ridiculing, Shaming**
   You are a sloppy worker.
   You are a fuzzy thinker.
   You're talking like an engineer.
   You really goofed on this one!

9. **Interpreting, Analyzing, Diagnosing**
   You're saying this because you're angry.
   You are jealous.
   What you really need is . . .
   You have problems with authority.
   You want to look good.
   You are being a bit paranoid.

10. **Reassuring, Sympathizing, Consoling, Supporting**
    You'll feel different tomorrow.
    Things will get better.
    It is always darkest before the dawn.
    Behind every cloud there's a silver lining.
    Don't worry so much about it.
    It's not that bad.

11. **Probing, Questioning, Interrogating**
    Why did you do that?
    How long have you felt this way?
    What have you done to try to solve it?
    Have you consulted with anyone?
    When did you become aware of this feeling?
    Who has influenced you?

12. **Distracting, Diverting, Kidding**
    Think about the positive side.
    Try not to think about it until you're rested.
    Let's have lunch and forget about it.
    That reminds me of the time when . . .
    You think you've got problems!

Source: Adapted from T. Gordon (2001). *Leadership effectiveness training,* pp. 65–68. New York: Random House.

the helper. Besides these 12 major detours, Wolberg (1967) has identified some other helper responses that can weaken or disrupt the therapeutic relationship. These include:

Exclamations of Surprise

Client: "I spanked the living daylights out of my kids last night."

> **Helpful:** "What led you to do this?"
> "You must have been really frustrated to have resorted to that. What other things might you have done?"
> **Not Helpful:** "You what?!"
> "That's awful!"

Being Punitive

Client: "I don't think that you are giving me the help I need."

> **Helpful:** "You feel stuck, that you are not making any progress."
> "What kind of help do you think would be useful to you at this time?"
> **Not Helpful:** "Then I will just refer you to someone else."
> "You are not making progress because you are not working on the problem."

Giving False Reassurance

Sometimes clients want us to give them hope that the helping process will be successful. This can backfire if the helper makes promises that cannot be kept.

Client: "Will I ever get over this completely and be normal?"

> **Helpful:** "First, tell me how you would like your life to be. What would normal look like to you?"
> "Right now, you are feeling unsure about whether you can conquer this problem. I am hopeful that we can make a significant change if we work together."
> **Not Helpful:** "Of course you will."
> "I think that you are normal now!"
> "You will be better in 6 weeks. I guarantee it."

Psychobabble and Premature Interpretations

Psychobabble is a word describing the overuse of psychological terminology. When the helper identifies a technical term for every issue, the client feels that his or her problems are trivialized or that they have become clinical syndromes. *Premature interpretation* is suggesting deep meanings before adequate data have been collected to support these interpretations.

Client: "My father was an alcoholic and my mother seemed to tolerate it. We lived in denial our whole lives."

> **Helpful:** "Tell me more about what you mean by denial."
> "Tell me something about your family relationships."
> **Not Helpful:** "That's because your mother was codependent and that makes you ACOA (adult child of an alcoholic)."
> "That is why you are a dependent personality."

Probing Traumatic Issues When the Client Strongly Resists

Respecting the client's wish to avoid a topic can be handled by noting it, reflecting, and suggesting that it can be put off until later. Damage to the relationship can take place when the helper mercilessly pursues a topic. It is often a question of timing. Sometimes it is best to nurture the relationship and address the topic later.

Client: "I don't want to talk about sex."

> **Helpful:** "It is a painful subject for you."
> "All right, we can come back to that another time if you want."
> **Not Helpful:** "We have to talk about it sometime."
> "Then, let's talk about your past sex life."

Transference and Countertransference

If we look closely at the relationship components and relationship consequences in columns 2 and 3 of Table 3.1, we can see that as the relationship develops, a sort of intimacy grows. An atmosphere of openness, liking, respect, and trust is developing. This kind of therapeutic intimacy is generally seen as a positive state of agreement and mutual caring. It creates favorable conditions for change (Rogers, 1957) and increases client involvement and compliance with treatment.

However, intimacy also tends to elicit strong feelings—feelings that may have had their genesis in previous relationships. *Transference* and *countertransference* are terms that originated among psychoanalysts to denote these powerful feelings that develop when client and helper bond. As client and helper grow closer, a client may experience the same emotions of self-doubt, fear of abandonment, and other residue from parental or love relationships. This is *transference reaction*. On the other hand, the helper may also see the client as a reflection of a past or present relationship or may experience strong emotions for the client. This is called *countertransference*. When the helper finds that the client's progress is stymied by the relationship itself, the helper must be trained and willing to examine the therapeutic relationship itself as a living model of the client's social world. When the helper finds personal needs spilling over into the therapeutic setting, he or she needs to consult with a supervisor and deal with these issues privately.

Stop and Reflect

It is said that we make first impressions in less than 4 seconds. So it is possible to experience transference reactions immediately on meeting an individual, that is, without having a close relationship. Most of us are familiar with automatic feelings of liking or disliking a person on sight. These emotional reactions are most likely due to experiences with a similar person in the past, and they may be vague and impressionistic, in other words, unreasonable. One simple way to categorize such reactions is to label them positive, neutral, or negative.

As an experiment, take a look around at your classmates and mentally note your feelings for each one—especially for those you have never met before this class or know only slightly. List each person's name or indicate some memorable feature such as "blue shirt." Next to each person, put a plus sign (+) next to those for whom you feel a positive attraction and a minus sign (−) if you have a negative feeling. If there is neither attraction nor a negative feeling, write N for neutral. You may think that it is unfair to assign a value to your feelings without taking into account the fact that you do not really know all your classmates well. That is true, but these impressions, like all first impressions, can be powerful. As mentioned earlier, we experience these first impressions within the first 4 seconds and act on them whether or not they are valid. Are there any real reasons for the positives and negatives you recorded? Are they the result of experiences with similar people? Think about the names of your classmates. Does any evoke an emotional reaction? If you had to choose two people in the class to play your parents in a role play, whom would you choose? Are you transferring any of your experiences with your parents or significant others to these people?

What Is Transference?

Transference is a client's carryover of feelings from past relationships into a new one—the client/helper relationship. Relationship-building activities, such as listening and providing conditions of safety, increase feelings of intimacy and enhance the possibility of transference. Clients' feelings can be described as positive, ranging from liking to sexual attraction, or negative, ranging from suspiciousness to hatred (Watkins, 1986). Negative transference reactions are thought to be an important reason for treatment failures (Basch, 1980) because clients often drop out of therapy rather than face them. Although it may be impossible to avoid transference altogether (Gelso & Carter, 1985), in many helping relationships, transference never endangers the relationship or the client's progress. For others, it is vital to examine the therapeutic relationship as a first step in setting other relationships straight. A client may experience such strong feelings toward the helper that they become a roadblock that must be overcome in order for treatment to continue. When issues of transference interfere with the attainment of goals, they must be dealt with, either in an isolated fashion or in conjunction with other relationship problems the client may be experiencing.

Why are we looking at a complicated issue like transference so early in your skill training? Dealing with such issues is certainly an advanced skill. But this is a chapter about all the things that can delay or prevent the formation of a therapeutic relationship, and it is crucial to address some of the initial challenges that you will face as you learn the art of helping. You may find that this chapter is most helpful when you start seeing clients in a school, agency, or clinical setting, although it is background for the basic skills you will learn and something to refer to when real relationship breakdowns occur.

Psychodynamic Conceptions of Transference

Some believe that transference is caused by unfinished business from the past. This notion is central to psychoanalysis, which asserts that issues surface from the unconscious because they are unresolved. Freud believed that resolution of transference was the most important aspect of therapy because it allowed the client to address emotional issues about parents and siblings. One alternative viewpoint that has emerged is to conceptualize transference as a set of cognitive distortions, rather than as unresolved conflicts or unfulfilled needs (Sullivan, 1954). These distortions are learned patterns of thinking, not unlike the irrational ideas that have been described by Albert Ellis (1985). Still, there is a common thread that binds the modern viewpoint to the psychoanalytic idea. In both conceptualizations, the client is seen as focused on the outside (external causes of behavior) versus the inside (self-direction). The client is thinking about the attributes of the helper, rather than focusing on self-awareness. Even if it is a positive distortion, it is not reality. Hero worship may damage self-esteem if one compares oneself in a negative way to the helper (Singer, 1970).

To summarize, on the one hand, the client may have distorted ideas about the helper and the helping relationship that should be addressed. These may appear as inflated expectations about the helper, believing that he or she will solve all the problems single-handedly. Alternatively, the client may have strong negative feelings for the helper, especially when overblown expectations are not met. Watkins (1986) has identified five major transference patterns that are based on the concept of transference as cognitive distortion. Table 3.2, adapted from Watkins, shows these patterns along with the client's attitudes and the helper's reaction to them.

Table 3.2
Major Transference Patterns

Client Behaviors/Attitudes	Counselor Experiences
Counselor as Ideal	
Compliments counselor profusely	Feels pride, satisfaction, and
Imitates counselor	all-competent
Wears similar clothing	Experiences tension, anxiety, confusion,
General idealization	anger, and frustration
Counselor as Seer	
Ascribes omniscience and power to the counselor	Experiences "God complex" and self-doubt
Views counselor as expert	Feels incompetent and pressure to
Sees self as incompetent	be right and live up to client's
Seeks answers, solutions, and advice	expectations
Counselor as Nurturer	
Experiences profuse emotion and sense of fragility	Experiences feelings of sorrow, sympathy, depression, despair, and depletion
Cries	Has urge to soothe, coddle, and touch
Feels dependent, helpless, and indecisive	
Desires to be touched and held	
Counselor as Frustrator	
Feels defensive, cautious, guarded, suspicious, and distrustful	Feels uneasy, on edge (walking on eggshells), tense, hostile, and hateful
Tests counselor	Withdraws and becomes unavailable
	Dislikes and blames client
Counselor as Nonentity	
Shifts topics	Feels overwhelmed, subdued, taken
Lacks focus	aback, used, useless
Is voluble and desultory	Experiences resentment, frustration,
Meanders aimlessly	and lack of recognition
	Characterizes self as a nonperson

Countertransference: Dealing with the Helper's Feelings

Countertransference is defined as the helper's strong emotional reactions to a client. To give an example of this, consider this true story that a practicum student tells about one of her first clients:

> My client is a 35-year-old woman who owns her own business. She showed up for her first session 5 minutes late. When I came to the waiting room, she complained loudly that she had been waiting for 10 minutes and then followed me to my office in a huff. Although I was pretty sure that she had been late, not me, I was on the defensive from the beginning, and I felt very uncomfortable and intimidated by her. As I watched the tape, I saw the many unreasonable demands she made. For example, she said that she needed to change seats with me because there was too much glare in her eyes. She criticized the decorating and quizzed me about whether or not I had read the notes of the previous counselor. I watched myself on the tape just back down and become silent. I talked this over with my supervisor, who also noticed my passive behavior. I think that I reacted this way partially because this was my typical behavior with my previous boyfriend. Although he was not violent, he was verbally explosive, and I learned to become quiet and back off during his rages. Now I am doing the same thing with this client.

Countertransference is an issue not fully appreciated by the beginning helper. When intellectualizing about the therapeutic relationship, one can hardly imagine the powerful feelings that some clients may elicit. In the example above, it would be easy to blame the client for her behavior and label her as uncooperative. Although her interpersonal behavior may have to be addressed later in the helping process, the helper's reaction merits examination too. In practice, helpers need ongoing supervision to monitor the tendency to be too helpful and to deal with feelings of sexual attraction, as well as fear and insecurity. Anger toward clients is one of the most common issues (Fremont & Anderson, 1986). Normally such issues are dealt with between helper and supervisor and not in the presence of the client. However, because countertransference can seriously disrupt the client/helper bond, it merits discussion in this chapter on the therapeutic relationship.

Some helpers try to deal with their own feelings simply by disclosing everything to the client. Such disclosure is a mistake if motivated by the helper's need to relieve his or her own discomfort: The therapeutic relationship is based on a contract that implicitly agrees that the helper should disclose information only if it is beneficial to the client. The therapeutic relationship is not a friendship, nor is it a two-way street. It involves a helper and the person being helped. The helper agrees to set his or her own needs aside and to do what is best for the client. Table 3.3 describes common helper emotional reactions, based on information collected by Corey, Corey, and Callanan (2003). The essential point of the information in the table is that countertransference issues are generally emotional reactions to clients, which can then lead to certain behaviors on the part of the helper. Instead of helping the client achieve mutually derived goals, the helper develops a second (you might say unconscious) agenda that changes the helper's view of the client as a contractual partner in the therapy process. The helper has come to see the client as a project, as a sexual object, as a friend, or even as a reflection of the self.

Table 3.3
Common Patterns of Countertransference

Counselor Emotional Response to Client	Counselor Behavior	Client Seen As
Paternal/maternal nurturing	Overprotective Failure to challenge	Fragile
Fear of client's anger	Reduction of conflict Attempts to please	Aggressor
Disgust, disapproval	Rejection	Needy Immoral
Need for reassurance	Socializing	Friend
Need for liking	Failure to challenge	
Anxiety	Avoidance of emotionally charged topics	
Insecurity		
Feelings of identification	Advice giving Overinvolvement Failure to recognize client's uniqueness	Self
Sexual	Seductive behavior	Sexual object
Romantic	Inappropriate self-disclosure Reduced focus on presenting problems Inappropriate exploration of sexual topics	Romantic partner
Frustration	Extreme confrontation	Product
Anger	Scolding Criticizing	Success

Countertransference is as common as transference, and most helpers regularly have strong feelings about their clients. Much of the unethical behavior in which helpers indulge is probably due to the strong emotions elicited in the therapeutic relationship, which make us forget our "asocial," contractual role. This is one reason why a supervisory relationship is so crucial for every helper. The supervisor's role is to appeal to the helper's professional and ethical sense and to remind the helper to act in accordance with therapeutic goals.

Dealing with Transference from a Client

A client's strong emotional reactions to the helper may be the result of transference or may be honest reactions to the helper's behavior. In both cases, the task of the helper is the same: to help the client gain more awareness and to nondefensively explore the source of these feelings. As examples, let us look briefly at how a helper can react therapeutically when a client expresses strong feelings of anger.

Step 1: Convey acceptance of the client's remarks but don't retaliate.
Dealing with an angry client is one of the most difficult and delicate issues in helping. One reason is that it tends to evoke anger in the helper. Retaliation or a defensive response can be perceived by the client as a weakness, as an admission of guilt, or as a punishment. The client's anger may be triggered by frustration over lack of progress

or by the perception that the helper is unfriendly, inept, or destructive. After having expressed this hostility, the client may be concerned about angering or hurting the helper or may fear abandonment.

Example:

Client: I don't think we're getting anywhere. When are we going to deal with the real issues? I'm sick of coming in here and paying all this money.

Helper: I can tell you're angry. I'm glad you had the courage to be so honest. I can't think of anything that will be of more help to you than dealing with this issue.

Step 2: Explore the client's feelings.   Following an expression of hostility toward the helper, the client may retreat, fearing he or she will be punished, lose control, or hurt the helper. Exploration of a client's hostile feelings involves continuing to encourage the expression and labeling of feelings while trying to clarify the source of the anger.

Example:

Client: I don't think this is working, and I am tired of coming in here and being told that it is all my fault.

Helper: What made you feel that it was all your fault?

or

Helper: Do you have the sense that I am blaming you for not changing?

or

Helper: You wish I would be more supportive.

Step 3: Utilize self-involving statements to help the client become aware of the helper's genuine thoughts and emotions about the client and the client's behavior.   Self-involving statements are the helper's thoughts and feelings that are shared with the client as information about the relationship.

Example:

Client: You are darn right you should be more supportive. Nobody supports me, not my wife, not my boss. I have to blow my top before they will even listen.

Helper (self-involving statement): I can tell you're angry with me because you think I am siding with these other people. I don't see it that way. I feel very much on your side, but I also feel a duty to help you look at what you are doing. And I can see where your anger is hurting your relationships.

Here is another example of a self-involving statement given by a helper when his client expressed feelings of romantic attraction:

Example:

Helper: I must say I am flattered and a little uneasy when you say you feel this way about me. I am uneasy because I don't want this to interfere with the progress we're making. At the same time, I need to tell you I don't share your feelings. I don't want to hurt your feelings, and I don't want to make you feel embarrassed.

I also don't want to lose the closeness that we have felt going through all the crises over the past year.

Step 4: Use the experience to help the client to find new and better ways of expressing feelings and meeting his or her needs. If the helper can avoid blaming, embarrassing, or shaming the client, the client's expressions of strong emotions such as anger or attraction can be used to examine the client's interpersonal life. Clients who exhibit excessive anger or who are indirect or revengeful may be alienating others and thereby engaging in self-defeating patterns. Clients who romanticize all close relationships may need to find ways of developing more intimate friendships that are not sexual in nature. Dealing with transference by listening, exploring, and disclosing has the effect of making clients aware of these patterns, but clients still may need assistance either individually or in a structured group to learn new and more productive ways of behaving. These interpersonal patterns are automatic and reflexive. Clients need to utilize the therapeutic relationship as a tool to examine new situations as they arise and to design alternative responses.

Example:

Client: I don't know why I blow up. But I don't know what else to do.

Helper: In this session, you have mentioned a number of situations besides this relationship in which you feel that you have to explode in order to be heard. I am not at all sure that is your only alternative. I think it would be helpful to learn and try out some new ways of relating, and you can practice on me. How do you feel about that?

Summary

In this chapter, we discussed the therapeutic relationship as a keystone in the process of change. In the stages of the helping relationship, the relationship is seen to empower all the other activities that a helper uses to aid a client, including assessment, goal setting, intervention, and evaluation. There are a number of helper behaviors that can enhance the relationship, including nonverbals such as physical closeness, posture, and warmth. In addition, empathy, expertness and credibility, self-disclosure, and a good helper/client match can make the helping relationship stronger. The attribute of empathy was discussed in some detail because it seems to be a foundational skill, as well as an attitude that allows us to enter more deeply into relationships.

There are also issues and behaviors that can strain the budding alliance. Among these are the 12 roadblocks of Thomas Gordon, a number of therapeutic faux pas, a poor office environment, and the challenges of transference and countertransference. Some time was taken in this chapter to deal with the issue of how to handle differences between client and helper when they seem to weaken the relationship. Extreme differences in culture, socioeconomic status, family background, and ethnic origin have their primary impact early in the session. Unless the therapeutic bond is forged quickly, there may be slow progress or clients may simply drop out. Although it may be impossible to cross all the barriers between people, because of the changing nature of our world, the helpers of tomorrow must possess the skills, knowledge, and attitudes that help them appreciate different people, different families, and different cultures. One of the subtle points of this chapter is that a helping relationship is not a social relationship. It is more important that there be a working alliance than a friendship. The social skills of making clients feel comfortable, talking about the weather, and being a friendly person can reduce anxiety in the beginning stages, but the helping relationship should not be constrained by the social forces of politeness and cultural tendencies to avoid certain topics for fear of embarrassment or controversy. Entering a helping relationship requires you to boldly go where few have gone before, using the relationship as the fuel to explore more and more deeply into the mystery of another person.

Exercises

Group Exercise 1

Take a look at the list of six characteristics of a therapeutic relationship described in the beginning of this chapter. Compare a therapeutic relationship with a friendship or a relationship with a favorite teacher. What are the similarities and differences? Discuss this in a small group.

Group Exercise 2

Barriers to Communication

Divide into groups of three to five students. The instructor will assign each group one of Thomas Gordon's roadblocks in Table 3.1. (Roadblocks 4, 7, 10, and 12 are especially effective.) Each group is to put together a presentation that demonstrates its roadblock to the class in a role play between a helper and a client and then show helper behaviors that could enhance the relationship in that situation. Following each demonstration, the class can discuss the effects of the roadblock on the helping relationship. It is especially useful for the "clients" to describe what it felt like when the helper used one of these roadblocks.

Additional Exercises

Additional Exercise 1: Case Study

In a small group, read and discuss the following example: Ricardo is a counselor in private practice. The following is his discussion of a client who was referred for counseling by her family physician when she came to the medical office crying and needing to talk.

> The client began the therapeutic relationship with much enthusiasm and high expectations for achieving her goals. She was a 23-year-old only child who felt that she could not maintain a serious relationship. After a few weeks, her enthusiasm waned, and she expressed disappointment in me as a helper. By this time, enough assessment had been done to identify this denouement as being similar to her history of intimate relationships. She began relationships with an idealized picture of her boyfriends and then was quickly disappointed. She came to the session one day indicating that she was angry that I had not been able to give her an earlier session. During her earlier phone call, she had said it was important but not urgent that she see me soon. She admitted that she expected me to

know how upset she was and to set up an emergency appointment. When we examined our relationship, the client was able to pick out several times when she left hints and clues about her needs but failed to ask for things directly.

I shared my feelings of surprise, being unaware of her real feelings. Naturally, this led to a discussion of how her behavior might have affected other relationships. It was a very significant insight when she realized that she was undermining relationships by her failure to send clear messages about her needs. In her case, this pattern of behavior could be traced back to her upbringing, which did not require that she state her needs and rewarded indirect suggestions. In therapy, she was able to learn some assertiveness skills and practice them in a group setting.

a. Do you think it was necessary to examine the client's past to help her with the problem in the helping relationship?
b. Is it possible that the client has a legitimate gripe and that Ricardo is "saving face" by making it the client's problem?
c. In a case such as this, how much responsibility should the helper take for the miscommunication about the client's needs? Would it have helped the client if the helper had apologized or assumed partial responsibility for the misunderstanding?
d. If you were Ricardo, how would you have handled the client's expression of anger?

Additional Exercise 2

Part 1. Take a look at the common transference reactions in Table 3.2. Now think back on the

case of Alicia B. that introduced this chapter. Which of these reactions did she experience in her relationship with Jim?

Part 2. Have you ever experienced any of these feelings for someone in authority? Think for a moment about the concept of authority. You have probably heard it said that a person has "authority issues." How is this similar to or different from transference reaction discussed in this chapter? Discuss your findings with a small group.

Additional Exercise 3

In groups of three, role-play a scenario in which the client expresses strong feelings toward the helper. As the "client" fumes, the "helper" is to try and utilize the four steps given in the section "Dealing with Transference from a Client":

Step 1: Convey acceptance of the client's remarks but don't retaliate.

Step 2: Explore the client's feelings.

Step 3: Utilize self-involving statements to help the client become aware of the helper's genuine thoughts and emotions about the client and the client's behavior.

Step 4: Use the experience to help the client to find new and better ways of expressing feelings and meeting his or her needs.

The observer in the group keeps track of any helper statements that seem to help the client explore this issue.

Homework

Homework 1

Make a list of your five favorite teachers from elementary school to present. List the traits or qualities of these persons. Identify any similarities. Are there also glaring differences? Now contrast them with some teacher or learning situation that was either very unpleasant or simply

unhelpful. What do these experiences say about how you like to learn? Based on your experiences with teachers, what kind of helper do you think might be the best fit for you? What kind of helper is likely to "push your buttons" and elicit some of the feelings you have had in previous helping relationships? Summarize your reactions to this exercise in two or three paragraphs.

Homework 2

One of the most common countertransference reactions is to feel sorry for a client and help the client too much. Another reaction is strong feelings of attraction for a client. Research the ethical codes of one of the helping professions. What guidelines can help you determine ethical action in such situations? In each case, what could be harmful about this particular countertransference reaction? In two or three paragraphs, discuss how you would handle each of the two situations, ethically and therapeutically.

Journal Starters

Remember that starters are designed to warm you up to the issues. You may take them in whatever direction you like. You need not answer all of them if they distract you from an important thought or stop the flow of ideas.

1. Think for a moment about an important friendship in your life; reflect on the ups and downs in the relationship and the stages that the relationship has gone through. What is it that makes this relationship special?
2. Consider the topic of anger in your journal. Look back over the past few months and think about times that anger has surfaced in your life. Now reflect about the ways in which anger was expressed in your family. Have there been times when anger has caused significant problems in your relationships? Has suppressing your needs and trying to be a "nice person" always been helpful? As a helper, how do you think that you might deal with a client's anger? What about your own feelings of anger when they arise in the helping session?

For more journal ideas, as well as more practice with the therapeutic relationship, refer to Chapter 3 in *Exercises in the Art of Helping*.

References

Bachelor, A., & Horvath, A. (1999). The therapeutic relationship. In M. Hubble, B. Duncan, & S. Miller (Eds.), *The heart and soul of change: What works in therapy* (pp. 133–178). Washington, DC: American Psychological Association.

Bannikotes, P. G., Kubinski, J. A., & Purcell, S. A. (1981). Sex role orientation, self-disclosure, and gender related perceptions. *Journal of Counseling Psychology, 28*, 140–146.

Barak, A., Patkin, J., & Dell, D. M. (1982). Effects of certain client behaviors in perceived expertness and attractiveness. *Journal of Counseling Psychology, 29*, 261–267.

Basch, M. F. (1980). *Doing psychotherapy*. New York: Basic Books.

Beier, E., & Young, D. M. (1998). *The silent language of psychotherapy: Social reinforcement of unconscious processes*. Chicago: Aldine de Gruyter.

Belkin, G. S. (1980). *Introduction to counseling* (2nd ed.). New York: Brown.

Benjamin, A. (1969). *The helping interview*. Boston: Houghton Mifflin.

Bloom, L. J., Schroeder, D., & Babineau, W. (1981). Reputation, training, fee and androgyny: Their comparative effects on impressions of therapist credibility. *Journal of Clinical Psychology, 37*(1), 90–95.

Bloom, L. J., Weigel, R. M., & Trautt, G. M. (1977). "Therapeugenic" factors in psychotherapy: Effects of office décor and subject-therapist sex pairing on the perception of credibility. *Journal of Consulting and Clinical Psychology, 45*(5), 867–873.

Cashwell, C. S., Shcherbakova, J., & Cashwell, T. H. (2003). Effect of client and counselor ethnicity on preference for counselor disclosure. *Journal of Counseling & Development, 81*, 196–201.

Corey, G., Corey, M. S., & Callanan, P. (2003). *Issues and ethics in the helping professions* (6th ed.). Monterey, CA: Brooks/Cole.

Corrigan, J. D., Dell, D. M., Lewis, K. N., & Schmidt, L. D. (1980). Counseling as a social influence process: A review. *Journal of Counseling Psychology, 27*, 395–441.

Covey, S. (1990). *The seven habits of highly effective people: Powerful lessons in personal change*. New York: Fireside.

Edwards, C., & Murdock, N. (1994). Characteristics of therapist self-disclosure in the counseling process. *Journal of Counseling and Development, 72*, 384–389.

Ellis, A. (1985). *Overcoming resistance: Rational-emotive therapy with difficult clients*. New York: Springer.

Erskine, R. G. (1998). Psychotherapy in the USA: A manual of standardized techniques or a therapeutic relationship? *International Journal of Psychotherapy, 3*, 231–234.

Fiedler, F. E. (1950). The concept of an ideal therapeutic relationship. *Journal of Consulting Psychology, 14*, 239–245.

Frank, J. D. (1961). *Persuasion and healing*. Baltimore: Johns Hopkins University Press.

Fremont, S., & Anderson, W. P. (1986). What client behaviors make counselors angry? An exploratory study. *Journal of Counseling and Development, 65*, 67–70.

Fromm-Reichmann, F. (1960). *Principles of intensive psychotherapy*. Chicago: University of Chicago Press. Gelso, C. J., & Carter, J. A. (1985). The relationship in counseling and psychotherapy: Components, consequences and theoretical antecedents. *Counseling Psychologist, 13*, 155–243.

Gelso, C. J. & Carter, J. A. (1985). The relationship in counseling and psychotherapy: Components, consequences and theoretical antecedents. *Counseling Psychologist, 13,* 155–243.

Goleman, D. (1995). *Emotional intelligence: Why it can matter more than IQ*. New York: Bantam.

Goodyear, R., & Schumate, J. (1996). Perceived effects of therapist self-disclosure of attraction to clients. *Professional Psychology, 27*, 613–616.

Gordon, T. (1986). *Leadership effectiveness training, L.E.T.: The no-lose way to release the productive potential of people*. New York: Bantam.

Heppner, P. P., & Dixon, D. N. (1986). A review of the interpersonal influence process in counseling. In W. P. Anderson (Ed.), *Innovative counseling: A handbook of readings* (pp. 8–16). Alexandria, VA: American Association for Counseling and Development.

Hubble, M. A., Duncan, B. L., & Miller, S. D. (Eds.). (1999). *The heart and soul of change: What works in therapy*. Washington, DC: American Psychological Association.

Johnson, D. W., & Matross, R. (1977). Interpersonal influence in psychotherapy: A social psychological view. In A. S. Gurman & A. M. Razin (Eds.), *Effective psychotherapy: A handbook of research* (pp. 395–432). Elmsford, NY: Pergamon.

Johnson, J. A. (1990). Empathy as a personality disposition. In R. C. McKay, J. R. Hughes, & E. J. Carver (Eds.), *Empathy in the helping relationship* (pp. 49–64). New York: Springer.

Jourard, S. (1971). *The transparent self*. New York: Van Nostrand Reinhold.

Kanfer, F. H., & Goldstein, A. P. (1986). Introduction. In F. Kanfer & A. Goldstein (Eds.), *Helping people change: A textbook of methods*. New York: Pergamon.

Kelly, E. W. (1994). *Relationship centered counseling: An integration of art and science*. New York: Springer.

Knox, S., Hess, S., Petersen, D., & Hill, C. E. (1997). A qualitative analysis of client perceptions of the effects of helpful therapist self-disclosure in long-term therapy. *Journal of Counseling Psychology, 44*, 274–283.

Kopp, S. (1978). *If you meet the Buddha on the road, kill him!* New York: Bantam Books.

Kottler, J. A., & Blau, D. S. (1989). *The imperfect therapist*. San Francisco: Jossey-Bass.

Lambert, M. J. (1986). Implications of psychotherapy outcome research for eclectic psychotherapy. In J. C. Norcross (Ed.), *Handbook of eclectic psychotherapy* (pp. 436–462). New York: Brunner/Mazel.

Loesch, L. (1984). Professional credentialing in counseling. *Counseling and Human Development, 17*, 1–11.

McCarthy, P. (1979). Differential effects of self-disclosing versus self-involving statements. *Journal of Counseling Psychology, 26*, 538–541.

McCarthy, P. (1982). Differential effects of counselor self-referent responses and counselor status. *Journal of Counseling Psychology, 29*, 125–131.

McCarthy, P. (2001). Differential effects of self-disclosing versus self-involving counselor statements. In C. E. Hill (Ed.), *Helping skills: The empirical foundation* (pp. 389–396). Washington, DC: American Psychological Association.

Nilsson, D., Strassberg, D., & Bannon, J. (1979). Perceptions of counselor self-disclosure: An analog study. *Journal of Counseling Psychology, 26*, 399–404.

Nuttall, J. (2002). Modes of therapeutic relationship in brief dynamic psychotherapy. *Journal of Psychodynamic Process, 89*, 505–523.

Pietrofesa, J. J., Hoffman, A., & Splete, H. H. (1984). *Counseling: An introduction.* Boston: Houghton Mifflin.

Pressly, P. K., & Heesacker, M. (2001). The physical environment and counseling: A review of theory and research. *Journal of Counseling & Development, 79,* 148–160.

Purkey, W. W. (1987). *The inviting relationship: An expanded perspective for professional counseling.* Englewood Cliffs, NJ: Prentice Hall.

Ritter, A., Bowden, S., Murray, T., Ross, P., Greeley, J., & Pead, J. (2002). The influence of the therapeutic relationship in treatment for alcohol dependency. *Drug & Alcohol Review, 21,* 261–268.

Rogers, C. R. (1957). The necessary and sufficient conditions of therapeutic personality change. *Journal of Consulting Psychology, 21,* 95–103.

Rogers, C. R. (1972). Client-centered therapy. In J. Huber & H. Millman (Eds.), *Goals and behavior in psychotherapy and counseling* (pp. 117–141). Columbus, OH: Merrill.

Schroeder, D. H., & Bloom L. J. (1979) "Therapeugenic" factors in psychotherapy—Effects of therapeutic orientation on the perception of credibility. *Journal of Clinical Psychology, 35*(3), 682–687.

Sermat, V., & Smythe, M. (1973). Content analysis of verbal communication in the development of a relationship: Conditions influencing self-disclosure. *Journal of Personality and Social Psychology, 26,* 332–346.

Singer, E. (1970). *Key concepts in psychotherapy* (2nd ed.). New York: Basic Books.

Strong, S. R. (1968). Counseling: An interpersonal influence process. *Journal of Counseling Psychology, 15,* 215–224.

Sue, S., & Zane, N. (1987). The role of culture and cultural techniques in psychotherapy. *American Psychologist, 42,* 37–45.

Sullivan, H. S. (1954). *The psychiatric interview.* New York: Norton.

Watkins, C. E., Jr. (1986). Transference phenomena in the counseling situation. In W. P. Anderson (Ed.), *Innovative counseling: A handbook of readings.* Alexandria, VA: American Association of Counseling and Development.

Watkins, C. E., Jr. (1990). The effects of counselor self-disclosure: A research review. *Counseling Psychologist, 18,* 477–500.

Weiner, M. F. (1979). *Therapist disclosure: The use of self in psychotherapy.* Boston: Butterworth Press.

Wolberg, L. R. (1967). *The technique of psychotherapy* (2nd ed.). New York: Grune & Stratton.

Yalom, I. (1985). *Theory and practice of group psychotherapy.* New York: Basic Books.

Helping Someone Who Is Different

4

The ways of the fish are more important than the tools of the fisherman
Fred Duhl

In this statement, a well-known family therapist is suggesting that techniques you use are much less important than understanding your client's unique needs and attributes. If you want to catch fish, you have to know where they live, what they eat, and what their patterns of behavior are. Similarly, to become a credible helper with someone who comes from a completely different background, you have to know as much as you can about the client. This is why so much time in this book is spent learning basic relationship skills rather than more complex and technical interventions.

The building block skills you begin to learn in the next few chapters will help you in building a good foundation.

It is not only the relationship that is affected by these differences. A client may refuse to do homework, try a role-playing exercise, or even talk about family problems when these activities are culturally proscribed or unfamiliar. You must have a sensitivity, skills, and knowledge of differences to communicate acceptance, understanding, and credibility to clients. You must recognize that the power of a technique is dependent on the degree to which the client cooperates. The client must have some faith not only in the helper but also in the method.

Depending on the client's background, the client may feel intimidated, angry, or excited when he or she first seeks help. Or perhaps the client believes he or she is being punished. Many of these issues come from the client's past or result from a clash between helper and client. Is it possible to overcome the barriers that are in place such as race, gender, culture and ethnicity, group history, language, family background, religion, and socioeconomic differences? At times, the gulf between two people may be so great that it is impossible to make contact. At other times, people, who are seemingly worlds apart, can find a way not only to work together but to actually bond. In the next section, we will look at differences that can affect the client/helper bond and some ways of coping with these challenges to rapport.

Differences That Can Affect the Therapeutic Alliance

In the last chapter, we examined the therapeutic relationship in some detail including its qualities and some of the techniques for enhancing the alliance. In this chapter, we will explore the issues related to differences between helper and client that threaten but also enrich the relationship. Chances for success in the helping relationship are maximized when there is a good match between helper and client. We sometimes use the term *chemistry* to describe a good fit in a relationship. On the other hand, a poor match can create problems that take time away from achieving the therapeutic goals. Let us look first at problems caused by a poor match.

Elkind (1992) suggested that "lack of fit" in the helping relationship can be due to differences in the stage of life between helper and client. Sometimes clients want older, "wiser" helpers, whereas others may find a better match with someone closer in age. Younger helpers sometimes find that their clients discount them because of their youth. Mismatches can also occur when the client brings issues or life experiences of which the therapist has no knowledge. Groups of people with common experiences are sometimes called *special populations*. Special populations include, but are not limited to, war veterans; those from a distinct socioeconomic stratum, such as the homeless; those with serious or chronic illness and pain; prison inmates; gay and lesbian people; children of alcoholics; non-Christians; ex-convicts; and those with physical or mental disabilities (Campbell & Witmer, 1991).

A number of other differences can lead to a relationship breach, such as holding racial or ethnic stereotypes. Personality differences can also cause mismatches. Clients who are very practical and concrete may not relate to a helper who wants to explore ideas and possibilities. Extroverted helpers may find introverted clients difficult to reach. Introverted clients may find extroverts annoying. As we discussed earlier, gender is another difference that can potentially separate client and helper.

Finally, Elkind identifies mismatches that occur as a result of differences in theoretical orientation, religion/spirituality, or life philosophy. For example, a feminist client might have difficulty accepting the premises of a traditional psychodynamic approach. Some religious ideas might clash with assertiveness training or ideas about the marital relationship. Similarly, differences in sexual orientation can make helper and client uneasy and mistrustful of each other.

It would be impossible in this chapter to cover all the ways that a client and helper can differ, and you will undoubtedly be asked to take an entire course on this subject later on. So, in this chapter, we will look at two of the most basic issues: cultural differences and gender differences. We will discuss them in terms of three traditional categories of learning—skills, knowledge, and attitudes. We will try to address the skills and attitudes that are important at this phase of your training. Knowledge about different cultural groups, special populations, and developmental groups will be part of your learning in other courses. Later, when you encounter differences between yourself and your client, you will still have some homework to do (because no one can be knowledgeable about all potential differences), but the hope is that you will have fundamental listening skills and an open, nonjudgmental attitude in place.

Challenges Caused by Differences in Culture

Culture is the system of shared beliefs, values, taboos, customs, behaviors, and artistic products that a group of people transmit from generation to generation and that members of the group use to understand their world and each other. Family and institutions such as churches and cultural organizations are the primary ways in which culture is passed on. Members of a group can vary in terms of how much they accept their cultural conditioning. In other words, the transmission of culture is not automatic, because people have different experiences. In general, the culture of ethnic minorities diminishes and they begin to take on the values of the dominant culture. For example, third-generation Italians in the United States may never have visited Italy, rarely eat Italian food, and do not speak the language. This demonstrates that just knowing someone's race or ethnic background is not enough to understand his or her culture. You must also know the degree to which the person is *acculturated*, or soaked in that culture. The fact that people are acculturated differently reinforces the fact that each person is culturally unique. He or she may share common beliefs with the culture of origin but is also different in terms of how much of the culture has been absorbed. It is quite possible, for example, that two siblings raised in a Greek-American household will be poles apart on the amount of Hellenic culture each has adopted. The helper must recognize that, because of these differences, stereotypes cannot serve as useful guides to understanding a person. But neither is culture to be ignored. We take our cultural attitudes and behaviors for granted. For example, in the movie *My Big Fat Greek Wedding*, the main character, Tula, is talking with her non-Greek boyfriend about how he spends his summers at the family cabin. She cannot imagine that his American nuclear family would spend that time alone. Having 25 first cousins means that family time includes the extended family. He could not imagine that much family involvement.

Thus, whether we know it or not, culture colors our worldview and our ideas about life that have relevance to the therapeutic process. For instance, it affects our notions about change and about the role of human effort and will. Many people in the United States, for example, believe that everyone can get ahead if he or she just works hard enough. But a little understanding of the economic and political conditions of other countries makes us aware of the fact that this is not the case everywhere. Therefore, it is quite possible that client and helper will have different ideas about the role of responsibility and motivation—key issues in change.

We can highlight the variability in cultural attitudes by examining the notion of internal versus external locus of control (Rotter, 1966). Keep in mind though that internal/external locus of control is just one way we could look at cultural differences; it is not the most important or the only method for comparing cultures. Still, it is a well-known psychological concept that may help us understand how cultural background affects a client's viewpoint about change.

Internal/external locus of control is a term that describes the degree to which an individual sees his or her behavior as due to personal effort (internal locus of control) or due to external forces such as luck, chance, or the influence of others. Cultures are thought to differ in regard to how much emphasis they place on responsibility for things that happen to us. Table 4.1 is a brief survey that you can use to get a feel for a concept similar to Rotter's internal/external locus of control. We call this the trait of inner-directedness. Do not forget that this trait is the construction of Western psychology.

Table 4.1
Are you inner-directed?

Instructions: Answer the questions in the survey as either true or false and then reflect a moment in the space provided.

	True	False
1. I can usually get what I want.	○	○
2. What is happening in world events has no great impact on me.	○	○
3. I do not believe in luck.	○	○
4. I do not think that I could win the lottery.	○	○
5. I persist when I encounter difficulties rather than give up.	○	○
6. I am often able to convince others to do things my way.	○	○
7. People can make a difference in fighting crime.	○	○
8. My successes are mostly due to chance.	○	○
9. I believe that I control my own destiny.	○	○
10. My vote counts.	○	○
11. I earn the things I receive.	○	○

Table 4.1
Are you inner-directed? *(Continued)*

	True	False
12. Hard work and sticking with it usually lead to success.	○	○
13. Other people do not control my life to any great extent.	○	○

Although this survey is not scientific, it shows some of the dimensions of a belief in "inner-directedness." If you answered, say, 10 questions as true, you probably believe that you are the "captain of your fate." If you answered most of them false, you may believe that luck, chance, the environment, or other people are mostly responsible for your successes and challenges in life. If you are somewhere in the middle, you probably believe that the good and bad you receive is due both to your own efforts and from external forces.

Do the results of this survey fit with what you know about yourself? _____

Do you think that cultures vary on this dimension? If so, why?_____

Let us suppose your family experienced a setback of some kind. Would it likely be attributed to bad luck, other people, or bad judgment? _____

Is it necessarily better to believe in hard work and persistence than in luck? Are there times that believing in luck, God's will, or fate might actually be more useful than believing in individual blame? _____

The lives of most Westerners are not greatly affected by political, economic, or even weather disasters, in contrast to those of many people in developing countries. Do you think the American dream that we can individually overcome hardships and go from rags to riches is because of our culture and that such an idea might actually be irrational in other societies? _____

Suppose you had a client who believed that he or she lacked the ability to make a difference in his or her life. How would you deal with this belief? Are all cultural ideas to be respected—even if they are antithetical to your ideas about male/female equality, mental health, justice, or morality? _____

Helping a Client Whose Culture Is Different from the Helper's

One of the biggest shocks to the beginning helper is dealing with someone whose world-view clashes sharply with his or her own. It is hard for the helper to remain neutral and nonjudgmental at first because it seems that the client is clearly mistaken or is operating from a distorted viewpoint. We have gathered some suggestions for dealing with cultural differences that could pose a problem in helping clients. These suggestions fall under the categories of (1) knowledge that the helper should possess, (2) skills that may be helpful in bridging the cultural gap, and (3) attitudes that will facilitate dealing with someone who is different.

Knowledge

There are three ways to gain knowledge about your client's cultural background: cultural study, cultural experiences, and a tutorial stance.

Cultural Study

Cultural study involves gaining some basic facts about a culture. While such training may lead to stereotyping, it is often useful to begin to appreciate the diversity of belief systems and to have a basis for comparison when we try to understand the acculturation of a particular client. At the minimum, helpers should have studied the culture and history of Asian Americans, African Americans, Hispanic Americans, and Native Americans (Sue & Sue, 2003). A helper should probably have training in more than one language.

In addition, helpers must be sensitive to nonverbal communication and to uses of language that might be offensive to special groups. In Chapter 5, we will talk about the cultural differences in eye contact and physical distance. There are also differences in the use of touch, gestures, facial expressions, etc. Although we cannot usually predict the effects of these differences, the helper must be open to discussing them and pay close attention when they seem to be interfering with communication.

Helpers must become sensitive to differences in emphasis on the role of the family among different cultures. Because families in North America are mobile and less cohesive, we usually assume that becoming independent from the family of origin is a sign of maturity. However, in some Asian and Latino cultures, becoming independent of the family is not a valued goal of adulthood.

Cultural Experiences

Immersing oneself in a culture (cultural experiences) can provide information about a culture you simply cannot obtain otherwise. Traveling abroad, having friends from different backgrounds, or going to a cultural event can correct stereotypes and help you appreciate the richness and beauty of a culture that is not really evident in the written descriptions. While both study and experiences are helpful, we must also try and understand the specific client and his or her relationship with the culture if we want to help. To do this, we recommend a tutorial stance.

A Tutorial Stance

Beginning helpers may feel overwhelmed when they realize the amount of information that they need to assimilate to become culturally sensitive. A rational approach to an overload of information is to accept that any helper cannot be prepared for all possible differences between helper and client. The best approach is a tutorial one. Let your client teach you about his or her background. Be open and sensitive and do not try to examine the client under the lens of the dominant culture or from your own moral perspective. I remember being lectured by a client with diabetes when she realized that I did not know the difference between Type I and Type II. She gave me a brief course in diabetes. When I followed up with questions and did some reading, she appreciated the fact that I showed interest and was willing to put forth effort to understand. What could have been a rift became an opening for dialogue.

Skills

Listen

Especially at the beginning of the relationship, a helper should focus on listening rather than on telling. Recently, a famous radio "doctor" told a welfare mother with three daughters that she should go back to work, even though she could not arrange good day care for her 3-year-old. Because this advice was offered in the first 60 seconds of the interview, the professional advice giver had not taken the time to assess the client's support system, the ages of the other children, or the importance the client placed on being a good mother. Anyone who offers advice so quickly is not respecting or understanding a client's worldview. Such advice is likely to be culturally insensitive, potentially damaging, and ultimately irrelevant to the client.

Tap into Cultural Support Systems

Helpers must recognize that the Western method of therapy may be unacceptable to some groups and that in many cases indigenous methods should be explored. For example, the World Health Organization recommends that Western medical personnel work jointly with traditional and folk medicine providers. Closer to home, a minister or priest in the African-American or Mexican-American communities may have more influence and insight than an external helper. Professional helpers need humility in dealing with unfamiliar situations and should work in concert with natural support systems.

Achieve Credibility

Sue and Zane (1987) identify credibility as a crucial relationship issue in helping someone who is culturally different. Although knowledge of the client's culture lends credibility to a helper who is dealing with someone from a different background, other factors are also important. Sue and Zane distinguish between ascribed and achieved credibility. *Ascribed credibility* is the status given to the helper by the client that is often due to sex, age, experience, and similarity of culture or life experiences and attitudes. For example, in some cultures, an older person is ascribed more credibility than a younger person. *Achieved credibility* refers to the helper's skills and demonstrated abilities. If the helper cannot be ascribed much credibility with an individual from a different background, he or she may be able to achieve it over time. For instance, a helper who is not recovering from alcohol or substance abuse will be ascribed very little credibility by clients in treatment programs for these problems. Or because the helper has never been addicted, clients are skeptical about how much he or she really knows. If the helper possesses special knowledge and skills, however, it may be possible to achieve some measure of acceptance, even without a history of personal addiction.

According to Sue and Zane, the helper can achieve credibility by conceptualizing problems in a way that is congruent with the client's beliefs and values. For example, it has been suggested that framing a problem as medical, rather than psychological, is more acceptable to a Hispanic client (Meadow, 1982). It has also been suggested that African-American clients prefer educational and practical strategies for dealing with problems more than methods that focus only on feelings (Parker, 1988). However, prejudging a client's values and beliefs or making a treatment plan based on a single characteristic such as race, ethnicity, or religion without a complete understanding of the client's background and unique personality is a serious mistake (Wohl, 1995). Counselors lose credibility when they fail to take into account the full complexities of the person and try to simplify a client by identifying him or her as a member of a particular culture, socioeconomic group, sex, or age group.

A significant issue in dealing with those who are culturally different is that the helper may not have much ascribed credibility coming from outside the client's ideas of what a helper should be. Therefore, the helper must work hard during the initial phase of the relationship to achieve credibility. Early studies suggested that as many as 50 percent of Asian-American clients did not return after the first session (Sue & McKinney,

1975). This is probably true of clients from other backgrounds who encounter culturally different helpers. When clients do not return, we can only speculate about their reasons, but it seems obvious that many clients have concluded at the first session that they have not been understood or that they cannot be helped. One way that a helper can achieve credibility under these circumstances is to do something tangible to help the client as soon as possible. Another is to utilize members of the client's community such as clergy and traditional healers as allies in helping the client.

Use an Eclectic Approach

A final point is that helpers who hope to work effectively with those who are culturally different should become truly eclectic, using skills, methods, and techniques and forming goals that are congruent with the views, values, lifestyles, and life experiences of each client. Helpers must recognize that strategies and techniques useful with the majority population will probably need to be modified or even eliminated when dealing with someone from a different background. There are some that argue that the basic building block skills that we present in this book are culturally Western. In essence, the basic skills you will be learning all depend on a basic nonjudgmental listening stance. We believe that this approach, while not value-free or culture-free, is one of the easiest ways to ensure that the client is being heard. If the client is being heard, interventions are less likely to be incongruent, disrespectful, or ineffective. If the helper is trying to understand the client, rather than fix the client, the basis for a respectful helping relationship is more likely and the possibility for harm is diminished.

Attitudes

Listed below are some of the attitudes that culturally competent helpers possess. *Culturally competent* means that one does not merely possess the skills and knowledge but that one also is psychologically open and accepting of people who are different.

1. The helper must have or adopt attitudes of empathy (rather than sympathy), tolerance for ambiguity, open-mindedness, and an openness to experience (Corey, Corey, & Callanan, 2003).
2. In addition, helpers should understand their own value systems and basic assumptions about human behavior and appreciate that the views of others will differ. Helpers may be unaware, for example, how their therapeutic training and views of mental health are based on several strictly Western assumptions. Some of these assumptions include an emphasis on individualism versus duty to family and society, an emphasis on independence and a neglect of client support systems, Christian morality, a focus on changing the individual rather than the system, and a neglect of history and a focus on immediate events (Pedersen, 1987; Sue & Sue, 2003).
3. Culturally competent helpers understand that other cultural groups have been shaped by social and political forces that may have also been important in shaping client attitudes and values.
4. Helpers understand the worldview of the client, are able to share it in some way, and constantly strive to avoid being culturally encapsulated. *Culturally encapsulated* means refusing to acknowledge that other cultural viewpoints have worth and are as valid as one's own.

Stop and Reflect

A helper is not always aware that his or her assumptions about good mental health are culturally bound. In this case, a counselor named Don was tempted to encourage a client to accept a Western concept of maturity even though she comes from an Eastern culture. As you read the case, think how you might help such a client solve the problem in a way that is best for her.

> Don was a counselor practicing in a small town near Denver, Colorado. He was born and raised in that area. One of his clients was a 25-year-old woman named Mira who had been born in the United States, although her parents were from northern India. She described the difficulties she was encountering with friends because she still lives at home. She was embarrassed because many raise their eyebrows when she tells them she is living at home. However, in her culture and family, any other living situation would be considered unacceptable before marriage. A previous helper had pushed her to move out of the house and told her, "If your parents don't like it, too bad."

- If the client were from an ordinary American background, aged 25, still living at home, what assumptions might you make about her? Do you think you might be tempted to make these same assumptions about Mira?
- In talking about her previous counselor, what was Mira communicating to Don?
- What cultural values do you imagine Don might possess that would conflict with the client's upbringing?
- If you were Don, how might you begin helping this client? What more would you like to know about the client?

Jot down your answers to the questions raised here and discuss them with your classmates.

Challenges Caused by Differences in Gender

Sex refers to basic physiological differences between men and women; *gender* refers to the roles that each sex is taught (Gilbert & Scher, 1999; Taylor, 1994). Each culture has different expectations for men and women, boys and girls. In the United States, the dominant culture has historically portrayed men as more powerful, credible, and influential than women. Consequently, in the past, clients of both sexes most often preferred male helpers. We now see consistent evidence that both men and women prefer helpers of the same sex (Hall, Guterman, Lee, & Little, 2002). Nelson (1993) also found that helpers prefer same-sex clients. Nelson sees this as evidence that, in general, we all prefer people who are similar to ourselves (the "similar to me" effect). However, is having a same-gender helper always the best idea? It is possible that we could be perpetuating male stereotypes if men were to be counseled only by other men. Nor does it always seem best to allow clients to choose. Some women might choose male helpers when exposure to a good female role model would be more useful. At this juncture, a clear answer to this dilemma is unavailable.

In general, training programs should teach helpers to address the issues of gender and cultural differences directly with clients and to continue to address these matters throughout the therapeutic relationship—but they do not (Vogel, Epting, & Wester, 2003). Training should also allow the helper to examine his or her personal assumptions about gender and to engage in some consciousness-raising activities (Robbins, 1983). Consciousness-raising is an examination of one's life experience as it has been influenced by sexism (Devoe, 1990; Russell, 1984). In this section of the chapter, we will look at some elementary steps that helpers can take to deal effectively with gender difference using knowledge, skills, and attitudes—the same three-part distinction we utilized when thinking about cultural differences.

Knowledge

Let us suppose that you were doing counseling over the Internet and the client refused to identify his or her sex. Would you feel that vital data were missing? Most of us would. Knowledge of our sex is fundamental to our identity (Bem, 1975); it is the first thing we ask about a new baby. Yet just as we noted in the arena of cultural differences, knowing someone's sex does not give us all we need to help. We must also understand the degree to which an individual has been trained as traditionally male or female. We need to know a person's attitudes about gender and something about communication patterns and values that can separate men and women. For example, according to Tannen (2001), men traditionally value independence over emotional intimacy and women are better than men at creating and maintaining intimate connections. It has been said that men use communication to preserve independence and maintain their status, while women use conversation more often to express and create intimacy (Pearson, West, & Turner, 1995). It is also fairly clear that men and women talk about different issues in counseling, or at least they frame them differently. For example, it has been found that women talk more about assertiveness and men talk more about being "stuck" (Vogel et al., 2003). Just as when dealing with cultural differences, a big problem arises when you realize that not everyone is affected in the same way by gender role indoctrination. We run the risk of stereotyping when we assume that someone is a typical man or woman and communicates in a certain way. Thus, part of gaining knowledge about a person is through the assessment process when we look at the unique characteristics of the person. Still, it is useful to gauge the individual's outlook about gender, as it affects identity and relationships.

Skills

Every helper needs to have the skills of the reflective practitioner that we talked about in Chapter 1. If you recall that discussion, it was said that being reflective is particularly important when differences between helper and client produce misunderstandings. Reflection is the process of identifying a puzzling issue and looking at it from different angles. How can we use reflection in dealing with gender issues? These assumptions about ourselves and others are so deeply ingrained that it is very difficult to get free of them. Using a journal, participating in group discussion, and consulting a supervisor are all reflective ways of getting to a point of view outside your own lens. In addition to reflection, here are some general strategies or skills that helpers can develop to avoid gender becoming a wall between them and their clients:

1. Address gender in the assessment process. In Chapter 10 we discuss how to do this via the genogram or family tree that can reveal generational influences in our attitudes and behaviors. This can be the beginning of a consciousness-raising activity.
2. Be willing to discuss gender issues that surface in client/helper interactions and misunderstandings.
3. Utilize supervision to discover your attitudes about a client that may be the result of your own gender socialization.
4. Be particularly aware of how gender affects attitudes about family roles and family violence (Scher & Stevens, 1987; World Health Organization, 2002). Gender bias in career counseling is a major issue that can potentially stunt an individual's development (Kerka, 1999).

Attitudes

Just as cultural groups tend to stereotype each other, the same process occurs between men and women. These stereotypes can affect how we diagnose a person and how much weight we give to his or her symptoms (Lopez, Grover, Holland, & Johnson, 1989). Most of the male/female contrasts we are dealing with are those of attitude or perception rather than substantial divisions in behavior. For example, there appears to be no plausible evidence of variability in how men and women express and react to emotions (Wester, Vogel, & Pressly, 2002). Despite this, it is a common belief that women are more emotional and men less so. Popular books such as *Men Are from Mars, Women Are from Venus* (Gray, 1992) may be reinforcing these stereotypes. The main thing we know is that men and women are socialized differently and that each person's training is unique. These stereotypes do not just affect how we see ourselves but how we see the other gender. For example, a man's belief that he should be the main breadwinner necessarily affects his view of his spouse. If a woman believes that she should not work outside the home, she may expect that her spouse should provide all the income. These expectations create problems in couples, and they create issues between the men and women who face each other in the therapy hour as helper and client (Young & Long, 1998). In raising awareness of these roadblocks, it is certainly possible that we will be evoking stereotypes about men and women. It is difficult not to talk about general tendencies. But instead of deciding that all men or all women act in these ways, take a look at the following thoughts as potential difficulties that may arise. Let us examine the two basic scenarios: men counseling women and women counseling men.

Scenario 1. Male helper, female client

If you are a man counseling a woman:

- Be aware of the common position of "androcentrism," or belief that male experience is normal and is a common experience (Robinson & Watt, 2001). This belief system has shaped our ideas about what is mentally healthy and unhealthy. For example, is not an aggressive woman in a business setting viewed less positively than a male counterpart? If so, is it possible that you might pathologize in a woman what is acceptable or healthy in a male (see Wester & Vogel, 2002)?

- Understand that many women have had experiences of sexual abuse or misuse, and these memories can be evoked if the relationship becomes intimate. This may mean that your client will experience fear or mistrust that can be dealt with in the therapeutic relationship or may require a transfer.

- Understand and discuss the role strain and role conflict a woman experiences when she tries to fulfill personal and societal expectations that she be the perfect mother and wife while also trying to meet the demands of her employer. These experiences can elicit a sense of guilt and failure when one finds it is impossible to be everything to everybody. In the same vein, how do you, as a male helper, feel about a woman trying to manage both work and family?

- Ask yourself, "How much work am I doing compared with the effort the client is putting forth?" As a male, are you feeding into the social expectation that you will lead and the woman will follow? Would you be doing this much for a male client? When are you helping too much? Could you be creating a dependency in the client?

- Consider: "Am I treating the client as fragile?" Is this what the client wants, or has the client come to receive confrontation as well as support? To what extent am I letting the client off the hook because of my own beliefs about her inability to handle strong statements?

- If the client is a lesbian, are you treating partner issues any differently than if she were heterosexual? Are your ideas about what makes a healthy relationship or healthy person different in this case?

Scenario 2.   Female helper, male client

If you are a woman counseling a man:

- Be aware that a man, being in a less powerful position as a client, may be uncomfortable whether his therapist is male or female. In fact, many men prefer female therapists because they feel they can be more honest and do not have to hide weaknesses. They may also believe that they can more easily influence a woman.

- Are you, as a female therapist, prejudiced against men who are not highly motivated or driven to succeed? Are you sending subtle messages to a male client that he needs to accept the male "harness" and make career the most important thing in life?

- Understand that man's respect for a female therapist may turn into romantic affection. Can you help a male client recognize that this is an impediment and an issue he may need to deal with in other situations? Can you do it in a way that does not destroy the therapeutic relationship?

- Are you comfortable with a man expressing feelings of weakness or powerlessness? How would you feel if your male client cried? Would you see this as more indicative of pathology than if a woman expressed an emotion in this way?

- If your client is gay, are you treating partner issues any differently than if he were heterosexual? Are your ideas about what makes a healthy relationship or healthy person different in this case?

Summary

The riddle that every successful helper must solve is "How can I use the training I have with a client who is totally different?" The first answer to this question is that you may not always be able to use your particular theory or armory of techniques. You will have to continue to learn and grow and find out *what* works for *whom*. It is recommended that the helper consult with the client at each step of the process. Just as the client is a partner in the setting of goals, the methods and techniques must also be compatible if the client is to become engaged and the therapeutic relationship is to be supported. By doing so, the helper reduces the chance that a method or technique is objectionable.

In this chapter, we have focused on dissimilarities and problems caused by cultural and societal conditioning, but we cannot forget that there are also places where everyone connects. Existentialists claim that all people are struggling with the human condition: coping with death, freedom, isolation and loneliness, meaninglessness, and anxiety (Robinson & Jones, 2001). If we have lived, we can relate to these stressors and challenges. Of course, we are different culturally and in our gender conditioning, but we can connect with people on these core elements of life and form relationships across spectacular distances of personality, culture, faith, and politics. This frequently means leaving behind dearly held hatreds, judgments, prejudices, and preferences and embracing a truly unconditional positive regard (Rogers, 1957). We have tried to say in the last chapter and throughout this book that the therapeutic relationship is the medium for the kind of understanding Rogers has advocated and that the basic core of nonjudgmental listening provides an avenue for connecting. But the hard work of bridging the gap is an internal struggle that each helper must eventually face. Can we begin to look through the eyes of others, or will we remain in the shackles of our limited experiences? Can we deal with the foreign and what is distasteful? This is not a safe kind of empathy. It requires courage. Karen Horney, the famous therapist, described three orientations for human relationships: to move away from others, to move against others, and to move toward others. We believe that the first step in dealing with differences is to adopt the courageous strategy of "moving toward" either finding commonalities or appreciating differences.

Exercises

Group Exercise 1: Cultural Expectations of Helping

Read the following case study in a group of five or six and discuss the questions that follow. Assign a recorder to write down some of the key points made by members of the group.

A therapist in Ohio related the following story about counseling a couple who had recently emigrated to the United States from Hong Kong. Because they did not speak English well, a Chinese translator was hired to be present during the sessions. Near the end of the first hour, it seemed that the translator was going beyond the helper's statements, and his simple reflections were turning into long paragraphs in Chinese. The couple left the session quite satisfied and smiling, promising to return. They even jotted down a few notes. When the therapist quizzed the translator about what he had said, the translator replied, "What you did was all right, but they came to you because you are an older and wiser person. If you didn't tell them how to handle their situation, they would have felt that the session was wasted. So I gave them some advice on your behalf."

- Suppose you were confronted with this therapist's situation. How do you think that you might handle the counseling situation with someone from a completely different culture? Should the helper adapt to the clients' expectations, or should the clients be inducted into the helper's way of doing things?
- This therapist's clients had expectations about helping based on a culture that looks to elders for wisdom. When you think about a helping relationship, what are your expectations? How would you expect to be treated? How would you have reacted to a helper who doled out advice in the first session?
- Just because a client culturally expects some action of the helper, such as advice, does this mean that the helper should supply it? Or should the helper think about what is best for the client?

- Can a helper ever really be value-free or culture-free?
- This story tells us that in the very first encounter, a client's cultural background can be a significant factor. In the United States, it is likely that many clients gain their ideas about the counseling relationship not from personal experience, but through television and movies. Can you think of some presentations of the counseling relationship in the media that might be priming clients for the wrong experience?
- How likely is it that you will be faced with a language barrier or see a deaf client who uses American Sign Language? Do you think that it is important for every helper to speak a second language or to learn an alternative form of communication such as signing?

Group Exercise 2: Role-Play a Traditional Relationship

Conduct a role play in a group of five students. One person plays the role of the husband with traditional values (see below) and one group member acts as the helper. The helper tries to listen and remain nonjudgmental. The rest of the group listens to the role play and discusses the helper's effectiveness in remaining nonjudgmental while exploring the full range of the client's situation.

Scenario: A man says he is supportive of his wife's return to work after 8 years at home with the children. The youngest is now in first grade. Because his wife is working, additional child care tasks, chauffeuring, homework monitoring, and housework fall to him. He resents the intrusion on his free time, and he is experiencing a lot of pressure. He says that his wife feels guilty when he complains, but he is very unhappy with their relationship, which has been eclipsed by all the responsibilities.

Additional Exercise: Remembering Your Gender Training

Identify two or three scenarios in your childhood where you learned or were instructed on the proper way for a boy or girl to behave. This may have been the result of your having violated a social norm about gender. Write a few words that will remind you of the incident.

Incident 1:
Incident 2:
Incident 3:

In a small group, each person, if he or she feels comfortable, is invited to describe this situation and get reactions from the other group members. As you discuss, consider the following:

- What method was used to teach you this lesson?
- Why do you think you were taught this lesson?

- Are all methods of teaching gender behavior subtle, or are some direct?
- Based on your experience, how do you want your children to be raised?

Homework

Homework 1

If you have never been a minority, consider placing yourself in that position by attending an event in a part of town where your ethnic background is not highly represented. Write a brief reaction to this experience. One of the things that those in the minority talk about is the sense of being observed. Did you have this sense? If so, how would it feel to deal with this on a daily basis?

Homework 2

Spend 30 minutes with someone whom you consider to be quite different from you. This person might be culturally different or religiously or politically at the opposite end of the spectrum. He or she may be from a different socioeconomic or educational background. Consider, after talking with him or her, what it would be like to work with this person as a client? Would you be able to develop an egalitarian relationship? What do you think you would find to be the most difficult things about this person to accept? What might the person have trouble understanding about you?

Journal Starters

1. It has been said that one of the emotions that white counselors in training have to deal with is shame (Parker & Schwartz, 2002). Shame arises as one realizes the misdeeds of one's ancestors and the amount of privilege that he or she has enjoyed. Shame and feelings of helplessness to undo the situation can lead to defensive reactions. For example, we ignore the homeless person on the street so that we do not have to face the fact that we should be helping. As a helper, you will be exposed to stories of horrible prejudice and the psychological effects of brutal injustice. How do you think you will personally react to these stories? Do you think you can help people deal with an unjust world?

2. Thinking back on your upbringing, what messages about men and women do you think you received? Take a look at the additional exercise in the section above that is titled "Remembering Your Gender Training." If we are right that this training is sometimes quite subtle, how will you be able to spot this bias in your own work?

For more journal ideas and practice, refer to Chapter 4 of *Exercises in Learning the Art of Helping*.

References

Bem, S. L. (1975). Sex-role adaptability: One consequence of psychological androgyny. *Journal of Personality and Social Psychology, 31*, 634–643.

Campbell, J., & Witmer, J. M. (1991). *Working with special populations: Guidelines for treatment and counselor education.* Unpublished manuscript.

Corey, G., Corey, M., & Callanan, P. (2003). *Issues and ethics in the helping professions* (6th ed.). Monterey, CA: Brooks/Cole.

Devoe, D. (1990). Feminist and nonsexist counseling: Implications for the male counselor. *Journal of Counseling and Development, 69*, 33–36.

Elkind, S. N. (1992). *Resolving impasses in therapeutic relationships.* New York: Guilford.

Gilbert, L. A., & Scher, M. (1999). *Gender and sex in counseling and psychotherapy.* Boston: Allyn & Bacon.

Gray, J. (1992). *Men Are from Mars, Women Are from Venus.* New York: HarperCollins.

Hall, J., Guterman, D. K., Lee, H. B., & Little, S. G. (2002). Counselor-client matching on ethnicity, gender, and language: Implications for counseling school-aged children. *North American Journal of Psychology, 4*, 367–381.

Kerka, S. (1999). *Career development and gender, race, and class* (ERIC Digest No. 199). Columbus, OH: ERIC Clearinghouse on Adult Career and Vocational Education.

Lopez, S. R., Grover, K. P., Holland, D., & Johnson, M. J. (1989). Development of culturally sensitive psychotherapists. *Professional Psychology: Research & Practice, 20*, 369–375.

Meadow, A. (1982). Psychopathology, psychotherapy and the Mexican-American patient. In E. E. Jones & S. J. Korchin (eds), *Minority mental health* (pp. 331–362). New York: Praeger.

Nelson, M. L. (1993). A current perspective on gender differences: Implications for research in counseling. *Journal of Counseling Psychology, 40*(2), 200–209.

Parker, W. M. (1988). Becoming an effective multicultural counselor. *Journal of Counseling and Development, 67*, 93.

Parker, W. M., & Schwartz, R. C. (2002). On the experience of shame in multicultural counselling: Implications for white counsellors-in-training. *British Journal of Guidance and Counselling, 30*, 311–318.

Pearson, J. C., West, R. L., & Turner, L. H. (1995). *Gender and communication* (3rd ed.). Dubuque, IA: Brown & Benchmark Publishers.

Pedersen, P. B. (1987). Ten frequent assumptions of cultural bias in counseling. *Journal of Multicultural Counseling and Development, 14*, 16–24.

Robbins, J. H. (1983). Complex triangles: Uncovering sexist bias in relationship counseling. *Women and Therapy, 2*(2–3), 159–169.

Robinson, E. H., & Jones, K. D. (2001). Existential counseling. In D. C. Locke, J. E. Myers, & E. L. Herr (Eds.), *The handbook of counseling* (pp. 159–169). Thousand Oaks, CA: Sage.

Robinson, T. L., & Watt, S. K. (2001). "Where no one goes begging": Converging gender, sexuality, and religious diversity in counseling. In D. C. Locke, J. E. Myers, & E. L. Herr (Eds.), *The handbook of counseling* (pp. 589–600). Thousand Oaks, CA: Sage.

Rogers, C. R. (1957). The necessary and sufficient conditions of therapeutic personality change. *Journal of Consulting Psychology, 21*, 95–103.

Rotter, J. B. (1966). Generalized expectancies for internal versus external control of reinforcement. *Psychological Monographs: General & Applied, 80*, 1–28.

Russell, M. N. (1984). *Skills in counseling women.* Springfield, IL: Thomas.

Scher, M., & Stevens, M. (1987). Men and violence. *Journal of Counseling and Development, 65*, 351–354.

Sue, D. W., & Sue, D. (2003). *Counseling the culturally diverse: Theory and practice.* New York: Wiley.

Sue, S., & McKinney, H. (1975). Asian Americans in the community mental health care system. *American Journal of Orthopsychiatry, 45*, 111–118.

Sue, S., & Zane, N. (1987). The role of culture and cultural techniques in psychotherapy. *American Psychologist, 42*, 37–45.

Tannen, D. (2001). *You just don't understand: Women and men in conversation.* New York: Quill.

Taylor, M. (1994). Gender and power in counselling and supervision. *British Journal of Guidance and Counselling, 22*(3), 319–326.

Vogel, D. L., Epting, F., & Wester, S. R. (2003). Counselors' perceptions of female and male clients. *Journal of Counseling & Development, 81*, 131–140.

Wester, S. R., & Vogel, D. L. (2002). Working with the masculine mystique: Male gender role conflict, counseling self-efficacy and the training of male psychologists. *Professional Psychology: Research & Practice, 4*, 370–376.

Wester, S. R., Vogel, D. L., & Pressly, P. K. (2002). Sex differences in emotion: A critical review of the literature and implications for counseling psychology. *Counseling Psychologist, 30*, 630–652.

Wohl, J. (1995). Traditional individual psychotherapy and ethnic minorities. In J. F. Aponte, R. Y. Rivers, & J. Wohl (Eds.), *Psychological interventions and cultural diversity* (pp. 74–91). Boston: Allyn & Bacon.

World Health Organization (2002). *World report on violence and health*. Geneva, Switzerland: Author.

Young, M. E., & Long, L. L. (1998) *Counseling and therapy for couples: An integrative approach*. Pacific Grove, CA: Brooks/Cole.

Invitational Skills

5

Yes, there is no doubt that paper is patient and as I don't intend to show this cardboard covered notebook . . . to anyone, unless I find a real friend, boy or girl, probably nobody cares. And now I come to the root of the matter, the reason for my diary: it is that I have no such real friend.

Anne Frank (in Moffat & Painter, 1975, p. 15)

This entry from Anne Frank's diary reminds us of the great human need to be understood and to communicate. This desire to explain oneself has been met in various ways through the ages such as by keeping journals and diaries, by taking part in religious confession, by confiding in friends, and by praying. Last, but not least, the therapeutic relationship, described in the previous chapter, is specifically designed to invite the client to communicate openly by providing a nonthreatening atmosphere with the safeguards of confidentiality. The act of disclosing can be a great relief and is the first step in the healing process.

James Pennebaker has conducted some of the most interesting research on the benefits of self-disclosure and confession (1989, 1990, 2002). He became interested in the phenomenon while talking to polygraph operators who gave lie detector tests to people suspected of crimes. These technicians told him stories of suspects who admitted their guilt under questioning and who even thanked the operators. Some operators said they had even received Christmas cards from some of those they helped to convict! This suggested to him that there is a powerful need to confess. Pennebaker found in his own research that college students who regularly wrote diaries about their most troubling experiences showed better immune system responses and significantly better health compared with those who did not write. Pennebaker's work exemplifies a growing body of evidence that opening up is good for the soul *and* the body.

Table 5.1

The Building Blocks for Invitational Skills

Nonverbal Skills	
Nonverbal skills are the use of attentive silence, eye contact, appropriate voice tone, body position, and nonverbal encouragers such as head nodding or hand gestures that invite the client to talk.	
Nonverbal Skill	**Example**
Eye contact	Direct eye contact with occasional breaks for client comfort
Facilitative body position	"Open" attentive body position, squarely facing the client
Appropriate use of silence	Allowing the client to fill in the "voids" in the conversation
Voice tone	Using a voice tone that reflects the client's and is appropriate in volume and rate and shows warmth and support
Gestures	Encouraging the client to open up with appropriate gestures and head nodding

Opening Skills	
Opening skills are verbal encouragers. They ask the client to explore a little deeper but are not very invasive. They also reassure the client that you are following the story.	
Opening Skill	**Example**
Encouragers	
Door opener	"Say some more about that."
Minimal encourager	"Uh, huh," "Okay,"
Questions	
Open question	"Could you tell me what has been going on?"
Closed question	"Is she your ex-wife?"

Pennebaker's work about disclosure also underlines the fact that when clients come for help, they are seeking to explain themselves to a nonjudgmental listener (Pennebaker, 1990). Clients want to untangle the knots of traumas, miscalculations, and resentments that are troubling them. However, they do not simply want absolution; they desire to understand how things got so mixed up and how to deal with the unfinished business. The therapeutic relationship can provide the opportunity to heal the body and the mind if the helper can get out of the way and allow the client to open up and investigate all the nooks and crannies of the problem.

In this chapter, you will learn and practice the first set of techniques you need in the art of helping. They are called *invitational skills*. Invitational skills are broken into two general categories: nonverbal skills and opening skills (see Table 5.1). Nonverbal skills such as using eye contact and body position set the stage for an open and confiding relationship. Opening skills are verbal catalysts that consist of encouraging statements and questions. Together, these two categories of invitational skills will allow you to convey to clients that you are listening to them and that they are invited to open up. The invitational skills are especially useful early on in the helping session when they do not interfere with the client's recitation of the story. However, these skills are used throughout the entire helping process, session after session, as the helper listens to the client relate his or her progress, report setbacks, and describe new issues as they emerge.

Listening to the Client's Story

> *"My wife says I don't listen to her . . . at least I think that's what she said."*
>   Lawrence Peter

The quote by Peter points out how often we fail to fully listen to those around us—even those closest to us. Most people do not expect others to solve their problems, but they do want someone to listen, and they want to have a chance to hear themselves as well. Can listening all by itself have a powerful effect on another person? Is it possible that merely giving someone your full attention is healing? Some writers have called this *active listening*, a way of attending and encouraging without intruding on the client's telling of the story. It is called active because the listener is fully absorbed and communicates this to the other. But listening is difficult. A number of competing thoughts and urges assail us.

One of the biggest distractions is the need to help. A client's story can create tremendous pressure on the listener. We want to ease the client's pain, help him or her decide upon a course of action and create a change. It is this impulse that prompts friends to offer quick advice. Frequently, however, the best approach in the professional helping relationship is to allow clients to completely describe the situation to you and to themselves before jumping into an instant solution. If you think about it, the client has probably heard a lot of advice already. What makes you think that your ideas are likely to be any better than a close friend's? It is through listening to the client's story that client and helper are able to find the keys to change, not by attempting to solve the problem in the first few minutes.

Therapists such as Sheldon Kopp (1978) have emphasized the importance of clients' "telling their tales." The tale is a full recitation of the problem from the client's unique perspective. It is the client's story of his or her life. Michael White, the Australian therapist, calls these stories "narratives" (White, 2000). Hidden in each story are the keys to understanding how that person views the world. Helpers who take the time to let the client's story unfold will design helping interventions that fit the unique client and his or her special worldview. So besides the therapeutic effects of allowing the client to disclose, we also gain greater insight into the client's world.

Stop and Reflect

Many beginning helpers get stuck because they feel that they have heard the whole story in the first 5 minutes. They become nervous because they think that if they spend more time listening, they will end up covering old ground. They also anticipate the client's unspoken question, "What should I do?"

Consider the first few minutes of this actual counseling session between a 30-year-old African American woman, Tia, and her counselor, Renee. Tia is living with her mother and her 4-year-old son.

"My mother wants everything done her way. I can't do anything right, even with my son. For example, I have to call her at the end of today's session and let her know I came. She thinks I need counseling. But really I just need her to get off my back. I have a job possibility, and it's walking distance from home. But my mother thinks that it doesn't pay enough. But I have to start somewhere, and I think I would like it. If it weren't for her, I would probably be living on the street. But when I try to get more independent, it's like she doesn't want me to. There are so many things I want to do. I want to go to school, have my own place, but she just won't let me."

After the session, Renee met with her supervisor, Marcy, to discuss the case:

Renee: "I had a hard time in the session because I just wanted to tell her to take the job and move out. I also wanted to agree with her that her mother is overbearing."

Marcy: "Do you know enough yet to make that kind of statement to her?"

Renee: "I guess not, but I wanted to help her figure out what to do."

Marcy: "Resist the temptation to intervene until you know more about the situation and about her."

Renee: "So I just listen? For how long?"

- How would you answer Renee's question? As you look back at Tia, what more would you like to know about her before you feel that you have enough information to help? As you look at Tia's story, do you see any way in which the helper might actually be hurting the client by intervening?
- What cultural, family, and religious factors are in the background of this client's story? How important are these things in understanding the client? What assumptions have you already made about Tia based on her background? How can you test them?

- In this situation, would you be tempted to find ways for the client to change her mother?
- Why is Marcy cautioning Renee to listen more? What other issues does Tia struggle with besides her relationship with her mother?
- What parts of Tia's story would you like to hear more about? Why do you think that would be helpful?
- What specific issues does Tia need to address in herself? Would encouraging her to take a job or move from her mother's house solve her problems?

Like Tia, in the "Stop and Reflect" section, some clients will open the floodgates of the story during the first session, pausing only to take a breath and perhaps ignoring most of the helper's questions and comments. It often seems that a client wants to get the story told as completely as possible before he or she will allow the helper to make an intervention. For others, it is a grueling process as the client's story is extracted drop by drop. In either case, the role of the helper *seems* passive, waiting for the client to finish the tale. Actually, the helper is listening with full attention so as to understand the facts, the feelings, and the unique perspective of the client. At times the helper is stopping to clarify a very important point of fact. Many client stories are as ironic and full of twists and turns as a Shakespearean comedy or tragedy. You cannot make a comment that a client will respect until you know the names of all the players and their relationships. It is difficult for many beginning helpers to listen to all these details. They cannot see where the story is going, and their own personal anxiety and desire to help propel them to fall back on the skills they have used all their life: offering praise, giving advice, and trying to track the client's problems back to some original cause. The art of helping, however, requires the helper to initially place his or her own concerns, questions, and theories on the back burner and to focus on the client's story, waiting until all the wrinkles have been explored.

Nonverbal Communication Between Helper and Client

You can tell whether someone is listening or not by body position and a sense of interest in the eyes. A helper must communicate this willingness to listen with his or her whole body. Before we look at specific messages that we want to communicate as helpers, let us focus for a moment on the wider area of nonverbal communication, because it helps us understand our clients.

Nonverbal communication is also called body language. We generally talk about seven nonverbal ways that we speak to others without talking: eye contact, body position, silence, voice tone, facial expressions and gestures, physical distance, and touching. Nonverbal behavior communicates additional information beyond words, regulates the interaction (indicates pauses and stopping points), enhances intimacy, and is persuasive (cf. Argyle, 1987). From this, it is obvious that nonverbals add crucial information to messages, but we often fail to recognize their power. Some writers have suggested that as much as 80 percent of communication takes place on the nonverbal level. Where strong emotions are being expressed, nonverbals are even more significant. For example, the difference between a written letter from a family member and his or her voice on the phone illustrates that most communication about emotions is nonverbal. It has been estimated that only 7 percent of emotions are conveyed by verbal means, whereas 38 percent are conveyed by the voice and 55 percent by the face (Mehrabian, 1972).

Nonverbals can be compared to the musical score in a movie. They can affect us tremendously, but we may not notice their presence. For example, researchers studying couples communication were at first confused when they examined written transcripts of troubled marriages. Everything appeared normal. It was not until they watched the videotapes that they were able to see the subtle nonverbal signals of contempt such as rolling of the eyes. Even very minor movements and expressions can set off an argument. For example, it has been found that a raised eyebrow takes only a sixth of a second, but it can be detected at distances of over 150 feet (Blum, 1998).

A clue to the importance of nonverbal communication in daily life is illustrated by the fact that many important decisions are handled in person. For example, I have a friend who spends thousands of dollars each year traveling to local offices of her company scattered around the state. If communication simply consisted of an exchange of words or data, all her business could be transacted by e-mail, telephone, or written correspondence, but, in fact, these approaches are only the "next best thing to being there." To communicate fully, you have to be face-to-face. Think about the difference between telling a friend over the phone that you are concerned, compared with personally communicating your caring by placing an arm around his or her shoulder.

Occasionally, we are required to interact with others without having access to all the nonverbal clues that the person is sending. Have you ever participated in a conference call on the telephone? In face-to-face conversations, cues about when to speak and when to listen are communicated nonverbally. Without access to these regulators, everyone talks at once or there are long periods of silence.

Nonverbal communication is also a powerful component of persuasion. The gestures and voice tone of famous orators such as Martin Luther King are evidence of this. Certainly the most persuasive communication takes place when we can see another person's face and when we are in the same room. It is much easier to say no to the salesperson on the phone than to the one who is standing right in front of you. The art of helping also relies on persuasive nonverbal messages to encourage the client to open up. Helpers use specific nonverbal behaviors to communicate listening, attention, openness, and safety. Your willingness to take the time to set the most inviting nonverbal atmosphere will ultimately affect your client's perception of you and his or her willingness to open up.

Nonverbal Skills in the Helping Relationship

One maxim says that you can't *not* communicate. Our bodies are not very good liars (Archer & Akert, 1977). Folded arms and drooping facial muscles tend to give us away. Astute helpers learn to read the body language of their clients as clues to the depth and meaning of the client's problems. However, helpers must be aware of the signals that they are sending, too. The client is interpreting and reacting to the nonverbal messages of the helper. Clients react to helper nonverbals from the very first contact by voice tone on the phone and even by the arrangement of the office where client and helper meet. This discussion brings up an important caution about nonverbal messages. They are *ambiguous*. A client whose voice seems monotonous and depressed may actually be suffering from a cold. Crossed arms may be a better signal that the air conditioning is too high than that the client is "closed." Although many emotions come through loud and clear regardless of culture, there is a wide variation in gestures and facial expressions because of one's upbringing (Kim, Liang, & Li, 2003). Because of the ambiguous nature of nonverbal communication, most helpers are cautious about interpreting a client's posture, facial expressions, or voice tone, or about drawing serious conclusions about a client's mental state from a single piece of data. On the other hand, we have no control over what conclusions clients may draw from inadvertent nonverbal signals that we as helpers send. For this reason, from the initial meeting, helpers try to present the most welcoming, nonthreatening, and facilitative nonverbals that encourage the client to talk and do not interfere with the client's telling of the story. Recall that there are seven ways to communicate nonverbally: eye contact, body position, attentive silence, voice tone, facial expressions and gestures, physical distance, and touch. In the sections that follow, we will address each of these as they are best used in the helping relationship.

Eye Contact

Eye-to-eye contact is the first and most important indicator of listening. It conveys the helper's confidence and involvement (Ridley & Asbury, 1988). In Western culture, we normally associate lack of eye contact with dishonesty, indifference, or shame. By contrast, those who sustain eye contact are seen as more ambitious, confident, assertive, intelligent, independent, and decisive than those who do not (Brooks, Church, & Fraser, 1986; Droney & Brooks, 1993).

Further, speakers who maintain eye contact with their audience are considered to be more credible and create more interest than those who do not. One study showed that graduate students in a seminar class are more likely to participate when they receive more eye contact from the professor (Caproni, Levine, O'Neal, McDonald, & Garwood, 1977). This suggests that eye contact can have an important interpersonal effect. It can stimulate involvement.

Clearly, eye contact is a powerful communication tool, but one should also be cautious in making assumptions about eye contact made by clients, especially those from different cultural backgrounds. For example, some African-American clients may have been trained to look away when listening (LaFrance & Mayo, 1976). Care must be taken when dealing with Asians and others who may be offended by direct eye contact. In some situations such as the military and with some cultural groups, direct eye contact can be considered an act of defiance, a rude gesture, a sexual invitation, or a sign that you consider yourself to be superior. If cultures seem to clash, it might be useful to discuss this with the client. Depending on the situation, it might be best merely to respect the client's own way of using eye contact and try to mirror it. Discussing it with the client might be distracting and make the client feel overly self-conscious.

There is also evidence to suggest that eye contact may be more effective in some situations than others. When people discuss difficult situations, are struggling for words, or do not trust the other person, they tend to look away (Brooks et al., 1986; Droney & Brooks, 1993). In such cases, a fixed stare may be disconcerting and should be broken naturally and intermittently if the client becomes uncomfortable. A rule of thumb is to maintain a moderate amount of eye contact while closely monitoring its effect on the client. Still, eye contact by the helper can be a powerful tool because it forces intimacy on the client and increases the helper's ability to persuade (Goldman & Fordyce, 1983). During times when the helper wants to be heard, eye contact will make his or her message more potent.

Body Position

Actions speak louder than words. Posture may be the most often noticed aspect of body language, so it becomes important to have a "posture of involvement." A relaxed alertness communicates "I am comfortable with myself and I have time to listen to you." A relaxed and attentive posture is one of the fundamental tools for putting the client at ease (Maurer & Tindall, 1983). Lounging or sprawling in the chair might add an air of informality, but it may also communicate that the level of the helper's involvement is minimal. It is suggested that the helper lean *slightly* forward, because leaning forward conveys attentiveness. Helpers normally maintain an open posture—no crossed arms or legs. Open postures seem to relax the client and encourage less defensiveness.

Attentive Silence

In social settings, it is considered vital to keep the conversation flowing. A deadly silence is a disaster at a party, but the art of helping does not follow the same rules. Allowing for small periods of silence gives the client moments for reflection and the helper time for processing. At times, silence is often the most appropriate response, such as when a client has experienced a great loss. Words often seem somehow to deny the validity of a person's grief or are perceived as attempts to sweep feelings under the rug. At these times, the helper falls back on attentive silence in order to be present without interfering. Finally, the most powerful use of silence is to nudge the client to disclose. When there is a gap in the conversation, there is a social norm that one talks to fill the awkward void. If the helper is able to endure the discomfort caused by these silences, the expectation to keep the discussion going may prompt the client to open up.

Voice Tone

A client's voice can give clues to his or her emotional state. We can tell from the client's tone which issues are the most painful and which are the sources of the greatest motivation and excitement. Similarly, clients respond to the helper's voice tone. Helpers attempt to show calm concern and empathy with their voices, and at times they try to mirror the client's emotional tone. When clients come to counseling, whether they are adults or children, they may be in a state of emotional turmoil. The helper who conveys a sense of calm with the voice can help stabilize the situation and give the impression that the helper will not be overwhelmed by the problem. Consequently, the client feels more calm and hopeful.

Sometimes, helpers use the voice to communicate that they understand how intensely the client is experiencing the problem. When a helper uses his or her voice to mirror the client's emotion, the helper does not try to *match* the intensity of the client's feelings but, instead, raises the voice slightly or gives emphasis to words that convey that the client's experience has been understood. Let us suppose, for example, that a client describes a situation in which he or she did not get an expected promotion at work. The helper may respond to the client's situation by saying. "You were really angry," or by saying. "You were *really* angry." In the second sentence, the helper's voice tone emphasizes the word *really* to more closely reflect the intensity of the client's feelings. This slight lifting of the voice can quickly let the client know you are listening very closely, not just to the facts but to the emotions as well.

Facial Expressions and Gestures

All human beings express the six primary emotions of sadness, joy, anger, surprise, disgust, and fear with the same basic facial expressions regardless of culture (Ekman, 1975), but interestingly, many of these expressions have cultural "accents." In other words, although Americans can identify sadness in pictures of Japanese people, there is something culturally distinct about their expression as well (Marsh, Elfenbein, & Ambady, 2003). Setting aside the basic emotions, human beings can also discern about 5,000 different facial expressions, many of which are culturally specific (Blum, 1998). Thus helpers must pay close attention to facial expressions, especially when it is important to determine if these signals match the clients' words. Incongruities between facial expression and verbal messages are clues to deceit, lack of self-awareness, and conflict.

Besides carefully attending to a client's expressions, the helper must consider what messages he or she is sending nonverbally. The first Freudian analysts were trained to avoid reacting to the client's expressions of emotion, while those trained in the client-centered approach of Carl Rogers felt that gestures and facial expressions shown by the helper should be genuine responses to the client's emotions. Regardless of one's theoretical persuasion, it is clear that facial expressions that convey the helper's reactions to the client's joy or sadness, anger or fear, excitement or boredom can serve as invitations to greater disclosure or potentially close the door if the client detects disdain, laughter, or boredom (Fretz, Corn, Tuemmler, & Bellet, 1979; Maurer & Tindall, 1983).

Gestures are physical motions we use to convey emotion or emphasize important points. At the two extremes, excessive movement may signal anxiety, whereas a motionless statuelike pose communicates aloofness. Fidgeting, playing with a pencil, drumming one's fingers, frequently shifting body position, checking a watch, and other such movements can be read by the client as nervousness, impatience, or disinterest. The listener who is moderately reactive to the client's content and feelings is more likely to be viewed as friendly, warm, casual, and natural. Specifically, this includes occasional head nodding for encouragement, a facial expression that indicates concern and interest, and encouraging movements of the hands that are not distracting.

Physical Distance

One's personal space, or "bubble," varies considerably from culture to culture. You may have noticed that people from Northern Europe require more space during a conversation than do Southern Europeans or Middle Easterners. It has been said that some Italians, for example, are perfectly comfortable with a conversation that is almost nose to nose (4 inches or less). Most one-on-one dialogues among Americans take place at a distance of 1 to 4 feet. Normally, about 3 feet is a comfortable space for personal interaction. In general, the smaller the physical distance, the more personal the interaction. Physical barriers such as desks increase distance and add a feeling of formality to the relationship. On the other hand, extremely close quarters can also feel intimidating and create anxiety. Stone and Morden (1976) suggest 5 feet (knee-to-knee sitting down) as an optimal distance between client and helper in a Western setting; however, most social situations are closer, with people sitting about 18 inches apart. Many helpers like to set up office chairs at about this distance, allowing the client to rearrange the chair in a comfortable way if it feels too close or too distant.

Touching and Warmth

Touch has a long history in the helping professions, dating back to Freud's "pressure technique," which involved placing a hand on the client's forehead to encourage free association (Smith, Clance, & Imes, 1998). Touch can communicate caring and concern, especially during moments of grief (Driscoll, Newman, & Seals, 1988). Willison and Masson (1986) contend that research supports the appropriate use of touch, which can have a positive impact on the therapeutic relationship. Holroyd and Brodsky (1980) recommend touch with socially immature clients to foster communication and bonding and with clients who are grieving, depressed, or traumatized as a way of showing support. They also encourage the use of touch as a greeting or at termination. In addition, touch may be used to emphasize or underline important points (Older, 1982). Touching another person does increase one's ability to influence that person (Goldman & Fordyce, 1983).

Although there is much to be said for the healing power of the human touch, certain taboos must be observed (Goodman & Teicher, 1988; Hunter & Struve, 1997). Touch can also engender powerful sexual and transference reactions in the client (Alyn, 1988). For a client who has been sexually abused, a good deal of anxiety may be aroused, and any kind of touch might be inappropriate (Hunter & Struve, 1997). Perhaps fears about physical contact are overblown in the literature, but many writers have cautioned that it is important to know the client well before initiating even the safest forms of touch, such as a pat on the shoulder or back. One guideline is to use touch only sparingly to communicate encouragement and concern, with the knowledge that even slight gestures may evoke sexual or fearful feelings in the client. The helper must be prepared to recognize this reaction in the client and be willing to discuss it.

Fisher, Rytting, and Heslin (1976) established three useful guidelines for helper touch: (1) Touch should be appropriate to the situation, (2) touch should not impose a greater level of intimacy than the client can handle, and (3) touch should not communicate a negative message (such as a patronizing pat). It must be recognized here that there is a "pro-hug" school of thought among some helpers. A hug may be a special gesture at the end of the counseling relationship, but it may be experienced as forced intimacy when used routinely. An embrace may be seen as phony, and the helper may actually be seen as less trustworthy (Suiter & Goodyear, 1985).

Table 5.2

Nonverbals That Communicate Warmth or Coldness

Nonverbal Cue	Warmth	Coldness
Tone of voice	Soft	Hard
Facial expression	Smiling, interested	Poker-faced, frowning, uninterested
Posture	Lean toward other; relaxed	Lean away from other; tense
Eye contact	Look into other's eyes	Avoid looking into other's eyes
Touching	Touch other softly	Avoid touching other
Gestures	Open, welcoming	Closed, guarding oneself, and keeping other away
Spatial distance	Close	Distant

Source: David W. Johnson, *Reaching Out: Interpersonal Effectiveness and Self-Actualization*, 7/e, Copyright 2000. Reprinted with permission of Allyn and Bacon.

Although touch has its dangers, the helper can still convey caring nonverbally by communicating warmth. Warmth is not a skill but a synthesis of nonverbal communications that can have a powerful effect on a client's willingness to open up. Warmth is difficult to define, but when it is present, we recognize it and respond by opening up. In Table 5.2, David Johnson (2000) shows how nonverbal messages can communicate either warmth or coldness.

Stop and Reflect

Differences in nonverbal communication can be a stumbling block in forming a relationship with someone from a different cultural background. We make assumptions about people based on the way they talk, look, or dress. In this section, Dr. Andrew Daire, who worked in a university counseling center, describes how talking about these perceived differences can lead to a better helping relationship and turn a negative first impression into a source of growth for helper and client.

I was the only black counselor at a small, private, predominantly white institution in the South. Once I was called to the office to meet a new client named Ray. When I came downstairs, I saw a burly young man in Western wear and cowboy boots who possessed a strong Southern drawl. He seemed very guarded initially, which I attributed to his discomfort in talking about his relationship problems. Soon I realized that we were not talking about the obvious differences between us, so I made the decision to cautiously open a discussion about his upbringing and how it differed from my own.

During that first session, he talked about his father being a racist and then admitted that he had almost walked out the door when he saw that his counselor was black. Despite this first encounter, we were able to form a good counseling relationship, and over the next nine sessions, we talked about his relationship issues as well as stereotypes and prejudice. When I saw my client for the first time, based on his clothing and accent, I expected him to be racist, and I was tempted to pull back and not even address our differences. I now believe that treating him in that way would probably have reinforced his stereotypes and prejudice, rather than providing an opportunity for him to examine them. I also began to understand a little about the fears that drive the attitudes of people like Ray and his father. Most important, we were able to develop a relationship that helped him deal with the issues he had come to work on. Had I not brought up the impressions we shared of each other, he probably would not have come back after the first session.

- Have you ever thought about attitudes you might have about people from various parts of the country? Do certain accents lead you to make unfair assumptions about people? What does a Southern, New York, Appalachian, or British accent imply about someone?
- Have you ever thought of clothing, hairstyle, or jewelry as a form of communication? All of these can be culturally influenced. For example, many people wear religious jewelry, giving a glimpse of their background. What customs can you identify in your own culture that help you decide what clothes or jewelry to wear? Are certain colors best for certain occasions, such as black for funerals?
- What can you really tell about a person from his or her clothing? Is there a risk of "pigeonholing" people based on their clothing choice or the kind of car they drive?
- Think for a moment about your experience with people from different cultural backgrounds. Which cultural groups do you have the most experience with through friends or family? Which groups do you know the least about? How important do you think it is for a helper to experience a variety of cultural groups during his or her training? Do you think it is possible for a helper to cross over cultural lines, as Andrew did, and help someone who seems to be so different?
- In Andrew's story, both helper and client reacted to the nonverbals of the other person—clothing, accent, skin color, and probably many other tiny cultural differences—but they were hesitant to mention them. When do you think it might be important in a helping relationship to notice these and talk about them? When do you think it is best to ignore them? Is part of your job as a counselor to open up areas of discussion that are traditionally taboo? Discuss this with your classmates.

We have now see that nonverbal communication can invite or dissuade a client from revealing himself. Next, we turn to opening skills, which are verbal prompts that encourage clients to disclose themselves even more deeply.

Opening Skills: How to Invite

The nonverbal skills say to the client, "I am ready to listen," but the opening skills say, "Tell me more." Because opening skills are demands that the helper makes of the client, they must be presented in a way that the client feels that he or she has the opportunity to refuse. They are soft commands. Opening skills include two broad skills: encouragers and questions.

Encouragers

Encouragement means "to cause to have heart." Encouragers are words the helper uses to bolster the client's courage to confide. We have divided these encouragers into two categories, but both types—door openers and minimal encouragers—are brief interventions to kindle the fire of self-expression. We will discuss them separately here, but later in the book, we will simply refer to them both as encouragers because both serve the same basic function: to spark disclosure without taking over the conversation.

Door Openers

The first kind of encourager is called a *door opener*, which is "a noncoercive invitation to talk" (Bolton, 1979, p. 50). The door opener is initiated by the helper, but the client determines the depth of the response. More than a passing social response or greeting, the door opener signals availability on the part of the listener and encourages exploration and discussion. By contrast, evaluative or judgmental responses are "door closers." Some parents and teachers use door closers and wonder why their children or students clam up. Here are some examples of door closers:

> "I suppose you are going to sulk again this morning, aren't you?"
> "When will you ever learn?"

By contrast, a door opener is generally a positive, nonjudgmental response made during the initial phase of a contact. It may include observations by the helper such as the following:

> "I see you are reading a book about Sylvia Plath [observation]. How do you like it?"
> "You look down this morning [observation]. Do you want to talk about it?"
> "What's on your mind?"
> "Tell me about it."
> "Can you say more about that?"
> "What would you like to talk about today?"

Door openers are invaluable to helpers because they can be used to get clients to expand on what they have been saying, to begin conversations in the first place, and to allow helpers additional time to formulate a response.

Minimal Encouragers

Minimal encouragers are brief supportive statements that convey attention and understanding. Most of us are familiar with minimal encouragers from the media's image of the Freudian analyst behind the couch, stroking his beard and saying, "Mm-hmm." Minimal encouragers are verbal responses that show interest and involvement but allow the client to determine the primary direction of the conversation. They are different from door openers in that they communicate only that the listener is on track. Such phrases reinforce talking on the part of the client and are often accompanied by an approving nod of the head. Examples of minimal encouragers include:

> "I see."
> "Yes."

"Right."
"Okay."
"Hmm."
"I've got you."
"I hear you."
"I'm with you."

Of course, these responses are not sufficient to help a client achieve the goals of therapy, but if they are *not* used frequently enough (especially in the beginning of the session), the client feels stranded and uncertain. Minimal encouragers tell the client, "I am present," but they do not interrupt the story's flow.

Questions

Be patient toward all that is unresolved in your heart.
Try to love the questions themselves.
Do not seek the answers which cannot be given,
Because you would not be able to live them.
And the point is to live everything.
Live the questions now.
Perhaps you will then gradually without noticing it,
Live along some distant day into the answers.

Rainer Marie Rilke

The great poet's words underline our common tendency to think that questions provide the ultimate road to understanding. Frequently, we can learn the most by patiently living with our questions until the answers come of themselves. We fall back on questioning when silence fails or when we feel uncertain about the direction of the conversation with someone we are trying to help. Sometimes questions get in the way of understanding for both helper and client.

Of all the opening skills, *questions* are the most easily abused. Excessive questions distract us from listening, and on the other side, the client may feel interrogated and evaluated. Questions can sidetrack the client from the story that is emerging because a question is a demand. In the beginning, questions interfere with the need the client has to tell the tale. Still, the helper must ask some questions in order to gain key information. So the problem is to know when to ask questions and which questions to ask. In general, specific questions about facts are best used (1) when an important part of the story is unclear and (2) as a means for encouraging the client to open up. In our experience, beginning helpers tend to ask too many questions, and they ask the wrong kinds of questions. Research suggests that helpers ask fewer questions as they gain experience (Ornston, Cichetti, Levine, & Freeman, 1968).

In the next section, we take aim at two common pitfalls, "why?" questions and leading questions. After that, we will talk about the appropriate use of questions in the beginning stages of helping.

"Why?" Questions

Asking the client *why* they behaved or felt a particular way is very enticing because this inquiry seems very psychological and appears to be getting to the root of a problem. The assumptions here are (1) that the client knows why and (2) that knowing why will be helpful. In fact, asking a client, "Why did you get a divorce?" may put him or her on the defensive rather than stimulating deeper thought (Brodsky & Lichtenstein, 1999). Adults tend to respond to "why?" questions with intellectualizations and rationalizations. On the other hand, if you ask a 5-year-old why he or she stepped in the mud, the inevitable and truthful answer is "I don't know." In reality, a few decisions people make, such as buying a car or a house, may have been the result of a lengthy, rational process, but the best answer to most "why?" questions is usually "It seemed like a good idea at the time." This may be true even for important life decisions such as getting married or changing jobs. Over time, helpers learn to ask fewer "why?" questions and learn to extract the motivations, or "why," of the client's behavior from the whole of the story.

Frequently the reason for asking questions is that the helper feels stuck. When you encounter a sullen, reluctant, silent, or angry client, you may find the almost irresistible urge to revert to questioning because listening is such a challenge. This feeling generally leads to desperate measures that do more harm than good. At such times, the helper should fall back on attentive silence and encouragers to keep the door open.

Leading Questions

Leading questions have an embedded message. The message usually is "If you follow my logic, you will soon see the answer to your problem." Leading questions are usually grouped together as a subtle argument or a secret way of giving the client advice. Consider this example:

Raymond (client): Since I was diagnosed with cancer, my entire life has changed. People have started looking at me differently. They look down on me like I can't do the job anymore. I am sick of being pitied.

Leila (helper): Are you letting other people affect your mood? (leading)

Raymond: "I guess so."

Leila: "Would you let other people affect you so much if you had more faith in yourself?" (leading)

Raymond: "No, probably not."

Leila: "Do you think that if your self-esteem were higher, you would feel better?" (leading)

Raymond: "Yeah."

These questions are *leading* because they are really disguised attempts to push through the client's acceptance of the helper's agenda. Can you see what the helper is trying to tell the client? Notice that the client agrees but does not respond with more information. Unfortunately, this type of questioning is very common among those who are trying to work with children and adolescents, but the evidence suggests that this approach shuts down the conversation (Sternberg, Lamb, Hershkowitz, Yudilevitch, Orbach, Esplin, & Hovav, 1997).

Open and Closed Questions

Besides leading and "why?" questions, we can put questions into two other broad categories: open and closed.

Closed questions *Closed questions* ask for specific information and usually require a short factual response. Some closed questions can be answered with a yes or no; others demand information such as when you ask someone's age. Closed questions are important when you need to get the facts straight—especially when there is an emergency situation or when an understanding of the complicated facts is crucial to your understanding of the client's story. This became apparent in a recent demonstration session during which a client discussed the trauma and aftereffects of a serious two-car accident. The helper, using door openers, minimal encouragers, and appropriate nonverbals, was able to get the client to talk about many of the important issues. However, the student helper failed to ask if the other victim of the accident had been killed or injured, an event that was the key to the client's shame and remorse about the incident. The student helper felt that the client should have volunteered this vital piece of information, but clients often talk about a problem on a superficial level at first. Sometimes, the helper must delve and pry to get the important facts. The difficulty is in knowing which aspects of the story are likely to be important. In this incident, for example, it was the seriousness of the accident that needed to be explored. Many beginning helpers might ask about less relevant details. They might ask when the accident occurred, how bad the damage was to the cars involved, where the incident took place, and so forth. These are the sorts of questions that sidetrack the client from the important issues.

Although there are times when closed questions are called for, they can have a dampening effect on the relationship and on the conversation. If a helper begins with a series of questions such as name, address, and phone number, the client may begin to believe that his or her job is to respond to the helper's questions rather than to tell the story. The client can become passive, waiting for the right line of questioning before speaking. Sometimes the deadly silence in the session is due to the fact that you trained the client to wait for questions rather than initiate conversation. It may also be true that, depending on a client's cultural background, the role of a helper is analogous to that of a physician. The client might feel that it is only respectful to wait for a question. At such times, the helper should not let the client suffer in silence, but instead let the client know that helping means a partnership in which both people have the opportunity to contribute. The use of open questions will help these clients make a transition to greater involvement.

Open questions Compared with closed questions, *open questions* allow more freedom of expression and are perceived as more helpful (Elliott, 1985). Open questions do not request specific information but encourage one to speak about the general topic. Because open questions are less coercive than closed questions, clients who are reluctant to seek help may respond better to these questions (Brodsky & Lichtenstein, 1999). Here are some examples of open and closed questions. Consider how you might respond to them.

"Could you tell me about the kinds of problems you have been having?"
"Last week, we discussed your relationships with men. Would you mind going into that again?"
"Can you tell me what has been happening at school?"
"You say you have self-esteem problems. What do you mean by that?"

Now consider the following closed questions:

"How old are you?"
"What school do you go to?"
"Are you planning to go to college?"
"Would you describe your marriage as happy?"

The difference between the two question types is something like the comparison between multiple-choice and essay exams. Multiple-choice tests check your knowledge of the facts, but essays ask you to show a deeper level of understanding. Here are some pairs of open and closed questions that each explore a similar topic. Note the differences in the client's typical response to open versus closed questions.

Closed

Helper: "Are you getting along with your parents these days?"
Client: "Yeah. Pretty good."

Open

Helper: "Can you tell me how you and your parents have been dealing with your differences recently?"
Client: "Well, we haven't been, really. We're not fighting, but we're not talking, either. Just existing."

Closed

Helper: "Are you married now?"
Client: "No, divorced."

Open

Helper: "Can you tell me a little about your personal relationships during the past few years?"
Client: "Well, I've been divorced for 6 months from my second wife. We were married for over 7 years, and one day she left me for this guy at work. Since then, I haven't really been up to seeing anyone."

As these examples suggest, open questions eventually elicit more information than closed questions, even though they may not seem as direct (Johns Hopkins University, 1998). They tend to enhance the therapeutic relationship (Boyd, 2003). Open questions also persuade the client to answer by giving the client the opportunity to refuse. They do not box the client in by forcing him or her to answer directly. When you feel the need to ask a closed question, try and transform it into an open one first.

In summary, there is a tendency for beginners to ask too many questions including "why?" questions, leading questions, and unnecessary closed questions. Yet it is also important to get crucial information. Good questioning is an art (Goldberg, 1998), and we will consider it in greater detail when we discuss its use in the assessment stage of the helping process. For the time being, keep a close watch on the overuse of questions in the exercises and practice sessions. See if you can do without closed questions, and let your nonverbal skills and other encouragers be the workhorses of your helping conversation.

Stop and Reflect: Are You an Opener?

The Opener Scale was developed by Miller, Berg, and Archer (1983) to identify individuals who are good listeners and are able to get others to disclose information about themselves.* If you score yourself as low on this scale, it does not mean that you cannot learn the basic helping skills in this book. It is a self-assessment of where you are right now, not what you can become. When you have finished this book, write down your answers again to see what changes you have made. As you fill out the scale, try to be as honest as you can. Do not compare your score with other people's results—this scale was not devised for that purpose.

Rate each statement as it applies to you on a scale of 1–5 (4–5 strongly agree, 3 agree, 2 disagree, 1 strongly disagree).

1. People frequently tell me about themselves.
2. I've been told that I'm a good listener.
3. I'm very accepting of others.
4. People trust me with their secrets.
5. I easily get people to "open up."
6. People feel relaxed around me.
7. I enjoy listening to people.
8. I'm sympathetic to people's problems.
9. I encourage people to tell me how they are feeling.
10. I can keep people talking about themselves.

Although the Opener Scale does not have any guidelines about what constitutes a high or low score, let us arbitrarily set 0–10 as a low score and 30–40 as a high score. It has been found that people with higher scores on the Opener Scale are more successful in eliciting self-disclosure, even in people whose self-disclosure is normally low. High scorers are also able to take the viewpoint of others (be empathic) more easily than low scorers. Purvis, Dabbs, & Hopper (1984) found that high scorers show more comfort, enjoyment, and attentiveness than low scorers and are more verbally and nonverbally engaged.

What reaction do you have to your results? Some beginning helpers wrongly believe that everyone has these interests and skills. They are surprised to find that the opening abilities tapped by this scale are not as common as they thought. Discuss this idea with classmates or record your reactions in your journal.

*Used with permission of the author, Lynne C. Miller.

Summary

Every client has a story to tell, and invitational skills let the client know that we are interested in that story. Invitational skills have two basic components: nonverbal skills and opening skills. Nonverbal skills are messages used by helpers to provide the right conditions for the client to open up. The skills are eye contact, body position, attentive silence, voice tone, facial expressions and gestures, physical distance, and touching. Opening skills are the verbal messages the helper

Table 5.3
Quick Tips: Invitational Skills

- Once you have adopted a facilitative body position, take a deep breath and relax.
- Remember that the ball is in the client's court: Invite the client to talk and to tell the story.
- After an open question or two, use the first few minutes to listen to the client, using minimal encouragers and head nodding.
- When a silence occurs, don't rush to fill the void. Wait for the client to do it first.
- Rely on door openers such as "Go on" and "Say some more about that," rather than asking too many questions at first.
- Use closed questions sparingly, but ask yourself if you have understood the most important facts. If you are unsure, stop the client and ask a closed question or two.

sends to facilitate the client's disclosure. Opening skills include encouragers and open and closed questions. Invitational skills are relatively simple to learn, but they count for so much in the relationship between client and helper. A summary of suggestions about how to use invitational skills effectively is presented in Table 5.3.

Getting the relationship off on the right foot means establishing the norm that the client has free rein to explore his or her deepest issues in a nonjudgmental atmosphere. Besides their importance in the beginning, invitational skills are needed at all stages of the helping process. As each new issue comes to the surface, the helper relies on invitational skills and a nonjudgmental attitude to provide the atmosphere of warmth and safety that allows for the deepest exploration of the client's needs, fears, and dreams.

Exercises

Group Exercise 1

Practice and feedback session using invitational skills

Some Notes on the Helper/Client/Observer Training Group

For many of the practice sessions in this book, we will be asking you to break into groups of three or four. This works in a circular fashion with person A counseling person B. Later, person B counsels person C, and person C counsels person A. Depending on how your instructor likes to work, you may be assigned to the same groups for all practice sessions, or you may

frequently change groups. Practicing on fellow students is a method used in medical and dental schools as well as in the training of mental health professionals. Recently, I met a dental student who told me the dental students practiced giving numbing shots to each other in class. Just as in giving an injection, there is some risk involved in role-playing, but one of the prime benefits is that you learn something about being in the client role. You learn how it feels to be challenged or supported. You also get a feeling about what is too invasive or too superficial. On the other hand, in the role of observer, you are able to step out of the helping situation and look at the situation more objectively. All three roles are instructive. Finally, as a member of a practice group, you will be challenged ethically, too. Although you may be role-playing part of the time, some of the situations are real; you should have an agreement for confidentiality just as if it were an actual problem. It has been our experience that students respect this confidentiality and take it very seriously. Still, confidentiality and its limits need to be explicitly discussed in each group.

Instructions for Group Exercise 1

Break up into groups of four. One person is the helper, another the client, and two act as observers. Before the "session" begins, the helper should take time to review the tips about invitational skills given in Table 5.3. Meanwhile, the client decides on the topic he or she wants to discuss, and the observers look over their checklists. Observer 1 will use Feedback Checklist 1 to give the helper data on his or her nonverbal skills. Observer 2 will use Feedback Checklist 2 to rate the helper on opening skills. For 5 to 8 minutes, the helper invites the client to discuss one of the following topics:

- How I chose my present job
- A trip I took that was very important to me
- My relationship with a close friend
- A topic of the client's choice
- The problem of a friend or acquaintance whose role the client assumes

Feedback

At the end of the time period, the observers and client give feedback to the helper. The client is encouraged to give qualitative feedback that may include general impressions of the helper's manner. The client should indicate whether or not he or she felt genuineness, empathy, and respect from the helper. The observers will give feedback based on their checklists. The participants switch roles, giving each person a chance to experience helper, client, and observer roles. The entire process will take about 45 minutes.

Feedback Checklist 1 (to be completed by Observer 1)

During the practice session, try to work through the checklist systematically, recording your comments for each skill as you observe it. The helper may want you to write these observations directly in his or her book. If you have time, start at the beginning and review each skill again to check your observations. When you are finished, write down any suggestions for improvement. Be as honest as possible so that the helper can benefit from feedback.

1. Draw a stick figure sketch of the helper's body position.

   What does the body position convey? (Circle all that apply)

   Openness   Relaxation   Tension
   Stiffness   Interest   Aloofness

   Comments for improvement:
2. Evaluate the helper's ability to maintain appropriate eye contact (circle one).

   Avoids
   Occasional
   Constant with breaks
   Stares

   Comments for improvement:
3. Circle all that apply as you listen to the helper's voice tone:

   Too loud   Cold
   Too soft   Soothing
   Confident   Clipped
   Hesitant   Interested
   Moralistic or smug   Bored
   Warm   Other

   Comments for improvement:
4. Evaluate the helper's gestures and facial expressions (circle all that apply).

Gestures:

   Nervous movement
   Occasional

Inviting gestures
Rigid

Nodding:

Head nodding appropriate
Head nodding too frequent
Head nodding too infrequent

Expression:

Helper's face shows concern and interest
Face shows disinterest
Face reflects client's feelings
Face is unchanging/masklike
Other (e.g., warmth or use of touch)

Comments for improvement:

Feedback Checklist 2 (to be completed by Observer 2)

You are to give feedback on the helper's use of encouragers (door openers and minimal encouragers) and questions (open and closed). Your task is to write down everything the helper says during the interview. At the end, categorize each response and give the helper feedback.

Categories

Encourager (E)—include door openers and minimal encourager under this same category
Open question (OQ)
Closed question (CQ)

Helper Question or Statement	Category
1.	
2.	
3.	
4.	
5.	
6.	
7.	
8.	
9.	
10.	
11.	
12.	
13.	
14.	
15.	

Feedback on the Use of Encouragers

1. Did the helper supply enough encouragers during the initial 2 minutes of the interview to let the client know he or she was listening?

2. Were minimal encouragers used too often, instead of open questions that might have given a direction to the discussion?

Feedback on the Use of Questions

1. Look at the list of closed questions used by the helper. Based on the client's response, were they vital or merely asked out of curiosity? How many "why?" questions did you detect?

2. Were there more open or closed questions? Does this helper need to increase the use of open questions or decrease the use of closed questions?

Group Exercise 2

Open versus closed questions

Each member of a small group (two or three students) should individually turn the following closed questions into open questions. Write your answers down and later get feedback from the group. Remember, an open question can expand a topic beyond the original closed question. For example, the closed question "Are your parents still married?" can be "opened" by changing it to "Can you tell me something about your family?" Share your open questions with others in a small group. Think how you might answer your own open questions. Does it give you room to expand and disclose?

- Where are you from?
- What is your problem?

- Why do you need help?
- When did all of your problems begin?
- Do your mom and dad fight?

- Did you have fun on the class trip?
- Was it suicide?

Additional Exercises

Exercise 1: Watch a videotape of a practice session between another helper and a client.

View 10 to 15 minutes of a videotape that shows a client/helper interaction. While watching, write down any observations you may have concerning the client's body posture, gestures, and movements. Afterward, discuss the relationship of these nonverbal messages to the client's concerns. Alternatively, half of the class can observe the client and the other half can focus on the helper. Check the helper's invitational skills against the list in Table 5.2.

Exercise 2: Eyes closed

Form dyads (groups of two) and sit facing each other with your eyes closed. Discuss your activities over the past week for about 4 to 5 minutes. In the class discussion that follows, take turns giving your reactions to the experience. What nonverbal behaviors did you and your classmates find it most difficult to do without?

Exercise 3: The effect of distance

Set up a simulated office for a role-playing situation. Provide one chair for the client and another for the helper. Use a third chair to represent a desk if one is not available. Place the chairs about 10 feet apart and ask two participants to hold a conversation at that distance concerning a minor problem one of them is having. Ask the group to comment on how the distance has affected the conversation. Next, allow the participants to move the chairs to a comfortable distance. Once the chairs have been moved and the participants are seated, measure the distance from knee to knee with a yardstick or tape measure and see if it is approximately 18 inches,

an average social distance. Does it seem too close or too far away? Next, move the chairs so close that the participants feel uncomfortable. Measure that distance. If participants from diverse ethnic backgrounds are members of the group, interesting variations can occur. Try the exercise with participants standing instead of seated. You will find that some people will feel comfortable with an interpersonal distance of 6 inches or less.

Exercise 4: Touch with caution

Conduct a group discussion on the implications of touching clients. What constitutes sexual touching? Whose needs are being fulfilled by touching? Is it all right for the helper's emotional needs to be met by hugging a client? Under what circumstances would a hug be beneficial or harmful? What about hugging in group therapy?

Exercise 5: Try a 15-minute videotape session

Make a 15-minute videotape of two trainees, one of whom acts as the client and the other as the helper. The client discusses a minor problem he or she is having at work or at school. Focus the camera for half of the session on the helper's face and the other half of the session on the helper's whole body. Replay the tape and ask the helper to evaluate his or her own facial expressions, body position, and gestures. While this is a very simple exercise, it may help students who are feeling camera shy. Our experience is that the more opportunities students have to be videotaped, the better their final sessions will be. As the normal fear of being observed lessens, the helper's responses become more natural and more attention is focused on the client.

Exercise 6: Sustained eye contact

In this exercise, students form dyads. The leader or instructor will keep time and signal the completion of the activity at the end of 2 minutes. Maintain eye contact with your partner and assume the appropriate helper's posture while remaining completely silent. Afterward, discuss your personal reactions to this exercise with your partner and then with the larger group.

Homework

Homework 1: Sound off

Record a television show or movie and replay it with the sound turned off. Try to see if you can guess emotional content by examining the characters' body language. Write a one-page reaction to this assignment. If you want to have the voice tone added, try watching a program in another language and see if you can still get the gist of the story without understanding the words.

Homework 2: Hug survey

Conduct a survey among a few friends or family members. How would they feel about being hugged or touched by a professional helper? Try to be objective and prepare a one-page summary of their answers and your conclusions.

Homework 3: Experiment with silence

In conversations with coworkers, family, and friends, instead of immediately responding to what they say, build in attentive silence and notice the effect. The purpose of the assignment is to observe the effect of silence on the communication of others. Make notes and report findings to the group. Write a one-paragraph reaction to this exercise. If your silence is too long, your friends and family will complain. If it is just right, they will say more and not feel uncomfortable.

Journal Starters

1. Many nonverbal skills such as touching, distance, and eye contact are learned in one's family of origin and reflect cultural values. Think for a moment about the rules about touching, eye contact, and personal space that you learned growing up. How might you unknowingly create a barrier by being too familiar or too aloof with a client? How will you be able to tell when your client is uncomfortable? What would be comfortable for you and what would you object to as a client?
2. Think about a secret that you have not shared with anyone. How do you think you would feel if a helper urged you to share this private information? Would it be easier to share it with a close friend? What kind of response would you expect if you told a close friend about this issue? How do you think you would feel after sharing this information? What are your fantasies about what might happen if you disclosed this secret? Do you imagine the helper telling others, or is it simply disquieting to think about the secret? Would any of these expectations affect your willingness to share the information with a professional helper?

References

Alyn, J. H. (1988). The politics of touch in therapy. *Journal of Counseling and Development, 66,* 155–159.

Archer, D., & Akert, R. M. (1977). Words and everything else: Verbal and nonverbal cues in social interpretation. *Journal of Personality and Social Psychology, 34,* 443–449.

Argyle, M. (1987). Functions of nonverbal communication. *Semiotica, 67,* 135–140.

Blum, D. (1998). Face it! *Psychology Today, 31*(5), 32–70.

Bolton, R. (1979). *People skills: How to assert yourself, listen to others, and resolve conflicts.* Upper Saddle River, NJ: Prentice Hall.

Boyd, G. E. (2003). Pastoral conversation: Relational listening and open-ended questions. *Pastoral Psychology, 51,* 345–361.

Brodsky, S. L., & Lichtenstein, B. (1999). Don't ask questions: A psychotherapeutic strategy for treatment of involuntary clients. *American Journal of Psychotherapy, 53,* 215–221.

Brooks, C. I., Church, M. A., & Fraser, L. (1986). Effects of duration of eye contact on judgments of personality characteristics. *Journal of Social Psychology, 126,* 71–78.

Caproni, V., Levine, D., O'Neal, E., McDonald, P., & Garwood, G. (1977). Seating position, instructor's eye contact availability and student participation in a small seminar. *Journal of Social Psychology, 103,* 315–317.

Driscoll, M. S., Newman, D. L., & Seals, J. M. (1988). The effect of touch on perception of helpers. *Counselor Education and Supervision, 27,* 113–115.

Droney, J. M., & Brooks, C. I. (1993). Attributions of self-esteem as a function of duration of eye contact. *Journal of Social Psychology, 133,* 715–723.

Ekman, P. (1975). Universal smile: Face muscles talk every language. *Psychology Today, 9*(4), 35–39.

Elliott, R. (1985). Helpful and nonhelpful events in brief counseling interviews: An empirical taxonomy. *Journal of Counseling Psychology, 32,* 307–322.

Fisher, J. D., Rytting, M., & Heslin, R. (1976). Affective and valuative effects of an interpersonal touch. *Sociometry, 39,* 416–421.

Fretz, B. R., Corn, R., Tuemmler, J. M., & Bellet, W. (1979). Counselor nonverbal behaviors and client evaluations. *Journal of Counseling Psychology, 26,* 304–311.

Goldberg, M. C. (1998). *The art of the question.* New York: Wiley.

Goldman, M., & Fordyce, J. (1983). Prosocial behavior as affected by eye contact, touch and voice. *Journal of Social Psychology, 121,* 125–131.

Goodman, M., & Teicher, A. (1988). To touch or not to touch. *Psychotherapy: Theory, Research and Practice, 25,* 492–500.

Holroyd, J., & Brodsky, A. (1980). Does touching patients lead to sexual intercourse? *Professional Psychology, 11,* 807–811.

Hunter, M., & Struve, J. (1997). *The ethical use of touch in psychotherapy.* Thousand Oaks, CA: Sage.

Johns Hopkins University (1998). Why and how to ask questions. *Population Reports, 26,* 5–6.

Johnson, D. W. (2000). *Reaching out.* Boston: Allyn & Bacon. Kim, B. S. K., Liang, C. T. H., & Li, L. C. (2003). Counselor ethnicity, counselor nonverbal behavior, and session outcome with Asian American clients: Initial findings. *Journal of Counseling and Development, 81,* 202–208.

Kim, B. S. K., Liang, C. T. H., & Li, L. C. (2003). Counselor ethnicity, counselor nonverbal behavior, and session outcome with Asian American clients: Initial findings. *Journal of Counseling and Development, 81,* 202–207.

Kopp, S. (1978). *If you meet the Buddha on the road, kill him!* New York: Bantam.

LaFrance, M., & Mayo, C. (1976). Racial differences in gaze behavior during observations: Two systematic observational studies. *Journal of Personality and Social Psychology, 33,* 47–52.

Marsh, A. A., Elfenbein, H. A., & Ambady, N. (2003). Nonverbal "accents": Cultural differences in facial expressions of emotion. *Psychological Science, 14,* 373–377.

Maurer, R. E., & Tindall, J. H. (1983). Effect of postural congruence on client's perception of helper empathy. *Journal of Counseling Psychology, 30,* 158–163.

Mehrabian, A. (1972). *Nonverbal communication.* Chicago: Aldine. Miller, L., Berg, J. H., & Archer,

R. L. (1983). Openers: Individuals who elicit intimate self-disclosure. *Journal of Personality and Social Psychology, 44*, 1234–1244.

Miller, L., Berg, J. H., & Archer, R. L. (1983). Openers: Individuals who elicit intimate self-disclosure. *Journal of Personality and Social Psychology, 44*, 1234–1244.

Moffat, M. J., & Painter, C. (Eds.). (1975). *Revelations: Diaries of women*. New York: Vintage.

Older, J. (1982). Touching is healing. New York: Stein & Day.

Ornston, P. S., Cichetti, D. V., Levine, J., & Freeman, L. B. (1968). Some parameters of verbal behavior that reliably differentiate novice from experienced therapists. *Journal of Abnormal Psychology, 73*, 240–244.

Pennebaker, J. W. (1989). Confession, inhibition, and disease. In L. Berkowitz (Ed.), *Advances in experimental social psychology* (Vol. 22, pp. 211–214). New York: Academic Press.

Pennebaker, J. W. (1990). *Opening up*. New York: Guilford.

Pennebaker, J. W. (Ed.). (2002). *Emotion, disclosure and health*. Washington, DC: American Psychological Association.

Purvis, J. A., Dabbs, J. M., & Hopper, C. (1984). The "Opener": Skilled use of facial expression and speech pattern. *Personality and Social Psychology Bulletin, 10*, 60–66.

Ridley, N. C., & Asbury, F. R. (1988). Does counselor body position make a difference? *School Counselor, 35*, 253–258.

Smith, E. W. L., Clance, P. R., & Imes, S. (1998). *Touch in psychotherapy*. New York: Guilford.

Sternberg, K. J., Lamb, M. E., Hershkowitz, I., Yudilevitch, L., Orbach, Y., Esplin, P. W., & Hovav, M. (1997). Effects of introductory style on children's abilities to describe experiences of sexual abuse. *Child Abuse and Neglect, 21*, 1133–1146.

Stone, G. L., & Morden, C. J. (1976). Effect of distance on verbal productivity. *Journal of Counseling Psychology, 23*, 486–488.

Suiter, R. L., & Goodyear, R. K. (1985). Male and female counselor and client perceptions of four levels of counselor touch. *Journal of Counseling Psychology, 32*, 645–668.

White, M. (2000). Reflections on narrative practice. Adelaide, Australia: Dulwich Centre Publications.

Willison, B. G., & Masson, R. L. (1986). The role of touch in therapy: An adjunct to communication. *Journal of Counseling and Development, 64*, 497–500.

Reflecting Skills: Paraphrasing

6

> *The unexamined life is not worth living.*
> Socrates

The invitational skills you learned in the last chapter send the following message to the client: "I am ready and willing to listen." Although invitational skills, such as eye contact, convey that you are present and available, they do not adequately indicate that you really understand what the other person is trying to convey. Invitational skills are commonly used by friends, family, and acquaintances, as well as by helpers.

Reflecting skills, on the other hand, are specialized interventions used by helpers to stimulate deeper exploration of the facts, feelings, and meanings that coexist in the client's presentation of the problem.

Reflecting Content and Thoughts, Reflecting Feelings, and Reflecting Meaning

Every client message has three basic components: (1) the client's understanding of the facts and his or her thoughts (a cognitive level), (2) the client's underlying feelings (an emotional level), and (3) hidden meanings (existential level) (see Figure 6.1). Each of these three dimensions of experience can be evoked by specific skills. As Figure 6.1 suggests, you might want to think of them as three separate boxes that have to be unpacked if you are to really grasp the whole story.

In this chapter, you will learn to reflect content and thoughts, a skill that is called *paraphrasing*. Chapter 7 focuses on learning the skill of *reflecting feelings*, and Chapter 8 addresses the skill of *reflecting meaning*. You will learn these skills separately and then practice putting them together in a complete helping session. In this section, we will distinguish paraphrasing from reflecting feelings and leave the discussion of meaning for a later time. Table 6.1 gives examples of these three building block skills.

To gain a clearer idea of the distinction between the parts of the client's message, consider the following story in which a helper describes how he began to recognize that parts of a story are suppressed and must be reflected.

> Once I ran a private practice in a small town. The house next door to my office was guarded by a huge German shepherd dog that frequently growled at my clients when they approached the front door. When I greeted my clients, I was always interested in how they framed their reaction. They often said, "That is the biggest dog I've ever seen." If I had responded to the content of the message, I might have said, "Yes, that is exceptionally large for a German shepherd," or, "Actually, I've seen bigger," or even, "Yes, he weighs over 100 pounds and is in excellent health!"

This example illustrates that every communication has at least two dimensions: the explicit and the implicit. In this case, the hidden message is an emotional one

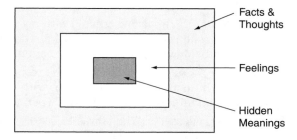

Figure 6.1
Components of the Client's Message

Table 6.1
Three Building Blocks in Reflecting Skills

Skill	Examples
Paraphrase	"So this week has been very difficult, at work and at home." "You've been thinking about spending more time with friends and visiting your family less frequently."
Reflection of feeling	"It was a shock when they announced your promotion." "After all that had happened, you were wary about continuing your friendship."
Reflection of meaning	"Family has always been important to you, and this event has really affected your faith in that." "The promotion was a big moment for you because it meant that you had finally arrived professionally."

concerning the fear that the dog evoked but that very few people felt comfortable in expressing. From culture to culture, people vary in their willingness to openly express their feelings, and frequently these are specific to the topic. Gender also affects what a person feels is permissible. For example, many men will not acknowledge feeling fearful or weak. In general, we are all much more comfortable talking about content or facts. That is why weather but not politics is most likely to be an early conversation starter.

In helping, the content and the emotional side are equally important if we are to really know someone. A response that recognizes both will lead to the deepest communication of understanding. At the beginning of the helping relationship, clients find it more comfortable if the helper is able to reflect the content of their stories. Later, a helper can show that he or she also grasps the underlying, or hidden, emotional side.

During a session, the helper makes a series of reflections. As the client responds to the reflections, the helper gets more information about the accuracy of paraphrases and reflections of feelings until the helper understands the whole message. Eventually, the helper begins to grasp the meaning behind the story, and the deepest reflections acknowledge the importance of these values and beliefs.

To demonstrate how a helper can lead a client to fully explore a story, let us look at the case of Phillipe, a single father who has come for help with his adolescent daughter.

Phillipe (client): "I am having trouble with my daughter. She has just started driving. I think she is a good driver, but I am not so sure about the kids she hangs around with. My wife says I am overreacting, that I don't want her to grow up."

Joyce (helper): "So the main reason you're here is to think about how you are handling the conflict you are having with your daughter, and it sounds like driving is an important part of that." (paraphrase)

Phillipe: "Yes, I guess it is. When I was 16, I stole a car with some other kids. We went joyriding and had an accident. The driver was drunk, and one of the kids in the car was killed. Every time my own kid goes out on Saturday night, I think of that. I yell and scream, and maybe I am too strict with her."

Joyce: "You remember that incident and worry that the same kind of thing might happen to her." (reflecting feeling—worry)

Phillipe: "Yes, sometimes I get really scared. My own parents didn't care what I did. I don't want to keep her at home all the time, but I don't want her doing something stupid."

Joyce: "It seems that you're wondering, 'Am I being a good parent.' " (reflection of meaning—being a good parent and not repeating his parents' mistakes is a deeper level of meaning)

The reflecting skills in this example go beyond invitational skills by bringing out a deeper level of the story—the emotional reactions of the client and the potential meanings. To use a metaphor, recognizing these deeper levels adds color to the black-and-white facts. With the example of Phillipe and Joyce in mind, we are ready to explore what reflecting involves and what functions are served by reflecting skills in helping.

Reasons for Reflecting

In general, reflecting entails repeating back to the client his or her own thoughts and feelings and implied meanings in a condensed way, using different words and in a manner that communicates nonevaluative, nonjudgmental understanding.

Four functions are served by reflecting skills in helping:

1. *Reflecting is a verbal way of communicating empathy.* In Chapter 3, we discussed the concept of empathy, or trying to "feel oneself into" another's experience. We indicated then that the helper tries to share a client's deeper experiences and that it is also important to convey this understanding to the client. Reflecting feelings communicates, "I hear your deeper thoughts and emotions as well as the facts." In the preceding example, Joyce does not have to say to Phillipe, "I understand what you are going through." Instead, she communicates his worry, confusion, and fear, trying to understand the situation through his eyes rather than a similar experience of her own.

2. *Reflecting is a form of feedback or a mirror that enables the person to confirm or correct the impression he or she is giving.* In Joyce's second response to Phillipe, she uses the word *worry*. For a number of reasons, this word might not have exactly fit what Phillipe was trying to communicate. He might have responded, "No, I don't worry that the same thing will happen. I just get mad at her for not listening to me!" This demonstrates that a reflecting statement, even if inaccurate, can give the client an opportunity to clarify the experience to others and to oneself. In other words, beginning helpers should try to reflect without being concerned that every reflection is perfect. If the helper does not hit the bull's-eye, in many cases the client will expand and explain the situation more clearly.

3. *Reflecting stimulates further exploration of what the client is experiencing.* Notice that when Joyce identifies Phillipe's feelings of worry in the first reflection, Phillipe begins discussing his own upbringing and talks about the conflict between being overprotective and too lenient. This shows that accurate

reflection has an opening effect, bringing out more facts and deeper feelings. Reflecting could also be compared to the soliloquy in a Shakespearean play or in an opera where the main character turns to the audience and expresses what is going on inside of him. Because clients do not always express or even recognize these deeper thoughts and feelings, the helper primes the pump with reflections.

4. *Reflecting captures important aspects of the client's message that otherwise might remain camouflaged.* In Phillipe's opening statement, he makes no mention of the fact that he is scared or worried about his daughter. Many people have difficulty admitting to negative feelings such as fear and anger. Perhaps, at this first meeting, Phillipe does not wish to appear foolish in his concerns. It is the helper's reflection that extracts this feeling that is hidden in his first statement.

The Skill of Paraphrasing: Reflecting Content and Thoughts

In the discussion of invitational skills, you were warned not to ask too many questions at the beginning stages of the helping relationship. Questions, especially closed questions, can interrupt the flow of the client's story and make the client feel that he or she is under a microscope. However, it is important to have a clear grasp of the facts relating to the client's problem and also, at times, to repeat some important thoughts or intentions embedded in the client's statements. So how can we get more information without quizzing the client and also let the client know we are on board? Paraphrasing is a reflecting skill that serves both purposes.

The paraphrase is *not* a word-for-word reiteration. The paraphrase is a distilled version of the content of the client's message that restates the facts and thoughts in different words and in a nonjudgmental way. As a client tells his or her story, the paraphrase is used as a mirror to let the client know that you are following but does not pressure the client by asking a question. It is short and sweet and therefore does not slow the client down while he or she is disclosing. It does not take sides with the client by supporting his or her version of the story but, rather, points out that this is the client's perspective.

Paraphrasing means reflecting what the client knows to be factual, but these facts are those that are uniquely perceived by the client. Facts and the client's thoughts and perceptions are intertwined. In order to accurately reflect them and at the same time remain nonjudgmental, the helper must take a neutral stance. Here is an example of a typical helper/client exchange:

Client: "Okay, I came in 2 hours late. And then my mom sent me to my room for the rest of the day. I am 17 years old. She treats me like a baby just because she likes to be in control all the time."

Helper (paraphrasing): "So you were punished again for breaking curfew. You think it is unfair and that she is doing it to control you."

Can you see that the helper is not taking sides in this paraphrase? Instead, the aim is to convey that the message was heard and to make the client aware of his or her perceptions of the events. This exchange illustrates some of the differences between social communication and therapeutic communication. The helper is not merely supportive but asks the client to reflect on his or her own words.

How to Paraphrase

Paraphrasing involves two steps: ①listening carefully to the client's story and then ②feeding back to the client a condensed, nonjudgmental version of the facts and thoughts. The second step in paraphrasing involves finding the important information in a large volume of client material and repeating it in a succinct summary. If the paraphrase goes on too long, it can fatally disrupt the client's story, and he or she will not stay on track. Using a boxing analogy, the paraphrase is more like a jab. The helper gets in and out quickly. The paraphrase is actually a miniature version of the client's story. A good paraphrase keeps the client's story on track by mentioning only the important aspects, not issues that sidetrack the client.

Here is an example of a conversation between a helper and a client in their first meeting. Notice how paraphrase assists the helper in understanding the facts of the story and also allows the client to feel the helper is on track:

Melvin (helper): "So what brought you in today?" (encourager)

Fred (client): "Well, I am a teacher, and I have been having some problems at school recently."

Melvin: "Okay, can you tell me about that?" (encourager)

Fred: "I have a group of sixth graders this year that are just wild. They won't listen, and they constantly challenge me. I've sent more kids to the office this year than I can ever remember. I've sent notes home and scheduled a lot of parent conferences."

Melvin: "Uh-huh. Okay." (encouragers)

Fred: "I guess you get a bad group sometimes. I've been teaching for 13 years, and I am used to working with rowdy kids. But this year it seems like it's getting on my nerves even more."

Melvin: "So you are not sure if it's just a wild class or if you are overreacting." (paraphrase)

Fred: "For some reason, I am really feeling the stress. This year, one of the teachers was fired during the first week for some unknown reason."

Melvin: "I see." (encourager)

Fred: "That has left a lot of people upset. With that kind of support from the principal, I just don't know what this year is going to be like."

Melvin: "So on top of the new students, you're dealing with a new atmosphere at work." (paraphrase)

Fred: "I guess this atmosphere isn't new. But it never really affected me before. I tried to stay out of all the politics and the complaining in the teachers' lounge. This year, all the teachers do is gripe. At meetings and after school, somebody is always talking about it."

Melvin: "So for the first time, it's hard to escape the gossiping." (paraphrase)

Fred: "Yeah. And I am wondering if the gossiping is worse or if it is me. There are a lot of other things happening in my life."

Melvin: "You are wondering if the things going on in your life are coloring your whole viewpoint about work." (paraphrase)

Fred: "That's it. That's what is so confusing."

Now that you have read the dialogue between Melvin and Fred, take a look at Melvin's reflections. Do you notice how Melvin does not repeat Fred's statements exactly? Melvin rewords Fred's statements to show that he grasps the essence. This is the art of distilling or collapsing the client's words into a brief statement. It is tempting to think that paraphrasing is just mimicking the client, but as you can see in Melvin's paraphrase, "You are wondering if the things going on in your life are coloring your whole viewpoint about work," Melvin is also picking out something said very softly guiding and highlighting a key issue. Now Fred is being asked to talk about what is going on in his life outside of school that may be contributing to his feelings.

Stop and Reflect: Secrets

"You are only as sick as your darkest secret." In Alcoholics Anonymous, this aphorism is used to remind those in recovery that being truthful and open about themselves is much healthier than putting on a false front. Admitting one's actions to others is considered a necessary step in overcoming the past. By admitting these things to others, one is also admitting them to oneself. When a client comes for help to a mental health professional, how important is it that he or she be completely honest? Is it all right for a client to retain some privacy and under what circumstances? How can we invite clients to share but show respect for their refusal to examine every nook and cranny?

The notion of secrets is an important issue for helpers to grapple with. Many of the ethical guidelines of professional organizations deal with the issue of secrets because of the notion of confidentiality. Compelling or forcing people to deal with all their secrets could be considered as undue pressure and therefore unethical. It is a paradox that we are to keep our client's secrets yet we can not force them to be completely honest with us. Consider the following scenarios and think about how you might handle them. If possible, discuss them with a small group of fellow learners.

- Your client is a 43-year-old married man who has just returned from alcohol treatment. He does not want to attend Alcoholics Anonymous for aftercare but comes weekly for counseling. During his sessions, he is open about his substance abuse issues but is very quiet about his family relationships and his feelings about everyone. Apparently he has no friends and confides in no one. How would you deal with this issue? How far would you go in insisting that he learn to open up?

- You are conducting outpatient group therapy for twelve women. One of the rules of the group is that there will be no socializing outside of the group. One evening while shopping, you happen to see two of the women sitting together at a restaurant in the mall. They are deep in conversation and they do not notice you. How do you think their secret relationship might affect their interactions with each other and with the group? As the group leader, what should you do? Should group leaders have rules about keeping secrets?

- You have been seeing Isabel for 4 weeks for individual counseling. At first, she discussed her dissatisfaction with her job and concerns about her parenting of her teenage son. On the fifth week, Isabel admits she is having an affair with a coworker, unbeknown to her husband. Isabel says that her husband senses something is wrong in the relationship and wants marriage counseling. Isabel believes they could benefit by being seen as a couple and asks you to do the counseling, but not to reveal the affair. What would be the best response to Isabel? Can you agree to keep this secret? What are the consequences if the secret is uncovered?

When to Paraphrase

Paraphrases can be used early on in any helping session, as soon as the helper gets a grasp of the facts or, conversely, needs to clarify the facts. Later in the session, paraphrases go a little deeper by reflecting the client's thoughts and perceptions of the event. Paraphrasing should follow a sequence of opening and invitational skills. Figure 6.2 shows the typical sequence of a helper's using invitational skills and paraphrasing in the beginning of a session. The helper begins with door openers and minimal encouragers, perhaps going on to an open question before paraphrasing. Paraphrasing after every client statement would be excessive and might seem to make the helper's responses trivial. It is therefore better to wait until the client has gone on at some length.

A general guideline is to use a sequence of invitational and reflecting skills from encouragers to open questions to paraphrasing. This slowly allows the client to open up and discuss more difficult issues.

In this book, we use the term *topic* to refer to a specific subject that the client is discussing. In Figure 6.2, all the helper responses are on a single topic. It is quite possible to discuss more than one topic in a given session. For example, a client might, in 1 hour, discuss the topic of her relationships, the topic of her problems at work, and the topic of her family. In early assessment-oriented sessions, a large number

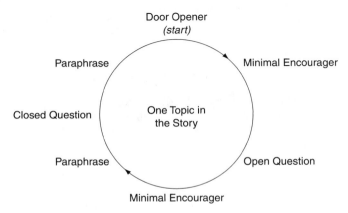

Figure 6.2
A Typical Sequence of Helper Responses in the First Few Minutes of a Session

of topics are explored because the helper is trying to get a grasp of all the different issues that a client is dealing with. However, when these assessment sessions are completed, helpers tend to focus on a particular subject until the *topic* has been fully explored. These topics are those that are associated with the client's key issues or problems.

As a beginner, you might have the tendency to rush a client through a topic without discussing all the facts, feelings, and meanings, going on to the next issue and then the next. More experienced helpers take time to ask open questions, check out key facts with closed questions, and paraphrase to make sure the story is being understood. They try to have a clear understanding of the surface issues and then use reflecting feelings to go even deeper. Beginning helpers become impatient at this point. They would like to do something to alleviate the client's discomfort and to solve the problem, and they quickly find themselves at the end of a topic. It turns out that trying to solve the client's problems prematurely is one of the quickest ways to lose a client. As you practice, see for yourself how a gradual buildup can lead to deeper sessions.

One way of understanding the process of easing into a topic is to take a look at the typical sequence of skills (see Figure 6.2). In the following conversation between a child and a school counselor, a paraphrase is shown in the normal examination of a topic. Later, you will have a chance to identify these elements and to practice paraphrasing along with all the other skills you have learned thus far.

Chris: "The teacher said I have to tell you what happened yesterday."

School counselor: "Do you want to give me an idea about what went on?" (encourager)

Chris: "Well, I was walking around the playground, not really looking at anything, you know? I was bored."

School counselor: "Yes; um-hmm." (encouragers)

Chris: "And then these three second graders came around the corner and started calling me names. I said, 'Shut up.' And later I punched William in the nose. It was bleeding, and he was crying, but I didn't care because he's mean."

School counselor: "Can you tell me more about what you mean when you said, you didn't care that William was hurt?" (open question)

Chris: "Well, I didn't mean to hurt him, but I am not saying 'Sorry' because he started it."

School counselor: "So, you got into a fight with William. He got hurt but you don't think it was your fault." (paraphrase)

Can you see how the counselor used encouragers and an open question before paraphrasing? These invitational and opening skills allowed more of the story to come out. Notice that the counselor's paraphrase is not just a restatement of what Chris said. It is a summary of the child's story, giving its essence in a nonjudgmental way. The paraphrase is brief and therefore does not interrupt the child unduly as he talks. It does not take sides by supporting one version of the story, but recognizes instead the child's perspective. It also identifies the child's thoughts, "You don't think it was your fault." Let us now look at the importance of understanding and reflecting the client's thoughts as well as what the client says happened.

The Concept of Depth

Later in the book, we will discuss the concept of "depth" in greater detail, but it is worthy of mention here because just as in the game of chess, the opening moves of the game affect its outcome. Every client story has a number of layers, and if you want to get to the center, you have to move patiently as the client allows. As a general rule, when you first meet a client, you begin with the least intrusive activities (opening and invitational skills), and then you will discuss the event and the client's thoughts about it (paraphrasing). Eventually you deal with the client's feelings (reflecting feelings) and finally with the client's most deeply held beliefs (reflecting meaning). Each of these steps represents a deeper layer, and each is more difficult for the client to reveal.

Some clients are quite open and will be able to reveal their deepest, most embarrassing experiences, thoughts, and feelings immediately. Others will require much more time before they feel ready to disclose the intimate aspects of the problem. Thus, even though paraphrasing may appear to be a relatively innocuous helping response, paraphrases can challenge a client to examine issues more deeply.

The Depth Scale

Let us utilize a scale of -1, 0, and $+1$ to indicate how much a paraphrase stimulates the client to respond more deeply. The rating -1 means that the helper's paraphrase moved the client to a more superficial level, to a discussion of less important, new topics or less relevant aspects of the problem. A rating of 0 refers to a response where the helper accurately paraphrases the client's situation and thoughts. Finally, a rating of $+1$ indicates that the helper has brought up something that the client has not really articulated but has implied. Let's take an example from a counseling situation in which the helper, Harry, and the client, Cho, are discussing Cho's recent decision to leave home and go to graduate school in another city.

Cho: "The main reason I left was that I was living at home with my parents. They wanted me to get a job near them until I knew what I wanted to do. My boyfriend wanted me to move in with him, but he really has nothing going for himself right now and we don't want to get married."

Harry (1): "In some ways your decision was based on the fact that you thought, 'I am going nowhere in my life right now'."

How would you rate this paraphrase: -1, 0, or $+1$?

Cho: "That's true. Everybody had a plan for me. But I didn't know what I wanted to do. I had to do something. So I escaped by returning to graduate school. Now I am not sure this was the best decision."

Harry (2): "So you made the decision primarily to produce some kind of movement, to get out of the doldrums. Now you're saying, 'Have I just taken the easy way out?'"

How would you rate this paraphrase: -1, 0, or $+1$?

Cho: "Yes, I am not sure if I've made the right decision. When I was younger, it seemed pretty clear—you go to school, you get good grades, and then you graduate. Now it is all up in the air."

Harry (3): "It sounds like you are at a crossroads in your life. Up to now, things have been rather prescribed. Now there are a lot of different possibilities."

How would you rate this paraphrase: −1, 0, or +1?

Cho: "I guess that is why I came to counseling. I am not sure how to handle my relationship with my boyfriend, and I am not sure about school. How do you know when you are doing the right thing?"

Do you think Cho is thinking about things a little more deeply at this point in the conversation? In what way?

Harry (4): "You have a lot going on!"

How would you rate this paraphrase: −1, 0, or +1?

This little exercise is designed to help you identify deeper paraphrases from more superficial ones. There is nothing wrong with a 0 paraphrase—one that accurately summarizes the client's thoughts and the facts in the story. But a deeper paraphrase will move the client to feel more comfortable in examining the more confusing, embarrassing, anxiety-provoking, and troubling issues. I would rate the helper (Harry's) responses above as follows: (1) +1, (2) 0, (3) 0, and (4) −1. Do you agree that the first response goes beyond what the client has said? In a sense, the helper is taking a risk or playing a hunch. Harry is suggesting something that the client has not yet quite verbalized, "I made this decision because I thought that my life was going nowhere." How did Harry know this? It is the kind of "artistic guess" that a helper learns to make by imagining what it would be like to be in that person's situation.

Common Problems in Paraphrasing

Simply Reciting the Facts

A common mistake is to simply list the major points the client has made in exactly the same way that the client said them. The best way to illustrate this mistake is to take an example from Melvin and Fred's earlier dialogue. Following the statement by Fred (the client) are two alternative paraphrases by Melvin (the helper): The first one is copied from the actual dialogue, and the second is a less effective paraphrase that merely recites the facts.

Fred: "I guess this atmosphere isn't new. But it never really affected me before. I tried to stay out of all the politics and the complaining in the teachers' lounge. This year, all the teachers do is gripe. At meetings and after school, somebody is always talking about it."

Melvin: "So for the first time, it's hard to escape the gossiping." (paraphrase)

Melvin: "So this atmosphere isn't new, but now it is affecting you. You don't like to get involved in all this backbiting, but the teachers are complaining, and it is everywhere you go, at meetings and after school. You can't escape it."

Besides the fact that this last reflection is too long and tends to parrot the client's words, the helper would be merely reflecting the content without recognizing the thoughts and perceptions of the client. Remember the deeper paraphrase that was made by Melvin, "You are wondering if the things going on in your life are coloring your whole viewpoint about work." This gets at the essence of the story.

Difficulty Hearing the Story Because of "Noise"

A second problem is caused by distractions. Of course, helpers must select quiet environments so that listening is not impaired by external noises. However, the biggest distractions come from "mental noise." You cannot grasp the client's message when you are listening to your own thoughts. Helpers sometimes experience mental noise when the client's story evokes a personal memory of a similar situation. Internal noise may interrupt because the client is expressing something you find distasteful or evokes moral outrage. When you realize that you have lost track of the client's story because of mental noise, stop and request that the client repeat the last part of the story again. Then respond with an appropriate paraphrase. Even though it is a distraction, it is better to stay on track than to miss the key elements of the story. If you find a client boring, morally repugnant, sexually attractive, or pitiful, you are probably going to have difficulty in really listening. You can start now to identify those issues that trigger mental noise and discuss or write about them in your journal.

Worrying About What to Say Next

Worrying about what to say next is perhaps the biggest source of mental noise. Rather than responding to the client's statement, the helper is sidetracked into thinking about what his or her response ought to be. This is especially true when you are being observed by others such as your instructor. One thing to remember is that almost everyone becomes less anxious as time goes on. Practicing in front of others may expose your weaknesses, but it is also the best way to get feedback and to learn. Still, there are a few things you can do to cope with this kind of worry.

The first antidote is to shift your attention to the client. Because it is difficult to do two things simultaneously, when you become focused on your own thoughts, you lose track of the client's story. This happens to everyone at some time. Your mind will go blank! The remedy is to refocus your attention keenly on the client's story. One other helpful hint is to remember that your job is to respond to *the last thing the client said*, rather than stimulate a new topic or ask a question. This will lead to greater exploration of the topic rather than shifting topics.

Being Judgmental and Taking the Client's Side

Beginners are often too quick to take the client's side and agree that the problem is caused by other people. You may think you are being supportive, but you may be accepting the client's version of the story prematurely. For example:

Rachel (client): "At work, the other women ignore me because I don't go drinking with them on Friday night, and they think I am the boss's favorite. The boss always compliments me on my work. I can't help it if they don't work as hard as I do."

Santiago (helper): "Things aren't going very well at the job because your coworkers mistreat you." (judgmental paraphrase)

With a judgmental paraphrase, the helper has essentially agreed that the co-workers are at fault. Shifting the blame to other people will not widen the client's perspective or help the client change his or her behavior. The following is a non-judgmental response to Rachel's problem:

Santiago: "So you see yourself as a hard worker, but you think your coworkers may be critical of you because of your dedication."

Here Santiago is subtly telling Rachel that his mind is open about who is causing the problem and that this may be Rachel's perception. It is possible that her coworkers have no such thoughts.

Being Judgmental of the Client

This error is made when the helper feels strongly about the client's behavior and thinks the client ought to correct it. This is an error, especially in the early sessions, because it will undermine the trust that has been building.

Rachel: "At work, the other women ignore me because I don't go drinking with them on Friday night, and they think I am the boss's favorite. The boss always compliments me on my work. I can't help it if they don't work as hard as I do."

Santiago: "You're having trouble at work because you haven't been a team player." (judgmental)

Sometimes helpers show a judgmental attitude when they try to sneak in a little free advice. In the previous example, there is a hidden message, "If you want to be liked, be more a part of the team." A nonjudgmental response would be:

Santiago: "So you're saying that your boss appreciates you, but otherwise you don't believe that others like you." (nonjudgmental)

In summary, the purpose of a paraphrase is to make sure that you understand the facts and the client's thoughts. It is not to supply a solution or place blame. Other errors include the tendency to recite only the facts and ignore the client's thoughts and to become distracted by mental noise and worrying about what to say next.

Quick Tips: Paraphrasing

- Don't paraphrase too early. Wait until you have a firm grasp of the important details and thoughts, and then compress them into a short paraphrase.
- Early on, use encouragers liberally to invite the client to supply essential information.
- Don't repeat the client's exact words. Give a distilled version in slightly different words.
- Don't add a moral tone to your paraphrase.
- When you can, paraphrase the client's thoughts and intentions as well as the basic facts.

- If you get lost, ask the client to repeat his or her last statement and try another paraphrase.
- Keep on track by responding to the last thing the client said.

Summary

Paraphrasing is the first of three reflecting skills, all of which involve feeding back to the client a distilled version of the story. The challenge is to construct the paraphrase so that it does not mimic the client's words but encapsulates the essence in a slightly different way. At the same time, the paraphrase should be nonjudgmental, not implying any advice or taking sides. Good paraphrases will let a client know that you really understand the facts and the client's thoughts.

Some paraphrases are deeper than others. Deeper paraphrases are better if they are not too intrusive, disrupting the relationship. The notion of depth implies that these are thoughts that the client has not yet expressed but are implied. Thus paraphrasing may seem like a very minor skill, but it is deceptively simple. A good paraphrase can convey understanding and even push the client to examine his or her version of the story more objectively.

Exercises

Group Exercise 1

Following are parts of three clients' stories. Try to paraphrase the facts of the stories and also unspoken thoughts. See if you can use slightly different words than the client did. In your responses, leave out the client's feelings for now. Compare your paraphrases with those of your small group and discuss any differences in your approaches.

1. "I had to tell one of my coworkers he couldn't go on the trip. He had not put in enough time with the company. I was forced to follow the rules. It wasn't really my fault, and I couldn't do anything about it. When I told him, he didn't say much. He just walked away."
2. "I met this woman. She seems too good to be true. I don't know too much about her. We only met last week. But since then, everything I find out about her makes me feel more like she is 'the one.' I believe there is only one person out there for everyone, you know. But how can you be sure?"

3. "I called my husband's hotel room Tuesday night, and when the phone was picked up, all I heard was the sound of a woman giggling. Then she hung up. I tried calling back and there was no answer. The next morning I called my husband's room again. He answered, and I told him what had happened the night before. He said I must have dialed a wrong number. I guess I believe him. But we went through something similar before when he was younger. There was more than one woman then. I won't go through that again."

After you have read and responded to these short stories, answer the following questions for yourself:

- Do any of these stories challenge your ability to be nonjudgmental?
- What feelings are aroused in you?
- Which one is the most challenging to remaining nonjudgmental? Why?
- What might you be tempted to say that would indicate that you are taking sides?

- How well were you able to distill the story, including the client's thoughts, rather than just reiterating the facts?
- Did you find it hard to leave out the feelings? Is there a time for listening to the facts of a story without reflecting the feelings?

Group Exercise 2: Practice Using Invitational Skills, Opening Skills, and Paraphrasing

In groups of three, divide into helper, client, and observer. The helper should review the "Quick Tips" section while the client takes a moment to think about a story that is often told in his or her family. Alternatively, the client can talk about career goals from childhood to the present. During the discussion, the client will describe the story and talk a little bit about the family. The helper will try to demonstrate all the opening and invitational skills first and then try to paraphrase once or twice during the practice session. The observer will use the Feedback Checklist: Paraphrasing to record the helper's responses. The observer may want to write these observations in the helper's book so that the helper can

retain a record of the practice session, or the observer may simply write the responses on lined paper. Following the session, all three participants join in categorizing the helper responses as indicated in the checklist.

Feedback Checklist: Paraphrasing

Observer Name:_____   Helper Name:_____

During the session, the observer records the helper's responses verbatim. After the session, the group categorizes the responses with the following symbols: E for an encourager (either door opener or minimal encourager), CQ for closed question, OQ for open question, or P for paraphrase.

Category*	Helper Response	Client Feedback
____ 1.	_____	_____
____ 2.	_____	_____
____ 3.	_____	_____
____ 4.	_____	_____
____ 5.	_____	_____
____ 6.	_____	_____
____ 7.	_____	_____
____ 8.	_____	_____
____ 9.	_____	_____
____10.	_____	_____

Homework

In the last chapter, it was suggested that you watch a television program with the sound off to see if you could guess the emotional content based on body language alone. For this assignment, watch a television program where one individual is speaking. An interview on a news program works well for this activity. Using a

remote control, listen to a couple of minutes of the dialogue, and then press the mute button. See if you can paraphrase the content of the last two or three minutes in a couple of brief sentences. This activity can provide anxiety-free practice because you can turn the "client" off while you are paraphrasing.

Journal Starters

1. Reread the "Stop and Reflect" section in this chapter about secrets. Dostoyevsky says in *Notes from the Underground* that there are things that we are afraid to tell even to ourselves and that every

decent person has several of these things stored away. Can you mentally identify one of these issues for yourself? Instead of describing the secret in writing, imagine telling your secret to a nonjudgmental listener. What reaction do you imagine? Do you think such confessions are helpful?

2. Think for a moment about a time when you disclosed too much to another person. Or perhaps you found yourself a recipient of someone else's disclosure that was far beyond what you expected or wanted. Perhaps the disclosure was poorly timed—too much, too early. Based on this experience or on other more positive experiences, what guidelines or private rules have you developed about disclosing to others?

For more journal ideas, as well as more practice with reflecting skills, refer to Chapter 6 in *Exercises in the Art of Helping*.

Reflecting Skills: Reflecting Feelings

7

The Importance of Understanding Emotions

Daniel Goleman, the author of *Emotional Intelligence* (1995), describes an incident on a flight that underlines how crucial it is that we understand how to deal with the emotions of others and in ourselves. One Super Bowl Sunday, the flight was crowded, and most of the businesspeople were obviously anxious to get off the plane to get home in time for the big game. In fact, they began collecting their luggage and moving around before the arrival at the gate. The flight attendant, instead of repeating the federal regulations, used the kind of voice used to chide a naughty child and said, "You're staaanding!" The reaction of the passengers was to laugh, and they exited the plane in a better mood. Goleman's story is in support of his thesis that there is a kind of intelligence that is quite different from what IQ tests capture (Goleman, 2003). Simply reminding the passengers of FAA regulations would be logical, but not emotionally smart! Emotional intelligence has been described as the "ability to monitor one's own and other's feelings and emotions, to discriminate among them, and to use this information to guide one's thinking and action" (Salovey & Mayer, 1990, p. 189).

There is little doubt that helpers must possess this emotional intelligence in the same way that an engineer must have the intellectual ability to understand higher mathematics. The point is that many helpers go into the profession because they have this basic emotional intelligence about people and want to use it, but they may not realize that they possess it. We undervalue this ability probably because it is not widely acclaimed, because it does not show up on the Graduate Record Examination, and because we think everyone has it. This is not to say that possessing emotional intelligence or mathematical intelligence means that one does not have more to learn, but it does imply that understanding and being able to respond to emotions is a critical skill in all sorts of situations, especially a helping relationship where strong emotions may be the very reason for the encounter.

The Skill of Reflecting Feelings

The building block of reflecting feelings involves essentially the same technique as paraphrasing. This time, however, the focus is on feelings rather than on content and thoughts. Reflecting feelings involves expressing in one's own words the emotions stated or implied by the client. Feelings can be reflected from both verbal and nonverbal responses of the client.

A number of therapeutic events occur when feelings are reflected. For one thing, the client becomes more keenly aware of the emotions surrounding a topic. Let us suppose that the helper makes a reflection such as, "I can tell that you are terribly angry about that." The client's response may be one of surprise, "Yes, I guess I am." Because a reflection is done in a nonevaluative manner, it communicates understanding of feelings—anger, guilt, and sadness—that the client may not be conscious of and that the client may feel he or she has no right to feel.

More importantly, reflecting feelings brings the client to deeper and deeper levels of self-disclosure. An accurate reflection focuses the client on emotions and teaches the client to become aware of and to report feelings. Even if the reflection is not quite accurate, the client will provide a correction that is more on target. Many clients underdisclose, and any method or technique that allows them to more fully experience and express their feelings is thought to be therapeutic.

★ In addition, an accurate reflection of feelings has the almost magical power to deepen the relationship between client and counselor. Nothing transmits nonjudgmental understanding more completely. This is why this technique, which originated in the client-centered tradition of Carl Rogers (1961), has gained such wide usage.

It taps the enormous healing properties of the therapeutic factor of enhancing the relationship. A beginning helper who can accurately reflect feelings can provide supportive counseling and understanding without any other tools.

Finally, reflecting feelings brings on feelings of genuine relief. Take, for example, the client who found his wife in bed with another man. He came to counseling crying about his loss of the relationship. He ran the gamut, on an emotional roller coaster, from shock to disgust to affection to rage. Experiencing all these conflicting emotions in one session can make anyone feel "crazy." Even though there were still conflicting feelings, by the end, the client felt more in control simply because he had sorted out his feelings and labeled them. Untangling the emotional knots seems to be healing even if no real action is taken. Somehow we can accept our feelings as normal reactions when we bring them to the surface and sort them out. Reflecting feelings by saying, for example, "You feel so betrayed, and yet you still feel a bond of affection," can help to normalize what the client perceives as a deeply conflicting emotional experience.

Why It Is Difficult to Reflect Feelings

Reflecting feelings is one of the most valuable tools of the helper, but it is not an easy one to learn. Theodore Reik, the famous analyst, claimed that in order to hear these feelings, one must learn to become sensitive to the unexpressed and listen with the "third ear." Referring to the fact that the client may not even be aware of these feelings, Reik said, "The voice that speaks in him speaks low but he who listens with a third ear, hears also what is expressed almost noiselessly, what is said *pianissimo*" (Reik, 1968, p. 165).

Feelings are often implicit in a client's statements and require hunches and guesses on the part of the helper to identify them. The reason is that our upbringing, family background, and culture affect the way we express emotions (Tsai & Levenson, 1997). For example, many individuals with Appalachian and English roots may tend to express emotions in very subtle ways. Some Native Americans, East Indians, and Europeans may come from cultures where open expression of feelings is rude or is a sign of weakness. For instance, a recent conference was held in Amsterdam on the "underexpression" of emotions as a mental health issue in Europe.

When a client's family background or culture is constantly sending the message "Don't let anyone see your feelings," the job of helping is more difficult because the helper can only guess what the client is experiencing. Getting to feelings may require more time and effort, and even then expression may seem faint by comparison. This can be frustrating when the client does not seem to respond to your reflections. For some clients, even a small crack in the voice may be quite an unusual manifestation and should be valued as a rather deep disclosure.

Gender also has a bearing on emotional expression. Men, more than women, have been trained to "never let them see you sweat" and to believe that "big boys don't cry" (see Kottler, 1997). Consequently, it may be difficult for some men to openly display strong feelings in the helping relationship. When they do occur, a man may feel weak or out of control. Feminine socialization, on the other hand, is more relationship-oriented and is more likely to encourage telling another person how you feel (Workman, 1993). However, women, too, are asked to repress certain emotions, such as anger or even confidence, that are not considered "ladylike."

How to Reflect Feelings

Like paraphrasing, reflecting feelings involves two steps. The first step is identifying the client's feelings; the second step is articulating the underlying emotions that you detect in his or her statements. You can learn the first step in your practice sessions as you listen intently to a client's statements. Imagine how he or she feels in this situation, and then try to label the feeling. The best way to do this is to think of yourself as the client, taking into account all the facts and also thinking about what you know about the client's personality and history. In other words, do not try to think about how *you* would feel in this situation; instead, become the client and think about how he or she might feel. For example, read the three client stories in the "Stop and Reflect" section in Chapter 6. See if you can identify the main feelings. Take a look at the feeling words in Table 7.1 to see if another word is closer to what the client

Table 7.1
Feeling Words

Feeling	Mild	Moderate	Strong
Joy	at ease	glad	overjoyed
	pleased	happy	jubilant
	satisfied		elated
	content		
Sadness	down	glum	depressed
	sad	downhearted	dejected
	low	melancholy	despondent
	blue		
Anger	annoyed	angry	furious
	irritated	mad	outraged
	miffed		enraged
	ticked		
Guilt/shame	responsible	guilty	ashamed
	at fault	embarrassed	humiliated
	chagrined		mortified
Fear	apprehensive	anxious	frightened
	restless	scared	terrified
	uneasy	worried	panicked
	wary	afraid	
	insecure	nervous	
	on edge		
Disgust	offended	turned off	repulsed
	put off	disgusted	sickened
			revolted
			nauseated

Table 7.1
Feeling Words *(Continued)*

Feeling	Mild	Moderate	Strong
Surprise	perplexed puzzled stumped	amazed bewildered baffled surprised	awed stunned astonished shocked
Interest/excitement	bored interested	amused curious inspired engaged	excited stimulated thrilled
Feelings Associated with Power and Confidence			
Weakness	unimportant awkward unsure	inadequate incompetent inept powerless weak	worthless helpless dependent impotent
Strength	able capable	confident strong authoritative secure competent	self-assured potent powerful
Feelings of General Distress			
	upset concerned troubled bothered	frustrated disturbed perturbed	distressed pained miserable anguished agitated overwhelmed

seems to be expressing. Don't forget that nonverbals are major clues to the client's feeling state. While reading and responding to vignettes in this book will be helpful, practicing with classmates will mean that you must pay close attention to the expressions as well as the words.

The second step in reflecting feelings is making a *statement* (not asking a question) that accurately mirrors the client's emotions. The client may not have actually shared the emotions; they may be hiding in the client's story. Although this sounds easier than the first step, it is actually more difficult because you must *accurately* express emotions in words.

In my experience, these two steps to reflecting feelings are often learned independently. Learning to identify feelings seems to be a precursor to actually reflecting them. Take some time to practice identifying feelings, and then it will be easier to put them into words. Later in this chapter and in the accompanying *Exercises in Learning the Art of Helping*, you will find additional practice opportunities.

An Algorithm for Reflecting Feelings

Statements that reflect feelings take two forms. The simple version of reflecting feelings is a helper statement with the structure "You feel ____." As you look at the following interactions between helper and client, think about what the reflection of feelings brings to the client's story and to the relationship.

Latrice (client): "You can imagine how everyone in the family reacted when grandpa got married 6 months after grandma's death."

Kendra (helper): "It must have been quite a shock." (simple reflection of feelings)

After one or two reflections of feeling, a helper may then use a reflection of feelings that connects emotions and content. The format of this combination response is "You feel ____ because ____." The first blank is a reflection of the client's feeling. The second blank explains the feeling by paraphrasing the content while, at the same time, showing the connection between the feeling and the content (Carkhuff, 1987). As the conversation between Latrice and Kendra continues, Kendra begins to understand and articulate the reason for Latrice's resentment and anger:

Latrice: "I was floored. I always thought that they had the perfect marriage."

Kendra: "You feel let down now that you have discovered that things were not as they seemed."

The reflection of feeling "You feel let down" is connected to the paraphrase "now that you have discovered that things were not as they seemed." This last phrase is content. The connection is the word *because,* which demonstrates to Latrice that Kendra understands what has happened. Can you see that Kendra's statement is essentially a mirror image of Latrice's, containing both a paraphrase and a feeling?

Every reflection of feeling does not have to contain a paraphrase. Sometimes it is sufficient to reflect the feeling using the simple "You feel ____." When you understand the connection between feeling and content, you can then utilize the combined form to convey deeper understanding of the *reasons* for the client's feelings.

Students report that they often feel phony when they use a response such as "You feel ____ because ____." The formula, or algorithm, is merely a training tool that you can modify later when reflecting feelings has become second nature. Then you will want to vary the way you reflect so that it feels natural to you and sounds natural to the client.

Improving Your Feeling Vocabulary

To learn the first step in reflecting feelings—identifying feelings—it is important to recognize that emotions have many shades and variations. They also vary in strength. Thus, it is difficult to classify them in a manner that fully captures their scope. Table 7.1 is an attempt to categorize feelings in a way that will help you recognize the basic emotions. They are like the primary colors in the light spectrum. The color analogy is used here because the emotions of clients are often mixed together, producing a completely unique hue. The primary emotions are listed top to bottom on the left-hand side of Table 7.1.

The emotions that have been identified as primary, or basic, are *joy, sadness, anger, guilt/shame, fear, disgust, surprise,* and *interest/excitement.* People around the world can recognize facial expressions of these emotional states whether the people are from remote parts of New Guinea or New York City (Izard, 1977). These facial expressions appear to have deep biological roots. In addition to the primary emotions, three other categories of emotions are indicated in the table: *feelings of weakness, feelings of strength*, and *feelings of general distress*.

Normally, the helper should be trying to identify the specific feeling that a client is experiencing. Sometimes though, especially in the beginning of a client's story, it is necessary to reflect a sense of general distress before homing in on the target feelings.

Across the top of Table 7.1, the emotions are categorized by intensity, much as colors can be described in terms of brightness. Besides finding precise words that suggest different intensities, you can qualify your reflections by using terms like *a little, somewhat*, and *very* to zero in on the client's exact feeling. In fact, some clients do not have large feeling vocabularies, and it is better to say, "You were very angry," rather than, "You were filled with consternation." Use Table 7.1 to familiarize yourself with a wider variety of words. The more closely you express the exact shade of feeling, the more the client will sense that you understand his or her frame of mind.

Stop and Reflect

To consider further the distinction between content and feelings, take a look at a portion of a client's story and see if you can respond as a professional helper would, answering the related questions and comparing your responses with those of your classmates.

Teresa: "First, we went to the drugstore; then we went to the grocery. We went to two or three other places and ended up in a bad part of town. All because he wanted this particular kind of candy. I had a lot to do that day. And this wasn't the first time this kind of thing had happened. He's a lot of fun most of the time; other times, he is a pain! What can you do?"

- What might Teresa be feeling? Identify as many emotions as you can. Try and pinpoint her feelings using Table 7.1. Use qualifiers like "a little" or "very" as needed to try and get the right shade of emotion. Your answers and those of your classmates may vary because in a written example we cannot hear the client's voice tone to cue us in on how strong her emotions are.
- What nonverbals might give away her exact feelings?
- Why do you think Teresa does not express her feelings about the situation in this part of her story?
- Try to summarize the content of Teresa's message (not the feelings) in a single sentence. Remember that the content includes thoughts, intentions, and facts that she relates.
- Try to make a connection between what Teresa is feeling and the content of her story: Teresa feels _____ (emotion) because _____ (reason you identify from content).
- What facts about Teresa's cultural or family upbringing might affect her willingness to express her feelings about her friend?
- Now think for a moment about your own upbringing, family background, and culture. What rules does your own family have about expressing emotions such as anger or sadness? How do you express affection? What would be the most difficult feelings for you to admit to a helper if you were a client?

Common Problems in Reflecting Feelings

Learning to reflect feelings is one of the most challenging skills you will develop in this course. For this reason, you will want to practice as much as possible. In your practice sessions you may find it easy to use opening and invitational skills and even paraphrase, but the practice session seems to have gone by without a single reflection of feeling. At these times you may wish to review the following list of common problems. Under each problem are some suggested activities for dealing with that issue. If you find that you are having difficulty with one of these typical hurdles, let your instructor and fellow students know so that you can receive specific feedback during practice sessions.

Asking the Client, "How Did You Feel?"

Rather than using a reflecting statement, it is tempting to simply ask the client what he or she is feeling. One of the main benefits of a reflection is that it conveys empathy. When you ask a *closed question*, the client does not feel that you understand. He or she may feel misunderstood and may feel the need to clarify. Often, the client can't pinpoint the feeling when asked, and the conversation stalls.

Waiting Too Long to Reflect

In the opening minutes of the helping session, utilize invitational skills to help elicit the client's story, but don't wait too long. A common mistake is to wait 10 or 15 minutes before going on to reflect the client's feelings. It is better to reflect inaccurately than never to reflect at all. To avoid the mistake of waiting too long, work first on becoming proficient at identifying feelings. Make full use of the written exercises in this chapter. Look at exercises in previous chapters, read the client statements, and see if you can pick out the feelings. Also, watch television shows, particularly daytime dramas, to see if you can listen to people's statements and then reflect their feelings immediately after they speak, picking up on nonverbal as well as spoken cues.

Turning the Reflection into a Question

In the common error called "Asking the client, 'How do you feel?'" I suggested that questions do not enhance an empathic relationship. Often, you know what the client is saying, but you state it as a question. For example:

Xiomara (client): "I've had a very difficult time. My mother died about 1 month ago, and now my dad is in the hospital with pneumonia. I'm here 2,000 miles away, and I can't get any time away from work."

Tori (helper): "Are you feeling sad over the death of your mom and a sense of helplessness as you worry about your dad?"

Can you see how a client might respond with a simple yes or no? The question suggests that the helper is confused, and it does not provide as many options to explore. Had the helper reflected the client's feelings with a statement, he or she could have said, "It must be a very helpless feeling for you to be so far away when you are worried about your dad and still trying to deal with the sadness of your mom's death." Such a statement more effectively communicates understanding of the client's situation and is more compassionate. Rather than responding to a question, the client can go on to explore whatever issues seem important to him or her. If you have the tendency to turn statements into questions by raising your voice at the end of a sentence, let your fellow students know and see if they can alert you to this habit.

Combining a Reflection and an Open Question

In the early stages, it is tempting to add an open question after the reflecting statement. This confuses the client because he or she has been asked to do two things: respond to the reflection of feeling and answer the open question. For example, a helper might say, "You feel really alone since your best friend moved away. Do you have any other close friends?" Clients often respond by only replying to the open question rather than to the reflection of feeling. In this example, the client may go on to tell you about his close friends but fail to discuss his loneliness. If you have this tendency, try eliminating open questions altogether for a while in your practice sessions.

Focusing on the Wrong Person

A major aim of reflecting feelings is to make the client aware of his or her underlying emotions. Clients may lead us away from these emotions by focusing on other people and launching into long stories about them. Let us take a look at a couple of different ways the helper can respond to a client statement such as: "My best friend, Judi, and I are not as close as we used to be. Sometimes I think she just wants to neutralize our relationship. It seems like she has no time for me, like she doesn't care." On the one hand, the helper can paraphrase in a judgmental way, focusing on the client's friend: "She neglects you." Or the helper can keep attention centered on the client: "You miss the relationship you used to enjoy so much." Can you see how focusing on the other person can send a judgmental message about the friend? Because you do not know anything directly about the other person, such a statement is unfair and perhaps inaccurate.

Letting the Client Ramble

Many helpers tend to let their clients talk too long without responding. After all, it is not normally polite to interrupt. However, clients need paraphrases and reflections in order to know that their story is making sense to the helper. Because they are talkative or anxious, some clients leave little room for the helper to slow the pace and focus on a particularly important message. Beginning helpers need to give themselves permission to stop rambling clients and make reflections. Surprisingly, this often serves to reassure clients that each aspect of their story is being heard in a systematic way. Here is one example of a way that a helper politely requests a pause to verify that the right message is being received:

 Helper: "Let me stop you here for a second and see if I understand correctly. You feel both angry and hurt that your friend is not spending time with you, but you are afraid to mention it because she may simply terminate the friendship."

or

Helper: "I'm sorry to interrupt, but let me tell you what I know so far. You resent the fact that you and your friend don't get together much anymore, but it is too scary to think about bringing it up."

 A footnote to this discussion is that a helping relationship needs to have both people actively participating. By stopping the flow of the client's story to catch up, the helper is becoming involved with the client, creating a connection and *actively* listening, rather than becoming a "listening post."

Using the Word *Feel* Instead of *Think*

In the beginning, you may hear yourself or your classmates make a reflection along these lines: "You feel that your husband should have been more respectful of your need for privacy." This is not a reflection of feeling because the client's underlying emotions are not being identified. In this helper's statement, the word *think* may be substituted for *feel*: "You *think* that your husband should have been more respectful of your need for privacy." If you can substitute the word *think* without changing the meaning, you have not reflected a feeling; rather, you have paraphrased the client's thoughts, which are part of the content. In the preceding example, a true reflection of feeling would be "You feel angry (or hurt) because you think that your husband should have been more respectful of your need for privacy."

Some people use *feel* instead of *think* a great deal in their daily conversations. If you have this tendency, try to become aware of it and change your "feel" to "think" whenever you become aware of it. By being accurate in your word choice with clients, you are subtly teaching them to become aware of the differences between thoughts and feelings.

Undershooting and Overshooting

Undershooting and overshooting are two common mistakes in reflecting feelings (Gordon, 1975). *Overshooting* means that the helper has reflected a feeling that is more intense than the one expressed by the client. *Undershooting* is reflecting a feeling that is too weak to adequately mirror the client's emotion. Consider this client statement and three possible responses:

Client: "Becky told Mrs. Gordon that I was not a good typist, so she started giving the most interesting work to Rolando instead of me."

Helper: "You must have been mad enough to kill!" (overshooting)

Helper: "You were a little annoyed." (undershooting)

Helper: "You were angry." (accurate intensity)

Overshooting and undershooting are beginners' mistakes; this tendency normally corrects itself as you gain a larger feeling vocabulary. Like playing darts, you learn to hit the bull's-eye as you recognize your mistakes. In your practice sessions, note the difference between a polite "Yes, that's right" and "Yes!" when you hit the mark. If you undershoot, you can raise the intensity a notch, and you can lower it when you overshoot. If your feeling vocabulary seems limited at present, study lists of feeling words like those in Table 7.1. You may also try using qualifiers such as a *little angry, somewhat angry,* or *very angry* to convey various shades of emotional intensity.

Parroting

Parroting is another common mistake caused by an inadequate feeling vocabulary. *Parroting* means repeating back to the client the very same feeling words he or she has just used. For example, a client might say, "The whole party I planned was rather frustrating because no one came for the first hour and then people stayed past the time limit we had indicated in the invitation." The helper then responds (parroting): "You were frustrated that they disregarded your instructions." The paraphrase in this case is pretty good since it distills the facts. However, the feeling is an exact reproduction. The tendency to parrot arises when the client seems to have beaten you to the punch and to have already expressed a feeling in his or her story. What do you do? The answer is to discern what other feelings the client might have experienced at the same time or to identify a feeling more accurate than the one the client has expressed. Forget about the feeling of frustration that the client has expressed and imagine what else you might have felt in that situation. Here are two possibilities:

Helper: "I'd guess you were also a little angry that they didn't seem to get the message after all the planning you put into it."

Helper: "If I had been in your shoes, I guess I might have felt a little hurt that very few of the people seemed to have honored my wishes."

Letting Your Reflecting Statements Go On and On

Sometimes helpers tend to continue to reflect and paraphrase, not in sentences, but in chapters. This is a kind of shotgun approach that we use to make sure we reflect everything. In reality, the important aspects of your response are lost in the verbiage. The student thinks, "If I reflect several different things, one of them is bound to be right." Instead, try thinking of reflecting as a form of gambling, like playing poker. You must wait until you think you understand and then you place your bet on a single brief reflection, paraphrase, or combination. If you are wrong, the client will correct you and proceed to describe the accurate feeling, helping you to find the bull's-eye.

Summary

The reflecting skills are a quantum leap from the invitational skills because they do much more than encourage clients to tell their stories. The reflecting skills move clients to greater self-awareness and encourage the client to address deeper issues beneath the surface. They forge a bond between client and helper because the client senses that someone has taken the time to really understand.

Reflecting feelings involves identifying and labeling the client's feeling, whether or not such feelings have been openly expressed. The feeling component of the message is often hidden because disclosure of feelings is bound by cultural and family rules.

The emotions that helpers identify when reflecting feelings have many nuances and variations. There are, however, some basic or primary feelings that helpers can consider when trying to accurately sense and communicate the client's unique emotional experience. Helpers need to improve their feeling vocabularies in order to convey understanding of the client's message. Labeling and reflecting feelings can be one of the most difficult processes to learn. There is a great variability in how quickly students learn to reflect feelings. Some come to it very naturally and quickly. Others take longer but can learn the skill eventually through persistence and practice.

Exercises

Exercise 1. Practice in Identifying Feelings and Reflecting Feelings in Writing

Listed below are eight client statements. First go through and identify the major feeling or feelings in each client statement. Then go back and write out a full reflection of feeling. If more than one feeling exists, reflect all of them.

a. "There I was, standing in front of the entire assembly, and I froze. Everyone was staring at me. My heart was pounding and I started to shake. I thought I was going to die right there on the spot. I can never show my face again after that."

b. "And for the third time in a row, he failed to show. What a jerk! My daughter looks forward to these outings with her father, and I hate to see him treat her this way. Don't you think he is a jerk?"

c. "I can't wait to go to Europe with the French club. It's the opportunity of a lifetime! Yet it is going to be expensive. In addition to the obvious things, I'm going to need spending money, too. I would have to bring my boyfriend something. I don't know how I am going to come up with all the money I need.

d. "The more I do, the more the boss seems to expect. He's never satisfied and is always finding fault. I think I should start looking for another job because I can't take it any more."

e. "I can't believe I trusted my sister-in-law. She is such a back-stabbing witch. I hate her. She'd start bad-mouthing my mother-in-law and get me going. Then after she got me saying negative things, I found out she was going back and repeating everything I said to her! Now my mother-in-law hates me."

f. "We just moved here, and I'm working two jobs. But somehow I've got to find time to take my kids to their schoolmates' houses so they can get to know people and have some friends. I just don't seem to have time."

g. "My son keeps staying out late at night with his friends. He won't tell me where he goes. I'm afraid he'll get hurt. He's probably able to take care of himself. I don't know what to do."

h. "My boss just stays in her office doing her personal paperwork. She won't come out to help us, and sometimes we get so busy. We get tired and then we get behind."

Group Exercises

Group Exercise 1: The Alter-Ego Technique for Identifying Feelings

Identifying feelings precedes reflecting them. One of the best action methods for learning to identify feelings is the *alter-ego technique*, which comes to us from psychodrama (Moreno, 1958). The alter-ego technique asks the student to pretend that he or she is the client in order to imagine the client's feelings. This group exercise requires four members: the client, the helper, the alter ego, and the observer. It is in the role of alter ego that the student learns most about how to identify feelings.

The Client

The client discusses an experience with either positive or negative ramifications, such as a good or bad vacation, a relationship that ended abruptly, a missed opportunity, or another minor problem.

The Helper or Listener

The trainee who plays the part of the helper has little to do in this exercise. The job of the helper is to listen with appropriate body position, using only open questions and minimal encouragers, providing a focus for the client but rarely intervening.

The Alter Ego

The third student, the alter ego, stands behind the client and speaks for the client, identifying anything the client might be feeling but has left out. The alter ego speaks using the word *I* as if he or she were speaking for the client; "I am angry," "I am embarrassed," and so on.

The Observer

The fourth member of the group is an observer who records the alter ego's remarks on a blank sheet of paper. In the discussion phase, the client gives the alter ego feedback on the most accurate and the least accurate reflections and paraphrases. The observer should gently correct the alter ego if he or she forgets to speak as the client and lapses into "you feel" rather than "I feel."

Action Phase

Once roles have been assigned, the client tells his or her story to the helper/listener. The alter ego, standing behind the client, expresses underlying feelings in the client's story. The client should be directed to ignore the alter ego, except when the alter ego really hits the mark. At that point, the client should incorporate the alter ego's comment into his or her statements. For example, if the alter ego says, "I am angry and embarrassed," the client may then respond, saying, "I *am* embarrassed." The client always directs his or her response to the helper/listener, even when reacting to the alter ego. Although client and helper/listener may find this exercise frustrating, the alter ego learns to hear feelings, imagining himself or herself as another person.

Discussion Phase

After 5 to 8 minutes, the group members discuss their experiences, and the observer gives the alter ego feedback. Members then exchange positions until everyone has had a chance to experience the role of alter ego.

Quick Tips: Reflecting Feelings

- You will probably need to use invitational skills and paraphrasing before you have enough information to reflect feelings. When you have heard enough of the client's story to grasp the emotional content, stop the client to make a reflection.
- If you don't know how the client is feeling, imagine yourself in the client's shoes. What would you be feeling if you were the client?
- Use different feeling words than those used by the client to avoid parroting.
- Don't agree with the client when he or she is placing blame on someone else.

Convey that you understand the client's viewpoint without taking sides.

Group Exercise 2

The alter-ego technique is a good way to develop the initial skill of imagining oneself as the client and identifying thoughts and feelings. The next step is to incorporate the skill within the helping interview. Break into groups of three with a helper, client, and observer. During a 5–8-minute session, the client describes a small problem he or she has been having with a friend, a family member, or someone at work. The helper uses invitational skills, paraphrases and, whenever possible, reflects feelings. The helper's goal is to reflect *at least three feelings* during the practice session.

The observer makes certain that the time limits are observed and, during the period, records every helper statement on the Feedback Checklist. At the end of the time, he or she shares feedback with the helper. The client gives the helper feedback on which responses on the checklist were most accurate and which were least accurate. The client makes a check

next to those that seem to hit the mark. The group exchanges roles until everyone has had a chance to practice the role of helper and receive feedback.

Feedback Checklist: Reflecting Feelings

Observer Name: _____ Helper Name: _____

During the session, the observer records the helper's responses verbatim. After the session, the group categorizes the responses with the following symbols: E for an encourager (either door opener or minimal encourager), CQ for closed question, OQ for open question, P for paraphrase, RF for reflecting feelings, and P/R for a response that paraphrases and hits the feeling.

Category*	Helper Response	Client Feedback
_____ 1.	_____	_____
_____ 2.	_____	_____
_____ 3.	_____	_____
_____ 4.	_____	_____
_____ 5.	_____	_____
_____ 6.	_____	_____
_____ 7.	_____	_____
_____ 8.	_____	_____
_____ 9.	_____	_____
_____10.	_____	_____

Homework

Keeping an Emotions Diary

Make a copy of Table 7.1 and keep it with some blank paper on a clipboard near your bed. Think about an emotion you experienced today. For example, if you felt angry at work, at school, or with family, record that feeling as the answer to the first question below. Fill out this diary for two successive days and then write a one-paragraph reaction recording your discoveries.

- What was the emotion?
- Think of a synonym for the emotion as you experienced it today.
- Describe the situation in which you experienced the emotion.
- Who was present when you experienced the emotion?
- What do you think caused your emotion? Do you blame other people for your emotion? Which of your personal values and beliefs might have given rise to this emotion? In other words, what did you say to yourself that seemed to spark this emotional response?
- How did you express the emotion?
- What societal rules come to mind when you think about expressing this emotion?
- Record any other thoughts you have about your experience today.

Journal Starters

1. Think about the expression of emotion in your own family. Do you think that some emotions are more allowable than others? How do you think your own family or ethnic background might affect your willingness to listen to a client's feelings?

2. Think about the following negative emotions: sadness/depression, anger, and fear. If a client expressed one of these feelings frequently and with great intensity, which ones would be the hardest for you to deal with?

3. Now that you have begun to practice some of the skills, how has this learning affected your feelings of confidence? Are you experiencing any of the anxiety or awkwardness that was predicted? If so, how are you coping with it? Do you have times when you feel comfortable with your work and other times when you lack confidence? What is different about these two times?

For more journal ideas, as well as more practice with reflecting skills, refer to Chapter 5 in *Exercises in the Art of Helping*.

References

Carkhuff, R. (1987). *The art of helping* (6th ed.). Amherst, MA: Human Resource Development Press.

Goleman, D. (2003). Emotional intelligence: Issues in paradigm building. [Electronic version]. Retrieved August 30, 2003, from http://www.eiconsortium.org/research/ei_issues_in_paradigm_building.htm.

Goleman, D. (1995). *Emotional Intelligence*. New York: Bantam.

Gordon, T. (1975). *PET: Parent effectiveness training*. New York: Wyden.

Izard, C. E. (1977). *Human emotions*. New York: Plenum.

Kottler, J. (1997). *The language of tears*. San Francisco: Jossey-Bass.

Moreno, J. L. (1958). *Psychodrama* (Vol. 2). New York: Beacon House.

Reik, T. (1968). *Listening with the third ear*. New York: Pyramid Books.

Rogers, C. R. (1961). *On becoming a person*. Boston: Houghton Mifflin.

Salovey, P., & Mayer, J. D. (1990). Emotional intelligence. *Imagination, Cognition, and Personality, 9*, 185–211.

Tsai, J. L., & Levenson, R.W. (1997). Cultural influences on emotional responding: Chinese American and European American dating couples during interpersonal conflict. *Journal of Cross-Cultural Psychology, 28*, 600–625.

Workman, W. J. (1993). Relationship of counselor variables to preference for type of response in counseling. *Counselor Education and Supervision, 32*, 178–188.

Reflecting Skills: Reflecting Meaning and Summarizing

8

It is not just what we inherit from our mothers and fathers that haunts us. It's all kinds of old defunct theories, all sorts of old defunct beliefs, and things like that. It's not that they actually live on in us; they are simply lodged there and we cannot get rid of them. I've only to pick up a newspaper and I see ghosts gliding between the lines.

Henrik Ibsen, *Ghosts*, Act 2

In the remake of the movie *Father of the Bride*, the bride-to-be calls off the wedding when her fiancé buys her a blender for the 6-month anniversary of their meeting. She is tearful and angry because, for her, the blender is a sexist symbol. She interprets the present as an expression of his wish for her to take on a traditional female role—in the kitchen. Her husband-to-be responds with bewilderment because that is not what he intended.

This example illustrates two points about the perceived meaning of an event. First, each person's interpretations, values, and perceptions are unique. They are formed by the person's history, current needs, values, and beliefs. Two people experiencing the same event will have different takes on its significance. As many cognitive therapists like to quote, "It is not what happens to us, but what we make of it." Second, the meaning of an event for an individual can be uncovered only with some deeper knowledge of that person. Had the fiancé understood that being independent and being recognized as more than wife and mother were very important to his fiancée, he would have been able to anticipate her reaction to the gift of a blender!

If a helper wants to really understand a client, he or she must be willing to go beyond content and feeling and uncover the deeper meaning that the client assigns to life events. In this chapter, we will look at how a helper can identify and respond to the meanings behind a client's story by using advanced reflecting skills. We will also look at summarizing, a method of binding together the parts of the story into a capsule account. Summaries are ways of pulling together the loose ends of a client's story and communicating that the helper has grasped content, feelings, and meanings.

Meaning, Uncovering the Next Layer

Understanding the content of the story gives us an outline or picture in our minds about what has happened. The emotions add color to the story and help us imagine the sometimes overwhelming feelings that the client is experiencing. Reflection of meaning is a significant step beyond content and emotion because it taps the unique worldview of the client. If we know the meaning of the story, we will have learned why the client is troubled by it. It answers the question, "Why are we talking about this topic?"

Consider the case of Joan, who had been having problems at work for 2 years. Her coworkers had split into two factions that everyone on the job called "the redbirds" and "the bluebirds." There was considerable animosity because of a power struggle between the leaders of the two groups. Joan found herself allied with the bluebirds. During one of their after-work gripe sessions, she revealed that she knew one of the redbirds, Bob, had sought treatment for alcoholism. Bob had told her this several years ago when they were on good terms. Once this information leaked, Bob's boss called him "on the carpet" because the company was working on several government contracts, and Bob was investigated as a security risk. A couple of weeks later, Joan went to the company's employee assistance program and asked for counseling. During the interview, she and the counselor (Lynn) had the following exchange.

Joan: "There is just so much turmoil. It used to be a good place to work. Now it's dog eat dog."

Lynn: "You are sad because things have changed and now there is so much competition." (reflection of feeling and paraphrase)

Joan: "Yes, that among other things."

Lynn: "Go on." (door opener)

Joan: "Well, Bob told me about his treatment for alcoholism one night when we were working late, sort of offhand. I even thought of him as a friend."

Lynn: "You're afraid of his reaction when he finds out that you leaked the information." (reflection of feeling and paraphrase)

Joan: "Not really. It just seems a nasty thing to do to someone who was trying to be friendly."

Lynn: "In other words, you are disappointed in yourself for having betrayed a confidence." (reflection of feeling and meaning)

Joan: "Yeah, that's the thing. I think I did it just to be part of the club. I don't like that about myself. I wish I were secure enough to have my own opinions about people."

Lynn: "It sounds like it has always been very important for you to be approved of, and sometimes, to be part of the group, you find yourself doing something you don't agree with." (reflection of meaning)

If Lynn had merely paraphrased the story of Joan's problems at work, her thoughts, and her underlying feelings, they would have had a productive session. However, Lynn chose to dig more deeply, not only paraphrasing Joan's feelings about recent events but also looking at the underlying meaning—the perceptions and values her client attributed to the self, the office situation, and the other workers involved. Notice how Lynn understands Joan's disappointment in herself and this leads to a deeper response by Joan. Previous paraphrases and reflections of feeling were not nearly as effective as when the helper keyed in on what was really bothering Joan.

Figure 8.1 shows that every client story, like Joan's, has several layers. As if peeling an onion, a client is likely to give us first the content of the story, then the feelings it evokes and, finally, its personal meaning. The figure also portrays the fact that as the client's story becomes deeper over time, there are occasional returns to more superficial material. Increasing depth is due to the development of trust, but, at the same time, more threatening material emerges such as feelings and meanings that evoke embarrassment and shame. Therefore, depth varies as the client discloses. If the helper can keep the client focused on deeper issues and provide a safe environment, the full meaning of the story starts to emerge.

Why Reflect Meaning?

It is clear that the events in Joan's story have a deeper significance than Joan herself is able to identify at first. Meaning is the background against which the client's story is projected, but meaning needs to be noticed and brought into awareness. Why is it important for the helper to bring this deeper level of meaning to the surface? One reason is that the client takes these backdrop issues for granted. When the helper highlights them, the client begins to realize their significance in shaping the story and begins to understand that these meanings are part of the unique way he or she constructs the world.

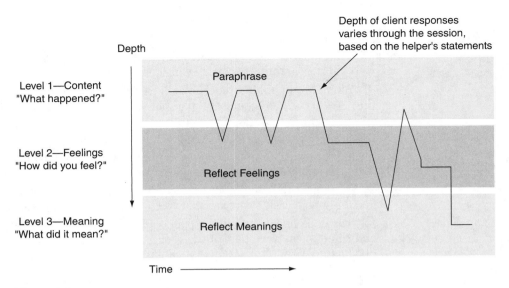

Figure 8.1
Levels of Disclosure

In *Reality Isn't What It Used to Be*, Walter Truett Anderson (1990) points out that, as far back as Plato, we have marveled about how people from different backgrounds can have such different views of the same situation. One of Plato's great metaphors is the allegory of the cave. With apologies, I am extending it here to make a point. In Plato's story, people are living in a cave chained together so they must all face the cave wall. They never see the outside world, and their ideas about it are based entirely on the shadows they see reflected on the walls, which constitute their reality. Similarly, we are all caught up in the restrictions of our cultures and backgrounds, and we see other people's points of view as odd, misguided, or even ignorant.

Like the people in the cave, those who possess similar views and a similar culture see things the same way and reinforce each other's views. Only when we look at ourselves from outside our usual vantage point do we perceive the chains that are holding us within a narrow range of vision. The helping relationship leads the client to look at himself or herself from a different perspective. The helper holds up a mirror to the client, "reflecting" rather than agreeing with what the client says. The helper lets the client get a good look at his or her own values and viewpoint about the self, others, and the world. When a client sees himself or herself through the eyes of another, he or she begins to envision how to make constructive changes. In Joan's case, by opening up to the meaning of the story, she begins to see that her actions were due, in part, to her long-felt need for approval. When she makes this connection, it paves the way to set a goal for becoming more self-directing.

Besides shifting the client's perspective, reflecting meaning inevitably has the effect of getting the client to discuss even deeper issues than those brought out in the first version of the story. Can you see how Joan's next statements in her dialogue with Lynn might progress? Perhaps she will discuss how she was raised, where her values came from, and in what other situations she has disappointed herself. While reflecting meanings leads to more disclosure and exploration of a topic, a helper's inability to tap meaning means that clients will stay with more superficial topics.

Beginning helpers are often confused when the client's story seems to have run its course. They feel that once the basic facts are known, where else can the conversation go? Very often this is because the helper has not gone deeper into the story. Figure 8.1 shows the concept of depth in a client's story over time. According to this model, superficiality is the result of traveling too rapidly through the story in a horizontal direction, rather than going deeper or vertically. The depth that a client is willing to reveal is dependent on a number of factors. Among these are helper responses, client readiness and willingness, and some attributes of the therapeutic relationship.

Questions and minimal encouragers do not invite the client to go deeper. They are supportive and keep the client at whatever level the discussion has reached. If the helper does not invite the client to reach deeper levels by reflecting feelings and meanings, the client will normally stay at level 1 (Figure 8.1). Of course, some clients are very psychologically minded and will quickly discuss the deeper aspects of a problem with little prompting, but even insightful clients will frequently miss the importance of meaning. On the other hand, some clients are not very talkative and are uncomfortable with expressing feelings and uncovering personal issues. In that case, going deeper takes a much longer time, even if the helper is very inviting and uses reflecting skills. Such clients may have trouble getting to the feelings level, and when they do, they only visit briefly. As we discussed in Chapter 3, clients are more likely to disclose deeply if the helper is perceived as competent, trustworthy, and nurturing.

Obviously, the only factors that the helper can control are his or her own actions. The helper cannot always break through a client's reluctance to open up. To increase the likelihood of greater depth in the client's explorations, the helper must avoid the overuse of questions and must also use reflecting skills to deepen the client's story whenever possible.

Challenging the Client to Go Deeper: The Inner-Circle Strategy

In Joan's case, the helper used questions and reflections of meaning to get at the deeper levels of the story. Sometimes clients have difficulty recognizing that their stories have these deeper layers, and it is useful to challenge them to move from a superficial recounting to the area of personal meanings. Arnold Lazarus, the founder of multimodal therapy, uses what he calls an "inner-circle strategy" for getting clients to identify deeper, more personal issues (1981, p. 55). The helper draws a series of concentric circles labeled A, B, C, D, and E (see Figure 8.2), identifying ring A as issues that are very personal, normally disclosed to only the closest friends. At ring E are issues that are essentially public and might be discussed with almost anyone on first meeting. Ring E issues may include discussion of the client's appearance and occupation. At ring A are very personal issues such as sexual problems, anger and resentment toward people, negative views of the self, and secrets that the client feels are immoral or dishonest. Rings B, C, and D represent increasingly secret areas. Once the circles are identified, the client might be asked to write in the names of individuals, including the helper, who have access to the various rings from A to D.

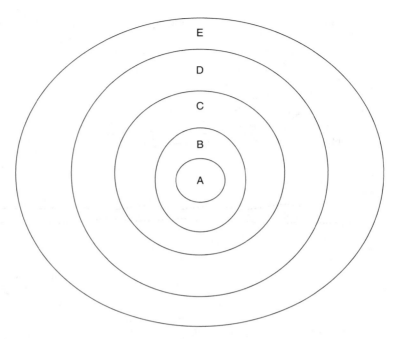

Figure 8.2
Inner-Circle Strategy

Lazarus likes to use the diagram to confront the client when therapy has become too superficial. For example, the helper might say, "It seems to me that we are discussing issues that fall in the D or C category. The most effective work occurs at levels A or B. I am wondering if you do not feel comfortable talking about these deeper levels yet."

Stop and Reflect

We have been talking about the fact that the best information is forthcoming, and the most therapeutic relationships are developed when clients reveal their deepest thoughts, feelings, and perceptions. Clients who venture to this level of disclosure are, however, risking a great deal. One way to realize this is to imagine yourself in the client's position. Think for a moment about what is unique about you. What would a person need to know about you before you would feel that he or she was sufficiently informed to help you? How long would you have to know someone before discussing your deepest secrets? Read each topic in the following list, and identify something relevant about yourself that you would be willing to discuss with a helper during the first session and something else that you probably would not discuss. Write down brief notes under each heading. What do you fear might happen if you disclosed the thoughts, feelings, and perceptions that you would prefer not to discuss?

Topic	I Would Disclose	I Would Not Disclose
• Your family values and family history		
• Your religion or spiritual beliefs		
• Your sexual history		
• Your personal dreams and ambitions		
• Happy and unhappy childhood memories		
• Physical limitations, disabilities, and illnesses		
• Times when you were dishonest or unethical		

Draw an inner circle for yourself like the one in Figure 8.2 and write down the names of people who have access to the deeper issues in your life. Now think of one or two issues that you would not discuss with anyone, even a professional helper. What would stop you? Are there also issues at rings B and C that would be difficult but not impossible to discuss with a helper? What issues would you discuss only if there were safeguards of confidentiality? Share your inner circle with a small group of classmates if you feel comfortable in doing so. There is no need to discuss the issues at each of the levels. However, it might be interesting to compare the numbers of people who have access to the various levels of your life. Who are these people, and how did they gain this kind of trust?

Worldview

Worldview is a term that refers to a person's view of self, others, and the world and one's values about what is right and wrong (Young & Witmer, 1985). Language, gender, ethnicity/race, religion/spirituality, age, physical abilities, socioeconomic status, and trauma all influence the development of one's worldview (Ivey, Ivey, & Simek-Morgan, 1997). In addition to worldview, a client's personal values are sources of meaning that can be brought to the surface. Recall the discussion between Lynn and Joan. The issue boiled down to Joan's feeling that she had strayed from what she believed was right. Violations of one's personal values are frequently background issues in client's messages. The helper's job is to understand both the client's worldview and values so that the client's viewpoint—and the meaning of his or her story—can be appreciated and an appropriate solution to the client's problems found. Without understanding Joan's moral dilemma and disappointment in herself, do you think it would be possible to help her deal with her situation at work? The appropriate solution must be consistent with her ideas of what is right and healthy.

Following are some other examples of client statements that give a window to worldview or values. A helper can listen for these kinds of statements as avenues for reflecting meanings.

View of Self

"I am essentially . . . (a good person) (evil) (selfish) (okay/not okay) (smart/dull) (damaged) (unlovable)."
"Nothing I do seems to work out."
"I always land on my feet."
"I am unlucky."

Notice that these statements express general notions about the self, rather than defining specific abilities such as being a good piano player or having a good sense of direction.

View of Others

> "People are . . . (unreliable) (essentially good) (selfish) (trustworthy) (kind)."
> "Men are all alike."
> "People will take advantage of you if they can."
> "White people are . . ."
> "Asians are . . ."

Beliefs About the Environment or the World in General

> "It's a jungle out there."
> "Life is a vale of tears."
> "You can't get ahead."
> "It's bad luck."
> "God punished you."
> "God rewarded you."
> "Things always turn out for the best."
> "Stuff happens!"

Values

> "People should treat each other fairly."
> "Men should be the head of the family."
> "Family secrets should be kept in the family."
> "Conflict is bad."
> "You should always try to do your best."

How to Identify Meaning Issues with a Client

Reflecting Meaning

Reflecting meaning is a technique that counselors use to attempt to restate the personal impact and significance of the event the client is describing. Meanings of events differ from person to person because of each person's worldview and values. For example, much work was done in the 1960s and 1970s on the effect of stressful life events (Holmes & Rahe, 1967). If you have ever been in a stress workshop, you may have taken a "stress scale" that lists life events such as moving, changing jobs, divorce, and so on. Each event is given a weight based on its predicted impact on your life. Initially it was thought that, by adding up the scores, one could anticipate how much stress a person would feel based on the number of changes during the past year. It turns out that the number of events is not very predictive of stress or illness, but the meaning and importance you place on the events is significant. For example, while divorce is highly stressful to most people and gets a high score on the stress scale, in conflict-ridden relationships, divorce may actually lead to a reduction in stress. It is not really possible to know how an event has affected someone until you understand his or her experiences, basic beliefs, and values.

Because meaning is even deeper below the surface than feelings, meanings are harder to detect. The meanings are implicit in the client's story, but one must learn to read between the lines to unearth them. This sometimes means employing intuition or hunches. The more you know about a client, the greater the likelihood that your hunches will be correct. Therefore, helpers are encouraged to be patient using invitational skills, paraphrasing, and reflecting feelings to help the meanings emerge. Helpers generally use two methods to get at meaning in a client's story. First, helpers can *pose open questions* that ask the client to focus on the perceived significance and meaning of the story. Second, helpers can *reflect meanings* by listening carefully and taking educated guesses about why the story is important to the client.

In Chapter 7, you learned to reflect feelings using the formula or algorithm: "You feel _____ because _____." The first blank was to be filled in with the client's emotion and the second with paraphrased content—for example, "You feel angry because you didn't get the promotion." To reflect meaning, we use the same formula, but in this case, we place an accurate reflection of feeling in the first blank and a reflection of meaning in the second blank, as in the statement, "You feel disappointed in yourself because being a good daughter is an important value to you." Sometimes it may be necessary to include both a reflection of feeling and a short paraphrase of content in the first blank so that the client knows exactly which event you are referring to—for example, "You were excited (feeling) when you received your driver's license (paraphrase) *because* it meant you were becoming an adult (meaning)." The word *because* shows the connection between the content and feelings of the story and their relationship to the underlying meaning for the client. In other words, it is quite possible, as one goes deeper into the story, to employ among reflecting meaning, reflecting feelings, and paraphrasing as needed. They can be delivered alone or in combination. How do you know when to use each? You try to reflect as deeply as you are able. If you can only grasp the feelings, then reflect those feelings and wait until you know more before playing a hunch about meaning.

Here are some examples of helper reflections of meaning. Assume that each reflection of meaning comes after a period of listening during a helping session.

Example 1

Client: "I don't know what to do now. Everything I worked for is going down the drain."

Helper: "You must feel pretty lost because the dream of having your own business was so important to you."

Here the helper reflects the feeling of being lost. The helper then ties this feeling with the unique meaning that the client's dream has died. The helper may only make a reflection like this when he or she has adequate knowledge of the client's hopes and ambitions from previous statements.

Example 2

Client: "My daughter isn't living right. She stays out late, and now she's moved in with that boy, and I don't have the heart to tell anyone where she's staying."

Helper: "You are ashamed about your daughter's living situation because you think you have failed as a parent to convey your values."

The helper reflects the client's feeling of being ashamed and briefly paraphrases by mentioning her "daughter's living situation" in a nonjudgmental way. Then the helper connects the feelings to the underlying meaning: The client feels that she has failed.

Example 3
Client: "I never thought about being divorced. We were married for so long that I never really considered it. Since he left 6 months ago, I don't know how to act."
Helper: "You feel disoriented by your husband's leaving. Never in your wildest dreams did you expect to get divorced."

Here the helper reflects the client's specific feeling of shock and disorientation. The meaning is that the client had developed a view of life that did not include the possibility of the marriage ending. The helper reflects this meaning by saying, "Never in your wildest dreams did you expect to get divorced." This variation of the client's own words is a bit risky, but if it is correct, the client might feel understood at a deeper level.

Reflecting meaning is one of the most difficult skills to learn. It requires that the helper think intuitively, and it also means that the helper must fully comprehend the client's unique situation and values. Although we can guess what meaning most people might derive from a situation to accurately reflect the meaning of an event, we frequently must have some understanding of its cultural context. The surest route to reflection of meaning is to patiently and persistently use the basic invitational and reflecting skills. These provide the best atmosphere for clients to tell their stories. The more fully we understand the content and feelings, the easier it will be to reflect the underlying meaning. We must patiently plod away at our reflecting until the lightbulb comes on and we see the meaning.

Using Open Questions to Uncover Meaning

Open questions focusing on meaning can be useful, especially when a client is not very forthcoming. You are already familiar with open questions as a building block from Chapter 5. There open questions were encouraged to delve deeper into some aspect of the client's story and to invite greater disclosure. Open questions can also be employed to facilitate a client's identification and expression of meaning. Consider the following exchange between a client, Sonia, and a helper, Chris:

Sonia: "There was a big family problem because I didn't pick up my sister at the airport. Everyone in the family jumped on me. I guess I was wrong, but I was busy and no one seemed to understand. Now my mom is mad at me and so is my brother."
Chris: "You feel confused about what happened." (reflection of feeling)
Sonia: "Yeah, and I am mad!"
Chris: "What is it about this situation that makes you so angry?" (open question focusing on meaning of the event)
Sonia: "My time isn't important. The family is important. My sister Camilla is important, but not me."

In this interaction, Chris correctly reflected a feeling of confusion, but Sonia added that she also felt angry, letting Chris know that she had only understood part of Sonia's emotions. Getting at these feelings seemed to pave the way for the client to expose more about the deeper significance of the problem. Because Chris could not quite identify the meaning in the client's statement, she used an open question to try to understand the deeper issue. The client responded by revealing the meaning of the event; she does not think her family cares about her needs.

Summarizing

Summarizing is the final reflecting skill you will need to learn. Although it is a relatively simple skill, we place it here because you cannot really use summarizing until you have paraphrased and reflected feelings and meanings. Summarizing pulls together everything a client has said in a brief synopsis of the session up to that point. The summary helps the client make some sense of the tangle of thoughts and feelings just expressed in the session. In other words, it serves a reflecting purpose, letting the client hear his or her viewpoint in a more organized way. The summary ties some of the major issues that have emerged into a compact version of the story. It may include any of the following: (1) content, (2) major feelings, (3) meaning issues and themes, and (4) future plans. Of the reflecting skills, it could be considered the broadest brush, bringing together main content, themes, and feelings in the client's story by concisely recapping them. But summaries are not to be used only at the end of a session. Summaries may be used at all points—beginning, middle, and end. This is because summaries have different purposes. Based on the reason for using the summary, they can be divided into four types: focusing, signal, thematic, and planning.

Focusing Summaries

At the beginning of a session, a summary may help to focus the conversation before it begins. A *focusing summary* is an intervention that brings the discussion to bear on the major issues and themes, places the spotlight on the client's responsibility for the problem, and reminds the client of the goals. For example:

> "In the last few sessions, it seems like we have been dealing with two major issues. The first is the way that you are trying to renew your social network and find some supportive friends since your breakup with Alicia. The other issue is your mixed feelings about living back home with your parents."

Focusing summaries are not only to remind clients about their goals from previous sessions. They can even be used at the first session with a new client. For example, a helper says:

> "Let's review what I know so far. Your mother called and made this appointment for you because you were arrested about a month ago for public intoxication. One of the conditions of your probation is that you receive help for your drinking problem. Your probation officer referred you to our agency. So you're here

to do something about the problems you've been having with alcohol. Is this about right?"

Brammer (1973) points out that a focusing summary at the beginning gets the client on track immediately. Contrast this with the normal opening statements such as, "How have things been going this week?" or "What would you like to talk about today?" When a client begins the session by reacting to a focusing summary, he or she immediately begins talking about the key issues and goals.

Signal Summaries

In the middle of a session, the *signal summary* tells the client that the helper has digested what has been said and that the session can move on to the next topic. If the helper does not summarize occasionally, the client may feel that it is necessary to go over an issue several times until full understanding is communicated. A good time for a signal summary is when the client seems to have come to the end of a story and pauses.

Client: "So that's about it . . . (pause)."

Helper: "Before we move on, let's just summarize where we've been so far. You have tried to get professional help for your daughter's drug problem, and she has rejected it. Because she is an adult, there is not much force you can apply. This makes you feel helpless, and when you see her, your relationship is very superficial because you can't talk about the drug issue without getting into a fight. You've always been the kind of person who likes to leap into action when a problem arises, and here is a situation where there is little to do. That's what makes it especially frustrating." (summary)

Client: "Yes, but that's the way it is. Now I guess I need to talk about how I can go on with my life under these circumstances."

Helper: "Okay, let's talk about that." (door opener)

Thematic Summaries

A theme is a pattern of content, feelings, or meanings that the client returns to again and again (Carkhuff, 1987). The *thematic summary* is an advanced reflecting skill because it means that the helper has to be able to make connections among the content, emotions, or meanings expressed in many client statements or even during many sessions. When this kind of reflection is made, it often provides new information to the client, who may be unaware that the issue is resurfacing so often. Rather than signaling a transition to a new topic, the thematic summary tends to push clients to an even deeper level of understanding or exploration. Here are some examples of thematic summaries:

- "There seem to be two issues that keep coming up. One of them is the anger you feel in a number of different close relationships (emotional or feelings theme), and the other is your sense that you haven't been able to reach your potential in your career (content theme)."

- "As you have been talking, I seemed to notice a pattern, and I'd like to check it out. You seem to want to end relationships when they begin to lose their initial excitement and romance (content theme)."
- "From everything we've talked about over these past few weeks, one major issue seems to be that, over and over again, you hesitate to make a commitment to a career or to a relationship or to take any important action because you are afraid you might let your parents down by failing (meaning theme). Is this right?"

It is difficult to practice using thematic summaries because it presumes that you have seen a client for some time and usually for more than one session. It takes time for important themes to emerge. Identification of themes is an intuitive process. The helper must think back on the whole of his or her experience with the client and try to cull the big issues. Even though identifying themes is an advanced skill, it is placed here because it is possible you may notice these themes as you practice. You may also have the opportunity to see advanced practitioners identify these themes in video-taped sessions. Remember too that themes are constructions of the helper; they should be used only when you have enough information to be fairly certain that you have identified a theme. It is best to propose themes tentatively because if incorrect, a thematic summary can have the effect of making the client feel analyzed.

Planning Summaries

Planning summaries entail a review of the progress, plans, and agreements made during the session. The planning summary brings a sense of closure and ends the session on a hopeful note. Here are two examples:

- "Well, it seems like we've identified several things in this first session that we want to pursue. First, you are unhappy with the way you tend to become overly dependent on your friends. You want to follow your own interests. In fact, you want to get to know yourself better. With this in mind, we thought about your entering a counseling group at the local mental health center. Besides that, you'd like to identify some goals for your career. That is something you and I can begin to work on right away. We'll set up an assessment program and talk more about this in the next several weeks. How does all this sound?"
- "Let's recap what we have talked about so far. On the one hand, you have accomplished your financial goals, but you are far from satisfied with your relationships with friends and family. You have said that this is because you are not very assertive. It sounds as if this is the area we need to discuss in our next session. What do you think?"

The Nonjudgmental Listening Cycle

When Do You Use Each Skill?

After learning the building block skills, students frequently ask, "In what order should the skills be used? When will we know it is the right time to use a particular skill?" Each client tells his or her story in a particular way and at a particular pace, depending on his

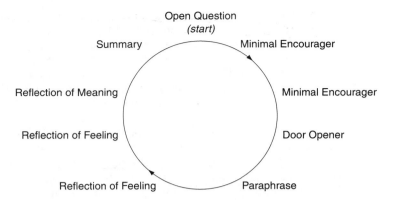

Figure 8.3
A Complete Nonjudgmental Listening Cycle Moving from Open Question to Summary

or her background, previous experiences with helpers, and present emotional condition. So it is not possible to predict the exact order of the skills you will use. However, we can assume that, in general, helping sessions will follow a fairly similar path. We call this the *nonjudgmental listening cycle (NLC)*, or just the *listening cycle*, to emphasize that it is a repeating pattern of basic helping skills. The nonjudgmental listening cycle is a way of conceptualizing a normal or average helping session during which you use the most common building blocks. The listening cycle is repeated with each major topic the client presents. The helper switches gears and begins a new listening cycle whenever the client opens a new topic, encounters difficulty, has a crisis, or needs to explain.

The nonjudgmental listening cycle can be thought of as a set of sequential procedures to be followed as each topic emerges, is discussed, and comes to closure. In our depiction, Figure 8.3, each topic forms a circle from open question to summary. The invitational skills open the topic, and the reflecting skills move the discussion to deeper levels. A summary normally makes the transition from one topic to another or ends the session. Because each person and each helping relationship is different, this map of the average session should not be seen as the way every helping session must unfold. Instead, it is designed to help you think about the whole session and give you an idea about what the pattern should look like. A cycle like that shown in Figure 8.3 is typical of an interchange that would occur later in a helping session or after a session or two. It is deeper and more mature because it shows reflections of feeling and meaning. Early on, a client and helper move through several more superficial cycles, as the client gives information and the helper paraphrases, asks questions, and collects data for the assessment process.

Why Is the Cycle Described as Nonjudgmental?

We have focused a great deal on the skills that a helper uses to understand a client's story, but the attitudes displayed by the helper can make a great difference in the willingness of the client to open up. Carl Rogers (1957), a pioneer in counseling and psychotherapy, identified unconditional positive regard as one of these important attitudes. Positive regard, as the name suggests, is not a neutral stance. The helper actively demonstrates a nonjudgmental approach to the client by showing respect and interest in the unique life of the client. It is a continual challenge to hold such an attitude, especially when we are confronted by clients who have perpetrated violence or engaged in self-defeating behaviors or have committed what we consider to be immoral acts. Positive regard means responding in an accepting and nondefensive way to others who are different in culture, language, ethnicity, or religion. The listening cycle is called nonjudgmental because the attitude of positive regard must be in place when the helping skills are being employed. Without this underpinning, the skills are perceived as cold and robotic. The client will feel dissected rather than understood. How can one develop such an attitude? One way is through vicarious learning. By watching videos or live demonstrations by helpers who have this nonjudgmental attitude, you may be able to acquire it. The ability to be nonjudgmental can be developed by putting yourself in situations where you can see another person's perspective.

Is the Nonjudgmental Listening Cycle All I Need to Know About Helping?

At this point, some students become restless to learn more advanced skills, thinking that their teachers are promoting the listening cycle as sufficient for all situations. The listening cycle is not the only set of skills used by helpers, but the listening cycle provides a safe pathway for the client to tell the story and builds openness and cooperation in the client/helper relationship. Without this foundation, the later processes of assessment, goal setting, and implementing advanced techniques are much more difficult.

Following is an example of helper responses to client statements that represent a complete nonjudgmental listening cycle. Although the helper summarizes here, actually, it may take more than one such cycle before the helper is able to summarize. The session is condensed here to illustrate the major components in sequence:

1. *Open question:* "Would you tell me more about the accident?"
2. *Minimal encouragers:* "Okay," "Uh-huh," "Yes," "Can you tell me more about that?"
3. *Closed question (important facts):* "How badly were you hurt?"
4. *Paraphrase:* "So you had to be in the rehabilitation center for several weeks and you're still unable to work."
5. *Reflection of feeling:* "You're embarrassed about what has happened and a little afraid that people blame you."
6. *Reflection of meaning:* "Your identity has always been tied up with your job. Now that you cannot work for several months, it is hard to feel good about yourself."
7. *Summary:* "Though you're recovering on a physical level, there are several issues that continue to worry you, including how you might perform at your job and how other people will see you."

A Questioning Cycle Typically Found Early in Training

Figure 8.4 shows a relatively unproductive but common cycle, called a *questioning cycle,* typically found in the beginning of training. In this cycle, the helper starts well with an open question and is able to paraphrase the content. Unable to use reflecting skills yet, the helper relies on a closed question to keep things moving.

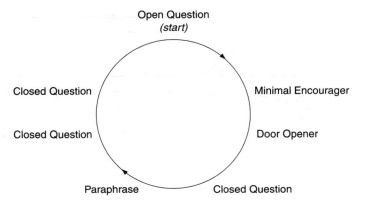

Figure 8.4
A Questioning Cycle Typically Found Early in Training

The question focuses the client back on content, and the helper follows this with a series of questions or minimal encouragers. After several such cycles, the helper is tempted to give advice because he or she has understood essential facts and expects that the client is simply in need of direction. In fact, because the helper is using encouragers and engaging the client's intellect with questions, the discussion does not deepen and the helper is surprised to find that the client has not really even scratched the surface.

One way of getting away from this trap is to *respond to the client's last statement* directly, using an encourager or open question. This will buy a little time as you search for a reflection. Closed questions, however, will lead to short answers that do not allow you this breathing room. In the example below, the helper has become snared in a questioning cycle. Note the client does not stay on the topic because the helper's questions do not respond to the client's last statement.

Helper: "Tell me more about the accident."

Client: "It was horrible—what can I say? It was a financial problem, I felt terrible for months, and there were the physical problems, too."

Helper: "Can you tell me more about the wreck itself?"

Client: "I ran into another car, and that car hit some people on the sidewalk."

Helper: "How badly were you hurt?"

Client: "I spent 2 weeks in the hospital with a broken femur and a broken ankle. I had to go to the rehab center for the month of May. I'm not walking yet without a cane. I don't know when I can go back to my job."

Helper: "Do you think you are getting better?"

Client: "Yes, but I am in no hurry to face people. I am a little afraid to see everybody."

Helper: "What is it like being out of work for so long?"

Client: "I am bored, and I focus a lot on the pain in my legs."

Helper: "Are they giving you some medication for that?"

Can you see that the helper's fifth question, "What is it like being out of work for so long?" is not responsive to the client's statement, "Yes, but I am in no hurry to face people. I am a little afraid to see everybody"? Here the helper has a golden opportunity to reflect the client's feelings of fear and embarrassment. Instead, the helper falls back on questioning, taking the client to a more superficial level. When the helper is struggling to understand but cannot make a quick response, he or she is better off using an encourager as a delaying tactic. It is crucial that the helper respond to the client's last statement rather than ask a question that sidetracks the conversation.

Here is an example of how responding to the client's last statement using encouragers, reflecting feeling, and reflecting meaning in that sequence can deepen the client's self-examination.

Helper: "How badly were you hurt?" (closed question)

Client: "I spent 2 weeks in the hospital with a broken femur and a broken ankle. I had to go to the rehab center for the month of May. I'm not walking yet without a cane. I don't know when I can go back to my job."

Helper: "So you had to be in the rehabilitation center for several weeks and you're still unable to work." (paraphrase)

Client: "Yes, but I am in no hurry to face people. I am a little afraid to see everybody."

Helper: "Go on." (door opener)

Client: "Well, I don't know what they are thinking."

Helper: "Okay." (minimal encourager)

Client: "I think that everyone blames me for what happened."

Helper: "You're worried that some of your friends will reject you because of the injuries to the other people." (reflection of feeling and paraphrase)

Client: "I guess it is not rational."

Helper: "When you think about it, it doesn't seem sensible, but all the same, it worries you." (paraphrase and reflection of feeling)

Client: "Sure. I guess I would feel even worse if my own friends blamed me."

Helper: "So it sounds like sometimes you blame yourself for what has happened." (reflection of meaning)

Summary

Reflecting feelings and content are important tools for communicating to a client that you understand the story, but for a client to deeply sense understanding from the helper, it is also important to identify and reflect the meanings behind the client's experiences. Meanings consist of the worldview and values that arise from upbringing, culture, family, and life experiences.

The inner-circle strategy is a method described in this chapter to indicate to clients that they are not disclosing at the deepest levels. The diagram also helps us to recognize that everyone maintains some secret areas. When we consider how scary it might be to expose these to others, we can begin to understand a client's need for a therapeutic alliance built on trust and time before deep disclosure can be expected.

Reflections of meaning are helper responses that go beyond the superficial, getting at the implicit messages rather than the explicit. This means that the helper must use intuition to go beyond the surface of what the client says, extrapolating the underlying meanings. When the facts, feelings, and meanings of a client's story are reflected, he or she feels that the helper has understood at a very deep level.

Summarizing is the second building block skill described in this chapter. Summaries pull together the content, feelings, and meanings in a distilled form. Summaries serve to focus the client on the major issues, identify themes, signal a transition in the session, and provide a basis for planning the next steps.

The nonjudgmental listening cycle is a way of explaining the deepening sequence of skills that a helper uses. Understanding the NLC can help new learners decide which skills to use at various points. By analyzing the NLC in transcripts or in classroom practice, a helper can determine if he or she is responding to the client's statements with deepening responses or is falling into the mistake of shifting topics by the overuse of questions.

Exercises

Group Exercises

Exercise 1

Form groups of three with a client, helper, and observer. The client is to pick a topic that is likely to evoke some deeper meaning such as:

> "My greatest ambition is . . . "
> "My biggest disappointment has been . . . "
> "Something I am not very proud of is . . . "
> "My ideas about divorce are . . . "
> "What I like about this country is . . . "
> "Something I would like to improve about myself is . . . "

The helper is to use encouragers and open questions to keep things moving, but the main goal is to advance hunches about the personal meanings that lie behind the client's disclosures. The helper should review the "Quick Tips: Reflecting Meaning" section that follows and make reflections of meaning to the client's story.

As the helper reflects, the observer is to write down all helper responses on a sheet of paper. Later the helper can record any useful feedback on this same sheet and take this record home for further examination. After 5 minutes or 10 attempts at reflection of meaning, the observer calls time. Together, look at the helper's responses and see how many of these are accurate reflections of meaning. The client, in particular, should give the helper feedback on key meaning issues that were missed. Group members should then change roles and continue until each person has had a chance to play the role of the helper.

Quick Tips: Reflecting Meaning

If you are having difficulty identifying the meaning behind the client's story, consider these tips:

- Use the following plan in your practice sessions: Ask an open question to start, use minimal encouragers as you get the details, and then strive for reflection of feelings. Whenever possible, make a reflection of meaning.
- Ask yourself, "Why is this story important to the client?" "Why is he or she telling me this?" "What is it that bothers the client so much about the event?"

- Be patient! Wait until you have heard enough of the story to understand its importance, and then reflect meaning.
- Think about the client's background, and then tie in what you know about his or her unique viewpoint from previous topics.
- Are you responding to the last thing the client said, or are you looking ahead to what you are going to say? If you stay with the client's statements, one by one, they will lead you to meaning.
- When you have established a good reflecting relationship and the client knows you understand the situation, take a risk and play your best hunch about some deeper underlying meaning.

Exercise 2

Look back in this chapter to the scenario of Joan and Lynn. After reading that dialogue again, write down a brief planning summary and share it with your classmates in a small group. Next write down a focusing summary that you might use to begin the next session. Summaries should be about two or three sentences in length. They should contain a brief synopsis of the thoughts, feelings, and meanings expressed by the client. Use the following

criteria to give each other feedback on the summaries:

- Was the summary no longer than two or three sentences?
- Did the summary essentially capture the major points?
- Did the summary include the key events, feelings, and meanings expressed?
- Is there a hopeful tone to the planning summary?

Quick Tips: Summarizing

- Use a summary when the client appears to be stuck. This will tend to get things back on track.
- At the end of a summary, it is often useful to finish with a quick "checking question" such as, "Have I got that right?" or "Am I correct?"
- When you feel like asking a question, try summarizing to signal the client to move on to the next topic.
- Use a summary when the client is moving too quickly and you want to slow the session down.
- Try to finish every session with a planning summary.

Additional Exercises

Exercise 1: Identifying Meanings

In this exercise, you are asked to separately identify content, feelings, and meanings in a client's statement and then put them together in a response that reflects all three areas. Take into account that there may be more than one possible answer because, in practice, inflection or word emphasis would certainly change the meaning of these statements.

a. "I am extremely depressed and have been for about 6 months. I am now taking medication, and things are a little better. But every day I go to the refrigerator and look in. I can't decide what to eat. In the morning, I can't decide what to wear. This isn't me. If a friend calls on the phone, I am not sure what I will talk about, so I dread anyone calling. How long do you think this is going to last? Never has anything like this happened in my family. I feel so bad that my daughter has to come and take care of me. She has a life, too. I even feel like I am a burden to you."

Paraphrase the situation (content):

_____

_____

Identify the client's feelings about the situation:

_____

_____

Client's underlying meanings or unspoken assumptions (why is this important?):

_____

_____

Your reflection of meaning (content, feeling, meaning):

_____

_____

b. "I am a 31-year-old construction worker. Lately I've had thoughts of hitting my child, Barbie. She is the light of my life. But she doesn't mind me. I have to yell and scream. My wife and I don't seem to see eye to eye on how she should be raised. Maybe we don't agree on a lot of things. When I tell my daughter something, my wife rolls her eyes and belittles me. So, of course, Barbie won't do what I say. I tried to talk to my wife, but she won't listen any better than my daughter does. Now, I was brought up with a belt. But only when I needed it. I don't necessarily think she has to be spanked, but she needs to learn to mind. I am embarrassed when I have to take her to my mom's house or anywhere else because she won't listen."
Paraphrase the situation (content):

_____

_____

Identify the client's feelings about the situation:

_____

_____

Client's underlying meanings or unspoken assumptions:

_____

_____

Your reflection of meaning (content, feeling, meaning):

_____

_____

c. "My main problem is that I am overweight. I know that. And I want to lose weight. Look at the television and magazines. Everybody's skinny! I guess I am supposed to go along with the crowd. But my husband doesn't realize that I have tried everything. He never says it, but I know he doesn't find me attractive anymore. But is a slim body all that is important? How about unconditional love? If I lost weight, what would I have to do next? Dress some particular way? He says he is concerned about my health, but do you believe that? Last week, my 7-year-old son and I went to the mall, and one of his classmates was there. In front of everyone, the other kid said to my son, "You have a big fat mom!" Children can be so cruel. And his mother didn't even correct him. Don't you think she should have?"
Paraphrase the situation (content):

_____

_____

Identify the client's feelings about the situation:

_____

_____

Client's underlying meanings or unspoken assumptions:

_____

_____

Your reflection of meaning (content, feeling, meaning):

_____

_____

Exercise 2. Analyzing your transcript

Once your training group has completed the first transcript (see Homework 2), you will have a way to look at the nonjudgmental listening cycle. Make a list of all the skills you used, in order, during your taped practice session. Can you discern a cycle from open question to minimal encouragers to paraphrases to reflection of feelings and meaning? Do you stick with a topic long enough to get at deeper feelings and meanings, or do you tend to go into a questioning cycle? Get feedback from your training group, your instructor, or a classmate about how you can deepen your nonjudgmental listening cycles.

Exercise 3. Identifying meaning in written examples

Form groups of four

Each member is to write down a three- or four-line statement that a fictitious client might give as a summary of a presenting problem.

It should be written in the first person, as follows: "I am having trouble getting my children to mind me. That's not all. I've been very depressed, and I'm not going to be able to pay my bills this month. I try as hard as I can. What am I supposed to do?" When writing the example, students should remember to include enough information so that a reflection of meaning is possible. The trainer or leader reads each one anonymously, and the training group takes turns giving a reflection of meaning using the formula "You feel _____ because _____." A good response to the preceding problem might be, "You are feeling really discouraged because your best does not seem good enough." The trainer or leader asks for feedback from the group concerning the accuracy of the reflection. Another option is to ask one participant to reflect the meaning using the formula and the next participant to rephrase it in more natural terms.

Homework

Homework 1: A Midcourse Checkup

You have now learned most of the building blocks skills presented in this book. Although you have probably not mastered all of them, it is time for a brief review and checkup. Try to be as honest as possible. This will help you identify areas where more practice is needed. Review the feedback you have received during group exercises. Then take a look at the building blocks that follow and rate your current level of mastery for each skill.

1 = I understand the concept

2 = I can identify it and give examples

3 = I can do it occasionally

4 = I can do it regularly

_____ Eye contact

_____ Body position

_____ Attentive silence

_____ Voice tone

_____ Gestures and facial expressions

_____ Door openers and minimal encouragers

_____ Open and closed questions

_____ Paraphrasing

_____ Reflecting feelings

_____ Reflecting meaning

_____ Summarizing

Examine the pattern of your responses. If you are like most beginners, your invitational skills are strong. You may also be doing fairly well with paraphrasing, but you may well be at level 2 or 3 on reflecting feelings, reflecting meanings, and summarizing.

Homework 2: First Transcript

Now that you have read about and practiced the building blocks of the helping relationship, it is time to make a record of your present skill level by recording a longer session (20–30 minutes) on audiotape or videotape. The next task is to convert the recording to hard copy, or as we will call it, a *transcript*.

Your goal as a helper in this transcript is to demonstrate your ability to move from cycles of questioning and paraphrasing to the use of the higher skills of reflecting feelings and meanings. Rather than asking questions, fall back on paraphrasing, encouragers, and even silence until you are able to make a reflection.

Step 1: With a partner from your training group, conduct and record a session based on a concern that he or she is willing to discuss. Alternatively, your fellow student may role-play the problem of a friend or acquaintance or fabricate a problem he or she might someday encounter in real life.

Step 2: Choose the best 15 minutes of the tape you made and transcribe every word of both client and helper using the format shown in Table 8.1. It is important that the client's comments appear directly *below* your helping responses, so that the connection between the two can be examined. Be sure you have permission to record from the client. You should do this aloud on the tape *and* in writing.

Step 3: Listen to the tape or read the transcript and make comments, naming each of the skills

Table 8.1
Typescript Example

In your write-up, include a short description of the client and the nature of the issue to be discussed. Note that each helper and client response is numbered so that the instructor can refer to them.

Client and Helper Responses	The Skill You Used	Comments
H1: "What would you like to talk about today?"	Open question	Looking at this now, it seems a little trite. I think I will try something else next time.
C1: "Well, I have been having a problem with a nosy neighbor."		
H2: "Really? Tell me more."	Minimal encourager and door opener	Seems appropriate at this stage.
C2: "Well, she comes over every day. I can't get anything done. I need to work on the computer. I need to do some work around the house. But she won't let me."		I notice that the client is blaming the neighbor. She is not owning the problem. Maybe next time I will get the client to focus more on that.
H3: "She doesn't have anything else to do?"	Closed question	Whoops, I missed the boat. I think it might have been better to reflect the client's frustration.

that your response exemplifies. Sometimes students describe their responses rather than categorizing them. It is important to identify the skills you are using to determine their frequency and appropriateness. Use only the names of the building blocks you have learned. The comments section is a place for you to reflect on your responses. Do not just note weaknesses; identify strengths as well. In the comments section, you may also wish to identify any other issues that come to mind as you review the transcript.

Homework 3: Alternative to the Transcript—Making a Video

Make a video as described in Homework 2. Instead of making a full transcript of the tape, watch the tape and classify each of your skills as you watch. The process of identifying skills can be a form of practice. Get feedback from fellow students and your instructor on your progress. Try not to be judgmental. One of the biggest mistakes at this point is to notice weaknesses. For example, many students see themselves on tape and do not like what they see. They see mistakes in body position or facial expression. Rather than reacting on a purely emotional basis, try to think about the following questions:

"Did I help the client to go deeper into the problem? In the brief encounter, did we form the basis for a therapeutic relationship?" Build on your strengths before focusing too much on your weaknesses. Here are some questions to ask yourself:

- Was I able to get the client to open up?
- Are any of my gestures distracting to the client?
- Are my body position, facial expression, and voice tone inviting?
- Do I allow silence sometimes to urge the client to open up?
- Do I appear relaxed?
- Do I seem engaged with the client, or am I too passive?
- How many paraphrases and reflections of feeling did I use?
- Did I rely too much on questions?
- Did I reflect soon enough?
- Did I overuse minimal encouragers rather than reflecting?
- How many reflections of meaning was I able to attempt?
- Are my words responsive to the client's last statement or to my own thoughts?
- What are my natural strengths as a helper?

References

Anderson, W. T. (1990). *Reality isn't what it used to be*. San Francisco: Harper.

Brammer, L. (1973). *The helping relationship: Process and skills*. Upper Saddle River, NJ: Prentice Hall.

Carkhuff, R. R. (1987). *The art of helping* (6th ed.). Amherst, MA: Human Resource Development Press.

Holmes, T. H., & Rahe, R. H. (1967). The social readjustment rating scale. *Journal of Psychosomatic Research, 11*, 213–218.

Ivey, A. E., Ivey, M. B., & Simek-Morgan, L. (1997). *Counseling and psychotherapy: A multicultural perspective*. Boston: Allyn & Bacon.

Lazarus, A. A. (1981). *The practice of multimodal therapy*. New York: McGraw-Hill.

Rogers, C. R. (1957). The necessary and sufficient conditions of therapeutic personality change. *Journal of Consulting Psychology, 21*, 95–103.

Young, M. E., & Witmer, J. M. (1985). Values: Our internal guidance system. In J. M. Witmer (Ed.), *Pathways to personal growth* (pp. 275–289). Muncie, IN: Accelerated Development.

Challenging Skills

9

My experience is what I agree to attend to. Only those items I notice shape my mind.

William James

In his book *Vital Lies, Simple Truths*, Daniel Goleman (1985) relates the following story told by a woman at a dinner party:

I am very close to my family. They were always very demonstrative and loving. When I disagreed with my mother, she threw whatever was

nearest at hand at me. Once it happened to be a knife and I needed ten
stitches in my leg. A few years later, my father tried to choke me when
I began dating a boy he didn't like. They really are very concerned
about me. (pp. 16–17)

Goleman claims this tale is a good example of how people deceive themselves.
Because the client cannot face the fact that she was the victim of child abuse, she
changes the story to its exact opposite, one of caring and concern. It is often the
helper's unhappy duty to awaken the client to this defensive maneuver. Irvin Yalom
goes so far as to compare this duty to that of an executioner (Yalom, 1990). The client
has found a refuge, and the helper's revelations kill off protective fantasies, potentially arousing resentment and discomfort. Sometimes it becomes necessary for
helpers to "dare" clients to examine the inconsistencies in their stories by *giving*
them feedback and, at other times, by *confronting discrepancies.* Making clients
aware of uncomfortable information moves them to act and change their circumstances. For most helpers, this step in the journey is a giant one. While the invitational and reflecting skills are supportive and convince a client to open up, these two
challenging skills push the client to examine critically his or her choices, feelings, and
thoughts. When the helper uses challenging skills, he or she is giving the client an
honest reaction or pointing out warring factions in the client's story. Invitational and
reflecting skills do not necessarily encourage the client to follow through with plans
and commitments, but challenging skills do.

Consider Figure 9.1, which depicts the relationship between support and confrontation. Depending on the mixture you use, the client will see you as someone who
is critical, as someone who is apathetic, as a helpful person, or as a friend. The ideas

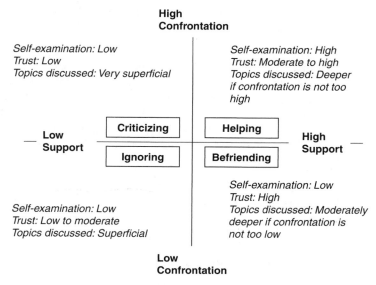

Figure 9.1
Effect of Helper Interventions Based on the Ratio of Confrontation and Support

behind Figure 9.1 are based on research in organizational settings that have identified managerial styles (Hersey & Blanchard, 1977). Supervisors in business situations can be roughly described as supportive or nonsupportive and challenging or not
challenging. It appears that good managers have a balance of pushing and supporting. Similarly, in the helping professions, much of what we do can be described as a
combination of confrontation and support (Keen, 1976) or "joining" and "kicking"
(Minuchin, 1974).

The ratio of confrontation to support has effects on the client's willingness to
explore his or her own thoughts, feelings, motives, and actions. This ratio also affects
the client's willingness to *trust* the helper and to *discuss deeper or more superfi-*
cial topics. On the bottom half of the chart in Figure 9.1, you can see that when a
helper does not use enough confrontation, the client does not engage in very much
self-examination; yet in the high-confrontation conditions, the client's trust in the
helper is reduced. When confrontation is high, the helper is bringing up topics and
inconsistencies that may be painful for the client, and this strains the relationship.
On the left-hand side of the figure, it also becomes clear that without support, the
client does not engage in self-examination, nor does the client wish to discuss deeper
issues because the trust level is so low. This figure suggests that the worst conditions
for helping are high-confrontation, low-trust situations.

When Should We Use the Challenging Skills?

When challenging skills are used, the aura of safety and support, so carefully constructed by the helper, is at risk. There is a fundamental shift from relationship building to a focus on the goals set by the client and helper, conveying to the client that
the helping relationship is not a friendship but a business partnership during which
the helper may have to hold the client's feet to the fire in order to attain the agreed-
upon outcomes.

During the initial stages of the relationship, the helper strives to understand the
client's unique worldview by getting the client to open up. As a client tells the story,
the helper listens attentively using the nonjudgmental listening cycle (NLC). After
several cycles, the helper begins to detect distortions, blind spots, and inconsistencies. He or she may then use feedback and challenging skills, not so much to
straighten out the client as to teach the client the method of self-challenging. The
essential aim of the challenging skills is to help clients operate with unclouded
information about themselves. With heightened self-awareness, they are better able
to make decisions and to operate free of illusions and "vital lies." This is consistent
with the goal of helping: to empower clients by encouraging them to explore their
own thoughts, feelings, and behaviors and to take steps toward their dreams and
goals.

Clients need to be challenged when:

- They are operating on misinformation about the self. For example, a client
  may underestimate her intelligence, feeling that she is not capable of attending college when there is evidence to the contrary.
- They are operating with mistaken ideas and irrational beliefs.

- They misinterpret the actions of others. This tendency is called *mind reading* and is a common problem among couples. A client may act on assumptions without confirming them, making statements such as the following: "I could tell by the way he acted, that he did not want to date me anymore."
- They are blaming others rather than examining themselves. For example, a client may blame the boss at work but refuse to look at his own responsibility for the poor relationship or his own work performance.
- Their behavior, thoughts, feelings, and values are inconsistent. For example, a client talks about how much she values honesty but, at the same time, discusses how she hides her financial difficulties from her husband.
- They are not operating according to their own values.
- They are not working on their goals.

In this chapter, we will focus on two building blocks, or basic skills, used to challenge clients and help them deal with problems more consciously. The first of these is giving feedback: your honest reaction to the client. The skill of giving effective feedback is one that has wide application in helping, including group work, couples counseling, and individual and family therapy. Second, we tackle the skill of confrontation itself, pointing out inconsistencies and blind spots in the client's story. Confrontation is a powerful technique that must be used with great caution.

Giving Feedback

Why Is Feedback Important?

Disclosing oneself to others and receiving feedback from others are the twin processes of personal growth. The invitational, reflecting, and advanced reflecting skills that you have already learned are the primary methods helpers use to encourage client self-disclosure. The mere act of confiding in another person seems to have many health benefits (Pennebaker, 1990), and the ability to be "transparent" to others has been linked with mental health (Jourard, 1971). Learning to receive feedback is the other key to self-awareness and growth. Clients need accurate feedback in order to confront inconsistencies in their own attitudes and to know how they are affecting others. Most problems that people face are "people problems." People come for help when they experience pain in their interpersonal worlds. Unfortunately, they often receive less-than-useful or conflicting messages about themselves from other people. Even family members and close friends may be afraid to give each other information about how they are affecting others. A friend or family member may say, "You look like a lunatic when you dance," or "Your driving makes me nervous!" during times of annoyance or stress. However, close friends and relatives are more likely to withhold feedback because they do not wish to jeopardize the relationship. What happens when you get a new haircut? People tell you they like it when, in fact, it may look terrible. We are all operating on too little information about ourselves. Rosen and Tesser (1970) called this unwillingness to transmit bad news the "mum" effect.

The Johari Window

The *Johari window* (Luft, 1969) is a visual way of explaining that information about the self comes from two sources: things we observe about ourselves and feedback from those around us (Figure 9.2). The Johari window (named by Joe Luft and Harry Ingram, who invented it) helps to explain how we can gain greater self-awareness through the two tools of growth: self-disclosure and feedback. The window has four "panes":

Information Known Both to Others and to the Self (Public Area)

According to the model, the behavior of self-disclosure widens the public area (windowpane I) and shrinks the private area (windowpane III). A client who has a broader public area is able to disclose more deeply, will experience greater relief, creates better relationships, and supplies the helper with more complete information about problems. The relative size of this windowpane compared with the other three areas and the information disclosed vary depending on how open or transparent an individual is. Overdisclosure can also be a problem when a person monopolizes conversations and drives people away.

Information Known to Others But Not to the Self (Blind Spot)

There is much about ourselves that we cannot know because we are not objective. As the poet Robert Burns said, "O wad some pow'r the giftie gie us to see ourselves as ithers see us." If only we could see ourselves from the perspective of those around us. Instead, we are operating with a number of blind spots in our vision. One example of a blind spot is the fact that, even when we look in a mirror, we are not seeing ourselves exactly. We are really seeing the reverse image, similar to a slide placed backwards in the projector. We often do not know if we have bad breath, if we are annoying someone, if we appear judgmental, or if we have a whining tone to our voice. Conversely, we may miss our positive traits as well, unaware that others see us as attractive, kind, or a good listener. Feedback shrinks the blind spot (windowpane II).

	Known to self	Not known to self
Known to others	I Public area	II Blind spot
Not known to others	III Hidden area	IV Unknown area

Figure 9.2
The Johari Window
Source: From J. Luft. (1969). *Of human interaction* (p. 13). Palo Alto, CA: National Press. Reprinted by permission.

Information Not Known to Others But Known to the Self (Hidden Area)

This is the area of secrets. People with large private areas usually are not known or liked by others. Because of fear of rejection, we engage in the neurotic behavior of keeping our mouths shut, which does not accomplish our goal of intimacy. There is a saying in Alcoholics Anonymous that you are "only as sick as your darkest secret." This phrase suggests that through appropriate self-disclosure, many problems that have been lurking in our minds—our deepest secrets—tend to vanish in the light of a confiding relationship. When we keep secrets from others, we do not have to face our negative traits and bad habits. Most people keep secrets about their sexual activities, their drug or alcohol use, and the times when they have been dishonest or cowardly. Not everything must be emptied from this area, but many individuals seeking help have low-quality interpersonal relationships because they have built strong walls around windowpane III, keeping their secrets safe and ironically depriving themselves of intimacy.

Information Not Known to Others or the Self (Unknown Area)

The helping relationship reduces the size of the unknown area (windowpane IV). Clients have moments of insight or "aha!" experiences that occur when they consolidate information gained through both self-disclosure and feedback. Invitational, reflecting, and challenging skills help clients gain more information about themselves and reduce this unknown area. When we think about whether a helping session has been successful, we can evaluate it in two ways. We can look at whether the helper has demonstrated the invitational and reflecting skills as well as other building blocks. On the other hand, the Johari window gives us a glimpse of the big picture, a truer test of whether help has occurred. A session is successful if the client has disclosed important material to the helper and if the client has reduced the blind spot by receiving feedback from the helper. Through disclosure and feedback, the client comes away from the helping session having probed deeper into the problem. The invitational skills set the stage to entice the client to think and experience more deeply, while the helper's feedback provides additional information that is not filtering through the client's defenses. Recall again William James's statement, "My experience is what I agree to attend to. Only those items I notice shape my mind." The helper can serve a valuable service of focusing the client's attention on unrecognized information.

How to Give Feedback

In the helping relationship, giving feedback means supplying information to a client about what you see, feel, or suspect about him or her. Feedback helps people grow when they are receiving constructive, specific information about themselves. When a professional helper gives feedback, the sole purpose is to help the client. Feedback from a professional—unlike that from family and friends—does not consider the needs of the helper or primarily concern itself with whether or not this will produce a strain on the relationship. Helpers only give feedback when clients ask for it or when the client needs information to progress. They give feedback for three purposes: (1) to indicate how the client's behavior affects the helper, (2) to evaluate a client's progress toward the goals, and ③ to supply a client with information based on the helper's observation. When a helper says, "You say you want to be assertive, but I experience your behavior as passive when you look away and avoid eye contact," the feedback indicates the effect of the behavior on the helper. The statement, "As I see it, you have now been successful in overcoming your anxiety by facing the situations you have been avoiding," is an evaluation of the client's progress. The helper is making an observation when he or she says, "I notice that you never seem to talk about your father."

Feedback may be rejected by clients because "the truth hurts." Clients use defense mechanisms to avoid accepting the information they receive. Therefore, helpers endeavor to present feedback so that it will be more palatable. In his classic book about raising children, *PET: Parent Effectiveness Training* (1975), Thomas Gordon described the process of delivering feedback as "I messages." Most feedback statements delivered by helpers are I messages because using the word *I* conveys that the helper is expressing his or her own perspective. When a person starts a conversation by saying, in effect, "This is my viewpoint," we are more likely to listen nondefensively.

Here are some suggestions about how to give effective feedback in all sorts of situations. These are good rules for helpers and for trainees, who may be giving feedback to each other in group exercises.

1. Do not give people feedback on their personality traits. It is hard to see how one can change a description of one's character.

    Poor feedback (boss to subordinate): "You are a procrastinator."
    Good feedback: "For the past 3 months, your report has been late. That is unacceptable."

2. Be specific, concrete, and nonjudgmental.

    Poor feedback: "You're bugging me."
    Good feedback: "I find it annoying when you whistle during my favorite music."

3. Ask permission before giving feedback.

    Helper: "You say that people at work are angry about your behavior. Would you like some feedback?"
    Helper: "I would like to give you some feedback on something I have noticed. Is that all right?"

4. Sometimes feedback about touchy subjects is accepted more easily if it is offered tentatively. You do not have to dilute the feedback; rather, find an acceptable route to get the client to think about what is being reported.

    Poor feedback: "Last time, we talked about your feelings that you deserted your father when he was ill. This time, you avoid the topic when I try to reopen it."
    Good feedback: "I got the impression last time that talking about your father was difficult for you and you seemed to steer away from that topic. Maybe it is because you think you deserted him when he was ill. Am I right about this?"

5. Give only one or two pieces of feedback at a time. When too much feedback is given, client defenses rear up like impenetrable walls and little gets through.

Poor feedback: "I think you should improve your appearance at work. You look disheveled, and you need to wear a tie. By the way, you left the copy machine on again last night, and you forgot to call Marlene back."

Good feedback: "I think you should improve your appearance at work. Your pants are wrinkled, and you need to wear a tie."

6. Do not forget to give feedback that emphasizes the client's strengths. It is easy to assume that clients are aware of their strengths and to focus on their foibles. We tend to give more feedback that points out unknown weaknesses than unrecognized assets. More often, clients need to know what is going right, what is working, and what resources the client has to bring to the problem. Try focusing on the positive aspects first and bringing up the negative later.

Poor feedback: "You asked someone out for a date, but you did not work on the other part of the assignment, where you were to confront your friend on her behavior. Let's talk about that."

Good feedback: "Based on what you've said today, I'm picking up that you have made real progress. Even though it was a little scary, you asked two people for a date and one of them said yes."

get feed back from c. to see how it was accepted.

7. Use an open question to determine whether feedback was received and how it was accepted.

Helper: "A minute ago, I pointed out that you have spent the last few weeks talking only about your ex-husband. What is your reaction to that feedback?"

Stop and Reflect

There is a parallel in our own optic system that can demonstrate the existence of blind spots, at least from a physiological viewpoint. You may know that the optic nerve attaches to the back of the eyeball. Where it connects, there is a small gap in the picture your brain sees. Because we have two eyes, we correct for this tiny blind spot and never know that it exists. Take a look at the X and the large dot shown in Figure 9.3. Now hold this book with your right hand and stretch it out to arm's length. Stare directly at the X on the left side of the page. Close your left eye and slowly move the book straight toward your face. At about 12 inches, the dot on the right side disappears.

The physical blind spot is only an analogy of the psychological phenomenon identified in the Johari window (windowpane II). Still it alerts us to the fact that our knowledge about the world and ourselves is not complete. The rub is that since

Figure 9.3
Blind spot

we are unaware of these things, how do we know what they are and how can we convince clients to listen to feedback? Consider the following questions:

- In this experiment, you learned about your blind spot through actual experience. Suppose I had merely told you about the blind spot? Which information is the most powerful in convincing you of its existence?
- How can we help clients have experiences of their psychological blind spots rather than merely talking to the clients?
- Suppose you gave the client some feedback that you were 98 percent sure was true and accurate, and the client's response was to dismiss it completely. How do you think you might react? How could you get the client to consider it further without damaging the relationship?
- Suppose that a client feels rejected in her personal relationships. In her interactions with you and with other personnel, you notice that she talks constantly, rarely allowing anyone else to control the conversation. First, write down a nonjudgmental feedback statement exactly as you would deliver it. Next, identify one or two other situations where the client might get this kind of feedback. What assignments might you give the client to make her more aware of this tendency?

Confrontation

Confrontations are interventions that point out discrepancies in client beliefs, behaviors, words, or nonverbal messages. As a result of confrontation, client awareness of inconsistencies is stimulated, and the client moves to resolve them. In essence, it is an educational process that brings information to the client's attention that has been previously unknown, disregarded, or repressed. A good confrontation urges the client to resolve the inconsistencies. Confrontation creates emotional arousal and can lead clients to develop important insights and to change their behavior. A discrepancy is an inconsistency, a mixed message, or a conflict among a client's thoughts, feelings, and behaviors. In fact, every problem a client presents contains discrepancies. For example:

- A client says that she wants an equal, sharing relationship, but she only dates domineering men.
- A client says that she loves her job, but she complains about it constantly.
- A client states that he wants to improve his marriage, but he forgets to go to marriage counseling sessions.

Why Should Inconsistencies Be Confronted?

Ivey and Simek-Downing (1980) say that "the resolution or synthesis of incongruities may be said to be a central goal of all theoretical orientations" (p. 177). In fact, most well-known therapeutic systems use confrontation in one way or another. For example, the Gestalt therapist Fritz Perls confronted clients about incongruities in their nonverbal and verbal behavior (which he labeled "phony"). Albert Ellis, the founder of rational emotive behavior therapy, likes showing clients the gap between their beliefs and rationality by directly exposing them to the "nuttiness" of their ideas and frequently uses curse words to create emotional impact. Albert Ellis used loud voice tones or even curses to intensify confrontations. Some early group therapy methods for substance abuse (the Synanon approach, Straight Inc.) used personal attacks and abusive confrontation to create movement in dealing with deeply ingrained behavior patterns. There is little evidence to support the use of such strong confrontation. In fact, it appears that, even with substance abusers, a consistent highly confrontational therapist style is not as effective as a moderately confrontational one (Miller, Benefield, & Tonigan, 1993).

These extreme examples are cited because many helpers feel they must emulate these master therapists who seem to be highly critical and judgmental toward their clients. Confrontation need not be a hammer. It can be a gentle push. In this chapter, we are urging you to consider how to raise inconsistencies in a client's mind without alienating him or her. I believe that confrontation is a skill that should be developed after the early helping building blocks are well established, namely invitational and reflecting skills. Research confirms that highly trained (doctoral) counselors used confrontation more often than students (Tracey, Hays, Malone, & Herman, 1988). At the same time, doctoral-level counselors demonstrated less dominance and verbosity than student helpers. It appears, then, that experience and training teach helpers to use confrontation more frequently, to talk less, and to simultaneously provide support.

Cognitive Dissonance and Confrontation: Why Confrontation Works

Do you remember the concept of cognitive dissonance from Psychology 101? Cognitive dissonance theory states that we are motivated to keep cognitions such as values, beliefs, and attitudes consistent (Festinger, 1957). When people experience inconsistencies in their thoughts, feelings, and behaviors, this creates tension, and they are motivated to reduce the tension. We convince ourselves that the incongruity is unimportant or try changing one of the incompatible elements. For example, a client, Donna, describes her job as good-paying but also as repetitive and boring. She needs the job to help her mother, who is struggling to survive on social security. Donna is aware that she wants to go to college because she is not intellectually challenged in her present position, but the costs are too great. This creates dissonance. She deals with the tension caused by these conflicting thoughts by telling others and herself that intellectual challenge is not really important; she needs to take care of her mother. We all use such defense mechanisms to distort reality so that we can reduce anxiety. In this case, the distortion is that Donna does really want to go to college: It may not be possible, but pretending that her desire to go to college does not exist is creating a giant "blind spot" in her life. Many times, clients use defense mechanisms to escape tension, rather than making choices based on thinking and planning. When helpers confront people with these discrepancies, anxiety often resurfaces.

Kiesler and Pallak (1976) reviewed dissonance studies and found a link between dissonance and physiological arousal (Cooper, Zanna, & Taves, 1978; Croyle & Cooper, 1983; Pittman, 1975; Zanna & Cooper, 1974). It seems that clients change their attitudes in order to reduce the arousal caused when the helper makes the client aware of the two incompatible elements in his or her life. The confrontation causes anxiety because the client must become aware of this split, which is normally kept out of awareness by his or her defenses. This is what Ernst Beier calls "beneficial uncertainty" (Beier & Young, 1998). The client's frozen position of security has been shaken up. In that state, the client becomes open to a shift. In the case of Donna, the helper might help Donna become more aware of her need to be intellectually challenged and ask her to talk about it, explore it, and even investigate options to use her mind. Without blind spots, we make decisions that are more reality-based and personally satisfying (Claiborn, 1982; Olson & Claiborn, 1990).

While we may use confrontation to bring buried elements into consciousness, we must remember that clients do not really like it (Hill, Helms, Tichenor, Spiegel, O'Grady & Perry, 1988). If the helper's confrontation is too powerful and the client's emotional arousal is too great, not only will he or she reject the message, but there will be less exploration of feelings and trust will diminish (Hill et al., 1988). Thus, therapists tend to use confrontations sparingly because it is strong medicine; and they should combine it with a liberal helping of support, or else they risk alienating the client (Barkham & Shapiro, 1986).

Types of Discrepancies

There are five elements of a client's story that can come into conflict: the client's worldview or beliefs, the client's previous experiences, the client's verbal messages, the client's nonverbal messages, and the client's behavior. They can occur in many possible combinations, but the six most common forms are illustrated in the following dialogues:

Incongruity Between Verbal and Nonverbal Messages

Client: "It's been hell. This whole thing. It's almost funny [laughs]. You know. Sometimes he loves me, sometimes he hates me."

Helper: "Your laughing and smiling make me think the problem is not serious, and yet I can tell by what you've said that it has been very painful for you." (confrontation)

Incongruity Between Beliefs and Experiences

Client: "I do the best I can. But I'm not really good-looking. I've been dating the same two guys for about 4 months now. They say I'm pretty, but I don't believe it."

Helper: "You tell me that you believe you're not attractive and then you describe going on a lot of dates." (confrontation)

Incongruity Between Values and How the Client Behaves

Client: "My son is the most important thing in the world to me. But I just don't have time to see him every week. I need some recreation, too. If I want to get ahead at work, I have to put in the hours."

Helper: "If I understand you, you say that your relationship with your son means a lot to you, but somehow you've let other things get in the way." (confrontation)

Incongruity Between What the Client Says and How the Client Behaves

Client: "I've been going to Cocaine Anonymous as I said I would. But it's not really helping. Every time I see one of my old friends, I'm back into it again."

Helper: "I'm confused. You say that you want to give up cocaine, and yet you continue to see your old drug friends." (confrontation)

Incongruity Between Experiences and Plans

Client: "Sure, my girlfriend and I have been having a lot of problems lately. But if we moved in together, I think things would improve."

Helper: "Isn't one of the problems that whenever you spend any length of time together, you fight violently for days? How will living together and spending even more time together help the relationship?" (confrontation)

Incongruity Between Two Verbal Messages

Client: "My wife makes twice as much money as I do. It doesn't bother me. But I always feel that she looks down on me because of it. I should be making a lot more than I do. I often think about starting a new career."

Helper: "Okay, on the one hand, you say that it doesn't bother you, and yet you also say that you feel inadequate in her eyes and talk about a career change!" (confrontation)

How to Confront

The helper's confrontational statement usually takes one of the following forms:

"You said _____, but your nonverbals said _____." (verbal versus nonverbal)
"You believe _____, but you experience _____." (beliefs versus experiences)
"You value _____, but you act _____." (values versus actions)
"You said _____, but you acted _____." (verbal versus actions)
"You plan to do _____, but your past experiences tell you _____." (plans versus experiences)
"You said _____, but you also say _____." (verbal versus verbal)

As you begin to identify discrepancies and present them to a client, you might find it helpful to memorize the following phrase, "On the one hand, _____; on the other hand, _____." Although you do not wish to overuse this statement with clients, this algorithm or template will help remind you to identify the conflicting aspects of a client's story.

Steps to Confrontation

Step 1: First, listen carefully and make sure the relationship is well established before confronting. Use the nonjudgmental listening cycle to fully understand the client's message and reflect feeling and meaning. Ask yourself if the timing is right or if a confrontation will prematurely place stress on the relationship. Have you earned the right to confront?

Step 2: Present the challenge in a way that the client will most likely accept it. The following example shows a helper using open questioning and reflection of feeling to gently usher in confrontation and reduce the negative impact.

Jung Sook (helper): "Can you tell me what you mean by the word 'independence?'" (open question)

Olivier (client): "Well, what I mean is that I am tired of having to report to my wife. I don't know what I'd do without her. But she is a pain in the neck most of the time."

Jung Sook: "You want to be independent, but you think you have to abide by your wife's wishes most of the time." (confrontation)

Olivier: "But she's a wonderful wife. I don't really mean it when I say those things, you know."

Jung Sook: "You think she's wonderful, and yet you find yourself angry with her a great deal of the time." (confrontation)

Olivier: "That's what bothers me; sometimes it's great, and sometimes it's terrible."

Step 3: Observe the client's response to the confrontation. In this case, the client does not fully accept Jung Sook's first confrontation. She notes this and tries something different.

Step 4: Follow up the confrontation by rephrasing or retreating. When the client does not accept or rejects the confrontation outright, the helper should try another tack. Because clients often respond to confrontation either by denial or by superficial agreement, the helper must be ready to follow up with additional exploration, another confrontation, or clarification. Jung Sook's second confrontation is accepted by the client because it is phrased in a way that the client can tolerate. Specifically, Jung Sook used the client's exact word, "wonderful," to gain the client's acceptance of the confrontation.

Evaluating Confrontation and Client Response

The Helper Confrontation Scale

The 5-point Helper Confrontation Scale (HCS) rates a helper's effectiveness in delivering confrontations (Hammond, Hepworth, & Smith, 1977). Higher-level scores (4–5) indicate that the helper is dealing with discrepancies in the client's story while providing support and encouraging action. Lower scores (1–2) indicate the helper is ignoring or failing to respond to discrepancies.

At level 1, the helper overlooks or accepts the discrepancies, inconsistencies, or dysfunctional expressions of the client or does not supply support and uses a harsh, abrasive, or "put-down" confrontation. For example, a helper might say, "Your unwillingness to make this decision shows that you are a dependent person," or, "When are you going to realize that you are knocking your head against a brick wall?"

At level 2, the helper does not focus on discrepancies, but responds with silence or reflects without noting the inconsistency. This category also includes poorly timed confrontations such as a strong confrontation that is delivered in the first few interchanges between helper and client before a therapeutic relationship is established.

At level 3, the helper focuses attention on a discrepancy by questioning or by pointing out the inconsistency. At level 3, the timing is appropriate and the confrontation is not abusive. For example, the helper might point out, "After hearing your story, I understand your unhappiness with the college you have chosen, but, at the same time, it sounds like there are things you like about being there as well."

Level 4 involves a direct confrontation by the helper that includes a challenge to the client to modify the behavior or to resolve the inconsistency while, at the same time, protecting the client's self-esteem. To guard the client's self-esteem, the helper uses a nonjudgmental tone and a tentative approach. For example, a helper might say, "What I am hearing is that, on the one hand, you love your mother, but, on the other, at age 30, you feel that you need a home of your own. This sounds like a really important issue for you to resolve, and I would like to help."

Finally, level 5 includes all the positive characteristics of the lower levels but is conveyed by the helper in a caring and helpful way along with encouragement or enthusiasm for growth. For example, the helper might say, "You really care for Angela, but you are afraid of the consequences when the boss finds out that you are dating his ex-wife. This sounds like a problem that really deserves some quick attention, and it could really help you because you desire to be more honest and straightforward about your feelings." In essence, the scale points out that the best confrontations are well timed, are direct, urge the client to act, and are delivered in a caring manner.

The Client Acceptance Scale

Unfortunately, many confrontations "bounce off" because the client is not ready to look at the discrepancy or the confrontation either is worded too strongly or is too vague. The Client Acceptance Scale (CAS) is a training tool to help you gauge the client's reaction to a confrontation. While you would not use the CAS in normal practice, in the beginning stages, it can make you aware of how the client is reacting to your confrontations. Clients can react to a confrontation in three basic ways. Each represents a different level of acceptance of the confrontation, and each reaction gives the helper important feedback and direction. A client response on the CAS can be rated as a 1, 2, or 3, depending on the extent to which a client agrees to the existence of a discrepancy pointed out by the helper. A client who fails to agree with a confrontation is not necessarily "resistant," because the confrontation may have been inaccurate, may have been delivered without support, or may be at odds with the client's experience. Very often, a client will tentatively respond at levels 1 and 2 before fully accepting a confrontation.

The three levels of acceptance on the CAS are:

1. *A client may deny that a discrepancy even exists*. Examples of denial include attempts by the client to discredit the helper, to change the topic, to seek support elsewhere, or to falsely accept the confrontation. The helper must decide whether to pound away continually until the confrontation is accepted or to bring the topic up again at a later date. The more combative approach is likely to be detrimental to the relationship.
2. *The client may choose to accept one part or aspect of the confrontation* as being true, while rejecting another part. This outcome is not all bad, because partial acceptance can lead to further dialogue on the issue. At such times, the helper is encouraged to focus the discussion on the areas of agreement.
3. *The client appears to fully accept the confrontation* and agrees to try to change his or her behavior to resolve the inconsistency that has been pointed out.

Previously, an example was given in which a helper confronted an individual (a) who stated that he wanted to give up cocaine and (b) who continued to associate with his old, drug-using friends. The continuation of their conversation is presented here to show how the helper can promote exploration even when the client does not fully accept the confrontation (responds at CAS level 2). The dialogue also shows how a confrontation can lead to the setting of a new goal when the helper points out a discrepancy and then asks the client to resolve it.

Client: "I've been going to Cocaine Anonymous as I said I would. But it's not really helping. Every time I see one of my old friends, I'm back into it again."

Helper: "I'm confused. You say that you want to give up cocaine, and yet you continue to see your old drug friends." (Helper Confrontation Scale—3)

Client: "I do want to stop using. But what am I supposed to do? Stay by myself all the time?" (Client Acceptance Scale—2)

Helper: "So what you really need is to be around people, socialize, have friends. How could you do this—stay away from cocaine and still have friends?" (helper moves on to setting goals)

Client: "You tell me."

Helper: "Hold it. I don't have all the answers to this. But you said you want to have friends and you want to stop using. Is this possible?"

Client: "It must be. People do it."

Helper: "Yes, but how do they do it?"

Client: "I don't know. I guess they have new friends that don't use. But it's hard to start all over again."

Helper: "I'm not an expert on this. But some people who have been off cocaine for a while must be familiar with this problem. It seems like it might be fairly common. Between now and when we next meet, would you be willing to think about this? Go to your next Anonymous meeting and ask one or two people about this. Then let me know what they have to say."

Client: "All right. And I'll talk to my friend Michelle. She's been sober for a year now."

Stop and Reflect

The following is a story by Cindy Yee Fong about how she was brought up and how her family and cultural values helped her become a nonjudgmental listener and also presented a challenge when she was forced to confront her clients.

Respect is a core value in Chinese culture. "Respect your parents and do as they say." "Respect your teachers and don't question or challenge them." "Respect your family and don't discuss concerns or problems outside the family circle." "Respect your elders and don't talk back to them." These were the values and expectations instilled in me by my parents, especially my mother. She was born in China and believed strongly in these rules.

When I first began working as a counselor, my job was to facilitate a group for court-ordered drunk drivers, one of the most angry and difficult client populations. You can imagine the challenges I had to face. For someone who is assertive, open, and willing to confront others, regardless of age or status, this would be a difficult job. For someone like me who was taught to listen, not interrupt, and agree with others, especially older people and those in higher positions, it was a daunting task.

Frequently, there were older clients in the group who tended to "ramble on" in their discussions. Interrupting them, in Chinese eyes, would have been very disrespectful. When doctors, lawyers, and teachers were in the group and expressed opinions contrary to my curriculum, it was nearly impossible for me, at first, to disagree with them. It has taken quite a while for me to overcome this reluctance to be what my culture would consider "disrespectful" and to develop the necessary skills as a counselor to be assertive in confronting others. This is still an area I am trying to improve. My cultural style of passive acceptance has helped me develop unconditional acceptance regardless of differences. This has helped me in developing rapport with clients and getting to the point in a relationship where they can accept confrontation. Chinese cultural values and beliefs have been both helpful and challenging to me as an emerging helper.

- Cindy Yee Fong indicates that respect is one of the core values in Chinese culture. Thinking back on your own upbringing, what cultural or family values would you describe as "core"?
- What were your family's values about contradicting others, keeping the peace, and disclosing weaknesses? Was family business to be kept within the family? Do you think any of your own core values might have an effect on your willingness either to talk with clients about their deepest issues or to confront certain individuals?
- One of the most common difficulties for most of us is overcoming the "mum" effect, the social rule that says to keep feedback to yourself. As a helper, your contract with the client implies that you will give honest feedback despite your personal discomfort. Think about some specific situations that will create discomfort for you such as refusing an expensive gift from a client, informing a client that his or her personal hygiene is poor, dealing with tardiness, talking about sexual problems, discussing whether the client is having an affair, or asking if the client is being honest with you. Which do you think will be the most difficult for you? How might you increase your comfort with these topics?
- Would you find it more difficult to confront someone of a different ethnic or racial background, someone older or younger than you, someone who has a high-status profession, or someone of the same or opposite sex? How do you plan to overcome these limitations? Discuss with a small group some strategies for overcoming some of these roadblocks to feedback and confrontation.

Problems and Precautions

One writer called confrontations the "thermonuclear weapons" of helping. They are powerful, and their force can help or harm. Confrontation may arouse the defenses of the client or damage self-esteem, rather than increase awareness and motivate action. Although the force of the confrontation should not be watered down with qualifiers, confrontation must be presented in a way that does not say, "Gotcha!", shaming the client. The target we are aiming for is to be able to deliver moderately confrontational statements with the client's best interests at heart.

Earlier we mentioned that timing confrontation could be important. Timing means knowing when in the relationship and when in the course of therapy confrontation will do the most good. Obviously, the time for confrontation is when the client/helper relationship is well established and the client trusts your motives. It has been my experience that frequent and premature confrontations based on very little information tend to erode the credibility of the helper. If you wait to confront an issue until after it has been raised on several occasions, the chances of acceptance by the client are high.

Before confronting, the helper must be clear that the reason for the intervention is to increase client awareness, not just to unload a sense of frustration. Helpers feel like confronting when they are stuck. This may or may not be a good idea. A cool head is required for confrontation, and the client's interests, not the helper's exasperation, should be the motive.

A general caveat is that any helper intervention that is in opposition to the client's social and cultural values may be not only disrespectful but also ineffective. Confrontation is an excellent example of a technique with important cultural implications. For example, Lazarus (1982) discusses how this technique can backfire with some Native American children in a school counseling setting. Others have recommended a gentle approach in using confrontation with African-American and Asian-American clients (Ivey, 1994).

Issues with... Culture and confrontation

Summary

In this chapter, the Johari window was introduced as a way of envisioning the big picture in the helping process. This diagram highlights self-disclosure and feedback as twin principles of growth. There are two main ways that a helper can facilitate growth. The helper can provide the client with information through feedback and confrontation, and the helper can provide the conducive atmosphere for opening up. Much of the material in previous chapters has been devoted to learning how to use the nonjudgmental listening cycle and adopting the attitudes that will create this ambience and allow the client to tell his or her story. However, the story also has inconsistencies and conflicts, or else the

client would not be seeking help. The problems the client is experiencing may be due to incompatible ideas and motivations. The helper must give the client feedback and use confrontational skills to help the client become aware of these discrepancies and also encourage the client to act to resolve them. Paradoxically, this places a strain on the therapeutic relationship because the client becomes uncomfortable, blames the helper for straying from safe territory, and may feel that the helper has abandoned his or her supporting role.

Compared with feedback, confrontation is a serious challenge to the client's version of the story, and the client feels a strong push from the helper. Confrontation is an art because one must point out these discrepancies clearly, yet kindly. The Helper Confrontation Scale in this chapter assists new helpers in evaluating the quality of their confrontations. On the other hand, the Client Acceptance Scale rates client reactions to confrontations so that you can determine how much of an impact your confrontation is having or whether another tactic should be tried. One reason that so much time has been spent on confrontation is that it is the stuff of therapeutic legends. Videos of famous therapists show them making startling confrontations. The beginning helper is advised to use confrontation sparingly and only when the relationship is firmly established.

Exercises

Group Exercise 1:
Feedback—the Fishbowl Activity

This exercise works best with groups of eight to ten people. Four or five people sit in chairs facing each other to form an inner circle. The same number of participants forms an outer circle. Each member of the outer circle is paired with an inner-circle member. The outer-circle members sit behind the inner circle and across from the members they are paired with so they can observe them (see Figure 9.4). For 10 to 15 minutes, the inner-circle members engage in a leaderless discussion on a topic such as "What are the most important personal characteristics of a helper?" or "What do you see yourself doing, personally and professionally, 5 years from now?"

During the discussion, outer-circle members are instructed to carefully observe nonverbals and listen to the words of their partners in the inner group. At the end of the discussion, the groups break down into dyads of the inner-circle members and their outer-circle partners. Outer-circle members give feedback to inner-circle members about *interpersonal style*.

Interpersonal style involves the verbal and nonverbal ways that a person communicates and includes the amount the person talks and how much he or she discloses. The outer-circle members offer their counterparts feedback using the tips given in Table 9.1. This should take about 5 minutes. Finally, inner-circle members identify, for their partners, any feedback that was especially accurate or helpful. Time permitting, the exercise can be repeated with inner- and outer-circle members changing places. Following the feedback in dyads, a class discussion can be held in which members compare their experiences of

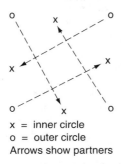

x = inner circle
o = outer circle
Arrows show partners

Figure 9.4
Fishbowl Activity Diagram

Table 9.1
Quick Tips: Giving Feedback

- Do not give people feedback on their personality traits.
- Be specific, concrete, and nonjudgmental.
- Ask permission before giving feedback.
- Sometimes feedback about touchy subjects is accepted more easily if it is offered tentatively.
- Give only one or two pieces of feedback at a time.
- Give feedback that also emphasizes the client's strengths, not just weaknesses.
- Use a checking question to determine whether feedback was received and how it was accepted.

giving and receiving feedback. Which role was more difficult, giver or receiver of feedback? Were you surprised by the accuracy of the feedback on your interpersonal style?

Group Exercise 2: Confrontation

Break into groups of three trainees, who will assume the roles of helper, client, and observer. As the exercise continues, each member should have the opportunity to assume each role.

The Client's Role

Discuss a problem that is causing an internal conflict or moral dilemma. The problem might be the result of:

- Conflict about a job or whether to relocate
- Conflict about whether or not to be honest in a relationship, for example, whether to tell a friend she depends on you too much
- Conflict about something you have done that you do not feel good about, that you regret, or that you wish you could change.

The Helper's Role

Review the list of quick tips for confrontation in Table 9.2. Use the nonjudgmental listening cycle to get the basics of the client's story. Do not spend too much time on setting up the relationship. Although this is critical in real helping situations, in this exercise the main purpose is to practice identifying discrepancies and delivering them to a client. As soon as possible, identify discrepancies by pointing them out, and then encourage the client to resolve the inconsistency.

The Observer's Role

Write down verbatim the helper's responses and then evaluate the helper on his or her ability to use confrontation using the 5-point Helper Confrontation Scale. Code the helper's responses using P for paraphrase, ROF for reflection of feelings, ROM for reflection of meaning, OQ for open question, CQ for closed

question, and CON for confrontation. Do not include encouragers.

Feedback Checklist: Confrontation

Observer Name: _____   Helper Name: _____

	Helper Statement	Coding*	HCS (1–5)	CAS (1–3)
1.				
2.				
3.				
4.				
5.				
6.				
7.				
8.				
9.				
10.				
11.				
12.				

Postexercise Discussion

The observer shares feedback with the helper, based on the Feedback Checklist and the 5-point Helper Confrontation Scale. The client

Table 9.2
Quick Tips: Confrontation

- Wait until you have heard the client's whole story before you identify discrepancies. What seems to be a discrepancy may be a minor point once you know more about the situation.
- If you are having trouble identifying discrepancies, remember that there would not be a problem if there were no discrepancy. Ask yourself, "What makes this a dilemma?" or, "What are the two sides to the client's problem that make this situation so bothersome? Use the memory aid, "On the one hand, _____; on the other hand, _____."
- Note the impact of your confrontation on the client. Does he or she deny, partially accept, or fully accept your identification of the discrepancy? Follow up denial and partial acceptance with invitational and reflecting skills.
- After you identify a discrepancy, try using a question such as, "Am I on target?" Often the client will correct you and clarify the discrepancy.

gives feedback to the helper concerning the effectiveness of the confrontations and the degree of discomfort they caused. For example, were the confrontations presented as observations rather than accusations? Were they presented nonjudgmentally? Helper and observer can also attempt to recall the client's reaction to the confrontation by scoring them 1, 2, or 3 on the Client Acceptance Scale.

Group Exercise 3: Collaborating to Identify Effective Confrontations

In groups of four, one member (the client) describes a problem situation to the group (use the suggestions described in Group Exercise 1). After the client has spent a few minutes describing the situation, each remaining member writes down a confrontation and delivers it verbally to the client. The client responds to each confrontation in turn. As the client does so, the member uses the Client Acceptance Scale to evaluate the client's response. In a group discussion, the helpers and client discuss which responses rated highest on the Helper Confrontation Scale and how confrontations might be phrased to achieve better acceptance by the client. After this discussion, members trade roles and continue until each has had a turn as client.

Additional Exercises

Exercise 1

Break into groups of three or four. Come up with a client problem, and then construct a role play in which the client has a clear discrepancy but denies that one exists. The helper's job is to point out the way the client is avoiding the issue and to encourage the client to reevaluate his or her choices. The challenge is to do this without alienating the client.

Exercise 2

Following are five client situations. Try to identify the discrepancy in each, using the formula "On the one hand, _____; on the other hand, _____." This will help you get a feel for identifying discrepancies.

In some of the situations below, the conflict is implied rather than actually stated. Imagine what conflicts you might be experiencing if you were in that situation. When you have written your answers, meet with a small group and discuss them. Looking at both the clients and the issues, which would be most difficult for you to actually confront?

a. An 18-year-old client describes how sad she is that she has to leave her parents and go off to college. She smiles as she talks about this.
b. The client is very religious and is very judgmental about nonbelievers. At age 22, he has only a few friends and has never had a longstanding romantic relationship. He comes for help because he has become "addicted" to 900-number telephone sex lines.
c. The client says that he loves his sister and that she is very important to him. During their last encounter, she "exploded" because he did not attend her wedding.
d. The client states that she has just been offered a job as a manager at a new company. They are very excited about having her because of her years of experience. She has worked at her current company on weekends and during the summer since she was 17. She says that she feels the owner relies on her, but her pay and responsibilities are unlikely to improve.

She feels that she has made as much advancement as she can and would like a new challenge.

e. The client is a 17-year-old high school student in an alternative school. She has worked hard and improved her poor grades to B's and C's. She failed her high school equivalency examination by 1 point. She is discouraged and has decided to drop out of school. She plans to continue working at her job, even though her boss has indicated she must have a high school diploma.

Homework

Homework 1

In a single page, identify an incongruity or discrepancy in your own life that you are willing to talk about. Alternatively, you may write about, in a disguised fashion, a discrepancy you have noticed in another person. Write down the two sides of the dilemma. How deeply does this discrepancy affect your life (or the other person's)? Do all problems contain discrepancies? Can you think of ways that you have used defense mechanisms or other methods of self-deception to decrease your discomfort? What action steps would be needed now to resolve the discrepancy?

Homework 2

Think about a particularly difficult piece of feedback you have received. It may have been about a weakness in your appearance, a job evaluation, or perhaps even feedback you received in this class. How did you respond emotionally to the feedback? Did it make you angry, hurt your feelings, or just make you feel incompetent? Did you try to protect yourself by denying or discounting the feedback? Did you learn anything constructive from the negative feedback?

Now think about a time when you received some positive feedback on a personal strength, for example, about a job well done or some aspect of your appearance or personality. What made the feedback positive?

Finally, have you ever had an experience where you received no feedback after expending considerable time and effort? What effect do you think a lack of feedback would have on a person's behavior in the long run?

Of the three kinds of feedback mentioned here—positive, negative and none—which helped you the most? How might you apply your reactions to your future dealings with clients? Summarize your reactions in two or three paragraphs.

Journal Starters

1. Identify three or four major problems you have had in your life. What conflicts were you experiencing internally? See if you can identify any patterns or themes of these conflicts. For example, do your conflicts seem to revolve around doing what you want to do versus doing what others want?

2. How comfortable are you with bringing up difficult issues with friends and family? Do you tend to be more tactful or more confrontational? When you go overboard, which end of the continuum do you approach? Where might this tendency have originated?

For more journal ideas, as well as more practice with challenging skills, refer to Chapter 9 in *Exercises in the Art of Helping*.

References

Barkham, M., & Shapiro, D. A. (1986). Counselor verbal response modes and experienced empathy. *Journal of Counseling Psychology, 33*, 3–10.

Beier, E. G., & Young, D. M. (1998). *The silent language of psychotherapy*. New York: Aldine de Gruyter.

Claiborn, C. D. (1982). Interpretation and change in counseling. *Journal of Counseling Psychology, 29*, 439–453.

Cooper, J., Zanna, M., & Taves, P. A. (1978). Arousal as a necessary condition for attitude change following induced compliance. *Journal of Personality and Social Psychology, 36*, 1101–1106.

Croyle, R. T., & Cooper, J. (1983). Dissonance arousal: Physiological evidence. *Journal of Personality and Social Psychology, 45*, 782–789.

Festinger, L. (1957). *A theory of cognitive dissonance*. Stanford, CA: Stanford University Press.

Goleman, D. (1985). *Vital lies, simple truths*. New York: Simon & Schuster.

Gordon, T. (1975). *PET: Parent effectiveness training*. New York: Wyden.

Hammond, D. C., Hepworth, D. H., & Smith, V. G. (1977). *Improving therapeutic communication*. San Francisco: Jossey-Bass.

Hersey, P., & Blanchard, K. H. (1977). *Management of organizational behavior: Utilizing human resources*. Englewood Cliffs, NJ: Prentice Hall.

Hill, C. E., Helms, J. E., Tichenor, V., Spiegel, S. B., O'Grady, K. E., & Perry, E. S. (1988). The effects of therapist response modes in brief psychotherapy. *Journal of Counseling Psychology, 35*, 222–233.

Ivey, A. E. (1994). *Intentional interviewing*. Pacific Grove, CA: Brooks/Cole.

Ivey, A. E., & Simek-Downing, L. (1980). *Counseling and psychotherapy: Skills, theories and practice*. Upper Saddle River, NJ: Prentice Hall.

Jourard, S. (1971). *The transparent self*. New York: Van Nostrand Rheinhold.

Keen, E. (1976). Confrontation and support: On the world of psychotherapy. *Psychotherapy: Theory, Research & Practice, 13*, 308–315.

Kiesler, C. A., & Pallak, M. S. (1976). Arousal properties of dissonance manipulations. *Psychological Bulletin, 83*, 1014–1025.

Lazarus, A. A. (1982). Counseling the Native American child: Acquisition of values. *Elementary School Guidance and Counseling, 17*, 83–88.

Luft, J. (1969). *Of human interaction*. Palo Alto, CA: National Press.

Miller, W. R., Benefield, R. G., & Tonigan, J. S. (1993). Enhancing motivation for change in problem drinking: A controlled comparison of two therapist styles. *Journal of Consulting and Clinical Psychology, 61*, 455–461.

Minuchin, S. (1974). *Families and family therapy*. Boston: Harvard University Press.

Olson, P., & Claiborn, C. D. (1990). Interpretation and arousal in the counseling process. *Journal of Counseling Psychology, 37*, 131–137.

Pennebaker, J. W. (1990). *Opening up: The healing power of confiding in others*. New York: William Morrow.

Pittman, T. S. (1975). Attribution of arousal as a mediator in dissonance reduction. *Journal of Experimental and Social Psychology, 11*, 53–63.

Rosen, S., & Tesser, A. (1970). On the reluctance to communicate undesirable information: The MUM effect. *Sociometry, 33*, 253–263.

Tracey, T. J., Hays, K. A., Malone, J., & Herman, B. (1988). Changes in counselor response as a function of experience. *Journal of Counseling Psychology, 35*, 119–126.

Yalom, I. D. (1990). *Love's executioner and other tales of psychotherapy*. New York: Harper-Collins.

Zanna, M. P., & Cooper, J. (1974). Dissonance and the pill: An attribution approach to studying the arousal properties of dissonance. *Journal of Personality and Social Psychology, 29*, 703–709.

Assessment and the Initial Interview

10

A question not asked is a door not opened.
M. C. Goldberg, 1998, p. ix

Why Assessment?

Assessment is the general term that describes the activity of gathering information about a client and the client's problems. Helpers collect information in a variety of ways, beginning with the first contact as the helper observes the client's behavior and listens to the story. Formal assessment methods include testing and filling out

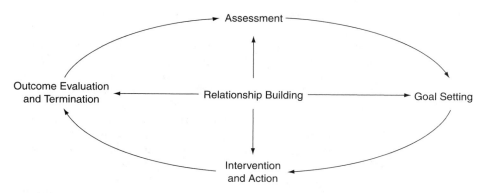

Figure 10.1
Stages of the Helping Process

questionnaires and forms. Informal assessment encompasses all the other ways a helper learns about a client, including observing and listening. Formal assessment may occur at a specific time in the helping relationship, but informal assessment is an ongoing process. In this book, I recommend that the helper set aside time for assessment during the second stage of the helping process (Figure 10.1).

Because each client is unique, it is impossible to be precise about how much time to give to each stage of the helping process. Still, one rule of thumb is to spend one session primarily in relationship building, with the only assessment activities being the collection of basic demographics, observation of the client's behavior, and whatever else you can glean from the client's story. The second and possibly a third session are spent in more in-depth assessment before moving on to a goal-setting phase, which might include testing. Therefore, if a client is seen for 10 sessions, about 10 per cent may be devoted to assessment.

In many places, it is common practice to have a formal period of assessment before the client and helper actually meet. In some agencies, the assessment may be done by an intake worker or a secretary before the client has any opportunity to talk about his or her problem. The decision to employ such an approach is based primarily on saving time and money, but it may also be a way of finding out if the client matches the services being offered. Beginning a relationship with formal assessment can be a mistake, even if it is conducted by the helper, because the initial moments of any human encounter are so important. Imagine how you would feel if you went for a doctor's appointment and were asked only to fill out forms, contribute blood samples, and answer questions, but you did not see the physician or receive any help for your problem.

Here are actual statements from two different client satisfaction forms at a community counseling clinic that relate the experiences of clients who underwent formal assessment in their first sessions:

> "I only came to two sessions. We had to fill out 21 sheets of paper before we could get started. It didn't seem worth it."
>
> "The helper didn't seem to care about my problem. He just kept writing on his papers."

The recommended approach is to focus on the relationship first and ask questions later.

When clients have been invited to tell their stories, they give much more information during the formal assessment period that follows. They leave the first session believing that they have made a start on solving problems, instead of feeling dissected by tests and probing questions. Key data need to be collected at the first interview, but there are several ways to handle this. For clients who can read and write, asking clients to come in early or stay later than the session can be an effective way of collecting information about the client's background and current status.

Although formal assessment should be a planned part of every helping relationship, assessment continues through the duration of the relationship and overlaps with every other stage (Drummond, 2000; Whiston, 2000). For one thing, the helper learns more and more about the client, the environment, and the client's problem as the relationship deepens. Second, the helper needs different kinds of information later in the relationship. For example, assume that a child is referred to a school counselor for excessive school absences that seem to be linked to problems at home (see Figure 10.1). The counselor spends time getting to know the client in the office *(relationship-building stage)* and later becomes familiar with the cumulative folder concerning the child's academic progress and behavior at school *(assessment stage)*. At this point, the child and counselor might set goals such as decreasing absences by 50 per cent during the next grading period *(goal-setting stage)*. To achieve the goal, the counselor contacts the parents for more information, and together they identify a course of action to solve the problem. During this process, the counselor learns a great deal about the client's family and begins to understand which interventions will work and which will probably fail. Next the school counselor suggests a plan involving parenting skills training for the parents and a change in math teachers for the child *(intervention and action stage)*. Once the plan has been established, the counselor regularly contacts the child, the teacher, and the parents to determine if the intervention is working *(outcome evaluation and termination stage)*. During each stage, information has to be collected. Otherwise the helper will set inappropriate goals, implement techniques that are rejected, or be unable to recognize success. In short, assessment is not a one-time activity but a continuous process that accompanies all the therapeutic skills that the helper is employing.

Testing as an Assessment Tool

Testing has gone through several stages of popularity and decline within the helping professions. Some of the ups and downs have been due to the enthusiasm and criticism associated with psychological testing. Psychologists embraced testing after World War II. Many other professionals also became enthralled with testing around this time. Later, in the 1960s, some realistic skepticism was directed at testing, as some of its abuses were uncovered. Many tests were found to be culturally biased (Anastasi & Urbina, 1997). Personality testing with instruments such as the Minnesota Personality Inventory and the Rorschach Test were routinely administered to all kinds of clients. Now they are used more judiciously.

Carl Rogers's client-centered approach was at its height in the 1960s and 1970s; its adherents rejected testing as being antithetical to the goal of seeing the client as a unique person. Family therapy proponents have also been leery of instruments that focus on a single person rather than on the family system (Gladding, 2002). This lent impetus to the anti-testing forces within the helping professions. Perhaps today we can look at testing with a more balanced perspective. We see testing as a tool, rather than as the only way of getting at the truth. Testing can certainly be valuable when diagnosis is difficult. Testing can alert you to dangerous behavior, substance abuse, and psychotic symptoms such as hallucinations and delusions. Testing can also give you insights into a client's functioning in areas you may not have inquired about, uncovering topics for discussion with the client (Hood & Johnson, 1997; Palmer & McMahon, 1997). At its worst, testing can be a waste of valuable time and reveal little beyond what could be found in a couple of sessions talking with the client. Testing can be inappropriate for those who are different culturally than those for whom the test was intended (Paniagua, 1998).

Assessment Is a Critical Part of Helping

Sometimes you will hear that gathering a lot of historical information about a client is not worthwhile. Many theories today emphasize the present and the future rather than the past. It is true that some helpers do spend an inordinate amount of time gathering background information and administering tests; on the other hand, by failing to collect critical data, one takes the chance of making a serious mistake. You must know your customer thoroughly (Lukas, 1993).

Once I interviewed a 65-year-old man who had been a shoe salesman in Cleveland. He had led an interesting life before retiring about 2 years before we met. He reported no real difficulties, and I couldn't seem to understand why he had consulted me. As a courtesy, I talked separately to his 28-year-old son, who had waited patiently outside. The son told me his father had been a physician in Texas and 5 years ago developed a syndrome, which was thought to be Alzheimer's disease, a severe brain disorder with a deteriorating course. The client had simply filled in the gaps of his history with very convincing fiction. That incident taught me that it is best to get as much information about a client as possible *and* from a variety of sources. If I had tested the client's memory or talked to his son first, I might have saved some time. More importantly, had I only relied on the client as the sole source of information, I might have sent him away without treatment.

Conducting superficial assessments, however, does not always lead to such spectacular embarrassment. It is very common, though, for helpers to accept the client's story without a critical thought. Even the most astute helper can make drastic mistakes. It is important to listen to what clients leave out and where they minimize or deny. Also, it is easy to forget to ask specific questions. Because someone is well groomed and comes from a prominent family does not mean that he or she should not be asked about drug abuse or suicidal thoughts. Our prejudices and worldview color our definition of pathology. Even the *DSM* of the American Psychiatric Association, the diagnostic bible, recognizes that misdiagnosis can occur when the helper is not familiar with a client's cultural background and interprets symptoms within his or her own cultural context (Paniagua, 1998).

Because of these common lapses in good assessment habits, helpers need to have a regular screening procedure. A systematic assessment assures us that we are helping the client with the most important issues, such as serious mental disorders, substance abuse, and danger to self or others (Sommers-Flanagan & Sommers-Flanagan, 1995). Perhaps you are thinking that you will never encounter serious problems like these in your future workplace. The reality is that nearly every helper comes into contact with these kinds of serious problems. Even school counselors deal with depressed parents and alcoholic coworkers.

Reasons to Spend Time in the Assessment Stage

Assessment Gives Crucial Information to Plan Useful and Realistic Goals

The main purpose of assessment is to gather information that will be useful in planning the goals that will guide the helper and client. Assessment must have both breadth and depth. As far as breadth is concerned, the helper must throw the net broadly enough to make sure nothing crucial escapes. Depth refers to focusing on specific issues such as suicide, the existence of mental disorders, and the crucial problems that catalyzed the client's decision to seek help.

Assessment Helps Clients Discover Events Related to the Problem

A woman came to a community clinic asking for help in dealing with problems at work. She recognized that her job was stressful, but she found that she was unusually irritable with her coworkers and wanted to work on that problem. After some reflection and homework by the client, we discovered that her angry outbursts all happened between 1 and 2 P.M. on days when she did not eat lunch. The client knew that she became grumpy when she was hungry, but she had never connected this with her behavior on the job. A physician helped the client to deal with a problem of low blood sugar, and her extreme irritability diminished.

Assessment Helps Us Understand the Impact of the Client's Environment on His or Her Mental Health

For example, is the client living with family, in a shelter, or with relatives? Does the client suffer isolation because he or she does not speak the dominant language or belongs to a religious minority? If the client is a child, what is happening at school every day that might be affecting the problem? Is the child bullied, rejected by classmates, encouraged by a teacher, etc.?

Assessment Helps Us Recognize the Uniqueness of Individuals

Unless we ask clients about family and cultural background issues, we make assumptions about them through our own cultural lens. People from a different cultural group may be judged as more pathological than someone who shares our own background. Attractiveness is another powerful social factor that may blind us to a client's problems, while unattractiveness may camouflage a person's strengths. A systematic assessment helps us be less manipulated by these strong social influences and more objective in recording everything about a client.

Figure 10.2
Timeline Assessment

Assessment Uncovers the Potential for Violence

Some clients are prone to harm themselves or others. Assessment can identify individuals who are at risk for violence. Although it is not possible to always accurately predict violent behavior, a history of self-inflicted injury or harm to others can cue us to examine the client's situation more thoroughly and take precautions.

Assessment Reveals Critical Historical Data

Figure 10.2 shows a simple assessment device called a *timeline*. Rafael was asked to fill in the boxes with critical life events in sequential order. His choice of key interpersonal events gave a glimpse of his worldview and his major concerns.

Assessment Can Highlight Strengths, Not Just Weaknesses and Pathology

More and more helpers are using assessment that focuses on client strengths and competencies (Lopez & Snyder, 2003; Snyder & Lopez, 2002). Strength-based assessment instruments such as the Behavioral and Emotional Rating Schedule (Epstein, 1998; Epstein, Harniss, Pearson, & Ryser, 1999) have been developed in recent years in response to this need. Strength-based assessment is, in part, a reaction to medical models based on pathology. It is also being recognized that building on client strengths enhances client self-esteem and helps client and helper use time more effectively (Miller, Hubble, & Duncan, 1996). Another direction is to base assessment on a wellness philosophy that emphasizes evaluation of client physical, emotional, social, cognitive, occupational, and spiritual issues (Witmer & Sweeney, 1992). By focusing on what the client already knows and can do, we can plan strategies that capitalize on his or her native abilities and coping assets.

Assessment Helps Clients Become Aware of Important Problems

Frequently, painful issues are pushed out of awareness or remain unrecognized until brought to the surface through assessment procedures. A common example of this is substance abuse. When clients are asked to discuss the problems that alcohol has caused, the resulting list can be an eye-opener. Many alcohol treatment centers take thorough histories as a beginning step in breaking down the alcoholic's denial system.

Assessment Keeps You Focused on the Most Important Areas

If you are able to immediately rule out medical problems, assess substance abuse, discuss suicide and violence, and identify clients who are suffering from psychotic disorders, you will probably save yourself and the client valuable time. These issues outweigh most of the other concerns that a client may bring to the table. By doing a broad screening assessment to identify these "hot" issues, you can deal with these first before spending time treating less important areas.

Categorizing Clients and Their Problems

Although helpers realize that each person is unique, the irony is that in order to simplify our work, we like to categorize and label clients as having this personality or that mental disorder. We construct pigeonholes so that we have some way of deciding how to help people with similar problems. However, with this simplification, we lose some of the important information we need. Labeling a child as possessing ADHD (attention deficit hyperactivity disorder) may illustrate something important to know about the client, but soon every action of the child is seen in light of this classification. Although diagnostic systems can paint humanity in broad brushstrokes, when it comes to an individual, so often the person does not seem to fit neatly into any of the categories we devise, and his or her unique strengths are lost behind a powerful and popular label.

Recently a magazine advertisement showed a photograph of people of many different nationalities wearing the company's T-shirts. The essence of the advertisement was that though people may look different and come from many cultures, from the company's perspective, there are only three types of people—small, medium, and large. While the clothing firm was trying to portray the oneness of the human family, the ad made me realize that by trying to see everyone as the same, we are probably ignoring something important. There must be many people who fall between small and medium and are not comfortable in either size. Compared to differences in clothing, the helping process is even more personal and must be tailored to each client.

This T-shirt metaphor also applies to the area of assessment and diagnosis, especially in cases where a helper becomes enamored with a specific tool. For example, if you use the Myers-Briggs Type Indicator (a commonly used test), there are only 16 types of people based on the configuration of preferences. Although 16 is quite a few, it is also not nearly enough to encompass all human differences. As the saying goes, "When the only tool you have is a hammer, everything looks like a nail." A familiar instrument can help you quickly summarize a person, but it will also limit your ability to describe an individual accurately, fairly, and in a culturally appropriate way. Instead of relying on a single test or intake form, it is suggested that you first listen carefully and gather information from any source that fills in the missing colors in the client's unique portrait. The more complete the picture, the better you will be able to design a treatment that really fits.

Organizing the Flood of Information: Making a Diagnosis

Professionals use paper-and-pencil tests, questionnaires, drawings, and similar instruments to gather data about clients and their problems. Besides formal testing, there are six other important sources of information to consider. Key information comes from *things the helper observes*, from *information provided by friends and family*, from *what the client supplies* (verbal descriptions, journals, recordings, and genograms), from *medical history*, from *other agencies*, and from *the legal system*. Because there is so much information that can be collected, it may be confusing to know which sources to tap and how to manage the incoming data. As you learn to be a helper, you will take a course in evaluation and assessment or tests and measurements and probably diagnosis. These courses will provide you with a more complete background. However, it is still important that you recognize that all assessment tools are attempts to simplify the process by placing clients in categories based on a theoretical system.

Figure 10.3 shows the flood of information from the seven sources of information entering a funnel that narrows as the data are examined and summarized into categories. Diagnosis is the simplifying process we use to organize the results of our examination. Diagnosis is identifying the overriding issues or problems that seem to encompass a large number of the client's complaints. Using this broad definition, all helpers engage in some form of diagnosis (Hohenshil, 1996).

Figure 10.3 also shows how the client's problems or diagnoses are placed on a treatment planning list, something like an in-basket to be sorted out during the goal-setting stage of the helping process. For example, a typical client's in-box might contain marital problems, career confusion, and low self-esteem, which become the focus of the client/helper discussions. Once the client's problems are identified, it is the helper's job to consult with the client and place them in order of priority, noting those issues that will take precedence and those that will be placed at the bottom of the box. The helper selects methods and techniques to treat each problem on the list. These methods might include referral to a physician, assertiveness training, group therapy, or any other method that the helper suggests. Typically, the treatment plan is constructed in conjunction with the client, who signs an agreement.

Beginning Assessment Methods

The Mental Status Examination

One way of systematically organizing an interview is by using the Mental Status Examination (Golden & Hutchings, 1998). This examination normally includes recording observations and the responses to questions during an initial interview. The Mental Status Examination is an effective way of making sure you do not miss organic (brain) problems and severe mental disorders. The examination can be criticized for dragging the client through many unnecessary questions, and because diagnoses have changed significantly in the past few years, the Mental Status Examination does not directly help the clinician make a DSM diagnosis (Othmer & Othmer, 2002). Still, many helpers in clinical settings use the Mental Status Examination as the basis for their initial screening of a client. It is mentioned here and shows you the basic categories. Learning to conduct a Mental Status Examination will be part of your basic training in assessment at some point, but it is too detailed for the current discussion. Table 10.1 shows the major categories of the Mental Status Examination.

This section presents four beginning methods of assessment: observation, questioning, genograms, and interviews using a brief intake form. With these four basic

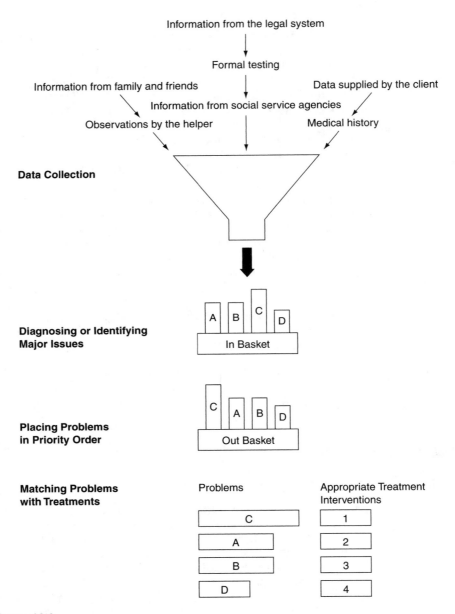

Information from the legal system

Formal testing

Information from family and friends

Data supplied by the client

Information from social service agencies

Observations by the helper

Medical history

Data Collection

Diagnosing or Identifying Major Issues

| A | B | C | D |

In Basket

Placing Problems in Priority Order

| C | A | B | D |

Out Basket

Matching Problems with Treatments

Problems

Appropriate Treatment Interventions

C		1
A		2
B		3
D		4

Figure 10.3
Process of Gathering, Sorting, and Matching Problems with Treatments
in the Assessment Stage

Table 10.1
Mental Status Examination

Category	Description	How Assessed
Appearance	Physical description and clothing	Observation
Behavior	In the interview	Observation
Attitude	Toward the helper and the examination	Observation
Motor behavior	Possible neurological problems or agitation/retardation	Observation
Reliability	Is the client too impaired or guarded to be a good source of information?	Observation
Mood and affect	Mood = general emotional state over time Affect = predominant emotion at the time of the interview	Observation and questions
Orientation	Is the client oriented as to place, person, and time?	Questions
Speech processes	Ability to express and receive, including unusual speech patterns suggestive of certain mental disorders	Questions
Thought processes	Including psychotic processes such as delusions	Questions
Perceptual abnormalities	For example, hallucinations	Questions
Memory, attention, and concentration	Impairments in this area may be symptoms of a number of mental disorders or brain dysfunction	Questions
Intelligence	A client's intelligence tells us what he or she is capable of intellectually and in therapy	Questions
Judgment and insight	Insight is recognizing that one has a problem Judgment is the ability to make decisions and solve problems	Questions

techniques, you can be confident that you have made a concerted effort to screen for major problems and to determine if the help you have to offer fits the needs of the client.

Observation

Yogi Berra once said, "You can observe a lot just by watching." His statement underlines the fact that observation is something of a lost art. It also emphasizes that observation is not a passive process, but a conscious, concerted effort. Experienced helpers are able to detect patterns from a number of small clues that, on the surface, may seem inconsequential. For example, some helpers can catch signs of alcohol abuse from a client's appearance. Some time ago, a cardiac surgeon called the national offices of a television network because he had seen an interview with a national figure on a talk show. He encouraged the broadcasters to inform the speaker that he was in imminent danger of a heart attack. Although the surgeon had not examined the person, he had seen hundreds of cardiac patients over a 20-year period. Unfortunately, the information was not passed along and the individual died before seeking treatment. Through experience and training, observation can be just as crucial in the helping professions. Clients often carry the clues to their problems on their faces and in the way they walk and speak.

The Helper as Detective

The fictional detective Sherlock Holmes relied on inferences (which he called deductions) to solve mysteries. These inferences were based on his keen powers of observation. In *The Sign of the Four* (Doyle, 1929), Holmes discusses with his partner, Watson, the two different processes involved in his art; observation and deduction:

> *Observation shows me that you have been to the Wigmore Street Post Office this morning but deduction tells me that when there you dispatched a telegram. . . . Observation tells me that you have a reddish mold adhering to your instep. Just opposite to the Wigmore Street Office they have taken up the pavement and thrown up bare earth which lies in such a way that it is difficult to avoid treading upon it . . . the earth there is of this particular reddish tint which is found, so far as I know, nowhere else in the neighborhood. So much for observation, the next is deduction. . . . Why of course I know that you had not written a letter since I sat opposite you all morning. What could you go into a post office for but to send a wire? Eliminate all other factors and what remains is the truth. (pp. 7–8)*

Like Holmes, Sigmund Freud was aware of the importance of observation and a thinking process (deduction). Freud believed that evidence of unconscious motivation was available in the everyday activities of clients, including unconscious movements and slips of the tongue (parapraxes). For example, Freud described clients with marriage problems who twisted their wedding rings throughout the session. From *observing* unconscious acts, underlying problems could be *deduced*.

The helper can learn much about observation from Holmes and certainly from Freud, but, unfortunately, human behavior is too complex to take the next step and conclude that we can leap from our observations to accurate predictions about people based on only a few clues. In this age, helpers are a little less inclined to jump to conclusions without validating them against data from the client. In the case of the wedding ring, there are several possible reasons for ring-twisting behavior, including weight gain and anxiety. Therefore, helper hypotheses are guesses, not deductions. Instead of arriving at Holmes's single inescapable conclusion, the assessment process of observation involves documenting observations and forming a list of hypotheses which, when linked to other information, may show a general pattern or theme. Instead of drawing swift conclusions, the helper confirms or disconfirms hypotheses more slowly through discussions with the client. By questioning and listening, a helper can determine if a client's disheveled appearance is due to depression, poverty, or apathy. Observation skills should be practiced, but conclusions should be drawn only when there is confirming evidence from the client and from other sources.

Avoiding Bias in Observation and Resisting Cultural Encapsulation

Our own cultural biases, assumptions, worldview, and experiences color what we observe. One of these biases is the human tendency to see and remember the things we are searching for. For example, if you are thinking about buying a new car, suddenly you may begin noticing more of them on the road than ever before (Goleman, 1985). Similarly, some helpers see pathology everywhere because their training has focused on seeing the half-empty glass rather than the half-full one. This is just one of the examples of how we tend to see what we are looking for.

Our expectations and experiences can also distort our observations. In a landmark article entitled "On being sane in insane places," Rosenhan (1973) studied individuals who faked their way into a mental hospital by reporting auditory hallucinations. Once admitted and labeled psychotic, all of their subsequent behavior was seen as abnormal. For example, one man's diary writing was classified as "obsessive" by hospital personnel. As you can imagine, being trained to identify mental disorders can cause us to see them in everyone we meet. Helpers must be careful not to diagnose except when strict criteria are met. In addition, we must balance our training to see illness by also recognizing client strengths and include this in the diagnostic process.

As the preceding discussion points out, observations are not objective. Our professional experience and training focus us on certain issues. In addition, our own family background and culture shape what we remember and pay attention to. We see clients through our own cultural lens and judge their behavior based on our standards. Freeing ourselves entirely from this conditioning is nearly impossible, but we can become more aware of our own limited cultural vision. Again, supervision allows us to reflect on our observations and involves another person who can help us identify our own lenses that may be coloring our vision. The reflective process described in this book suggests that you should think about and record your reactions to your learning. Keeping a diary and obtaining supervision can help avoid bias, the tendency to judge other people's behavior from our own narrow perspective.

Furthermore, helpers need to have firsthand contact with people from different backgrounds. Only by experiencing different cultures can we even begin to understand client behavior within the context of the client's own culture. Every helper should consider finding ways to have experiences in another culture. Although it is enlightening to be a visitor to another culture, we can also learn about other cultures by being curious and becoming students of every culture we come into contact with. For example, on a recent trip to Europe, my companions and I encountered a large group of Japanese tourists taking hundreds of pictures of a Dutch windmill. We found this to be, on the one hand, amusing, and on the other, excessive and annoying. I began talking with the Japanese tour guide about this. She explained that living on an island means that travel is more restricted and off-island vacations are relatively rare for most people. In addition, she indicated that pictures are a way of sharing experiences with family and friends back home, who may expect and eagerly await a slide show. When we heard these explanations, my colleagues and I were embarrassed by our cultural encapsulation, and we began to see the behavior in a completely different light. Since then, I have tried to take special care in recording and reflecting on my observations when a client is culturally different. In the following sections, remember that your impressions come through your own cultural lens. When you have the chance to record your observations with real clients, revisit this section and reflect on what you may be bringing to the picture you are painting.

What to Observe

Speech   Note all aspects of a client's speaking voice. Does the client's voice annoy or soothe? Is the client's tone slow and monotonous or excessively labile? Does the client have an accent of any kind? Is the client's speech hurried or forced? Does the client have a speech impediment of any kind? Does the client speak without listening?

Client's clothing   Does the client wear expensive, stylish, well-coordinated, seductive, old, or outmoded clothing? Is there anything odd or unusual about it? Does the client reflect a particular style (artistic, conservative, etc.)? Is clothing appropriate to the weather (several layers on a hot day), and is it appropriate to the occasion? Does the client wear a little jewelry? A lot of jewelry? Does the client wear appropriate amounts of makeup? Does the client wear glasses or a hearing aid? Does the client's clothing suggest a different cultural background?

Grooming   Is the client clean? Does the client exhibit body odor and a general disregard for personal hygiene? Even if the client shows concern for cleanliness, is there a disorganized appearance to the hair and clothing, perhaps suggesting disorderliness, depression, or lack of social awareness? Do cultural differences in grooming account for the client's appearance? If the client is a child, what does grooming suggest about family environment?

Posture, build, and gait   What is the client's posture during the session? What is the position of the shoulders and head? Does the client sit in a rigid or a slouched position or with head in hands? Does the client's posture reflect the present emotional state, or is the client's posture indicative of a more long-term state of anxiety, tension, or depression?

Build refers to the body habitus. Is the client physically attractive? Is the client obese, muscular, or thin? Are there any unusual physical characteristics, such as excessive acne, physical disabilities, or prostheses?

Gait means the person's manner of walking. Does the client's manner of walking reflect an emotional state, such as depression or anxiety? Does the client's walk seem to indicate confidence or low self-esteem? Is the client tentative and cautious in finding a seat?

Facial expressions   Facial expressions include movements of the eyes, lips, forehead, and mouth. Do the client's feelings show, or are the client's expressions flat, devoid of any emotion? Shakespeare wrote that "the eyes are the windows of the soul." Does the client maintain direct eye contact or avoid it? Do the eyes fill with tears? Does the client smile or laugh during the session? Is the brow wrinkled? Could the client's facial expressions be due to cultural injunctions about eye contact or posture with one seen as an authority?

Other bodily movements   A client may show anxiety by twisting tissue or by tapping restlessly with fingers, toes, or legs. One important way in which people express themselves is through their hand movements. Fritz Perls, the founder of

Gestalt therapy, was fond of making clients aware of how bodily movements expressed their inner conflicts and impulses (Perls, 1959, p. 83).

General appearance In writing an assessment of the client, it is sometimes useful to note initial holistic impressions, which may become less noticeable as treatment progresses—for example, "The client appeared much older than his stated age," "The client appeared to be very precise and neat and seemed to carefully consider all of his statements before speaking," "I had the feeling that the client was a super salesman." Many of these holistic impressions are due to cultural differences. Are you judging the client based on your own upbringing?

Feelings of the helper Basing his observations on Harry Stack Sullivan's (1968) theories, Timothy Leary (1957) hypothesized that we react automatically and unconsciously to the communications of others. Our reaction, in turn, triggers the other person's next response. We tend to instinctively react in a positive, friendly manner to individuals whom we find attractive and friendly. Similarly, we instinctively respond negatively to individuals who are combative or aloof. They, in turn, become more abrasive and the cycle continues. These *interpersonal reflexes* (Shannon & Guerney, 1973) occur outside of awareness and are rarely discussed, but they can be very important in the helping relationship and in the client's social world.

If the helper finds himself or herself becoming annoyed with the client, is it possible that most of the client's social contacts have the same response? What would motivate the client to push people away? Is the client even aware of his or her effect on others? According to Ernst Beier (Beier & Young, 1998), the helper can learn to use his or her personal feelings as an assessment instrument. It requires detaching and not reacting to the client's overtures. Instead, think about how others in the client's world must feel about the client and record this information to add to the assessment.

Questioning

Asking too many questions was criticized earlier as being apt to strain the relationship between client and helper. In fact, the most common mistake for beginning helpers is relying on questions in the relationship-building stage, rather than taking the necessary time to understand the client and provide an atmosphere of openness and trust. On the other hand, introductory questions are extremely helpful in signaling the transition to the assessment phase once a relationship is established. Questioning is an important part of the assessment process because answers to direct and indirect questions are part and parcel of taking personal and sexual histories, structuring genograms, and allowing the client to elaborate on his or her construction of the problem. It is not that questions are inherently bad; it is just that they are used too often by beginning helpers and at the wrong time.

Questioning is an art (Goldberg, 1998). When used artfully, questions can be therapeutic devices to spur the client's thinking or stimulate action. Questions can also be used to gain valuable information and to focus the client on the agreed-upon goals. They serve an "orienting" function in that they tell the client what is important (Tomm, 1988). Following are some questions frequently asked by helpers early in the assessment stage in order to begin focusing on a client's concerns.

"How can I help you?"
"Where would you like to begin?"
"What prompted you to make today's appointment?"
"Has something happened in the last few days or weeks that persuaded you that
    help was needed?"
"What is it that you want to stop doing or do less of?"
"What is it that you want to begin to do or do more of?"
"What would your life be like if the problem were solved?"

Genograms

The genogram is a pictorial representation of the client's family tree. It quickly shows
a family's history by depicting current and past relationships. Figure 10.4 shows
the symbols used to construct the genogram, and Figure 10.5 is an example of a
completed genogram for a client, Bob. Figure 10.6 is a skeletal genogram you can use
as a template.

When a client comes from a large family or one with many siblings or stepsiblings,
the genogram can assist the helper in identifying the individuals involved instead
of continually quizzing the client. The genogram is therapeutic when a client's main
concerns are family problems because the client gains insight into the issues by
describing them to the helper as the genogram is constructed. Finally, the genogram is
a tool to explore specific issues such as family influences on career choice (Dickson &
Parmerlee, 1980; Okiishi, 1987), alcoholism, or abuse (Armsworth & Stronck, 1998;
Young & Long, 1998).

Reasons to Consider Using the Genogram

1. To identify cultural and ethnic influences on the client
2. To represent the strengths and weaknesses in relationships between family
   members
3. To understand the present household composition and the relationships
   among the client's household, previous marriages, and past generations
4. To discover the presence of family disturbances that might be affecting the
   client, including alcoholism, abuse, divorces, suicides, sexual abuse, schisms
   and skews in marital relationships, mental illness in the family, and so on
5. To uncover sex role and other family expectations on the client
6. To assess economic and emotional support resources for the client
7. To identify repeated patterns in the client's relationships
8. To determine the effects of birth order and sibling rivalry on the client
9. To make the client and helper aware of family attitudes concerning health
   and illness
10. To identify extrafamilial sources of support
11. To trace family patterns of certain preferences, values, and behaviors, such as
    legal problems, sexual values, obesity, and job problems
12. To identify problem relationships
13. To document historical traumas, such as suicides, deaths, abuse, and losses
    of pregnancies

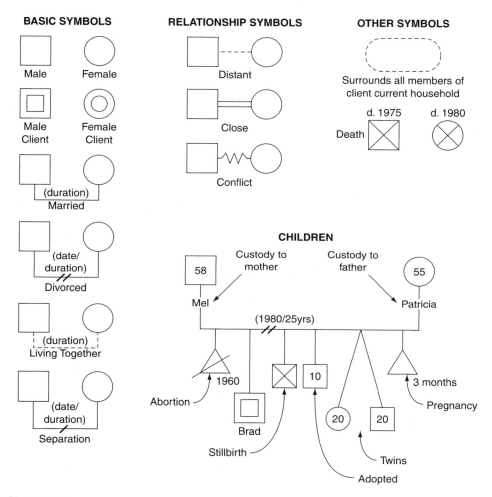

Figure 10.4
Genogram Symbols

Adapted from Figure 4.2, page 93, *Counseling Methods and Techniques: An Eclectic Approach* by Mark E. Young. Columbus, OH: Merrill/MacMillan, 1992.

Stop and Reflect

Construct your own genogram using Figure 10.6. Copy the skeleton on a separate piece of paper and begin by filling in your grandparents' names and ages in the appropriate row. Note that men are squares and women are circles. Now fill in your parents' names in the boxes of the "parents" row and then bring down a line for each sibling in your original nuclear family along the line that connects your parents. When a person has been married more than once, his or her previous spouses are connected to that person horizontally. In the sample genogram in Figure 10.5, Bob is the

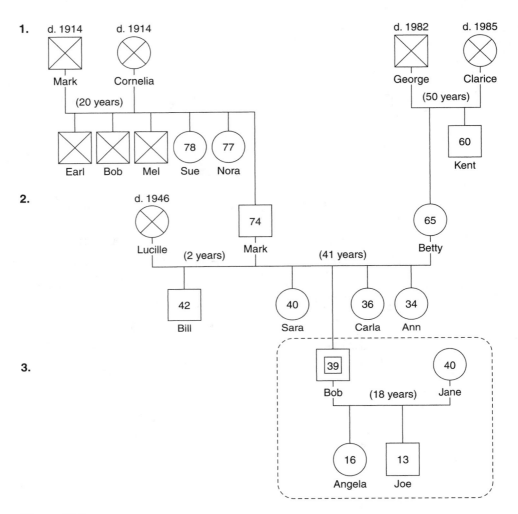

Figure 10.5
Sample Genogram

third of five children. His box is dropped to show a fourth generation, his children, but because Bob is the client, we place him in Generation 3 ("Generation of Client" in Figure 10.6). Drop your own box, below that of your siblings, if you wish to show your own marriage or children. Indicate your present nuclear family by encircling it with dashes as shown in the example in Figure 10.5.

Check your drawing to make sure you have not missed any family members in the three generations. If parents or grandparents have been married more than once, place their other spouses to the side (see the example of Lucille and Mark in Figure 10.5). Put an X in the box or circle of anyone who is deceased. Place the ages of each person in his or her box or circle. Place the approximate years of marriage and make slashes to indicate divorces or separations. Put this information on the

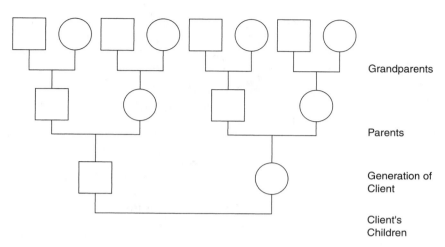

Grandparents

Parents

Generation of
Client

Client's
Children

Figure 10.6
Skeletal Genogram

lines between spouses as shown in Figure 10.5 (see also Figure 10.4, which shows a divorce).

Now review the genogram symbols in Figure 10.4. Add any additional symbols that you wish to include in your family genogram. Specifically, you may wish to depict relationships within your family as shown in the section entitled "Relationship Symbols."

When you have completed the genogram, answer the following questions:

1. What cultural or ethnic background characterizes each person in your family tree?
2. How do you think culture and history affect the values and rules around which your family functions?
3. Are differences in backgrounds ever the source of conflict in the family? Does cultural heritage beget closeness or conflict? If there are different cultural influences in your family, are you more a part of one specific side of the family, or do you embrace more than one culture?

Conducting an Interview Using a Brief Intake Form

One way of getting started in the assessment process is to systematically record your impressions about a client on some kind of standard form. A form is a good training device because it is a check to make sure you have not missed the big problems. In this chapter, you will find a prototype form to use for reflection, case presentation, and treatment planning. The form asks you to jot down your evaluation of the client's (A) affective or emotional issues and status; (B) behavior deficits, excesses, and strengths; and (C) thinking or cognitions. These three items will be referred to as A, B, and C, for short. In addition, you are asked to accumulate data about the client's (1) developmental level, (2) family history, (3) cultural and religious/spiritual background, and (4) physical challenges and strengths.

Within this brief assessment questionnaire, several trigger questions are embedded in each area. These are questions that prompt the helper to reflect on the client's answers and seek assistance from a supervisor or consider referring the client to a more qualified practitioner. The trigger questions are:

1. Does the client meet criteria for a major emotional disorder such as anxiety or depression? Such a diagnosis might require referral or special treatment, including medication.
2. Does the client show any evidence of suicidal thinking, have a history of self-destructive behavior, or indicate thoughts or history of harming others? If so, a close assessment must be made by a qualified practitioner.
3. Does the client show any evidence of thought disorders, highly unusual thought processes, hallucinations, or delusions (bizarre fixed false beliefs)? If so, the client may require a medication evaluation and specific support groups.
4. Is the relationship between helper and client moving toward a healthy alliance? Have cultural differences been addressed? Does the client feel the helper is a trustworthy and credible resource for helping to achieve treatment goals?
5. Could any medical problems or organic brain syndromes be causing or contributing to the client's problem?
6. Does the client need treatment for substance abuse?

Let us now take a brief look at each of the seven elements (ABC-1234) and why it is critical to collect these data on each client during a screening or intake interview.

A. Affective Assessment

Clients come for help because of overwhelming and confused emotions. They are seeking relief from anxiety, grief, depression, and anger. Whether these are disabling conditions or merely uncomfortable, the helper assesses the intensity, frequency, and duration of these negative emotions in order to plan effective treatment. It is similarly important to identify the client's positive affective states. If clients can identify the times when they feel satisfied and happy, they can attempt to re-create those states.

B. Behavioral Assessment

Many people are seeking assistance for *excessive* behaviors, ranging from smoking to sexual addiction. Others need help in learning new behaviors such as social skills or time management. Clients also have "positive addictions" or healthy habits that should be noted. If a client has a regular exercise regime, meditates, or is very organized, these behaviors can be identified and encouraged.

C. Cognitive Assessment

Cognition includes the client's thinking, images, and meanings (the client's worldview). For example, a client may be engaging in negative thinking and negative imagery about an upcoming event. By uncovering this in an assessment interview, the helper can help the client find specific constructive thoughts and images as an antidote. In this section of the intake form, the helper records intellectual deficits and strengths, any specific learning problems, or head injuries.

1. Developmental Issues

Helpers must have a basic knowledge of human development as major theorists such as Piaget, Erikson, Loevinger, and Kohlberg have described it. Then assessment and helping techniques can be modified to deal with life-stage differences. In this section, people are grouped according to the common age-related categories of children, adolescents, adults, and older people. The descriptions of these life stages are generalizations about groups of people. The discussion is meant to urge you to consider critical developmental issues. However, it is important to remember that each person is unique. There are some octogenarians who are physically and intellectually younger than their chronological ages; some 7-year-olds demonstrate an unusual amount of intellectual and emotional maturity.

Children   There are many specialized assessment and helping techniques that are specific to children (Sattler, 1998). School functioning for children is analogous to occupational functioning in adults and is an indicator of overall adjustment. Contact a teacher for insight into a child's behavior toward adults and peers. To understand a child's family and his or her relationship with parents, interview parents, grandparents, and siblings.

Adolescents   Adolescents are challenging but also intriguing and rewarding to work with. Issues of trust and betrayal, freedom, autonomy, dangerous behavior, and anger are just beneath the surface of their words. When assessing adolescent problems, it is particularly important to touch on drug and alcohol abuse, sexual behavior, and relationships with parents and siblings. Most adolescent deaths are not due to medical problems but to automobile accidents, suicide, homicide, and substance abuse. These areas must be carefully addressed in the assessment stage.

College students   College students are characterized by their focus on issues of self-esteem, separation from their family of origin, and their strong need to form close bonds with others. The helper who works with college students deals with alcohol and drug abuse, suicide attempts, eating disorders, intense love relationships and their dismal aftermath, problems with parents, pregnancy, and sexually transmitted diseases.

Older people   Understanding the problems of older people requires consideration of their unique histories. It is likely that your parents or grandparents lived through the Great Depression and World War II. These two events shaped their thinking and worldview. It instilled in them a cautious approach to life, especially where money is concerned. When choosing a career, for example, they might counsel, "Have something to fall back on!" In short, to know an older person, it may be important to get a sense of the time they grew up in because it affected their perspective on life and is the basis for their view of the future. Helpers who work with older people deal with issues of loss, deteriorating health, thoughts about lost opportunities, and fears associated with loneliness. Helpers frequently also assist older people who are trying to create new lives following the death of a spouse, who need to let go of past experiences, or who have disappointing family relationships.

2. Family History

Our family histories provide a deep insight into who we are. Our ideas of gender roles, parental roles, and what is normal and good all come from our original family group, or our *family of origin*. The visual nature of the genogram makes it an efficient way to understand a client's family history. In the absence of a genogram, you may simply want to question clients concerning important stressors in their family now and in the past.

A family history of depression, suicide, anxiety disorders, substance abuse, and sexual abuse is valuable information, as it may shed light on the client's current concerns. Our ideas about normal family functioning, what it means to be a spouse and parent, are based on our own families. Taking the time to get a sense of the client's family will be rewarded by insights into the forces that shaped the client's worldview.

3. Cultural and Religious/Spiritual Background

Besides identifying a client's ethnicity, race, or class, it is important to understand the client's acculturation. A client's acculturation is the degree to which he or she personally identifies with a particular culture. For example, two children in a bicultural family may feel close to one parent's culture but not the other's. In addition, a girl whose parents are Russian Jews but who was born in the United States might conceivably have a minimal relationship to her family's culture and religion. Following are some additional questions that stimulate thinking about the degree of a client's cultural identity and its impact on the helping process:

- What is the client's cultural/ethnic identity?
- What is the client's religion or spiritual orientation?
- How closely does the client identify with his or her cultural or ethnic background?
- According to the client, how is seeking help from a helper viewed within his or her culture?
- How can the client's goals and problems be viewed in a way that is compatible with his or her cultural background?
- How does the client's upbringing regarding appropriate gender roles relate to the presenting problems?
- Is the client's culture a source of pride or shame?

4. Physical Challenges and Strengths

For our purposes, physical challenges include medical diagnoses, physical disabilities and limitations, and drug and alcohol use and abuse. All these may have physical, social, and psychological effects. Focus on the client's physical assets and abilities in this category, too.

Medical diagnoses A number of physical disorders have psychological effects. A helper can go wrong by trying to work on a symptom that turns out to be the result of a treatable medical condition (Pollak, Levy, & Breitholtz, 1999). For example, a brain tumor or other serious problem, rather than stress, may be the cause of a client's headaches. Symptoms of depression, anxiety, sexual disorders, irritability, weight gain or loss, headaches, and fatigue suggest that the client should receive a thorough medical checkup as part of the helping process. It is irresponsible and unethical to treat someone for these symptoms until medical causes have been ruled out. When in doubt, helpers should refer clients for medical evaluation. On the other side of the coin, be sure to note positive health and wellness behaviors such as good diet and physical exercise.

Physical disabilities   The term *physical disabilities* suggests that there are normal and disabled people. Perhaps the term should be "physical differ-abilities," because abilities are probably better described on a continuum rather than within a disabled/abled dichotomy. It is not as important to know that a person is in a wheelchair as it is to know how he or she sees himself or herself in relation to other people, how he or she functions, and how this way of getting around affects that person socially and professionally.

Not all disabilities are as obvious as a prosthesis or wheelchair. Heart conditions, multiple sclerosis, arthritis, diabetes, and a myriad of other problems have an effect on mood, behavior, and thinking. It is helpful to know the normal psychological effects of common diseases, and it is important to explore with a client the impact of the disease on his or her overall functioning.

Drug and alcohol use and abuse   Alcohol and other drug use is difficult to assess because clients consciously and unconsciously minimize the amount they report. Prescription and nonprescription drug taking must also be discussed with clients because the mental, emotional, and behavioral effects can make other issues worse. For example, such medication can affect school or work functioning and family relationships. Once substance abuse is identified, many helpers try to treat this first because continued substance abuse undermines progress on other issues.

Because clients may not want to bring up substance abuse, one way to start a discussion and gain important information is by asking direct questions or by asking the client to fill out a questionnaire on substance use and history (see Evans, 1998). Table 10.2 contains a list of additional questions that you might use to follow up on suspected substance abuse.

Summarizing Important Background Information

Figure 10.7 shows a blank copy of the ABC-1234 Intake Form. It can be used as a worksheet to summarize data collected about the client in the initial interview. Figure 10.8 shows a completed form on a fictitious client. Each section should contain problems and strengths. It is important to emphasize the client's abilities as well as disabilities, because strengths give the helper useful information about what methods and techniques might be most effective. For example, a client who is an excellent reader and enjoys books might profit from bibliotherapy. A client who has

Table 10.2
Some Key Interview Questions for Substance Abuse

"Do any of your friends and family think you have a substance abuse problem?"
"Have you ever been arrested for driving under the influence?"
"Have you ever been physically injured or had an accident while using?"
"Have you ever broken any bones as an adult? If so, how?"
"How much do you drink or use each day?"
"Have you ever had a blackout or amnesia while using?"
"Has your substance abuse changed any of your close relationships or affected your work?"
"Looking back at your family tree, which relatives have had a substance abuse problem?"
"Have you ever felt the need to cut back on your use of substances?"

Demographic Data

Name: _____

Age: _____

Date of Birth: _____

Street Address: _____

City: _____ State: _____ Zip: _____

Home Phone: _____

Work Phone: _____ Okay to call at work?   Yes/No

Level of Education: _____

Occupation: _____

Marital Status: _____

Children's Names and Ages: _____

Reason for Referral: _____

Referral Source: _____

Client's Statement of the Problem

Write down a paragraph in the client's own words that describes why he or she came for help.

A. Affective Assessment

What major and minor emotions are troubling the client? _____

Is the client sad? Angry? Fearful? Anxious? _____

Are these due to the helping interview or longer-term states? _____

What emotional states does the client wish to reduce? _____

How does the client normally handle negative emotions?_____

What emotional strengths does the client have?_____

Trigger: Does the client require treatment for depression, mania, or severe anxiety?

_____

B. Behavioral Assessment

What does the client want to do that he or she is not doing? _____

What behaviors does the client wish to reduce or eliminate? _____

What behaviors does the client need to increase? _____

What behaviors does the client want to learn? _____

What habits does he or she want to eliminate?_____

What positive behaviors does he or she want to strengthen? _____

Has the client ever engaged in violence toward self or others? _____

Identify the client's strengths and positive social and health behaviors. _____

Trigger: Does the client now require treatment for dangerous behavior toward self or others? _____

C. Cognitive Assessment

Does the client show any signs of memory problems or other problems in thinking?_____

Does the client succeed in a typical classroom environment? _____

Does the client report *negative or positive* imagery about the problem? _____

What rational and irrational thoughts were detected in the client's statements?_____

Does the client show distorted thinking patterns such as overgeneralization, black-and-white thinking, etc.?_____

How would you characterize the client's worldview and values?_____

What positive thinking patterns exist? _____

Trigger: Does the client show any evidence of thought disorders, highly unusual thought processes, hallucinations, or delusions (bizarre fixed false beliefs)? Does the client think about hurting self or others? _____

Figure 10.7

ABC-1234 Intake Form Worksheet

1. Developmental Issues

How did the client handle major maturational milestones of childhood? _____

Compared with the client's peers, how is the client adjusting to normal developmental issues? _____

Describe the client's maturational level in terms of career, intellectual, sexual, moral, and social development. _____

Do any of the client's developmental issues relate to the statement of the problem? _____

2. Family History (Attach Genogram if Possible)

What does the genogram reveal about the client's family history as it relates to the statement of the problem? _____

How many brothers and sisters does the client have? What is the client's birth order? _____

What problems in family relationships are revealed by the genogram or by questioning?

What family support does the client have? _____

Is the client on good terms with family members? _____

Has the client achieved a healthy interdependence with family compared with others of the client's culture? _____

What traumatic events have affected the family? _____

What family changes have occurred recently? _____

What strengths has the client gained from his or family background? _____

3. Cultural and Religious/Spiritual Background

What is the client's cultural/ethnic identity? _____

What is the client's religion or spiritual orientation? _____

How closely does the client identify with his or her cultural or ethnic background? _____

How culturally acceptable is it for the client to seek professional help? _____

Does the client's attitude regarding appropriate gender roles relate to the presenting problems? _____

Is the client able to identify the positive and healthy aspects of his or her culture and the part they might play in solving problems? _____

Trigger: Does the client appear skeptical that the helping process and the helper are credible methods for achieving the stated goals? _____

4. Physical Challenges and Strengths

Does the client report any medical issues or disabilities? _____

How does the client view himself or herself in relation to diseases or disabilities? _____

What is the extent of the client's current use of alcohol and drugs? Previous use? _____

What is the client's level of knowledge about substance abuse? _____

Does the client have a family history of substance abuse? _____

Does the client have a good diet and physical self-care habits such as exercise? _____

Trigger: Could any medical condition be causing or contributing to the client's statement of the problem? _____

Trigger: Does the client need treatment for substance abuse? _____

Treatment Goals (Mutually Agreed Upon) Treatment Plans (Proposed Interventions)

1. _____   1. _____
2. _____   2. _____
3. _____   3. _____

Signatures: _____ Date: _____

Figure 10.7
(Continued)

Demographic Data

Name: Claudia O'Reilly

Age: 35

Date of Birth: 11/13/69

Street Address: 132 Shade St.

City: New Brunswick   State: OH   Zip: 45123

Home Phone: 614-555-2194

Work Phone: None   Okay to call at work?   Yes/No

Level of Education: H.S. diploma

Occupation: Homemaker

Marital Status: Married

Children's Names and Ages: Amber age 6, Heather age 4

Reason for Referral: Pastor felt she needed individual help to deal with feelings of depression.

Referral Source: Pastor, R. Brown, Central Community Church

Client's Statement of the Problem

"My main problem is learning to accept my husband for the way he is. I get very depressed over the fact that he does not seem to want to spend time with me and the kids. He is not motivated at work. He smokes marijuana and drinks with his friends. Because I don't work, I have no say-so about the money. I go to church and to Alanon and that is my total social life. I would like to go out more with him and have a life."

A. Affective Assessment

Client reported lack of direction in her life. She feels ineffective in her work taking care of the children and her home. Client also indicated feelings of sadness over her marital problems. At times, she reported feelings of "frustration" with her husband that would best be described as anger and resentment. She did not meet *DSM-IV* criteria for a mental disorder associated with her feelings of depression.

On the positive side, the client reports that religious activities, including attending church and reading her Bible, have helped her during her worst "down" periods.

B. Behavioral Assessment

Client admits that she lacks assertiveness skills. She believes that she "sulks" at times as a way of getting her husband to respond. She wants to "go out more and have a life." By this, she means that she would like to return to school, eventually go to work, and have some free time outside of the house. The client has no history of harming herself or others and does not appear to be a danger to herself or others. The client appears to be ready to return to school and has an interest in reading and learning.

C. Cognitive Assessment

The client shows no apparent problems with memory. She reports being an A and B student in high school. In fact, the client is aware of her above-average scholastic abilities, but sometimes berates herself for not developing her mind earlier in life. In assessing the client's thinking about herself, she reports low self-esteem. She is perfectionistic in her thinking and often engages in black-and-white thinking. For example, she said that she was not a good housekeeper because her home is rarely spotless like her mother's. She had difficulty seeing that her expectations were rather high for someone with two young children. She believes that expressing her feelings and stating her preferences is "generally rude."

Figure 10.8
ABC-1234 Intake Form Sample

1. Developmental Issues

The client is approaching midlife and feels unfulfilled in her work as a wife and mother. She was married at 25, but says she lived a sheltered life before that, living at home with her mother. She wants to work outside the home and wishes to begin training of some kind.

The client and her husband have been married for 10 years. The marriage was apparently a happy one in the first 2 years, but there have been major problems and upheavals over the last 5 years. Although the marriage is now stable in that there is no talk of divorce, apparently both partners are dissatisfied with the way they interact.

The client and her family are in transition because the youngest child is now entering preschool and will be gone most of the day. With two children in school, there are new pressures, including transportation. Because the children are in school, the client will also have some additional free time on her hands and conceivably might have enough time to take classes. She has received career testing at the community college and is interested in becoming a dental hygienist.

2. Family History

The client's parents were divorced 20 years ago. She has two older sisters, both of whom work in professional occupations. The client's mother is a retired bookkeeper, and her father is still working as a building contractor. The client related that as she was growing up, both of her parents, but especially her mother, had high, even impossible, standards for all the children. She feels that she has let them down by not achieving.

Today, Claudia and her mother are closer. Her mother helps with the children, and Claudia can talk to her about most problems. Both of Claudia's sisters live out of state, but she receives some support via telephone.

The client is most disturbed by the lack of support she receives from her husband. Her opinion is that he does not wish to be a part of the family. The family has little money, and she is angry that he spends any amount on alcohol and drugs. He gives her money with which she pays the bills. She regards him as her "third child." About 1 year ago, she began attending Alanon. She claims that his drinking is not as much of a problem as it was a year ago, but that he smokes marijuana daily and this bothers her a great deal.

3. Cultural and Religious/Spiritual Background

The client's family members consider themselves to be "Southern." Her grandparents and even her father at one time worked as peanut farmers in Georgia, where the family originated. The client had a strict religious upbringing, a fundamentalist Protestant denomination. She has continued to be a member of this church, and she takes her daughters every Sunday, although her husband does not attend. Her religion is definitely a support for her. Besides the time she spends at church, she also prays regularly and feels that her depression is reduced by both activities.

One of the cultural/gender issues surfaces when the client talks about "not being lady-like." She sometimes describes other people in this way and has indicated she has trouble standing up for herself because she does not want to "act like a man." In addition, the client has very traditional views about the roles of husband and wife that may clash with the mainstream of society and her own goals to have a more personally fulfilling life.

4. Physical Challenges and Strengths

The client has suffered from periods of chronic fatigue. Her physician indicates that this is not solely the result of feeling depressed, but is associated with an endocrine dysfunction. She takes medication for the condition but occasionally has periods when she is unable to do much for 2 or 3 days.

Figure 10.8
(Continued)

The client has no regular exercise regime and eats a diet that is very high in fat, salt, and sugar. She claims that she has to cook what her husband likes and so she cannot really change her eating patterns. The client has never used drugs or alcohol.

Treatment Goals (Helper and Client Contract) Treatment Plans

1. Increase assertive behavior	1. Client will be referred to assertiveness training class.
2. Decrease depression, increase self-esteem	2. Individual sessions will decrease depression and increase self-esteem.
3. Improve marital relationship	3. Following treatment for items 1 and 2, client will be referred with husband to couples counseling.

Signatures: _____ Date: _____

Figure 10.8
ABC-1234 Intake Form Sample *(Continued)*

a strong religious background can be implored to use this strength in understanding and dealing with fear or depression.

The intake form begins with a statement by the client, indicating what issue(s) propelled him or her to seek help and what he or she hopes to achieve. It is useful to record this statement in the client's own words because the client's view of the problem is critical to treatment planning. Let us say, for example, that in the client's statement she indicates that she is mostly concerned with her adolescent son's marijuana abuse. Even if the helper focuses on what seem to be more critical problems, the client may not feel that she has received the treatment she has asked for.

Each section of the intake form contains a trigger question. This question, when answered positively, prompts a referral to specialized treatment or, at the minimum, identifies an issue that should be discussed with a supervisor. The trigger question is a reminder to look for serious issues that should be dealt with first or that might jeopardize the helping relationship.

Summary

Assessment means gathering information about a client. The gathering begins the moment a client walks through the door. We observe, ask questions, review tests, and receive medical data and reports from social service agencies. We may even interrogate family and friends. One of the pressures from the beginning is to organize the flood of information from multiple sources. This process involves listing and then organizing problems in priority order. This is the process of treatment planning.

Assessment helps both client and helper. Assessment helps the client discover events that may be related to the problem which they may never have identified or recognize issues that were previously hidden. The helper uses assessment data to plan useful and realistic goals, identify the best treatment for the client's particular problem, determine whether the client is suicidal or dangerous, and become aware of client strengths and unique attributes.

The final section of this chapter presents four beginning assessment tools in some detail: Observation, Questioning, Conducting an Interview Using a Brief Intake Form, and the Genogram. Also, the Mental Status examination, a time honored method of acquiring basic data about a client, is outlined here.

Exercises for In and Out of Class

Group Exercise

In groups of three, one student acts as the helper, another is the client, and a third observes. The helper interviews a fellow student using the intake form. Before the interview, the client and observer identify and agree on a problem that the client is hoping to work on or that is fabricated for this exercise. The client should take a moment to look over the intake form and think about answers to key questions. The client should retain his or her real identity so that the other aspects of the intake are authentic even if the problem itself is concocted. After the exercise, the client gives specific feedback to the helper on the following issues:

a. Was the helper able to intersperse questioning and listening? Or was the interview too businesslike?

b. Did the helper find the key problems? If not, why not?
c. What other suggestions do you have for the helper in terms of the quality of the interview?

Within your group, discuss the following questions:

- What is your reaction to the use of a standardized form such as this one?
- What important areas do you think are missing that you would have like to explore?
- How long did it take to complete the interview?
- Did the client react negatively to answering so many questions? If so, how might this be handled better?

Additional Exercise

Conduct a classroom discussion on gender issues in assessment. In small groups, discuss popular books on gender issues. Do these books help people understand the role of gender in the helping process, or do they reinforce stereotypes? In your group, discuss the importance of including an assessment of gender-related issues in the assessment process. As you look at the intake form for Claudia (Figure 10.8), how important are these issues for her? If you were helping Claudia, would you bring up her perceptions about gender role? Why or why not?

Homework

Homework 1

Complete a genogram for yourself using the skeletal form in this chapter. Use the instructions in the "Stop and Reflect" section as a guide. Next to each person in your genogram, list his or her jobs or careers. If you do not know this information, do some research by asking other family members. Can you identify a family pattern in the selection of vocation? To go into a bit more depth, look up the Holland codes for each occupation in the *Dictionary of Holland Occupational Codes* (Gottfredson, Holland, & Ogawa, 1996) and see if you can see a family transmission of certain traits.

Homework 2

Search the Internet for resources for dealing with people who are HIV positive. What limitations do such people experience? What mythologies affect the way people look at them? What challenges would this present socially and professionally for an affected person? Looking at the various web sites, what must a helper know about current treatment, testing, and prevention? How would you feel about working with someone who tested positive for HIV? What issues might you expect them to bring to the helping session?

Journal Starters

1. Think back on assessment experiences in your own life. These may range from encounters with a high school guidance counselor to an intake interview at the college counseling center to a College Board Examination. What important decisions have you made based on testing or assessment results? What decisions have others made about you based on testing? Discuss any negative or positive experiences. How do these affect your views and feelings about testing clients?
2. This chapter suggests asking clients about religious and spiritual beliefs. How important are these issues to you? How

Homework 3. Assessment of Children

Do a brief research study on the symptoms of depression in children. Use articles, books, and Internet sources. What is different about the way that children express and experience depression?

often have you been able to discuss this part of your life with others? If you tend to hide this part of yourself, how do you think this affects others? How do you think others might react if they knew your religious or spiritual beliefs? If you were a client, how important would it be to discuss spirituality? If your spiritual or religious beliefs are not very well developed, how would you want a helper to approach this area?

For more journal ideas, as well as more practice with assessment, refer to Chapter 10 in *Exercises in the Art of Helping*.

References

Anastasi, A., & Urbina, S. (1997). *Psychological testing* (7th ed.). New York: Macmillan.

Armsworth, M. W., & Stronck, K. (1998). Intergenerational effects of incest on parenting: Skills, abilities, and attitudes. *Journal of Counseling and Development, 77*, 303–313.

Beier, E. G., & Young, D. M. (1998). *The silent language of psychotherapy* (3rd ed.). Hawthorne, NY: Aldine de Gruyter.

Dickson, G. L., & Parmerlee, J. R. (1980). The occupational family tree: A career counseling technique. *School Counselor, 28*, 131–134.

Doyle, A. C. (1929). *Conan Doyle's best books* (Vol. 2). New York: Collier.

Drummond, R. J. (2000). *Appraisal procedures for counselors and helping professionals* (4th ed.). Upper Saddle River, NJ: Merrill/Prentice Hall.

Epstein, M. H. (1998). Assessing the emotional and behavioral strengths of children. *Reclaiming Children and Youth, 6*(4), 250–252.

Epstein, M. H., Harniss, M. K., Pearson, N., & Ryser, G. (1999). The Behavioral and Emotional Rating Scale: Test-retest and inter-rater reliability. *Journal of Child and Family Studies, 8*, 319–327.

Evans, W. N. (1998). Assessment and diagnosis of substance abuse disorders (SUDS). *Journal of Counseling and Development, 76*, 332–336.

Gladding, S. T. (2002). *Family therapy: History, theory, and practice* (3rd ed.). Upper Saddle River, NJ: Merrill/Prentice Hall.

Goldberg, M. C. (1998). *The art of the question: A guide to short-term question-centered therapy*. New York: Wiley.

Golden, C. J., & Hutchings, P. S. (1998). The mental status examination. In M. Hersen & V. Hasselt, *Basic interviewing: A practical guide for counselors and clinicians* (pp. 107–128). Mahwah, NJ: Lawrence Erlbaum.

Goleman, D. (1985). *Vital lies, simple truths: The psychology of self-deception.* New York: Simon & Schuster.

Gottfredson, G. D., Holland, J. L., & Ogawa, D. K. (1996). *Dictionary of Holland occupational codes* (3rd ed.). Odessa, FL: Psychological Assessment Resources.

Hohenshil, T. H. (1996). Role of assessment and diagnosis in counseling. *Journal of Counseling and Development, 75,* 64–67.

Hood, A. B., & Johnson, R. W. (1997). *Assessment in counseling: A guide to the use of psychological assessment procedures* (2nd ed.). Alexandria, VA: American Counseling Association.

Leary, T. (1957). *Interpersonal diagnosis of personality.* New York: Ronald.

Lopez, S. J., & Snyder, C. R. (2003). *Positive psychological assessment: A handbook of models and measures.* Washington, DC: American Psychological Association.

Lukas, S. (1993). *Where to start and what to ask: An assessment handbook.* New York: Norton.

Miller, S. D., Hubble, M. A., & Duncan, B. L. (Eds.). (1996). *Handbook of solution focused brief therapy.* San Francisco: Jossey-Bass.

Okiishi, R. W. (1987). The genogram as a tool in career counseling. *Journal of Counseling & Development, 66,* 139–143.

Othmer, E., & Othmer, S. C. (2002). *The clinical interview using DSM-IV-TR.* Washington, DC: American Psychiatric Publishing.

Palmer, S., & McMahon, G. (eds.). (1997). *Client assessment.* London: Sage.

Paniagua, F. A. (1998). *Assessing and treating culturally diverse clients: A practical guide* (2nd ed.). Thousand Oaks, CA: Sage.

Perls, F. S. (1959). *Gestalt therapy verbatim.* New York: Bantam Books.

Pollak, J., Levy, S., & Breitholtz, T. (1999). Screening for medical and neurodevelopmental disorders for the professional counselor. *Journal of Counseling & Development, 77,* 350–355.

Rosenhan, D. L. (1973). On being sane in insane places. *Science, 180,* 250–258.

Sattler, J. (1998). *Clinical and forensic interviewing of children and families.* San Francisco: Author.

Shannon, J., & Guerney, B. G., Jr. (1973). Interpersonal effects of interpersonal behavior. *Journal of Personality and Social Psychology, 26,* 142–150.

Sommers-Flanagan, J., & Sommers-Flanagan, R. (1995). Intake interviewing with suicidal patients: A systematic approach. *Professional Psychology, 30,* 1–7.

Snyder, C. R., & Lopez, S. J. (2002). *Handbook of positive psychology.* New York: Oxford.

Sullivan, H. S. (1968). *The interpersonal theory of psychiatry.* New York: W. W. Norton. (Original work published 1953).

Tomm, K. (1988). Interventive interviewing: Part III. Intending to ask lineal circular, strategic or reflexive questions? *Family Process, 27,* 1–15.

Whiston, S. C. (2000). *Principles and applications of assessment in counseling.* Belmont, CA: Wadsworth.

Witmer, J. M., & Sweeney, T. J. (1992). A holistic model for wellness and prevention over the life span. *Journal of Counseling and Development, 71,* 140–148.

Young, M. E., & Long, L. (1998). *Counseling and therapy for couples.* Pacific Grove, CA: Brooks/Cole.

Goal-Setting Skills

11

Until one is committed, there is hesitancy, the chance to draw back, always ineffectiveness. There is one elementary truth, the ignorance of which kills countless ideas and splendid plans. That the moment one commits oneself, then Providence moves too. All sorts of things occur to help one that would never otherwise have occurred. A whole stream of events issues from the decision, raising in one's favor all manner of unforeseen incidents and meetings and material assistance which no man could have dreamt would come his way. Whatever you do, or dream you can, begin it. Boldness has genius, power and magic in it. Begin it now.

Attributed to Goethe

I have always had Goethe's quote hanging in my office because it reminds me that my job is all about the power of new beginnings. If we are to really help, not only must we understand a client's problems, but we must also decrease demoralization and ignite hope. Identifying and achieving goals help the client gain confidence even if the objectives are rather modest. If one can achieve a small goal, then discouragement, the biggest enemy of change, is diminished (Frank & Frank, 1991).

Goal setting separates the tangled mass of a problem into manageable units. Once a few goals have been identified, future sessions have a focus and the client begins to see the light at the end of the tunnel. Hope begins to dawn because the client now views the amorphous mass of trouble as a set of solvable problems. Figure 11.1 shows the client's difficulties as they first appear in the opening sessions and later after the assessment and goal-setting stages. Through this process, the intangible cloud of problems has been broken into identifiable segments.

The second reason I like Goethe's quote is that it reminds me that commitment is required for success. To use an analogy, frequently clients have started a number of dry holes in their life, never sticking with something but trying many different solutions, digging several shallow holes. If you commit to a goal, you are digging deeply in the same place and you will eventually hit water.

By setting goals and sticking to them, the helper mobilizes the magic of the beginning and also receives the benefit of persistence. Thus, every helping session should focus on the client's goals. When clients know clearly what their goals are, they are much more likely to think about them and work on them between sessions because they know that they will be reporting at the next session.

In this chapter, you will be learning about when to set goals and how to know if the goals you and your client devise are constructive. In addition, we will look at two building

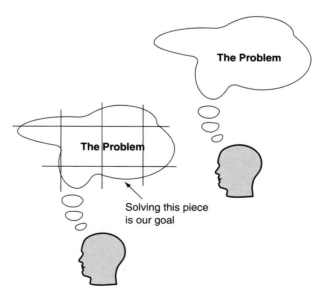

Figure 11.1
Breaking the Problem into Parcels and Working on One Part

block skills that narrow the discussion and identify the key issues: (1) focusing on the client and (2) boiling down the problem.

Where Do I Go from Here? Set Goals!

At this point in training, many students make the following statement: "I seem to be able to empathize with the client through the nonjudgmental listening cycle, but where do I go from here?" The helper feels that after a session or two, he or she has exhausted the client's story and explored the client's distress, but the helper does not feel that he or she has really helped. More than ever, the helper is tempted to give the client advice or introduce a new technique of some kind. The best answer to the question "Where do I go now?" is "Set goals!" When you have set goals, the techniques that you choose will make sense to the client. Much of the confusion about the purpose of the helping sessions will be alleviated. If these goals are mutually formed, the client will feel that he or she is part of the team and a partner in the therapeutic project. Partners are much more likely to make contributions than patients.

Why Must We Set Goals?

Steve de Shazer says that one of the most important questions a helper can ask is, "How will we know when therapy is done?" (de Shazer, 1990). This question can be answered in several ways. Some helpers use a time-limited approach, where the client attends counseling only for a certain amount of time or a certain number of sessions. Helping is finished when the time is up, typically between 6 and 20 sessions (Grayson, 1979). One of the reasons that time limits help, as Ben Johnson pointed out, is that the threat of execution tends to focus the mind. Setting a date for termination of the relationship motivates helper and client to work quickly to solve problems.

The problem with the time-limited approach is that we terminate the relationship regardless of success or failure. On the other hand, allowing the client to discontinue the helping process unilaterally makes the ending more of whimper than a bang.

If we have formulated goals at the beginning of the helping relationship, client and helper will have a shared vision throughout the relationship and will know when it is time to end. The best measure of whether the work is done is to determine if the treatment goals have been reached.

When to Set Goals

Certainly goal setting can be entered into prematurely. The helper must establish a relationship and conduct a thorough assessment. In this book it is said that helping progresses through five basic stages, as shown in Figure 11.2. At the initial relationship-building stage, most of the helper's activities are based on the invitational, reflecting, and challenging skills, which invite the client to open up and engage in self-examination within the confiding relationship. Early in the relationship, the helper does not narrow the field of discussion, but dares the client to go deeper and disclose more about a number of topics. In the assessment stage, the helper gets in-depth information about the client, the client's problems, and the environment. Without this knowledge, the goals might turn out to be irrelevant or ineffective if the

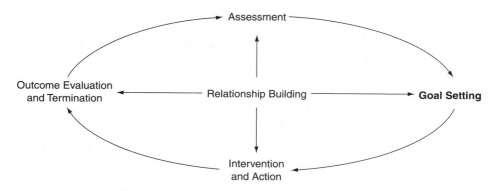

Figure 11.2
The Counseling Relationship: Goal Setting

client is not motivated, is being influenced by others, or is in a nonsupportive environment. As was mentioned in the last chapter, hidden areas of a client's life might not come to light without a thorough look at the client's history. These secrets, such as substance abuse, could seriously undermine the therapeutic plans.

While invitational and reflecting skills encourage clients to open up and assessment provides crucial data, the skills of the goal-setting stage are methods for narrowing down the information into a few specific tasks and goals. Like a funnel, helping begins with wide-ranging discussions, but eventually it narrows to focus on some particular areas. Goal setting is the stage when the helper begins to change the focus of counseling sessions from the introduction of new topics and assessment to the identification of the most crucial issues to be addressed in later sessions.

What Are the Characteristics of Constructive Goals?

This section is an argument for selecting goals that are specific, simple, stated positively (reflecting the presence of something rather than the absence of something), important, and realistic. Each of the following sections covers one of these topics, and each contains a set of questions or statements the helper can use to refine the goal with a client.

Goals Should Be Specific

Before a client and helper can agree on goals, the client must be questioned about which goals he or she wants to work on. Unfortunately, some clients have difficulty in selecting clear projects. Their goals when stated are vague and elusive (Rule, 1982). A vague goal is exemplified in this type of client statement: "I don't really know what's wrong; it's just that I am uneasy with everything," or, "I haven't been feeling right for about a year." A specific, clear, and easily restated goal sounds more like this: "I want to be able to be more assertive with my friends and coworkers."

When clients have clear goals, they make better progress (Borelli & Mermelstein, 1994; Hart, 1978). It has been found, for example, that having specific goals, even if they are difficult, is more likely to lead to progress than having fuzzy goals in the form of suggestions that you "do your best" or having no goals at all (Ponte-Allan & Giles, 1999; Smith, Hauenstein, & Buchanan, 1996). Specific goals make the direction of the helping process clear to the client. Clients then begin to feel that they have a handle on how to begin making changes. The client who is clear about goals will be able to work on them in and out of session.

It is not only clients that have trouble setting goals. For one reason or another, some helpers prefer to focus on the process of helping, letting the client deal with issues as they arise, rather than establishing landmarks of progress. This book argues that helping has changed radically in the last decade. Nearly all therapy is now brief therapy. Focusing on specific issues allows helpers to make the best use of therapeutic time. Besides these general advantages, at least five other favorable outcomes accrue from negotiating specific goal statements:

1. When based on specific individual goals for the client, the counseling process is more likely to be aimed at the client's needs rather than derived from the helper's theoretical orientation alone. A client who has the goal of overcoming shyness in work situations will perceive this as more relevant than "becoming self-actualized."
2. When goals are clearly understood by client and helper, the helper can determine if he or she possesses the requisite skills to continue with the counseling or if a referral is needed. Sometimes it is only during the goal-setting process that the helper realizes that the client needs some specialized assistance such as sex therapy, couples counseling, or even substance abuse treatment.
3. Many clients have problems imagining or envisioning success. Thinking about and imagining specific, positive outcomes have the effect of focusing the client's resources and energies and increasing hope. For this reason, goals that are stated positively such as the acquisition of skills are considered to be more useful than goals that are only focused on eliminating a negative behavior.
4. Identifying specific goals provides a rational basis for selecting treatment strategies that agencies, third-party providers, and supervisors can understand. Specific goals reassure others that the outcomes of helping will result in measurable changes.
5. Specific goals enable helpers to determine how successful helping has been for the client. Goal statements allow the client to gauge their progress as helping progresses. At termination, the helper can realistically evaluate the client's achievements.

Interventions to Help a Client Make a Goal More Specific
The following are helper statements that might help a client transform a vague goal into a clear objective:

- "I understand that you want to be 'happy,' but if you were happy, what would you be doing that you are not doing now?"
- "When you say things are not going well, specifically what things are you talking about?"
- "You say you want things to be better in your relationship with your husband. Specifically what would you like to be better?"

- "You have said that you want higher self-esteem. How would you like to see yourself exactly?"
- "Once you said that you live in the past. Where would you like to live?"

Goals Should Be Stated Positively

Frequently you will hear clients say they want to get over depression, stop drinking, stop binging on food, stop feeling anxious in social situations, reduce arguing, and so on. When goals are stated as negatives, they have less power to influence and motivate us. For example, I have heard it said that the goal of Alcoholics Anonymous is not "stopping drinking." AA's goal is to help people lead happy lives without alcohol. If you think about it, if we focus all our attention on "not drinking," we are still focusing on drinking! Instead, setting a goal to lead a happy life without alcohol allows us to consider what things we would like to have in our lives, what people we would like to interact with, and many other possible futures.

Another way of looking at this is that the helper should try to turn problems into goals. It seems like a small difference, but it would be much better to develop a list of goals than a list of problems. Although we must be willing to understand what problems brought a client for help, we should eventually focus on where we want to go. We spend too much time mapping the prison and too little time planning our freedom. When a clear vision of success is formulated, it is easier to see the steps needed to attain it (O'Hanlon & Weiner-Davis, 1989).

Questions to Help a Client Turn a Problem Into a Goal

We are now seeing that questions can be more complex than the open and closed varieties we discussed in an earlier chapter. These questions can be used to focus away from the problem and onto a future without the problem.

- "If a miracle occurred while you were asleep and during the night your problem just vanished, what would be some of the things you would first notice that let you know that the problem had disappeared?" (the miracle question) (O'Hanlon & Weiner-Davis, 1989).
- "You say that you and your husband argue constantly. If you were not arguing, what would you like to be doing?"
- "If the problem were solved, what would you be feeling, doing, or thinking that you are not now?"
- "If you were not procrastinating, what kinds of things would you be doing to get your work in on time?"
- "Suppose I gave you a job with all the money, benefits, and resources you required. Think about this for a moment and design your own job. Where would it be? With whom would you be working, and what would you be doing?" (Beck & Hoppock, 1998).

Goals Should Be Simple

A rule of thumb in developing a goal is that it should be extremely simple, so simple that "an eight-year-old could understand it" (Steiner, 1976). Developing simple goals that have a high probability of success is especially important when the client is demoralized. Whenever small goals are achieved, the client will be encouraged to continue with more difficult or more time-consuming projects (Dyer & Vriend, 1977). As Milton Erickson once said, "Therapy is often a matter of tipping the first domino" (Rossi, 1980, p. 454).

Many agencies require that helpers set quantifiable behavioral goals. Behavioral goals are concrete, measurable, and observable. They indicate the client's current behavior (baseline) and the target or goal behaviors that represent success. Here is an example of how you can develop a behavioral goal:

> **Client's Stated Goal (Client's Description of the Goal)** The client would like to increase comfort and decrease anxiety in social situations. The client's job entails several social functions each week, and they are necessary for his employment.
> **Target Behaviors (Described in Frequency, Duration, and Intensity)** The client would like to be able to attend a social gathering, hold two or more conversations (frequency), at least one of these with a woman, stay for a period of more than 1 hour (duration), and maintain a subjective distress level (SUDS) of 3 or 4. (The SUDS level is the client's feelings of discomfort in the situation and is measured on a 10-point scale of intensity, with 10 being the most uncomfortable and 1 being mildly uncomfortable.)
> **Baseline (Current Level of Target Behaviors)** The client states that he can currently remain at a party for only about 15 minutes before he leaves. He can hold a brief conversation with a male coworker, but has not recently talked to a woman in this setting. He currently experiences a SUDS level of 8 or 9 during social conversations with any woman.

Behavioral goals have advantages in that they specify exactly what must be achieved in the helping process. Many helpers will be required to set behavioral goals at their place of work because agencies use the numbers to quantify success. Other agencies look at goal attainment in other ways, including client feedback forms and helper and client assessments of success. Even when helping goals are not quantifiable, they can still be simple and concrete (Goodyear & Bradley, 1986). For example, the helper might not want to accept the following goal: "I want to improve my relationship with my mother." The helper might be willing, though, to accept the following revision: "Well, I would like to be able to politely stop her when she starts trying to give me advice." Whether goals are described behaviorally or not, simple goals make it easier for both helper and client to identify when helping is on the right track.

Questions to Help Simplify a Goal

The questions that simplify a goal are those that try to pin a client down to specific behaviors that the client would like to achieve and that would demonstrate success in a way that would be recognizable. For example:

- *Client's Goal:* "To decrease stress in my life."

Helper's questions:

- "What activities would help you reduce stress?"
- "How often would you like to engage in stress-reducing activities?"

- "How long would you like to meditate?"
- "If your stress level at work is a 10 now, what level of stress would represent an improvement to you?"

Goals Should Be Important to the Client

Clients will be successful when they are pursuing goals that are important to them (Barbrack & Maher, 1984; Bruce, 1984; Evans, 1984; Goodyear & Bradley, 1986; Hart, 1978; Miller & Rollnick, 1999). It seems obvious that clients will work harder when they are focusing on a goal that really matters to them. However, many people are referred by friends, families, courts, and student judiciary boards to solve problems that the client has little or no interest in solving. In cases where the court orders treatment for a particular problem, neither client nor helper has participated in the goal-setting process, and neither may feel personally involved or motivated to achieve the aims. Clearly, the likelihood of success in these conditions is low. The third-party problem is evident in the example of a client who has been referred by a probation officer following an incestuous relationship. The probation officer wants the client treated for sexual dysfunction to ensure that this kind of thing does not happen again. The client is divorced now and has had no contact with his teenage daughter, the incest victim. At this point, the client's concerns center on forming new relationships and dealing with family members' rejection. He is not willing to rehash the incestuous relationship and is resentful of the helper's intrusions. I use the example of incest because it seems so clear that this client has a problem that needs to be treated and yet we have little hope of making a difference if the client is not a partner in the process.

The "reluctant client" is quite common (Ritchie, 1986). In fact, clients pressured to attend by a third party may comprise as much as one-third of all new clients referred for counseling (Haley, 1989). Helpers must therefore be clear about whose goals will be the focus with each client. Sometimes they are forced to accept the goals of third parties, but goal setting involving both client and helper provides the best opportunity for success. In the case of the incest problem, one tactic that helpers frequently use is to accept a lesser goal by the client, hoping that, as the relationship improves, the client will eventually accept a goal of working on sexual dysfunctions.

Morally Objectionable Goals

Students often raise the question, "What if the client's goals are morally unacceptable to the helper?" Although helpers are generally nonjudgmental and accepting of differences, there are times when a helper cannot help a client to set and achieve a goal because of personal religious convictions or ethics. For example, many helpers will refuse to take sides in custody cases when they have seen a couple for marriage counseling. Some helpers may not choose to help clients achieve goals related to sexuality, such as accepting homosexuality or conducting extramarital affairs. Professional helpers inform clients early in the counseling process about issues they will not address, so that the relationship does not develop too far before a referral is needed.

Sample Questions to Gauge a Goal's Importance

Hidden in each of these questions about a goal's significance is a message from the counselor to the client. The message is, "We need to set goals that make a difference in your life."

- "How likely are you to follow through with this goal?"
- "How important is this goal to you?"
- "If we accomplished this goal, what difference would it make in your life?"
- "How are you likely to talk yourself out of trying to accomplish this goal?"
- "Is this your goal, or is it something other people want you to accomplish?"

Goals Should Be Realistic

The helper's expertise is important in defining goals when a client has unrealistic aims. Sometimes the client has insufficient information about the self or about the issue. At other times, the client wants to accomplish two incompatible aims. For example, a client recently said, "I want to be better paid at my job, but I don't want to work harder and give up my free time." One method of dealing with unrealistic goals is to confront the client with the discrepancy. Another way is to invite him or her to explore the goal and collect information to see if the goal is really possible. In some cases, it may be necessary for the helper to express doubts about the goal. Consider the following client statements and possible helper responses:

Example 1

High school senior: "I don't like science or math, and I am not very good at them. My aptitudes in those areas are not very good, according to the national exams. I want to be a doctor, because I need to have a good salary and I want to be respected as a professional."

Helper: "It sounds like you want the status and the money that being a physician might bring, but you are not sure you have the ability or the interest needed for the training. Perhaps we need to look at both of these things a little closer."

Example 2

Client: "I want to get my girlfriend back. She's living with someone else right now, and she won't even return my calls. She hates me because I was dating other people behind her back while we were going out. I still have a problem with being faithful to one person, but I know if I got her back, we could make it work."

Helper: "I'm not sure that reuniting with your ex-girlfriend is a realistic goal. For one thing, you say you're having trouble being with only one person, and, second, she is showing no interest in getting back together."

Example 3

Client: "I want to stay married and enjoy the safety and security of the married relationship. Myra and I have a problem with communication, and that is something we can work on. But there is someone else that I am seeing right now. The excitement and romance is something that is missing in my marriage. I can't hurt

Myra or the kids by letting it come out in the open. So I have decided to keep it a secret. When Myra and I come in for marriage counseling, I don't want to bring up this other relationship."

Helper: "I would like to help, but I don't believe you can improve your marital relationship while you are carrying on a secret affair."

When a client is operating with faulty information or is engaging in self-deception, as in the preceding cases, the helper uses challenging skills and helps the client gain self-knowledge or information about the problem that will help him or her set better goals. For example, in the case of the student who wants to be a physician, the helper might help the client gain experience and knowledge of medicine in several ways, including volunteering in a hospital, looking at the courses medical schools offer, and asking physicians directly about how important it is to enjoy and do well in math and science.

Stop and Reflect

There is a saying among career and life planning counselors that if you do not know where you are going, you will arrive somewhere else. The meaning is that if we do not set goals for our lives, other factors besides our own plans will intervene. A well-known football coach, Lou Holtz, has said, "Write down everything you hope to achieve in life, then make sure you do something every day to realize one of your dreams. You are going to encounter adversity but you will also . . . take big, satisfying bites out of life" (1998). Holtz set several hundred personal goals over 20 years ago. Recently he indicated that he had completed over three-fourths of them. Think about the following areas of your own life and write down a goal under each heading that you would like to accomplish in the next 5 to 10 years:

1. A job I would like to have:

   _____

   _____

2. A project I would like to be involved in:

   _____

   _____

3. The kind of friendship or intimate relationship I would like to develop:

   _____

   _____

4. An area of learning I would like to master or a formal degree program I would like to complete:

   _____

   _____

5. A hobby or interest I would like to develop:

_____

_____

6. A way I would like to improve myself:

_____

_____

Next evaluate each of the goals that you have identified according to the following criteria:

   a. Is the goal specific?
   b. Is the goal stated in positive terms?
   c. Is the goal simple enough for an 8-year-old to understand?
   d. How motivated are you to accomplish the goal?
   e. Is the goal realistic considering your abilities?
      • Choose one of the goals that appears to meet some or all of the preceding criteria and rewrite it in a simple, specific sentence or two. List the steps you must go through to accomplish this goal.
      • As you look at the steps that you have identified, does the goal seem more manageable or more difficult now that it has been broken down into parts?
      • Discuss this exercise with a friend who knows you well. Ask him or her to evaluate the goal as to how realistic it is and how clearly it is stated.

Who Owns the Problem? The Technique of Focusing on the Client

Thomas Gordon (1975) suggested that helpers think about a key question as they begin the goal-setting stage of the helping process: Who owns the problem? The question can be most clearly answered by determining who is emotionally upset by the problem. The emotional reaction not only provides the motivation to seek help, but acts as a red flag for the helper by identifying the person most affected. For example, if both members of a couple are unhappy with the relationship, the couple will "own" the relationship problem and may seek counseling together. On the other hand, the man who complains about his employer's stinginess "owns" the problem and must decide how to solve the problem by seeking another job, becoming more assertive, or modifying his feelings and perceptions to better handle the situation. It is unlikely that the employer "owns" the problem, since he or she is probably not upset by stinginess toward others.

One of the reasons this is such a critical question is that, early on in their practice, helpers can be easily sidetracked by agreeing to a client's goal that involves changing a third party: spouse, employer, or significant other. One of the clearest examples of this occurs in the case of a family affected by alcoholism. At first, the affected family members seek professional help to try to control the drinking of the alcoholic member. Sometimes they can actually force the alcoholic person into treatment. Eventually, however, the helper must confront other family members with the fact that they themselves are troubled and need to deal with their own emotional disturbance and develop their own goals. The family members must come to realize the senselessness of trying to stop the alcoholic's drinking and instead try to regain self-esteem and handle their own negative feelings regardless of the alcoholic member's behavior. The proper view of problem ownership is a central theme of the self-help organization Alcoholics Anonymous. The issue of problem ownership is crystallized in AA's prayer, "God grant me the courage to change the things I can change, serenity to accept the things I cannot change, and the wisdom to know the difference." In short, before clients can set goals or solve problems, they must recognize what aspect of the problem they can actually change and ask themselves, "What part of this problem is mine?"

Stop and Reflect

A 65-year-old widow, Rhoda, complained that her 40-year-old son, Jorge, was irresponsible with money. She indicated that her two other children, Verna and Marta, accused her of always rescuing Jorge financially when his drinking and gambling created a crisis. She was both resentful and worried about Jorge's spend-thrift ways, wanting suggestions about how to get her son to become more responsible. She was also defensive about her need to protect her son, whom she felt was incapable of controlling himself. Verna and Marta were angry and shocked when they recently learned that Rhoda had left most of her money to Jorge in her will. Rhoda explained to her counselor that she was fearful about Jorge becoming homeless after her death and wanted to provide for him as her daughters seemed to be doing well.

- If you were Rhoda's counselor, what would you identify as the main problem that Rhoda owns?
- What problems are owned by other members of the family?
- Assuming that you cannot help change any other family members, including Jorge, what do you think the main goals you and Rhoda might agree upon?
- If you saw the whole family together, what problem do you think everyone "owns" that might be the basis for family therapy?

How to Focus on the Client

A recent cartoon depicted a couple coming to their first counseling session. As they sit before the counselor, you can see the wife thinking, "Now, the counselor will find out how crazy he really is!" Meanwhile, the husband is thinking the same thing about her. As we discussed in the example of alcoholism in the family, one of the major issues we face in dealing with clients is getting them to deal with issues that they can control and trying to coax them to give up on the project of reforming others. The technique of focusing on the client is the skill of asking the client to take responsibility and ownership for his or her problems, rather than trying to convert everyone else. Nearly all major theoretical orientations agree that effective helping involves empowering clients to change themselves. The skill of focusing on the client is the elementary method for shifting the focus away from others and the environment and onto the issues that the client owns. The following is an example of a helper who has been seduced into listening to Bradley's story—a story that seems to point out that Bradley's life would be better if only others or the world would change:

Bradley: "With the economic slowdown and my bills, I can't change jobs right now, no matter how angry I get with my boss."

Helper: "Your boss makes the job miserable, but you can't leave because of money. You don't have many options right now." (Here, the helper is paraphrasing with a focus on others and the environment. The helper is buying into the client's pessimism and external focus.)

Bradley: "Yeah, my boss is a jerk, and all around me I see other people getting ahead because either they have connections or maybe they have a boss who helps them."

Helper: "You feel angry because your boss is unfair." (Here the helper is reflecting feelings with a focus on others and the environment. He has tacitly agreed to the client's viewpoint about his boss.)

Bradley: "Yeah, sometimes I get pretty steamed when he gets on his high horse."

Helper: "What does the boss do that makes you angry?" (Here the helper asks a closed question, with a focus on others as the cause of Bradley's anger. The helper has agreed that the boss is the cause of the client's anger.)

Bradley: "He is always on me, criticizing my work. He never has a good word to say."

This dialogue may seem exaggerated, but, in fact, it is typical of what can occur when the helper keeps the focus on external issues such as the boss and the economy. When the client responses center on others or the environment, he or she becomes dispirited and disempowered and does not gain any personal awareness of emotions or engage in thoughtful self-examination. In effect, when the helper asks the client to focus on others or the environment, the helper is agreeing that other people or external events are the cause of the client's problems.

On the other hand, focusing on the client is empowering and prevents the client from blaming other people and external circumstances, a time-draining sidetrack. Focusing on the client does not encourage passive acceptance of the behavior of others or the vicissitudes of life; rather, it challenges the client to become responsible for his or her own happiness and do something to change the world.

Let us take a look at how the dialogue with Bradley might be handled, this time keeping the focus on the client. Note that keeping the focus on the client is a general technique that uses many of the skills you have already learned, including reflecting feelings, asking questions, and reflecting meaning.

Bradley: "With the economic slowdown and my bills, I can't change jobs right now, no matter how angry I get with my boss."

Helper: "It is a difficult situation you find yourself in, caught among a stressful situation at work, financial pressure, and fewer job opportunities." (Here the helper is paraphrasing with a focus on the client. By paraphrasing, the helper is acknowledging that life is not easy right now.)

Bradley: "I really hate my job, but I need the money. One thing I would like to work on is getting rid of some of my bills so that I have more freedom."

Helper: "You feel trapped in your job right now, and you're experiencing stress from financial problems, too." (Here the helper is reflecting feelings with a focus on the client. Note that "You feel trapped" is different from "You are trapped," which suggests an external locus of control.)

Bradley: "I don't feel like I have one place in my life where things are calm and going right. I feel like everything is out of control."

Helper: "It's always been important for you to feel that you have a handle on things. Now, without that, you can't seem to find many peaceful moments." (Here the helper is reflecting meaning with a focus on the client.)

Bradley: "It's hard to feel in control when everyone else is putting pressure on you. I go from one pressure cooker to the next."

Helper: "In what part of your life do you experience the most pressure?" (Here the helper asks a closed question with a focus on the client. The client is urged to think about which problem pinches the most. The purpose is goal setting.)

Bradley: "I have a big car payment, student loans, and a lot of credit card bills."

Can you see that with these interventions the helper is keeping the focus on the client as the one who needs to make decisions and deal with the pressure? The helper acknowledges that external forces are at work and that they affect the client's decisions, but by keeping the focus on the client, the helper indicates that the client can be the one who does something about the situation. Focusing on the client rather than on other people and circumstances leads in a more productive and positive direction, with more client self-examination and empowerment.

The Technique of Boiling Down the Problem

Earlier in this chapter we identified some of the characteristics of constructive goals. Goals should be specific, stated positively, simple, important to the client, and realistic. As you might expect though, clients do not normally arrive with clearly defined questions and problems. More often, they present tangled stories of feelings, people, and events that spiral in different directions. At some point, the helper must choose areas to develop and others to set aside for the moment. Just sorting the work into "piles" or cutting the job into "pieces" reduces client anxiety and offers fresh hope. Most of us are aware of the experience of motivation and relief that accompanies making a "to-do list" when we feel overwhelmed. Similarly, clients need to narrow down the list of issues and focus on one or two to begin with.

One therapist used to say to clients, "Well, we've chased a lot of rabbits out of the bush; now let's track down a few of them." This metaphor worked well to signal that a more specific focus was needed. Boiling down the problem is also a metaphor for this process. First, the client is encouraged to open up, and then specific issues are identified and evaluated. Finally, the list is narrowed to a couple of the most critical. The steps in boiling down the problem are as follows:

Step 1: Summarizing and Enumerating All the Issues. The helper uses summaries, reflecting skills, and paraphrasing to determine agreement on the overall content of the counseling session to this point.

Helper: "So let me pull this together a little. You're living at home and feel embarrassed because you think that you should be out on your own. The man you have been dating for a year has called it quits, and in the middle of all this upset, your teenage sister is causing turmoil in the home. Meanwhile your mother's illness worries you. You're feeling overwhelmed since everything has happened at once."

Tricia: "That's about it. I'm living at home. My life is going nowhere, and right now everyone needs me to be strong."

Step 2: Asking the Client to Identify the Most Crucial Problems.

Next the helper uses one or more closed questions to ask the client to evaluate which problems are the most critical, thereby narrowing down the number of issues to be addressed.

Helper: "I realize that all these issues—your mother's health, your sister's problems, getting over your boyfriend, and becoming financially able to have your own place—are important issues to you. Of these, which do you think are the most critical and are ones that we can deal with in these sessions?"

Tricia: "There is nothing I can do about my mother's illness, and, unfortunately, there is not much I can do about my sister, either. But I want to get on my feet financially and emotionally. I need help in thinking about where I am going in my career so I can earn enough to live on, and I've got to think about how I am going to make it through the next few months without my boyfriend. I need to focus on myself for a little while."

Step 3: Selecting the Focal Problem.

In this activity, the helper uses a mental checklist to evaluate client goals and advocates for those that are:

- Specific
- Simple and easily restated
- Mutually agreed upon by helper and client
- Realistic

Helper: "So it sounds like one of the emergency issues is to help you find some ways to take care of yourself emotionally so that you can cope with your loss. At the same time, you want to look at the future a little bit, too. You want to explore some career ideas."

Tricia: "I know I can get some help with the career thing. You've already offered to do the tests and talk about that. The main thing is how I can deal with my angry and depressed feelings all the time. I am bored and angry and alone. I feel like a baby."

Step 4: Changing the Problem to a Goal.

In this step, the helper encourages the client to think about success. What will the problem look like when it is solved? This step helps us make sure that the goal is stated positively, one of the criteria for constructive goals.

Helper: "You have told me that you are in a lot of distress about losing your boyfriend, and we have discussed that topic pretty thoroughly. As you think about the future, I wonder if you can envision your life when this is no longer a problem. What would you be doing then that you are not doing now? What would you be feeling and thinking?"

Tricia: "I would be going out with my friends and enjoying life again. I wouldn't be thinking about him all the time, sitting there waiting for him to call. I would be able to concentrate at work."

Helper: "So these are the goals that you would like to work toward."

Tricia: "Sure!"

Step 5: Making Sure Client and Helper Are Clear and in Agreement.
Here the helper summarizes the mutually agreed-upon goals. In addition, the helper may ask the client to state them aloud or write them down, so that the agreement is clear. At this point, clients often need encouragement and a message from the helper that the goals are reachable.

Helper: "Let's see if I can restate them: You would like to go out with friends and enjoy life again, instead of spending so much time thinking about your ex-boyfriend. Is that about right?"

Tricia: "Yes, but it is not that easy."

Helper: "I agree. It won't be easy. Are we on the right track though? Are these your goals?"

Tricia: "Yes."

Helper: "Would you mind restating the goals as we talked about them so that I am sure we are both operating with the same understanding?"

Tricia: "Okay, I am going to find a way to have fun again and spend time with friends again."

Helper: "Like you said, it won't be easy, but I am confident that you can make this happen. Let's talk some more about how you can actually go about making this happen."

Summary

The first stage of the helping process can be summarized as "opening a relationship" and the second as "assessing." The next stage, goal setting, described in this chapter, might be called "narrowing": Once the client's important issues have been identified and a working relationship is under way, it is time to select and target the important issues. One of the key questions in narrowing is, "Who owns the problem?" Helpers develop the skill of focusing on the client to keep the client directed toward the issues that are causing pain. This compels the client to deal with issues he or she can really make an impact upon.

This chapter advocates that the helper develop goals collaboratively with the client, melding the helper's expertise with the concerns and needs of the client. Constructive goals are therefore mutually agreed upon; they are also specific, positively stated, and simple and are those that the client is motivated to achieve. The skill of boiling down the problem uses summarizing and questioning to help clients clearly define and negotiate specific achievable goals.

Exercises

Group Exercise

The purpose of this exercise is to practice the process of boiling down the problem to a workable agreement between helper and client. The activity involves a helper and client and one or two observers.

   To complete this exercise in a short period of time, the helper and client should spend only a little time of the interview (perhaps 5 minutes) on the invitational and reflecting skills—just enough to enable the helper to understand the basics of the problem. The helper should then jump immediately into a discussion of goals. While client and helper are engaged in goal setting, one observer (see "Instructions to Observer 1" below) can write down any of the helper's interventions that seem to help the client in setting the goal. A second observer (see "Instructions to Observer 2" below) writes down the final goal verbatim and facilitates a discussion about how closely the goal matches the ideal characteristics.

Part I: Instructions to Observer 1   Record what you believe are the key statements by the helper that help the client boil down the goal to a workable contract.

1. _____
   _____
2. _____
   _____
3. _____
   _____
4. _____
   _____
5. _____
   _____

Part II: Instructions to Observer 2   In the space provided, write down your understanding of the goal finally arrived at by client and helper.

   Read this to the client and helper to determine if your articulation of the goal is accurate. Then give the helper feedback on how closely the goal matches the following characteristics. Is the goal, as written:

- Specific?
- Positively stated? (the presence of something versus the absence of something)
- Simple?
- One that the client is motivated to achieve?
- Realistic?

Additional Exercise

In the helper/client interview, one of the mistakes beginners make is to ask too many closed questions that focus on others and the environment. Examine the client situations listed here and formulate one question or paraphrase that focuses on the client and another that would take the client off track.

High school student: "I don't know where I am going with my life. My grades are good enough to get into college, and my parents want me to go. But I am more interested in music. My music teacher thinks I should go that route. What do you think?"

Client Focus: _____
Other Focus: _____

Student who doesn't do homework: "In study hall, it's too distracting. There are these three guys who sit next to me, and all they do is talk. The teacher doesn't even try to stop them. I never have time to do it at home. My parents have a lot of chores for me."

Client Focus: _____
Other Focus: _____

Parent of a teenager: "He smokes pot continually. I am caught between him and his father. I found some pot under his bed. He says that he is not smoking now, and I am afraid to tell his father. He will blow up. What am I going to do about his drug problem?"

Client Focus: _____
Other Focus: _____

Client who has accepted a job out of state: "My family is upset with me. They can't see that this is my best chance for success. They want me around to come over for Sunday dinner. I want that, too, but it is so hard to balance these things."

Client Focus: _____
Other Focus: _____

Homework

Homework 1

In boiling down the problem, one aspect that takes practice is changing a problem into a goal. Create two short dialogues between client and helper whereby the client is helped through the five steps of boiling down the problem. The five steps are (1) summarizing all the issues, (2) asking the client to identify the most crucial problems, (3) selecting the focal problem, (4) changing the problem to a goal, and (5) making sure that the client and helper are clear and in agreement. After each dialogue, identify the problem as stated by the client and the goal as reformulated by the helper.

Homework 2

Talk with two friends about their personal goals. See if you can get each friend to identify five short-term and five long-term goals. In a single page, describe your experiences. Which friend has the clearest goals? Be sure to describe the reactions of your friends to this exercise. Do you think people often discuss their most important goals?

Journal Starters

1. Make a list of goals you would like to achieve in the next 5 years. Now look at each one and indicate what you think might keep you from accomplishing it. Do you notice any personal unwillingness to think about this issue? Does it raise any anxiety? Discuss your reaction.
2. Imagine that you are a very old person talking to your relatives about your life. What were the major things you enjoyed in your life? Don't just recount your accomplishments, but focus on those times when you were the happiest. It has been suggested that successful people are those who "follow their bliss." What things have you discovered that you really like to do? How can you incorporate them more into your present life? How can you use them to motivate yourself? What use can you make of this when you are trying to help another person?

For more journal ideas, as well as more practice with goal setting, refer to Chapter 11 in *Exercises in the Art of Helping.*

References

Barbrack, C. R., & Maher, C. A. (1984). Effects of involving conduct problem adolescents into the setting of counseling goals. *Child and Family Behavior Therapy, 6*, 33–43.

Beck, E. S., & Hoppock, R. (1998). Vocational fantasy: An empowering technique. In H. G. Rosenthal (Ed.), *Favorite counseling and therapy techniques* (pp. 34–36). Washington, DC: Accelerated Development.

Borelli, B., & Mermelstein, R. (1994). Goal setting and behavior change in a smoking cessation program. *Cognitive Therapy and Research, 18*, 69–83.

Bruce, P. (1984). Continuum of counseling goals: A framework for differentiating counseling strategies. *Personnel and Guidance Journal, 62*, 259–263.

de Shazer, S. (1990, May). Brief therapy. Symposium conducted at Stetson University, DeLand, FL.

Dyer, W. W., & Vriend, J. (1977). A goal-setting checklist for counselors. *Personnel and Guidance Journal, 55*, 469–471.

Evans, M. H. (1984). Increasing patient involvement with therapy goals. *Journal of Clinical Psychology, 40*, 728–733.

Frank, J. D., & Frank, J. B. (1991). *Persuasion and healing* (3rd ed.). Baltimore: Johns Hopkins University Press.

Goodyear, R. K., & Bradley, F. O. (1986). The helping process as contractual. In W. P. Anderson (Ed.), *Innovative counseling: A handbook of readings* (pp. 59–62). Alexandria, VA: American Association for Counseling and Development.

Gordon, T. (1975). *PET: Parent effectiveness training*. New York: Wyden.

Grayson, H. (1979). *Short term approaches to psychotherapy*. New York: Human Sciences Press.

Haley, J. (1989, May). Strategic family therapy. Symposium conducted at Stetson University, DeLand, FL.

Hart, R. (1978). Therapeutic effectiveness of setting and monitoring goals. *Journal of Consulting and Clinical Psychology, 60*, 24–28.

Holtz, L. (1998). *Winning every day*. New York: Harper Business.

Miller, W. R., & Rollnick, S. (1999). *Motivational interviewing: Preparing people to change addictive behavior*. New York: Guilford.

O'Hanlon, W. H., & Weiner-Davis, M. (1989). *In search of solutions: A new direction in psychotherapy*. New York: Norton.

Ponte-Allan, M., & Giles, G. M. (1999). Goal setting and functional outcomes in rehabilitation. *American Journal of Occupational Therapy, 53*, 646–649.

Ritchie, M. H. (1986). Counseling the involuntary client. *Journal of Counseling and Development, 64*, 516–518.

Rossi, E. (1980). *Collected papers of Milton Erickson on hypnosis* (Vols. 1–4). New York: Irvington.

Rule, W. R. (1982). Pursuing the horizon: Striving for elusive goals. *Personnel and Guidance Journal, 61*, 195–197.

Smith, J. A., Hauenstein, N. M. A., & Buchanan, L. B. (1996). Goal setting and exercise performance. *Human Performance, 9*, 141–154.

Steiner, C. (1976, April). Radical psychiatry. Symposium conducted at the University of Dayton, Dayton, OH.

Solution Skills

12

In this chapter, we will introduce four new building block skills: giving advice, giving information, brainstorming, and alternate interpretation. These building blocks are called *solution skills* because they are all methods that helpers use to help clients to find solutions to their problems. Solution skills can be used inappropriately. By their very nature, they place the helper in a superior position, which can change the client/helper relationship. Also, the helper could breed dependency in the client by overuse of these skills.

Properly applied, however, solution skills can stimulate clients to work toward resolving their own problems, aid clients in getting in touch with creative ideas, and help them to examine their self-limiting assumptions. Most important, when clients begin to focus on solutions, they are living in the future rather than ruminating over the past.

The solution skills represent the final set of building blocks. Although you will learn more advanced techniques, the building blocks can help you successfully navigate the

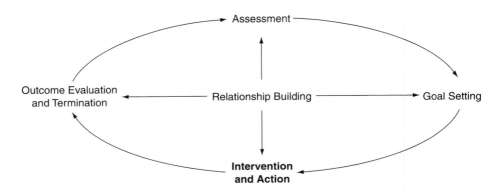

Figure 12.1
Stages of the Therapeutic Relationship: Intervention and Action

opening stages of the helping process from relationship building to assessment to goal setting. With the addition of solution skills, you will be able to begin mobilizing the change process by involving the client in problem solving and experimenting with new behavior. Figure 12.1 shows the stages of the therapeutic relationship that are described in earlier chapters. You learned the relationship-building skills (in the center of the diagram) in the first few chapters and some basic assessment skills in Chapter 10. Next, in Chapter 11, you learned some goal-setting skills to develop a vision of what is to be accomplished. The challenging skills you learned earlier and the solution skills in this chapter are part of the intervention and action phase. These skills are implemented to help a client move beyond his or her version of the story. When properly used, the client feels encouraged to consider new alternatives, to recognize inconsistencies, and probably to move out of the zone of comfort and safety. Again, this is why the relationship-building skills are so critical. During the intervention and action phase, the helper must continually reestablish the connection with the client so that the client has the courage to dream and change.

Giving Advice and Information

Giving Advice

Like salt, advice is beneficial, but only in the right amount. Giving advice can be crucial in emergency situations when a client is engaging in dangerous behavior, such as practicing unsafe sex, considering an affair, or using drugs, or when a client is being exposed to physical violence.

Because beginning helpers like to give advice too liberally, many teachers ban it outright in the initial stages, and, as a consequence, textbooks often have little to say about it. However, because advice giving is rarely addressed, students tend not to be aware of its drawbacks and may find it an easy habit to fall back on. For example, when college students come for counseling, they typically expect advice, and they freely dispense advice to their friends in an attempt to help. They feel that it is effective mainly because they view it as tangible assistance. In fact, advice giving is a veritable minefield. It lures us into thinking that we are actively helping a client. The next section explains some of the reasons for leaving this skill out of your practice sessions for the present. If you have a tendency to give advice, we urge that you consider "retiring" that skill at this point and develop other alternatives.

Why Are Professional Helpers Reluctant to Give Advice?

In the *Peanuts* cartoons, Lucy sits at the psychiatrist's booth with a sign that says, "Advice: 5 cents." Generally, this is how the media portray the helping professions. Someone pays and someone gives a good dose of advice. If helping were merely giving advice, we could set up such a booth at the local grocery store. However, as one writer notes, "Clients can get all the advice they want from acquaintances, friends, and family members. They hardly need to pay a therapist to tell them what to do" (Kleinke, 1994, p. 9). To give exactly the same advice as everyone else in the client's world makes the helper seem impotent.

Another reason that professional helpers avoid giving advice is that while others may listen politely, they simply do not act upon it. It is an established fact that about 50 percent of all medication prescribed by doctors is not taken. It is thought that a major reason that medical patients do not follow physician recommendations is that they have private medical beliefs that are more influential than the doctor's suggestions. Similarly, when helpers give clients advice and homework assignments, the helpers can expect no better than 50 percent compliance. Are we then to blame the clients or to recognize that the art of helping is more challenging than this?

Real helping is an art that involves getting people to solve their own problems and is much more difficult than supplying solutions by giving advice. Sometimes advice does stimulate a client's thinking about the problem, but, more often, it is simply disregarded (Mallett, Spokane, & Vance, 1978). Eric Berne identified a "game" that illustrates this point. Games are sequences of behavior that are frequently repeated and involve a payoff for at least one of the players. This advice-giving game involves a routine set of transactions between client and helper called " 'Why don't you . . . ' 'Yes, but . . . ,' " or WDYYB. When the helper gives advice, he or she begins, "Why don't you . . . ," and the client responds, giving reasons why the advice will not work, "Yes, but. . . . " Most of us are familiar with this "game" from work and social situations. The advice giver feels confused and frustrated when good suggestions are rejected. Even when clients ask for advice, they frequently refuse it. What we need to remember is that while a client may appear to be asking for advice, he or she is really looking for opportunities to think aloud, to be understood, and to explore the options.

Another crucial drawback to advice giving is that if the client follows the helper's advice, the helper is responsible for the resultant change. If the helper gets the glory for having supplied good advice, how has this empowered the client to solve future life problems? There is an aphorism that states, "Give me a fish and I will eat today; teach me how to fish and I will eat forever." The long-term goal of helping is not to supply a quick fix, but to help the client, even when the helper is no longer in the picture. Sometimes advice may be needed to solve emergent problems, but when clients resolve their own difficulties, they gain confidence and skills.

By solving a client's problem for the client, you may also be sending the client a message. Thomas Gordon (1975) considers lecturing and preaching to be one of the "dirty dozen" of bad communication practices because it communicates to a client that he or she is incapable of solving the problem. Lecturing and preaching are disguised advice giving (Patterson & Eisenberg, 1983). For example, during the goal-setting phase, a client identifies excessive anger as one of the areas she wishes to work on. Frequently, beginning helpers launch into a "sermonette" on expressing anger and self-acceptance. The effect on the relationship is that the helper moves into the role of expert and begins to speak in generalities, rather than focusing on the client's unique situation. If you can identify a sermonette in your practice sessions, you are probably using disguised advice giving.

Another persuasive argument against giving advice is that the consequences of giving the wrong advice can be severe, both to the client's life and to the client's faith in the therapeutic relationship. A final reason to avoid advice giving is that it may violate the values of an individual's family, culture, or religion. Such advice will probably be rejected, and it may also harm the therapeutic relationship. Consider these examples of inappropriate advice:

"I advise you to quit your job and go back to college."
"I suggest you learn to be more assertive with your mother."
"If you don't like all the arguing, why don't you get a divorce?"

When Is It Appropriate and Inappropriate to Give Advice?
A helper who gives advice must have the following knowledge or experience:

- Special knowledge and training in the specific issue the client is facing
- Firsthand experience or experience helping many people deal with the particular issue
- Understanding that the helper's experiences are not the same as the client's experiences
- Ability to give advice in a way that outlines the risks as well as the opportunities that following a certain course of action entails
- Through understanding of the client'is history, including the client's ethnic, religious, and cultural background

Appropriate advice is concrete and invites reaction and discussion. It is presented as one alternative along with other solutions generated by the client. It suggests that the client should alter the instructions to fit the circumstances. Advice about what to expect from certain courses of action may be quite helpful. Advice is also appropriate when the client is in some physical danger and a helper's directive can reduce the risk.

Here are some examples of advice that might be appropriate:

"Your statement that you are drinking too much has me concerned, especially since you drive home in that condition. If you continue to drink, you can expect to be in an accident or in court. I want you to go to an alcohol treatment center for an assessment interview. Would you be willing to do that?" This advice is given to inform the client about the likely outcomes of drinking and also identifies potential physical danger.

"You know, my wife and I always try to spend 15 minutes at the end of every day playing cards or backgammon. It has been a way of building in a moment of contact in our hectic lives. Do you think something like that might work for you?"

This advice invites discussion and asks the client to tailor the advice to fit his or her particular situation.

"You've outlined several possibilities. Let me add one more. Have you considered directly confronting your coworker about her unsafe behavior on the job? What effect do you think that might have?" This advice asks the client to think and to discuss the alternative suggested by the helper.

On the other hand, here are some situations in which advice is inappropriate and could be harmful to the therapeutic relationship:

- When the client seems to be dependent on others to make decisions and needs to learn to choose his or her own course of action. He or she might ask, for example:
  "Do you think I need a new haircut?"
  "Do you think I should go home this weekend as my parents ask, or should I do what my boyfriend wants?"
- When the client has not heeded advice previously.
- When the client is asking for assurance on issues with unpredictable outcomes, such as:
  "Should we have a baby?"
  "Should I get married?"
  "Should I move to Saudi Arabia?"
- When the purpose of obtaining advice is to influence another person:
  "My husband believes in spanking our child, but I don't. What do you think?"
  "My mother thinks I am too young to date. Do you agree?"
- When the client has information available and is capable of solving the problem without advice.
- When the advice conflicts with a client's basic values, upbringing, or culture. The helper is giving inappropriate advice, for example, when he or she says: "You may come from an East Indian culture, but you live in America now. You have to do what you want, and your parents will have to understand."

Clearly, the times when advice giving is useful are quite limited. Giving advice is appropriate only at carefully considered moments rather than as standard procedure. If advice giving is something you rely on in your natural helping style, try this experiment: Avoid advice giving altogether until you have learned to conduct an entire session using invitational and reflecting skills. There is an analogy in boxing training in which a left-handed puncher ties that hand behind the back in order to learn to operate only with the right arm. By letting go of an old way of responding, a new set of skills has the chance to take hold and become stronger. Similarly, if you can let go of your tendency to sermonize and give advice, you will have the chance to develop the subtler skills of helping the client find his or her own solutions.

Stop and Reflect

Think back for a moment on pieces of advice you have received from teachers, guidance counselors, friends, parents, grandparents, or other family members. It might have been about the purchase of a car or house, about which college to attend, or about what to do in a relationship. Identify one piece of good advice and one that was not very helpful, and then consider the following questions:

- What was it about each piece of advice that made it helpful or not helpful?
- When considering the helpful advice, did the person giving it have particular expertise in that area?
- What other characteristics did the person giving the advice have that encouraged you to accept it?
- If you cannot recall any advice given by friends, teachers, counselors, parents, or family members, what conclusions might you draw from this?
- When you have a problem, do you want advice, or is it more important to have someone listen so that you can figure things out for yourself?
- Have you ever given a friend advice that was really heeded? How did it turn out?
- What can you conclude about the role of advice in helping you to make decisions in your own life? Will your conclusions have a bearing on your willingness to give advice as a helper?

Discuss your answers with a small group of classmates.

Giving Information

Giving information means supplying data or facts to help a client reach his or her goal. Information giving might include making referrals to social services or community resources. It can include correcting erroneous ideas about topics such as sexuality, drugs, parenting, and stereotypes about different ethnic groups. Information giving can also take the form of a planned psychoeducational program such as teaching the client assertiveness training.

A helper uses information giving sparingly because too much information will overload the client and will likely be ignored. Information giving can also subtly change the relationship between client and helper. It can become a lecture that clients may disregard. Here is an example of an appropriate use of giving information:

> "Based on what you have told me, your financial problems are significant and you could use some professional help. I would like to refer you to the Consumer Credit Counseling Service. They can help you make the decision about whether bankruptcy is a good answer for you. Would you be willing to go?"

Recently, a student intern referred one of her clients to Alcoholics Anonymous after helping him identify his alcohol problem. She was elated after the session because "It really felt like I did something for a change instead of just listening." I tried to point out that it was the relationship that she had so painstakingly constructed that provided the atmosphere where the client could face his problem. If she had referred him for treatment at their first session, he would never have accepted the referral. It took time and trust to bring him to that realization. Like giving advice, giving information feels as if we are really accomplishing something. But the proof is in the pudding. Like the advice we give, most information we give clients does not sink in. Although the helper feels effective, it is important to find out if the client has really been helped. Therefore, the helper must follow up with clients to see if information or referrals have had an impact. We will talk more about the topic of referral and follow-ing up when we discuss termination of the helping relationship in the next chapter.

Brainstorming

Creativity and the Art of Helping

According to Holland's typology of personalities and career environments (Holland & Gottfredson, 1976), helpers frequently show three personality traits: investigative, social, and artistic. The investigative trait indicates an interest in solving puzzles. Clearly, a helper must have investigative interests and skills to untangle a client's story, just as a scientist tries to understand the riddles of nature or a detective tries to uncover the reasons for a crime. Helpers also have strong interpersonal interests, rep-resented by the social trait; they want to help people. The artistic aspect of helping is perhaps less obvious, but as the title of this book suggests, there is a side to helping that cannot be quantified and is purely artistic. Artists use different media to express themselves and create beauty. The helping arts are not focused on self-expression by the artist but on the helper's desire to create something beautiful out of human disar-ray: harmony, peace, wholeness, and fulfillment. This holistic sense cannot be achieved merely through application of a scientific process any more than it is possible to use a formula to reproduce a Picasso.

Helpers are often creative people. They are flexible and open to a variety of options when a problem arises (Gladding, 1995). They try to help clients devise novel ways of thinking and problem solving. Indeed, they may at times use artistic media—drama, poetry, painting, sculpture, and music—to help clients express themselves (Gladding, 1998). Helpers also encourage their clients to think creatively when they have prob-lems. A major difficulty in problem solving is that we tend to see things through the lens of our outmoded ideas, social conventions, and our personal history. As Emerson noted, consistency can be a hobgoblin, leading us into foolish repetitions when what we need is to break out of our old ways of thinking.

Stop and Reflect

Perhaps you have heard of the nine-dot problem. Take a look at the nine dots in Figure 12.2. The problem is to take a pencil and draw four straight lines that connect all the dots without lifting your pencil from the page. The answer to this puzzle appears in Figure 12.3, but try to solve it yourself before looking at the answer. Whether you have seen this puzzle before or not, it illustrates an important aspect of human thinking. We tend to rely on previous experience. In the nine-dot problem, we have usually been told to "color in the lines." We see a box shape represented by the points and conclude that we must stay within the shape rather than expand into the page beyond. This same kind of thinking affects us when we encounter a problem in life. As the nine-dot problem suggests, we see rules when none exists. Perhaps you have heard the story of the man who takes his son to the emergency room and the doctor exclaims, "I can't operate on this child, he's my son!" We do not automatically recognize that the doctor must be the child's mother. Because of our training and the

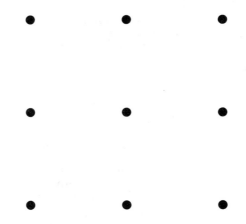

Figure 12.2
The Nine-Dot Problem

pervasive influence of the media, we unconsciously fall back on our usual way of thinking, that a doctor must be a man.

During crisis states, we become even more conservative and less creative. A sort of tunnel vision develops that convinces us that we have very few options. For example, people with suicidal thoughts may have concluded that killing themselves is the only option available. It is also well known that battered women see few options to their abusive relationships because their experience tells them that the situation has no exit. The concept of learned helplessness has been advanced to explain why people fail to look for alternatives following experiences of failure (Seligman, 1991). When people seem to find that nothing works to solve their dilemmas, they stop trying, even when circumstances change. The job of a helper is to be an "expander" (not a "shrink") who tries to help clients enlarge their viewpoint, jump-start their thinking, and engage their creativity.

What Is Brainstorming?

Brainstorming originally was developed by Madison Avenue advertising firms to increase the creativity of staff members responsible for commercials. To brainstorm, a group of people sit around a table and generate ideas. The conditions and ground rules, however, are a little different from those of an average meeting: The atmosphere is relaxed and even playful. Cooperation rather than competition is encouraged. Everyone in the group is called upon to participate, and no one is allowed to dominate. All ideas are recorded, but the focus remains on a specific problem that the group wants to solve. Beyond these general conditions for brainstorming, there are some specific rules that differentiate it from other problem-solving activities:

1. No ideas generated by brainstorming are evaluated. They are simply brought before the group and recorded. Evaluation involves a critical function of mind rather than a creative one. Creativity flows best in a nonjudgmental atmosphere.
2. Freewheeling is encouraged. Practical considerations are not brought up during a brainstorming session. In fact, the wilder the ideas the better, so that the

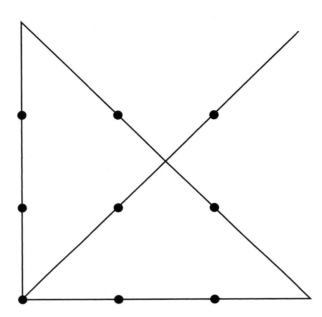

Figure 12.3
Solution to the Nine-Dot Problem

limits of creativity can be reached. A playful attitude by the facilitator can increase freewheeling.

3. The quantity of ideas is more important than the quality. A large pool of ideas is needed as a source of good solutions. Seemingly unimportant ideas actually can spark thoughts from other members of the group, and small ideas can be used to improve bigger ones.

4. Hitchhiking is encouraged. Hitchhiking, or piggybacking, is building on the ideas of other people. By combining ideas, a concept grows and develops. Thus brainstorming is a creative and cooperative process that has the power to unearth hidden solutions and engage both helper and client.

Research has suggested that sometimes when two or more people brainstorm together, they do not generate as many new ideas as they do when they compile their lists separately (Diehl & Stroebe, 1991; Mullen, Johnson, & Salas, 1991). The reason is "production blocking." Production blocking means that people are sometimes too polite in a group situation to spontaneously blurt out their ideas while others are talking. The flow of ideas dries up. Brainstorming requires that each person be allowed to express his or her ideas without having to wait for others to stop speaking (Johnson & Johnson, 1997).

Production blocking can also occur in a therapeutic relationship. The client is reluctant in that setting to really think in a spontaneous and freewheeling way because of the weight that he or she places on the helper's ideas. Sometimes it is more effective for each person in a brainstorming session to write down his or her ideas or for one person to generate ideas and the other to record them. This allows for more freewheeling than the start-and-stop approach that a conversation entails.

How to Brainstorm

Brainstorming between a helper and a client involves the same basic activities that groups use, with only slight modifications. The helper acts as a facilitator and participant, but a major aim is to help the client develop skills of creative thinking, which can generalize to other situations. While we are trying to help the client arrive at a solution, we are also teaching a valuable life skill.

In the helping relationship, brainstorming should not be an activity that merely keeps a client talking about options rather than taking action. Brainstorming is a solution skill. At the end of a brainstorming session, both helper and client should have a clear idea about the next steps to take to solve the problem. Its aim is to help the client arrive at a practical first step. Brainstorming takes a client through three basic phases:

1. Challenging the client's assumptions and identifying the problem
2. Generating ideas
3. Evaluating and agreeing upon potential solutions

Brainstorming with a client does not differ much from the steps in group brainstorming except that, at the outset, more attention is devoted to identifying and challenging assumptions. The client thinks about the assumptions he or she has about the problem and tries to shake free of them. Otherwise, preexisting ideas will color the next idea-generating step, leading the client to substitute previous solutions rather than to think creatively.

One tactic for dealing with assumptions is to reverse them. For example, while designing an innovative program for training school counselors, participants listed all their assumptions about school counselors. One of them was "School counselors work during school hours." This assumption was reversed and written down on the blackboard, "School counselors do not work during school hours." Ideas based on this new concept were then generated. Participants began thinking about how school counselors should be available to parents after school and in the evenings. This led them to include family counseling training as part of the curriculum. A nearby public school system is now incorporating this idea in its new school. The plans for next year allow flexible working hours for school counselors so that they can meet with parents several evenings per week.

Another story illustrates how assumptions about problems can be challenged and how, in turn, creative thinking leads to better solutions.

David and Gloria have been married for 5 years. David's job requires that he move to another state for a 2-year period to work on an exciting project. If David refuses the assignment, he risks losing his job. The couple came for help because they have come to an impasse in their decision-making process. David wants Gloria to quit her job as a part-time graphic designer and move with him. Gloria wants to stay where she is, and she wants David to stay, too, even if he gets demoted or loses his job. Neither wants to live alone for the 2-year period.

Acting as a facilitator, the helper took them through the three basic steps of brainstorming to help them arrive at a solution.

Step 1: Challenging assumptions and asking the right question.   The first step is to ask the right question. This can be determined by asking what is to be achieved in the end. What is the goal? The reason this step is so crucial is that often clients are examining previous solutions rather than the current problem. A good example of how this happens comes from the food industry. For several years, the question was often asked in this way: "How can we make a better can opener?" This formulation generated a number of new can openers, both manual and electric; however, a can opener is a previous solution, not the real problem. Someone ultimately was able to ask the question in a different way: "How do we open a can?" When the problem was stated in this way, a whole new set of creative opening features developed. Helpers assist clients in identifying the key issues by asking closed questions such as:

"What do you want to achieve by solving this problem?"
"What is it you are afraid of losing?"
"What is the most important thing you want to accomplish?"

Similarly, David and Gloria might argue over who is going to move, but what is the real question? With the assistance of the helper, the couple realized that the question that really needed to be asked was, "How will we be able to spend enough time together and feel close to each other if David goes out of state for 2 years? Previously, the couple had assumed:

"Someone is going to have to move."
"Someone is going to be unhappy."
"Someone is going to lose his or her job."

Once the problem assumptions had been put aside and the real problem identified, the couple were ready to start generating ideas.

Step 2: Generating ideas.   In a freewheeling and cooperative atmosphere, David and Gloria took a few minutes to identify creative answers to the question "How can we remain close if David takes the job for 2 years?" Since quantity is wanted, the helper insisted that they generate at least 10 ideas. They came up with the following list:

1. We will e-mail every day.
2. We will call every day.
3. We will meet halfway every weekend.
4. David will come home once a month, and Gloria will travel to see David once a month.
5. We can send telegrams.
6. We will spend our vacations and holidays with each other for the next 2 years, not with other family members.
7. We will install a videophone or videoconferencing software on the computer.
8. We will send recordings to each other.
9. Gloria will take some of her work with her to David's place and stay for a week at a time.
10. David will ask the company for time off to come home.
11. We can take pictures of things that happen and share them with each other.

12. We could both take a class to fill our time and discuss it with each other.
13. We can send smoke signals.
14. We can meet halfway in Mexico.

As the ideas got crazier, they began to hitchhike on each others' ideas. When Gloria said, "We could take a class," David suggested that they take a Spanish class and share their learning when they meet in Mexico.

Step 3: Evaluating and selecting a solution. The final step of brainstorming is evaluating and selecting a solution. David and Gloria went through the list at this point and discussed each possibility. They settled on four or five suggestions to implement that best fit the goal of keeping their relationship vital while they lived separately.

Although the case of David and Gloria may seem too good to be true, many clients and helpers have learned to use brainstorming in just this way. When a client and helper devise a creative solution to a knotty problem, the therapeutic relationship is enhanced and the client's confidence and sense of hope is increased. Not only have the clients been fully involved in the solution, but they have learned or relearned an important problem-solving skill.

The Skill of Alternate Interpretation

The skill of brainstorming encourages clients and helpers to collaborate and create new solutions. When we challenge our assumptions in the first steps of brainstorming, we begin to recognize that there are many different ways to frame a problem and that the way we conceptualize it has important implications for the eventual solution. *Alternate interpretation*, or *alternative interpretation*, is another method to help clients recognize that problem situations can be seen in many different lights (McMullin, 2000). The method of alternate interpretation does not attempt to reach into the past to find the correct interpretation or meaning of an event. Rather, its sole purpose is to convince the client that there are several possible alternatives to a negative first impression or catastrophic appraisal. For instance, many people continue, in adulthood, to misinterpret, minimize, or exaggerate events that happened when they were children. The method of alternate interpretation tends to loosen the hold of outmoded ideas and to convince clients that there are many possible ways of looking at a problem, some of them helpful and some of them self-defeating.

How to Teach a Client to Use Alternate Interpretation

The decision to use alternate interpretation usually comes within a session when a client describes an event that has occurred and then begins to catastrophize about it. *Catastrophizing* is the tendency to expect that an event will be devastating before one really knows what the outcome will be. In this case, the helper stops the process and asks the client to stop imagining the worst-case scenario and examine the premises that led to the conclusion that a catastrophe has occurred or is imminent. Consider the case of Jane, who has been working at a new job for only a short while. She was recently fired from another position and is feeling very insecure about her new situation:

Jane: "On Monday, my boss mentioned that I had not finished last week's reports. My boss is criticizing me. Things are starting all over again. I know I'll lose this job now."

Step 1: Using the skill of alternate interpretation, the helper proceeds as follows: The helper listens to the client's problem and then previews and explains the concept of alternate interpretation.

Helper: "I recognize that you are concerned about losing your new job, but I wonder if I could stop you for a moment and ask you to try something."

Jane: "Okay."

Helper: "This technique is called alternate interpretation. The way it works is that we take the situation and try to identify some different conclusions than the one that you have drawn. As I understand it, your boss stopped you and mentioned you had not done last week's reports, right?"

Jane: "Right."

Helper: "And your first conclusion was that the same thing is happening that occurred at your old job and that you will probably be fired, right?"

Jane: "It sounds kind of silly when you say it that way."

Helper: "Well, what I would like to do is get you to try and generate some other interpretations of the facts. For example, perhaps your boss needed that information for some reason and was more interested in the content of the reports than in firing you."

Jane: "All right, I see."

Helper: "Good, but I want you to come up with some ideas that make just as much sense as your first impression, okay?"

Step 2: The helper asks the client to make a list of three or four other interpretations that fit the facts at least as well as the catastrophic conclusion of the client.

Helper: "I am wondering if you would try and think for a moment about some other ways of interpreting the same situation."

Jane: "Well, in the past, I have not received this kind of criticism. It is unfamiliar. Perhaps she—my boss—is trying to help me improve and become a better employee."

Helper: "That's good. What else?"

Jane: "Um, I guess I could realize that I have just received feedback that will help my performance. Maybe it will actually help me keep the job."

Helper: "Very good. Can you think of any other way to interpret this situation?"

Jane: "Like I said, this is the first time that my work has been criticized. My boss probably doesn't place that much importance on a single instance like this. She's probably forgotten about it. I am just nervous because of my past history."

Step 3: The helper assigns a homework task of developing three or four alternate explanations to the first interpretation of any disturbing event that occurs between sessions. The only requirement for the alternatives is that they have as much likelihood of being true as the first impression. The helper does not try to "sell" any particular interpretation but is trying to loosen up the client's automatic, catastrophizing response.

Stop and Reflect

1. Think about the following scenario and consider how you might help the client develop alternate interpretations of the same situation.

   "My best friend Pam isn't talking to me. We were out together on Friday night. Well, I met someone that I knew from work and wanted to spend more time with. He and I left the coffee shop. It was crowded, I didn't see Pam, and so I didn't say good-bye. When I saw her at church, she waved but didn't stay to talk. I know she hates me now. We have been so close for 2 years and now it's over."

2. Now take a moment to consider an event in your own life where your first impression was incorrect. Might the skill of alternate interpretation have been helpful in your situation? As you think about it, list two or three other possible interpretations you might have made had you been able to be more objective.

3. What client problems do you think might respond best to the technique of alternate interpretation? Compare your ideas with those of your classmates.

Summary

Up to this point, we have looked mainly at skills for developing the therapeutic relationship, exploring client problems, and setting goals. In this chapter, we talked about four building blocks that help move clients toward solutions: giving advice, giving information, brainstorming, and alternate interpretation. Giving advice is the most controversial skill presented and the one that can potentially create the most harm to the therapeutic relationship. It is discussed because helpers need to understand the appropriate and inappropriate uses of advice rather than ignoring it completely.

The major focus of this chapter was on the skills of brainstorming and alternate interpretation. Both skills are aimed at getting clients to free themselves from their first interpretations of events or the mental constraints that keep them from developing creative solutions to their difficulties.

The solution skills are the final building blocks in the art of helping. Along with challenging skills, the solution skills if properly applied are collaborative attempts to move clients out of their current frames of reference and to have them consider new alternative ways of thinking and behaving. The ability to effectively introduce these activities is built on the carefully constructed framework of the therapeutic relationship. The nonjudgmental listening cycle allows the client to develop a sense of trust, and that begins to pay off as the client takes tentative first steps in changing his or her life. More importantly, as the client encounters obstacles on the path to solutions, these basic listening skills will be needed. You must shift back and forth between listening and working on solutions as long as a helping relationship lasts. Thomas Gordon (1975) used to call this "shifting gears." There are times to push forward and break new ground, and there are times to "downshift" and return to a listening stance. In other words, be patient when using solution skills. One cannot go full speed ahead at all times. The therapeutic relationship requires that the helper abandon forward progress at times and reestablish the vital therapeutic bond.

Exercises

Group Exercise: Practicing Brainstorming

Students work in groups of three or four. One student takes on the role of a client, another becomes the helper, and the others act as observers. The client discusses a dilemma with a helper. The dilemma should be a situation in which the client is forced to make a difficult choice between two alternatives. It may be a current dilemma or one that the client faced in the past. Suggestions of possible topics for the client to discuss include:

- Whether or not to commit to a relationship
- Whether or not to end a relationship
- Whether to move or stay in the same place
- Whether or not to begin an academic degree program

Before beginning the brainstorming process, the helper first reviews the "Quick Tips on Brainstorming" given below. Then the helper uses the nonjudgmental listening cycle for several minutes to understand a little more about the client's problem. Next the helper moves with the client through the three steps of brainstorming:

1. The helper challenges the client to review his or her assumptions about the problem and to identify the real issue.
2. The helper and client brainstorm solutions.
3. The helper and client agree on a solution.

Following the brainstorming session, the client and observer(s) give the helper general feedback on:

1. The handling of the nonjudgmental listening cycle.
2. The helper's success in getting the client to think creatively.
3. The final solution. Was it realistic and appropriate for this client?

Quick Tips: Brainstorming

- Use closed questions to help the client pinpoint the real problem.
- Create a playful and cooperative atmosphere in the session by modeling freewheeling. Come up with a few unusual ideas yourself to encourage the client's creativity.
- The helper should take the role of facilitator and write down all the ideas that are generated.
- Add humor when possible and exaggerate to encourage a sense of play.
- Make sure that the final creative solution between helper and client meets the "reality criterion": It must effectively address the problem.

Additional Exercises

Exercise 1: Giving Advice

This activity can be used as a whole-class activity or for groups of at least six or eight students. One student acts as the client and describes a real problem to the group. The client is asked to identify a problem that is not too personal so that he or she does not feel uncomfortable discussing it in some detail. The helper (student or teacher) uses the nonjudgmental listening cycle to understand the issue. When the story has been fully articulated to the helper, the group thinks about the client's story, and each person writes down a piece of advice.

In the second part of the exercise, the helper collects the written advice and reads each student's advice to the client. After hearing the advice, the client discusses with the class which advice he or she is most likely to follow and why.

In the third part of the exercise, the helper uses a brainstorming approach to get the client to think about the issue and to come up with his or her own plan. Finally, the client is asked to review both the advice-giving and brainstorming sessions and indicate what course of action he or she is most likely to take. The class or group discusses the results. If possible, on the following week, the student client is asked to report on what action he or she actually took.

Exercise 2: Reversing Assumptions and Increasing the Quantity of Ideas

This exercise can be done by the whole class facilitated by the instructor. Its purpose is to challenge basic premises we have about common objects as a way of highlighting the importance of thinking creatively.

Begin by requesting the class to list ideas about how to improve the blackboard. The task is to produce as many ideas as possible in 2 minutes. These are recorded on the board or on a flip chart so that everyone can see. For the first part of the activity, remember that it is important to let go of the mind's evaluative function and allow creativity to flow. Do not think about how practical the ideas are at first. Give equal time to wild ideas.

Next list on the board the assumptions you have about blackboards—for example, they are black, you write on them, and so on. Next to each assumption write a *reversal of the assumption*—for example, "Blackboards are not black," "You do not write on them," and so on. Then brainstorm any ideas about improving the blackboard that seem to come out of these reversals. Add any new ideas to the list of improvements. Now see whether you can force-fit any two ideas on the list together, or hitchhike (combine ideas), to devise any new creative ideas. If so, add them to the list.

As the final step in the process, evaluate each idea and select the best. Can any of the good ideas be combined to create a new product? The final design should meet the reality criterion: Is the product really an improvement? How likely would it be to sell?

Homework

Homework 1

Consider the case of Arnold, a 30-year-old man who had recently broken up with a woman he had been dating for a short time. The client described the problem like this: "I can't seem to make a relationship last. I thought this one was it! There must be something wrong with me. I think that women can see how incapable I am at maintaining a relationship." Identify three or four alternate interpretations for

Arnold's first impression. Next identify two alternate interpretations for each of these client statements:

- "My marriage is on the rocks. We're not in love anymore."
- "All people have a direction for their lives by the time they're my age. What's wrong with me?"
- "I can't stand this anxiety anymore. I want it to go away."
- "My life is not going anywhere. I am in graduate school and I am working, but when does it get to be fun?"

Homework 2

It has been said that creativity is an important trait of helpers. According to Witmer (1985),

creative individuals are said to possess the following characteristics:

Curiosity
Openness to new experience
Independence
Sense of humor and playfulness (spontaneity)
Persistence
Flexibility
Originality
Ability to accept that opposing points of view may both be right

Do you see yourself as a creative individual? Is this something you would like to develop? Write a paragraph or two about why you think creativity might be useful in helping others. Indicate specifically how you might employ creativity in homework assignments for clients.

Journal Starters

1. Some helpers use a technique in which the client sits in the counselor's chair and gives advice as if he or she were sitting in the empty client chair. This is a way of tapping into that wise person in each of us. Think for a moment about your relationships, your family, money, children, or your career. Imagine yourself as this older, wiser self and write down your advice. When you have finished writing, react to the activity by sharing your evaluation of the advice.
2. Begin your journal entry by writing a poem about your life. It doesn't have to rhyme.

The poem should be a picture of your life at this moment in time. Use metaphors to indicate how much effort you are putting forth, how you are dealing with problems and setbacks, and how you see your future goals. Reflect on your poem and decide whether this activity gave you any insight on your present situation. Now write a poem about how you would like to see your life. Is there a difference? How important is it for you to have a creative outlet in your life? Can you see any value in assigning this kind of activity to a client?

References

Diehl, M., & Stroebe, W. (1991). Productivity loss in idea-generating groups: Tracking down the blocking effect. *Journal of Personality and Social Psychology, 61*, 392–403.

Gladding, S. T. (1995). Creativity in counseling. *Counseling and Human Development, 28*, 1–12.

Gladding, S. T. (1998). *Counseling as an art: The creative arts in counseling* (2nd ed.). Alexandria, VA: American Counseling Association.

Gordon, T. (1975). *PET: Parent effectiveness training.* New York: Wyden.

Holland, J. L., & Gottfredson, G. D. (1976). Using a typology of persons and environments to explain careers: Some extensions and clarifications. *Counseling Psychologist, 6,* 20–29.

Johnson, D. W., & Johnson, F. P. (1997). *Joining together* (6th ed.). Boston: Allyn & Bacon.

Kleinke, C. L. (1994). *Common principles of psychotherapy.* Pacific Grove, CA: Brooks/Cole.

Mallett, S. D., Spokane, A. R., & Vance, F. L. (1978). Effects of vocationally relevant information on the expressed and measured interests of freshman males. *Journal of Counseling Psychology, 25,* 10–15.

McMullin, R. (2000). *The new handbook of cognitive therapy techniques.* New York: Norton.

Mullen, B., Johnson, C., & Salas, E. (1991). Productivity loss in brainstorming groups: A meta-analytic integration. *Basic and Applied Social Psychology, 12,* 3–25.

Patterson, L. E., & Eisenberg, S. (1983). *The counseling process* (3rd ed.). Boston: Houghton Mifflin.

Seligman, M. E. P. (1991). *Helplessness: On depression, development, and death* (2nd ed.). New York: Freeman.

Witmer, J. M. (1985). *Pathways to personal growth.* Muncie, IN: Accelerated Development.

Outcome Evaluation and Termination Skills

13

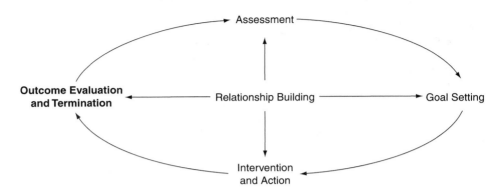

Figure 13.1
Stages of the Helping Relationship: Outcome Evaluation and Termination

How will we know when the helping relationship has come to an end? This question is a theme that binds together the assessment, goal-setting, and outcome evaluation and termination stages of the helping relationship (see Figure 13.1). Focusing on the desired outcomes of helping is not a one-time activity. It must be addressed in every session when we ask the client how he or she is progressing toward the goals. In the assessment phase, we select measurements that tell us how the client is functioning at the present time and that we can use again to assess progress. In the goal-setting stage, we develop a treatment plan that, if completed, becomes our definition of success. The final stage, outcome evaluation and termination, comes about when we revisit our treatment plan and compare our goals with the client's present status, and we conclude that significant progress has been made. This chapter addresses outcome evaluation and termination, completing the circle and addressing the final stage in the five stages of the helping process (Figure 13.1). In the first part of this chapter, we look at some ways that we can evaluate whether or not we have made progress and whether termination is appropriate. In the second part, we address the practical and emotional issues that termination raises for both helper and client and discuss how the transition can be made in the best possible manner.

Evaluating the Effectiveness of Helping

Because of the emergence of managed care and a growing awareness that many unsound treatments are being applied, there has been a burgeoning interest in outcome evaluation in the medical and other helping professions (Sexton, 1996; Sexton, Whiston, Bleuer, & Walz, 1997). In other words, insurance companies and researchers are asking clinicians to be more scientific, to show that they are using proven practices and that the client was actually helped by the therapeutic process. Today, whether you work in a school, hospital, agency, or private practice, someone wants to know if you can demonstrate that what you do is actually working (Granello & Granello, 1998).

Outcome research is at the heart of this new trend toward scientific helping. *Outcome research* is the general term for studies that look at whether what we do actually benefits the client. It must seem obvious that this is a very important line of inquiry, but when we look at the history of research in counseling and therapy, these studies are conspicuous by their absence. For example, relatively little research has been conducted that looks at the efficacy of the basic helping skills you have learned in this book. Most of the studies suggest that helpers can learn these skills and that some training methods are better than others. But very little has been said about how clients react to these skills. In other words, research confirms that the operation is a success, but nobody asks whether or not the patient survived. Many of our ideas about effective therapy and good training in the helping skills are based on clinical observation. The proponents of outcome research are quick to point out the limitations of this "seat-of-the-pants" approach to determining what works.

The extremists in this "evidence-based" camp suggest that we only use treatment methods that we can back up with research. Unfortunately, this idea is also limited. We know from medicine that two clients will react to the same prescription differently. We also know that two depressed people are depressed in different ways. So the helper's task is to determine "what treatment, by whom, is the most effective for this individual with that specific problem or set of problems, and under which set of circumstances" (Paul, 1967, p. 111). We must be able to adjust the treatment based on the individual person.

Finally, we do not have enough research to test the myriad of interventions that are available. Sticking to what has been fully studied would handicap the helper as promising strategies emerge. Still this does not exonerate the helper, regardless of setting, from recognizing that some approaches have been better studied than others and have more to recommend them.

Let me give an example. For more than 2 years, I utilized relaxation procedures to help clients with panic disorder because I had been trained in stress management and it seemed logical. I had very little success. These clients had trouble reaching deep states of relaxation through Jacobsonian relaxation procedures. I did not know whether to attribute this to the technique or to the intransigence of the mental disorder. Years later, research confirmed that other techniques are much more effective (Beamish, Granello, & Belcastro, 2002).

The competent, ethical helper must be a good consumer of research and be constantly watching the professional literature for these kinds of data. This monitoring of what works is important, because our clinical wisdom only extends to the breadth of our own clientele and our own limited perspective. This is where outcome research comes in. We can take measurements of our clients, and we will accumulate data about their progress.

Up to this point, we have discussed the rationale for outcome evaluation based on the fact that we are going to be externally evaluated. Let us now turn our attention for a moment to *internal* reasons for monitoring client outcomes. Through this book, you have been practicing the basic helping skills using a partner or small group. We have also encouraged you to get feedback, both qualitative and quantitative, from these fellow students. This feedback is a kind of outcome evaluation that you can conduct now and in the future. You can ask, "Are we going in the right direction? What has changed since we started meeting? And what is not working for you?" This kind of questioning assists the helper as well as the client. It keeps us from wasting our time or from potentially damaging the helping relationship.

Another personal or internal reason for conducting outcome evaluation is the issue of helper self-esteem and efficacy. Because of the wide variety of clients, disorders, problems, and treatment options, it is hard to feel effective, especially as a beginner. Frequently clients have very high expectation of the helping relationship and may not recognize when changes have been made. Outcome evaluation can give you periodic encouragement, and you can grow in confidence as you see the actual data collect, rather than only listening to your fears and discouraging thoughts. Just as the school counselor who started a character education program discovered, if you track outcomes, you can gain a personal sense of power and confidence that you are doing something that works. (This example is explained in more detail later in the chapter.)

Perhaps you have already received some positive feedback from your fellow students or your instructor. We continue to build on your strengths. Do what you are best at and then add new techniques as you are able. Outcome evaluation is a way for you to keep your confidence high and also to help you recognize when things are going in the wrong direction. Even if you are not particularly attracted to the scientific or research aspects of the helping profession, you can utilize some very simple methods to keep track of client progress. In this next section, we discuss the use of progress notes, global measures, specific measures, client satisfaction forms, and goal attainment scaling. All of these are minimally intrusive in the helping process and push both client and helper not just to dream but to fulfill dreams.

Basic Outcome Evaluation Methods

Use Progress Notes

When you begin seeing clients in a clinical, agency, hospital, or academic setting, you will be asked to document progress by the client using some sort of progress note form. There are a variety of systems for note taking; however, I recommend one that coincides with the outcomes that the client and helper have initially agreed to. For example, if a teenager wants to reduce anxiety in social situations, the notes should (1) restate the goal, (2) indicate what progress has been made during the week (outside of the session) that was relevant to the goal and the results of any homework assignments, (3) state what was talked about in the session that relates to the goal, and (4) specify what plans have been made for the coming week and next sessions as they relate to the goal. In short, the progress note should keep the helper on track, focusing on the agreed-upon aims and not becoming waylaid by tangential conversations. Figure 13.2 shows a sample case note that utilizes this method of evaluating client outcomes relative to goals at each session. In a sense, the helper is evaluating progress toward the goals at every session. This kind of note also reduces the time it takes to do paperwork because the focus is so specific.

Use a Global Measure to Detect Change

There are a number of global measures of psychological distress and psychopathology. Utilizing these measures periodically can help you chart whether the client is generally improving or deteriorating. The Brief Symptom Inventory (BSI) (Derogatis, 1975) and

---

Client Name __John Doe__   Session No. _3_   Date _4_ / _18_ / _2005_

Client/Counselor Negotiated Goal Statements

1. Decrease depression and suicidal thoughts.
2. Resolve family problems. Increase brief contacts.

Any Progress in Goals Since Last Session

1. Client indicates that depression decreased significantly but still having suicidal thoughts
    1 time per day.
2. No effort or progress toward this goal.

New Information (Changes in Client's Situation or Mental Status)
Denied that suicidal thoughts were intense or increasing.
Denied any planned method or available suicide means.

Counseling Activity During This Session

Goal 1. During session, client was confronted on self-downing and was taught to
    challenge negative self-statements.
Goal 2. We did not address this goal except for client to indicate that he is not quite
    ready to work on this issue. I suggested he consider attending Adult Children
    of Alcoholics as a preliminary step. He agreed.

Homework Assignments, Referrals, and Plans
Goal   Plan

1.   Client to challenge negative self-statements as homework and call if suicidal
          thoughts increase.
2.   Will call friend to accompany him to first ACOA meeting.

Counselor Signature B. B. James   REPLAN date _6_ / _9_ / _2005_

Figure 13.2
Sample REPLAN Record and Case Notes

the OQ-45 (adult and youth versions) (Lambert, Hansen, Umphress, Lunnen, Okiishi, Burlingame, Huefner, & Reisinger, 1996) are two well-established paper-and-pencil instruments used to identify global change. Both can be administered and scored in just a few minutes.

Use a Specific Measure

Sometimes you are looking for a specific change such as a decrease in depression. There are a number of specific brief measures such as the Beck Depression Inventory II that can be used routinely (Beck, Steer, & Brown, 1996). The 21-item Beck has been used extensively in research, and many clinicians like to administer it every week when they are seeing a depressed client because it appears to be sensitive to improvement in mood.

Use Subjective Scaling and Self-Report to Measure Improvement

A SUDS, or Subjective Units of Discomfort Scale, was described earlier in this book. Basically SUDS asks the client to indicate on a scale of 1 to 100 how uncomfortable (depressed, anxious, stressed, unhappy) he or she currently feels. Then the clinician regularly asks the client to reevaluate and makes note of the SUDS in the progress notes. Besides the fact that helpers can see and inform clients of improvement, it gets the clients thinking about their goal and about the changes they are making.

The helper might also ask the client to make a note of specific behaviors in frequency, intensity, or duration such as:

- How many cigarettes did you smoke?
- How many times did the child pull out his or her hair (trichotillamania)?
- How many times was the teenager able to start a conversation with peers?
- How many times did each member of the couple give the other a compliment during the counseling session?
- How intense was this marital argument (on a 10-point scale)?
- How intense was your fear of dogs in this situation (on the SUDS)?
- How long were you able to meditate today?

Use Another Person to Monitor Change

Frequently someone in the environment is better able to see changes than the client. For example, suppose a college student is trying to become more outgoing and talk more in class and in social situations. The counselor may utilize an ally of the client—a friend who will give the client periodic feedback when the friend sees the client behaving in a different manner or sees evidence of avoidance. There are pitfalls to the use of allies or aides, including the fact that they may take too much responsibility or they may not respect confidentiality. In addition, if the ally is a spouse or parent, his or her own needs and wants for the client can complicate matters. Still, having someone in the client's real world giving a progress report can be useful to the process and can also motivate the client.

Use Client Satisfaction Scales

Client satisfaction scales are measures of how happy the client is with the services rendered. Most of these are developed by agencies and schools to answer specific questions, but others are nationally normed and can give feedback on how satisfied clients are compared with those around the United States. It may be useful to look at overall satisfaction from a program evaluation standpoint, but helpers can also look at client outcomes by including a few useful statements to be rated (say, on a scale from 1 to 7), such as:

- I was able to achieve my goals as a result of these sessions.
- My relationship with the counselor was important in helping me improve.
- I have a more positive view of the future because of these sessions.

Use Goal Attainment Scaling

One graphic method for evaluating progress is goal attainment scaling (Kiresuk & Sherman, 1968). Goal attainment scaling has been advocated for demonstrating accountability, but its best use may be that it can provide helpful information to the client and counselor about progress (see Table 13.1).

The goal attainment guide in Table 13.1 is used in the following way:

1. Each goal is briefly described in the goal statement section.
2. Specific indications of success are noted in the sections just beneath the goal statement. A simple example of a goal is to "maintain social support for

Table 13.1
Goal attainment guide

Case of _____

	Goal Statement No. 1	Goal Statement No. 2	Goal Statement No. 3
	_____	_____	_____
	_____	_____	_____
	Specific success indicators	Specific success indicators	Specific success indicators
	_____	_____	_____
	_____	_____	_____
	_____	_____	_____
	Outcome Description	Outcome Description	Outcome Description
Least favorable likely outcome			
Less than expected level of attainment			
Expected goal attainment			
Better than expected outcome			
Best outcome			

Goal Attainment Scale				
1	2	3	4	5
Least Favorable Outcome	Less Than Expected Outcome	About Expected Outcome	Better Than Expected Outcome	Best Probable Outcome

Goal scale				
Goal no. 1				
Goal no. 2				
Goal no. 3				
Average goal attainment with this case _____				

Source: Reprinted by permission of Donald A. Blocher.

sobriety." The specific success indicators might be "regular attendance at support meetings."

3. The least and best outcomes for each goal are then described on the goal attainment guide. These descriptions should be as specific as possible since they will be used as a means for judging client progress. In this case, the best outcome might be "three meetings per week," and the least, "one meeting per month."

4. The client's current functioning is recorded on each of the goal attainment scales at the bottom of the guide. First the client's initial or baseline functioning should be arrived at by the therapist and client. Let us say that the therapist and client agree that the client, at intake, is functioning at less than expected outcome concerning attendance at support groups. Using the letter B for beginning or S for start, the therapist records this information on the goal attainment scale on the Goal no. 1 line at the 2 position.

5. At various points in therapy, additional notations can be made on the scale showing progress or relapse.

6. Besides the ability to monitor progress, the goal attainment guide provides a tool for review of therapy during the termination process. At times, the client may be discouraged because one of the goals has not been achieved. The guide may be able to show that even if the best outcome was not achieved, some progress was made (Blocher, 1987).

Use Program Evaluation

Program evaluation means looking at the effectiveness of an entire program rather than the outcomes of a particular student, couple, or family. Helpers are routinely asked to begin and participate in treatment programs, but frequently the reason these programs are begun and continued is that they sound like good ideas without regard to whether or not they work. Let us take an example in a school setting. Recently a first-year school counselor, Robb, was asked to set up a "character education" program at his school. In the state where Robb lived, character education was mandated, and this seemed like a good enough reason to implement the program. Most schools bought posters and instructed teaching faculty to discuss a particular value (such as "responsibility") with their students each month. When the school principal asked Robb to design and operate this treatment, the principal insisted that the counselor build in a system of evaluation. Together principal and counselor agreed that the program, if effective, ought to have an effect on the behavior of students, and so together they developed a set of outcomes that they hoped would reveal the effectiveness of the character education project. When the participants know what the outcomes should be, they work in a more focused way. In this case, Robb identified a decrease in disrespectful behavior toward fellow students (those that resulted in a referral to the office) as the hoped-for outcome. During the school year, principal and counselor tracked all the referrals to the office and kept a tally of the reasons for the referral. Over the school year, they were able to see a decrease as the character education program took hold. At the end of the year, the counselor received a grant from the school district to continue this work and teach it to others. The point of this story is clear.

Helpers who can prove that they are having an impact will benefit professionally. More important, we will be able to feel that we are administering treatments that are effective, and we can have more confidence that our clients are being helped.

Termination

Even the word *termination* sounds deadly or evokes an Arnold Schwarzenegger movie. Termination, here, is used to denote the period of time when client and helper negotiate the end to the helping relationship. The time for termination is when the established goals have been met. Emotionally, client and helper may not be ready, and there may be foot-dragging from both. It is not always a celebration for the client; sometimes it is just a relief. The helper can expect little in the way of thanks, because all along he or she has been encouraging the client to recognize their own accomplishments. Even termination is not about the helper; it is about helping the client to break the bonds and make the transition to life without relying on the helper.

How to Prevent Premature Termination

Before we discuss ways of accomplishing a smooth ending to the therapeutic relationship, let us look at a related problem. Frequently our issue is not how to exit the relationship but rather how to restrain the client from terminating until real progress has been made. It is discouraging to a helper when a promising client does not return after the first or second session, and the helper may think of this as a failure.

Sometimes early termination is a good thing. There is evidence that even one-session counseling is viewed as helpful by many clients. In general, clients expect a shorter duration in therapy than the counselor (June & Smith, 1983). Yalom (1995) has suggested that early termination by the client may be a good thing since it acts as a safety valve when the client/counselor match is not correct (see also Epperson, 1983).

Still, an argument can be made that it is preferable to complete therapy with a bang, not a whimper—to come to a formal ending or to refer the client after a few sessions rather than letting the relationship wind down. A positive ending may pave the way for the client to return to therapy (Kramer, 1986, 1990). A petering out may cast the therapist as ineffective or the client as a failure.

Certainly clients "vote with their feet"; that is, they leave the helping relationship when they feel it is not helping them meet their goals. But there are a number of reasons that clients terminate prematurely that have little to do with how much progress they are making. The suggestions listed below are a combination of observations and recommendations from the literature concerning ways of preventing clients from leaving therapy for reasons other than that therapy has been ineffective (Mennicke, Lent, & Burgoyne, 1988; Pekarik, 1985):

1. Avoid delays in seeing clients. Although some clients seem to come only during emergencies and fail to follow through, clients who must wait 2 or 3 weeks for an appointment may not arrive at all or may be hostile and less motivated.
2. In cases and settings where clients might be expected to drop out early, make contracts with clients for completing a small goal or a small number of sessions (6–10).

3. Do not process clients through several channels. Clients who are interviewed by an intake counselor or secretary for screening and then referred to the real therapist may be lost because they have been treated impersonally. It is difficult enough for many people to reveal their need for therapy by making the phone call for an appointment. Asking them to reveal their problems to several people may be too much.
4. Provide orientation to clients about therapy and offer information about the qualifications of the therapist. Some counselors use a written handout that describes the helper and the process of the helping relationship. Some helpers send this to the client through the mail before the first session; others provide it in the waiting room. Such a process can develop positive and realistic expectations and diminish client fears. Fees, billing procedures, expectations of client behavior, confidentiality, and other issues can be dealt with in this manner. It is also a good idea to talk about these issues in the first session.
5. Use reminders to motivate client attendance. Obtain the client's permission to call or to write a brief reminder just before the next session. This simple suggestion can improve attendance significantly. Think about your dentist. Do you get a call the night before reminding you of the appointment? A phone call midweek may also serve to remind the client of homework and encourage the client to work on therapeutic issues without the helper even mentioning them.
6. When a client terminates early, call him or her and find out why. There may be several unexpected reasons for the client's termination other than a feeling that the therapy is unproductive. These reasons range from the embarrassment of having seen an acquaintance in the waiting room, difficulty with transportation, or rudeness from support personnel.
7. In cases where the client decides to terminate before goal completion, the helper should try to go the extra mile (Kaplan & Sadock, 1997) by making it easy for the client to return at a later time. This may mean agreeing with the client's idea to interrupt therapy and directly inviting the client to come back later by setting a follow-up date.

How to Tell Whether Termination Is Needed

Clients should be terminated when they have attained their goals, when they have been receiving counseling or psychotherapy for some time and have not made progress, or when there are signs that they can handle their issues independently but have become dependent on the helpers. Most professional organizations, including the American Counseling Association, the American Psychological Association, the American Association for Marriage and Family Therapy, and the National Association of Social Workers, state in their codes of ethics that a client should be terminated if he or she is not making progress. In such cases, the client should be made aware of alternative sources of help, and a referral should be made. The decision about whether a client is making progress is not always easy because some of the signs that suggest a client is ready for termination, such as missing sessions, coming late for sessions, or failing to do homework, can be signals of resistance or problems of motivation as well.

How exactly do we know when helping has been successful? Should we consider success from the standpoint of the client or from the standpoint of the helper? Should we define success in terms of societal standards (dangerousness, employment, school grades) or from some ideal of mental health advanced by theorists? Mathews (1989) suggests reviewing one's caseload and asking oneself, "If I had a waiting list right now, would I be seeing this client?" (p. 37). Based on Maholich and Turner (1979), Sciscoe (1990) identified five questions a helper might ask himself or herself to assess a client's readiness for termination:

1. Is the presenting problem under control?
2. Has the client reduced the initial level of distress by developing better coping skills?
3. Has the client achieved greater self-awareness and better relationships?
4. Are life and work more enjoyable for the client?
5. Does the client now feel capable of living without the therapeutic relationship?

The first four of Sciscoe's questions highlight improvements that have been made and goals that have been achieved. The last question is especially important, because it asks the helper whether or not the client is able to maintain the gains of helping without the therapeutic relationship. Answering these questions in a dialogue with the client and arriving at a mutual decision can help in working out the knotty question of termination.

How to Prepare a Client for Termination

Most experts agree that sudden termination is not advisable (Brammer, Shostrom, & Abrego, 1989), but how soon should the topic of termination be brought up? Dixon and Glover (1984) recommend that at least three sessions in advance of termination be devoted to issues of termination, while Lamb (1985) recommends at least seven sessions. As much time as was spent in relationship building in the beginning of the therapy should be devoted to termination, say Cormier and Cormier (1985); and one-sixth of the time spent in therapy should be devoted to termination, according to Shulman (1979). In other words, there should be a period of preparation. How long this should take is a matter of judgment and should be determined by the length and quality of the therapeutic relationship.

During the preparation period, the helper leads the client in a discussion that reviews the counseling process and progress made. In general, it is important to emphasize the client's strengths and to end on a positive note; however, areas left untreated or unresolved must also be discussed (Anderson & Stewart, 1983). One way to review is simply to compare before-and-after client functioning from the viewpoint of both helper and client. This is where outcome evaluation using client goal attainment or testing can be extremely informative. At times, it is useful to discuss an early session when the client was at a different stage of functioning in order to examine the contrast. Some therapists like to read case notes that they wrote early on and other notes written later in the relationship to highlight changes. Finally, any unfinished business between client and helper should be addressed, and the client should be encouraged to think about how he or she will look back on the counseling experience in the future. How will the client evaluate himself or herself if a return to see the helper is needed?

Dealing with Loss at Termination

The general strategy to help clients deal with their feelings of loss at termination is to take time to prepare them and to ask them to identify both positive and negative feelings associated with the end of the relationship. Clients may be upset by termination because it is associated with other historical losses (Ward, 1984). Some suggestions to help prevent, explore, and resolve these feelings include (Cavanagh, 1982; Dixon & Glover, 1984; Hackney & Cormier, 1979; Munro & Bach, 1975):

1. Bring termination up early.
2. Reframe termination as an opportunity for the client to put new learning into practice.
3. Specify the number of counseling sessions at the very beginning, so both helper and client are prepared for termination.
4. Use a fading procedure; that is, space appointments over increasing lengths of time.
5. Avoid making the relationship the central feature of helping. Although relationship building is crucial, it may be unwise to employ only this curative factor. Help the client to see his or her own actions that led to success.
6. Play down the importance of termination; play up the sense of accomplishment and the value of independence.
7. Use reflective listening to allow the client to express feelings of loss.

The Helper's Reaction to Termination

Kanfer and Schefft (1988) suggest that helpers need to accept the fact that termination inevitably occurs at a point far short of perfection. Many clients leave with the helper feeling that the solutions are still under construction. Besides the fact the helper must frequently let go of what seems to be an incomplete project, the helper may have also become deeply involved in the client's life. Helpers may even postpone termination because of their own attachments and feelings of sadness and loss (Gladding, 2000).

Goodyear (1981, p. 348) lists several possible reasons that helpers have trouble letting go:

1. The relationship may be quite significant to the helper.
2. The helper may feel uncertain that the client will be able to function independently.
3. The helper may believe that he or she was not effective.
4. The helper may feel that his or her professional identity is challenged by the client's premature termination.
5. The termination may represent a loss of continued learning for the helper, who was looking forward to gaining experience from the client's peculiar problem.
6. The helper may miss the vicarious excitement of the client's exploits.

7. The termination may uncover historical events associated with loss in the counselor's life.
8. A helper's feelings of loss at termination may also be due to a reliance on helping relationships to meet needs for intimacy (friendship) as well as a conscious or unconscious sexual attraction.

Krantz and Lund (1979) feel that trainees may have special difficulty with termination. Beginning helpers may keep clients too long because they like the client or because they hope that the client will accomplish even greater goals. They may also be unprepared for their own feelings or for the powerful loss experienced by the client, no matter how much they are intellectually informed. A supportive supervisory relationship is the best way to help trainees through difficult terminations (Sciscoe, 1990).

How to Maintain Therapeutic Gains and Prevent Relapse Following Termination

The term *follow-up* refers to a brief contact the helper makes a few weeks or months following termination. The purpose of the contact is to determine how the client is progressing and to remind the client that the door is open if counseling is needed in the future (Wolberg, 1954). In addition to follow-up contacts, there are a number of activities that helpers employ. These techniques are designed to help maintain therapeutic gains and are actually means for extending help following termination. Here are some suggestions (Cavanagh, 1982; Perry & Paquin, 1987):

Fading

Fading means scheduling follow-up sessions with longer and longer intervals spaced over a 1-year period. The client can be informed of the follow-up system during the final sessions. For example, a helper can make brief phone calls to the client at 6 weeks, 6 months, and after a year. In other cases, it may be useful to actually have the client return for a single session at each of these times. When clients are learning specific skills, such as assertiveness training, stress management, and communication, these follow-ups can be called "booster sessions" or "refreshers," with the stated aim of reviewing learning and dealing with problems. One benefit of planning for follow-up as the relationship is winding down is that the client need not later feel a sense of failure if a return to counseling is needed. If the client decides to cancel the later visits, this can be reframed as a sign of success. These planned follow-up sessions are particularly useful with children and adolescents, because they may benefit most from reminders and may see them as a sign of the helper's continuing interest.

Home Visits or Observation

A possible follow-up to marriage or family counseling is to review progress after an interval in the family home. Observing the couple or family in this setting can convey a great deal about progress, though it is not an ideal therapeutic setting because of the many distractions.

Contracts with Paraprofessionals

Some agencies provide follow-up services for clients on a free or inexpensive basis. Mental health clinics, for example, may provide home visits by caseworkers to monitor medication and identify areas of continuing need in those suffering from severe mental disorders.

Self-Help Groups

Self-help groups, if improperly conducted, can be a case of the blind leading the blind, but they can also be extremely powerful supports for clients following treatment. The quality of such groups is quite variable, and so the helper must be familiar with groups in the client's vicinity before making a recommendation. Because clients are sometimes reluctant to attend self-help groups, therapists must strongly encourage clients to become involved. Sometimes clients do not want to attend self-help groups because it forces them to admit they have a problem. For example, college students who have alcohol problems rarely attend Alcoholics Anonymous because they do not see themselves as alcoholics and do not want to be different from their peers. It is crucial that the helper support attendance at support groups in these cases and encourage the client to attend a few sessions before giving up. In addition, the composition of these groups varies tremendously, and it is important to find one that suits the client.

Self-Monitoring Activities

Self-monitoring means that the client is asked to keep records of progress on the treatment goals. These reports can be reviewed at the follow-up sessions. A less formal way to encourage self-monitoring and self-reflection is teaching the client to use a personal journal to explore thoughts and feelings (Kalven, Rosen, & Taylor, 1981).

Self-Management Skills

Clients can learn to use behavioral principles to reward their own positive behaviors and to punish negative ones (Kanfer, 1975; Kazdin, 1980; Rudestam, 1980). For example, students can learn to make watching a 1-hour television show contingent on completing several hours of study. A helper can assist a depressed client to develop a system of rewards for engaging in physical activity. During follow-up sessions, helpers can monitor client progress and help clients develop new strategies and reward systems. Both printed and recorded materials can be sent by clients back to the helper as evidence of practice.

Letter Writing

Young and Rosen (1985) describe a group therapy activity in which clients write a letter to themselves during the last group session before termination. In their letters, clients remind themselves of their goals and also excuses they may use to try to avoid achieving their goals. The therapist mails the letters to clients about a month after the completion of group therapy.

Letter writing by the helper is an underutilized but powerful way to spark the client's motivation to continue working on goals as well as to remind the client that the helper is concerned and available. Narrative therapists, in recent years, have been the main champions of letter writing. Through letters, a helper can reinforce the client's new life story and help the client continue to see the new perspective developed in therapy (White, 2000).

Summary

This chapter focuses on evaluating the client/helper collaboration and dealing with the ending of the helping relationship. On the one hand, client and helper may decide to continue working on the stated goals or develop new ones. Alternatively, a decision may be reached that the maximum benefit has been achieved. While the door may be left open for future help, termination can evoke feelings of loss for clients and helpers. Developing a positive ending for the helping relationship helps clients celebrate their successes and can shape their attitudes about receiving help in the future. One important issue during the evaluation stage is building in a follow-up system to help clients maintain change and prevent relapse.

Exercises

Exercise: Role-Play a Termination Session

In a small group, two members role-play client and helper discussing termination, which is to take place in a week's time.

Observers give the helper feedback on the following:

- Did the helper review the history of the helping process and the therapeutic relationship with the client?

- Did the helper help the client celebrate success in attaining the goals?
- Did the helper leave the door open while expressing confidence in the client's readiness to terminate?

Homework: A Final Tape and Transcript

Homework 1: Self-Evaluation

Before you record and transcribe a final session with a client, take some time to review the feedback you have received during group exercises and your individual practice. Think about each of the following building blocks, and for each skill, rate your current level of mastery.

1. I understand the concept
2. I can identify it and give examples
3. I can do it occasionally
4. I can do it regularly

— Eye contact

— Body position

— Attentive silence

— Voice tone

— Gestures and facial expressions

— Door openers and minimal encouragers

— Open and closed questions

— Paraphrasing

— Reflecting feelings

— Reflecting meaning

— Summarizing

Compare the scores with your answers in Chapter 8. Where have you improved? Where do you still need improvement?

Homework 2: Final Typescript

In Chapter 8, you recorded and transcribed a session with a client. Now it is time to make a final tape in the same way.

Step 1 Make a tape of 20 to 30 minutes with a classmate who is discussing a real problem or who is role-playing. During the taping, your goal as a helper is to:

- Demonstrate the nonjudgmental listening cycle
- Demonstrate goal-setting skills
- Demonstrate challenging skills
- Close the session with a discussion of how the client will follow up on what he or she has gained

Step 2 Choose the best 15 minutes of the tape and transcribe every word of both client and helper, using the format of Table 8.1. It is important that the client's statements appear directly *below* your helping responses so that the connection between the two can be examined. Be sure you have permission to record from the client. You can do this aloud on the tape and in writing.

Step 3 Listen to the tape or read the transcript and make comments, naming each of the skills that your response exemplifies. Sometimes students describe their responses rather than categorizing them. It is important to identify the skills you are using to determine their frequency and appropriateness. Use only the names of the building blocks and techniques you have learned. The comments section is a place for you to reflect on your responses. Do not just note weaknesses; identify strengths as well. In the comments section, you may also wish to mention any other issues that come to mind as you review the transcript.

Most important, reflect for a few minutes on your progress from the start of your training until now. Make some comments about your progress. What impact has it had on you personally or on your professional goals or your relationships with others? Learning the art of helping is a journey. What steps have you taken so far? What must you do now to go farther?

Homework 3: Videotape Evaluation Form

In some training situations, a final transcript may not be required. Some instructors like students to watch and evaluate the tapes exclusively. Use the videotape described in the previous assignment. Watch the video twice.

During the first viewing of the tape, use Table 13.2 to evaluate your basic skills:

- Make tally marks in column 2 next to the skill in each of the first five skill areas. A tally make is made each time you see a particular skill demonstrated.
- Stop the tape, and in column 3 make any comments or reflections about "depth." How deeply have you been able to allow the client to explore?
- In column 4, make notes about any problems you are encountering.
- In column 4, list any question or problems you wish to share with your instructor. Make note of the video counter number or a quotation that will help you find that spot again.

Table 13.2

(1) Skills	(2) Tally	(3) Comment and Reflect on Depth of Client's Exploration	(4) Questions and Problems
Invitational skills			
Reflecting skills			
Advanced reflecting skills			
Challenging skills			
Goal-setting skills			

Journal Starters

1. In the first "Stop and Reflect" section in Chapter 1, you filled out an inventory of your attitudes about helping. Reread that section and think about how you might answer those questions now. In general, how has this training experience affected you? Has your level of confidence fluctuated during the training? What events have been helpful, and which have been difficult?

2. If you were to keep track of a client's progress toward his or her identified outcomes, do you think you would be performing a task that is somehow at odds with the helping role? In other words, when you put on the assessor/evaluator hat, are you distancing yourself from the client? If so, how do you think you might overcome this problem in a relationship with a client?

For more journal ideas, as well as more practice with new learning experiences and with evaluation of the effectiveness of helping, see Chapter 13 in *Exercises in the Art of Helping*.

References

Anderson, C. M., & Stewart, S. (1983). *Mastering resistance: A practical guide to family therapy*. New York: Guilford.

Beamish, P. M., Granello, D. H., & Belcastro, A. L. (2002). Treatment of panic disorder: Practical guidelines. *Journal of Mental Health Counseling, 24*, 224–243.

Beck, A. T., Steer, R. A., & Brown, G. K. (1996). Beck Depression Inventory–II (BDI–II). San Antonio, TX: Psychological Corporation.

Blocher, D. (1987). *The Professional Counselor*. New York: Macmillian.

Brammer, L. M., Shostrom, E. L., & Abrego, P. J. (1989). *Therapeutic psychology: Fundamentals of* counseling and psychotherapy (5th ed.). Upper Saddle River, NJ: Prentice Hall.

Cavanagh, M. E. (1982). The counseling experience. Monterey, CA: Brooks/Cole.

Cormier, W. H., & Cormier, S. L. (1985). Interviewing strategies for helpers: Fundamental skills and cognitive behavioral interventions (2nd ed.). Pacific Grove, CA: Brooks/Cole.

Derogatis, L. R. (1975). Brief symptom inventory. Baltimore, MD: Clinical Psychometric Research.

Dixon, D. N., & Glover, J. A. (1984). Counseling: A problem-solving approach. New York: Wiley.

Epperson, D. L. (1983). Client self terminations after one counseling session: Effects of problem recognition, counselor gender, and counselor experience. Journal of Counseling Psychology, 30, 307–315.

Gladding, S. T. (2000). Counseling: A comprehensive profession (4th ed.). Upper Saddle River, NJ: Merrill/Prentice Hall.

Goodyear, R. (1981). Termination as a loss experience for the counselor. Personnel and Guidance Journal, 59, 347–350.

Granello, P. F., & Granello, D. (1998). Training counseling students to use outcome research. Counselor Education & Supervision, 37, 224–238.

Hackney, H., & Cormier, L. S. (1979). Counseling strategies and objectives. Upper Saddle River, NJ: Prentice Hall.

June, L., & Smith E. (1983) A comparison of client and counselor expectancies regarding the duration of counseling. Journal of Counseling Psychology, 30, 596–599.

Kalven, J., Rosen, L., & Taylor, B. (1981). Value development: A practical guide. Ramsey, NJ: Paulist Press.

Kanfer, F. H. (1975). Self-management methods. In F. H. Kanfer & A. P. Goldstein (Eds.), Helping people change (pp. 309–355). New York: Pergamon.

Kanfer, F. H., & Schefft, B. K. (1988). Guiding therapeutic change. Champaign, IL: Research Press.

Kaplan, H. I., & Sadock, B. J. (1998). Synopsis of psychiatry: Behavioral sciences, clinical psychiatry (8th ed.). Baltimore, MD: Lippincott, Williams & Wilkins.

Kazdin, A. E. (1980). Behavior modification in applied settings. Homewood, IL: Dorsey Press.

Kiresuk, R. J., & Sherman, R. E. (1968). Goal attainment scaling: A general method for evaluating community mental health programs. Community Mental Health Journal, 4, 443–453.

Kramer, S. A. (1986). The termination process in open-ended psychotherapy: Guidelines for clinical practice. Psychotherapy, 23, 526–531.

Kramer, S. A. (1990). Positive endings in psychotherapy. San Francisco: Jossey-Bass.

Krantz, P. L., & Lund, N. L. (1979). A dilemma of play therapy: Termination anxiety in the therapist. Teaching of Psychology, 6, 108–110.

Lamb, D. H. (1985). A time frame model of termination in psychotherapy. Psychotherapy, 22, 604–606.

Lambert, M. J., Hansen, N. B., Umphress, V., Lunnen, K., Okiishi, J., Burlingame, G. M., Huefner, J., & Reisinger, C. (1996). Administration and scoring manual for the OQ 45.2. Stevenson, MD: American Professional Credentialing Services.

Maholich, L. T., & Turner, D. W. (1979). Termination: That difficult farewell. American Journal of Psychotherapy, 33, 583–591.

Mathews, B. (1989). Terminating therapy: Implications for the private practitioner. Psychotherapy in Private Practice, 7, 29–39.

Mennicke, S. A., Lent, R. W., & Burgoyne, K. L. (1988). Premature termination from university counseling centers: A review. Journal of Counseling and Development, 66, 458–465.

Munro, J. N., & Bach, T. R. (1975). Effect of time-limited counseling on client change. Journal of Counseling Psychology, 22, 395–398.

Paul, G. L. (1967). Strategy of outcome research in psychotherapy. Journal of Consulting Psychology, 31, 109–119.

Pekarik, G. (1985). Coping with dropouts. Professional Psychology: Research and Practice, 16, 114–124.

Perry, G. P., & Paquin, J. J. (1987). Practical strategies for maintaining and generalizing improvements from psychotherapy. In P. A. Keller & S. R. Heyman (Eds.), Innovations in clinical practice: A source book (Vol. 6, pp. 151–164). Sarasota, FL: Professional Resource Exchange.

Rudestam, K. E. (1980). Methods of self-change: An ABC primer. Monterey, CA: Brooks/Cole.

Sciscoe, M. (1990). The termination of therapy. Unpublished manuscript.

Sexton, T. (1996). The relevance of counseling outcome research: Current trends and practical implications. *Journal of Counseling & Development, 74*, 62–63.

Sexton, T. L., Whiston, S. C., Bleuer, J. C., & Walz, G. R. (1997). *Integrating outcome research into counseling practice and training*. Alexandria, VA: American Counseling Association.

Shulman, L. (1979). *The skills of helping individuals and groups*. Itasca, IL: Peacock Press.

Ward, D. E. (1984). Termination of individual counseling: Concepts and strategies. *Journal of Counseling and Development, 63*, 21–25.

White, M. *Reflections on narrative practice: Essays and interviews*. Adelaide, Australia: Dulwich Centre Publications.

Wolberg, L. R. (1954). *The technique of psychotherapy*. New York: Grune & Stratton.

Yalom, I. R. (1995). *Theory and practice of group psychotherapy* (4th ed.). New York: Basic Books.

Young, M. E., & Rosen, L. S. (1985). The retreat: An educational growth group. *Journal for Specialists in Group Work, 21*, 157–171.

Curative Factors and Advanced Skills: Part I

14

There comes a stage in the development of every helper when we begin to search for the perfect technique or "silver bullet" that will work for all clients or at least for the client that is confounding us right now. At this juncture, the helper begins a search of literature and attends conferences to find the answer. The helper begins to wonder if what he or she learned in graduate school is really relevant to the real world of unique individuals where one counseling method does not seem to work for every client.

There is nothing wrong with the desire to have the most knowledge and widest range of therapeutic techniques that one can accumulate. But the systematic kind of eclecticism recommended by this book starts with the agreed-upon goals and leads to choosing methods and techniques that are aimed at those goals. This is not a trial-and-error method that begins when we hear about a new technique and then experiment with it. Rather, ethical guidelines suggest that when we are learning something new, we should seek supervision and make sure that we are using the technique because we believe it will help the client, not because we feel desperate or because we have a new toy. We can only reasonably use methods that are appropriate and sensitive to the client's unique background and current situation.

Curative Factors

In this chapter and the next, we will address each of the six curative factors first identified in Chapter 2. As we discussed in Chapter 2, a curative factor is a common or underlying element that explains why many different therapy systems seem to be effective. This viewpoint suggests that they are all evoking the healing potential in one or more of these curative elements. The concept of curative factors is useful because it provides a way of organizing the techniques you are learning and because it will help you to understand the purpose of the techniques you are choosing. The whole range of helping skills and techniques can be linked with one or more of these six factors and this provides you with a rational way to home in on the special techniques that might be effective for your client. For convenience sake, we refer to each of the factors by a letter. Together, they form the acronym REPLAN, which is a way of remembering them when we think about planning the course of helping.

R = Maintaining a Strong Helper/Client Relationship

The therapeutic alliance was discussed in Chapter 3 and in later chapters when you learned invitational and reflecting skills. Enhancing the helper/client bond involves both the nonjudgmental listening cycle on the part of the helper and the client's willingness and ability to enter the relationship. Differences between the two people (Chapter 4) also affect the therapeutic alliance. Not only must the helper provide a therapeutic atmosphere, but he or she must also take into account the unique background, family, religion, and culture that can influence the client's reaction to the helper and to the helping process. In addition, the helper must deal with transference and countertransference issues when they interfere with achieving the client's goals.

E = Enhancing Efficacy and Self-Esteem

In this chapter, we will look at techniques that improve a client's confidence in his or her abilities and also deal with an underlying lack of self-worth. Nearly all helpers agree that improved self-esteem is a desired goal, but changing long-held beliefs is a challenge.

P = Practicing New Behaviors

Later in this chapter, we will look at ways of helping clients practice a new behavior once it has been learned. For example, clients may learn communication techniques to improve the couple relationship, but they need to practice both within sessions and between sessions so that the new skills are firmly established. Many practice techniques are available to strengthen fragile new learning.

L = Lowering and Raising Emotional Arousal

The next chapter (Chapter 15) introduces techniques to quiet strong emotions and methods to arouse emotions. Quieting techniques involve such activities as relaxation training, whereas arousing techniques include asking clients to become more aware of suppressed feelings.

A = Activating Client Expectations, Hope, and Motivation

Chapter 15 also introduces ways that a helper can help motivate a discouraged client, including the use of encouragement. That chapter also discusses ways of identifying the techniques that match the client's level of motivation.

N = Providing New Learning Experiences

The number of techniques in this category far surpasses all the other groupings. Helpers stimulate new learning by provoking insight, directly teaching social skills, reframing, and many other methods. These will be discussed in Chapter 15.

Treatment Planning and the REPLAN System

There are many different methods for treatment planning. Most people are familiar with the diagnostic treatment planning method. It is the medical methodology that begins by assessing the client and arriving at a diagnosis. The diagnosis becomes the basis for determining what treatment the client will receive. If you have major depression, for example, you receive a certain treatment; if you have obsessive-compulsive disorder, you receive another (cf. Antony & Barlow, 2002).

Alternatively, many clinicians construct treatment plans based on the theory to which they subscribe. The techniques one eventually chooses may come from the Gestalt, Adlerian, psychodynamic, or behavioral theories. As indicated earlier in the book, there is good reason to think that an eclectic or integrative approach to treatment planning is useful, particularly early in training. Before one is entrenched in a particular viewpoint, one can utilize the techniques of different theories.

This brings us to how the concept of curative factors can aid us in setting up a general treatment plan. The first step in treatment planning is to make a list of problems that have been identified by the counselor, the client, or both. The next step is to order the problems in priority, choose one or more problems to focus on, and then identify techniques to address these problems (Woody, Detweiler-Bedell, Teachman, & O'Hearn, 2003). REPLAN is the goal-oriented, treatment planning model using six curative factors. The REPLAN system does not conflict with making a DSM-IV diagnosis or using theoretically oriented models, but it does assert that nearly all clients with the same diagnosis need different treatments. Therefore, treatment strategies must be tailored to the client's goals and the unique characteristics of the client rather than to a specific diagnosis.

The REPLAN system is distinguishable from other forms of treatment planning because it focuses on a relatively few number of client goals, using strategies associated with one or two curative factors. This makes it a brief treatment model. This approach has the benefit of focusing clients on a few goals at a time, rather than planning an elaborate treatment regimen that may collapse over time as the client's situation changes. The approach is not incompatible with long-term therapy, but it approaches client problems as distinct goals that must be regularly evaluated and replanned. Replanning occurs frequently during the helping process because client goals shift as some problems are resolved and new insights on old problems emerge.

Steps in Treatment Planning Using the REPLAN Model

The three basic steps in REPLAN treatment planning are:

1. Formulate mutually agreed-upon treatment goals, as a result of assessment, that are understandable to both client and helper. These goals are then boiled down to a workable, solvable form and placed in priority order.
2. Use the curative factors (maintaining a strong helper/client relationship; enhancing efficacy and self-esteem; practicing new behaviors; lowering and raising emotional arousal; activating client expectations, hope, and motivation; and providing new learning experiences) to generate a list of possible treatment strategies or techniques to achieve the goals.
3. Replan the treatment on a regular basis, say, every 6 weeks, to move new problems into focus as old issues are dealt with.

Once an overall treatment plan has been constructed, the helper generates a list of potential techniques by asking himself or herself two questions: "What curative factors are most likely to help the client reach the goals?" and "What strategies, methods, or techniques will be most effective and acceptable to the client?" To illustrate how this works in practice, let us look at the case example of Matthew, a 25-year-old single white male, a chemist, who is shy and wishes to meet and date women but has not been successful. Matthew's main problem is anxiety in social situations. Together he and the helper, Nadia, identify the following positive goal: to be able to go out with a woman and have fun.

To initiate the REPLAN method, Nadia asks herself, "Which curative factors would be most helpful for Matthew in achieving his goal?" Based on her knowledge of Matthew's situation, it seems clear that practicing new behaviors and new learning experiences would be the most useful place to begin. Now that Nadia has identified the major curative factors, she asks herself a second question, "What specific methods under these therapeutic factors would be most effective with Matthew?" She then selects strategies to evoke the therapeutic factors. Following is part of the treatment plan that she developed for Matthew, with a set of strategies or steps to help him learn social skills and then practice new behaviors. Under the curative factor Practicing New Behaviors, the objectives are shown so that you can see specific steps that Matthew and Nadia designed.

Curative Factor	Strategy
New learning experiences	1. Learn basic communication theory, listening, and self-disclosure.
Lowering emotional arousal	1. Learn a basic relaxation technique to reduce anxiety before entering social situations.
Practicing new behaviors	1. Practice self-disclosure and listening skills with helper and a friend.

Objectives

a. Role-play asking someone out for coffee.
b. Ask any friend out for coffee.
c. Ask female friend out for coffee.

In summary, the notion of curative factors is a way of identifying what the client needs and selecting a general approach to the client's problems. The use of curative factors is a heuristic, or method, for stimulating thinking about possible techniques to employ. Then the helper narrows down the list of potential techniques based on the client's needs. The rationale for this kind of approach is that it encourages the helper to weigh a wider variety of planned interventions than a theoretically oriented or a diagnostically oriented treatment planning model. I leave you with this idea and now begin to address more advanced techniques. One or two advanced techniques are presented as examples under each curative factor to give you a sampling of commonly used methods across the therapeutic spectrum.

The Therapeutic Factor of Enhancing Efficacy and Self-Esteem

The first curative factor we take up is enhancing efficacy and self-esteem (see Figure 14.1). There is wide agreement that a positive self-concept is a keystone of mental health and that raising self-esteem is a fundamental task of helping (Bednar & Peterson, 1995; Carlock, 1998; Kurpius, Rockwood, & Corbett, 1989; Walz, 1990). Humanistic theorists have identified the helper's task as increasing "can-ness." For example, Carl Rogers focused on reducing the gap between one's perceived self and one's ideal self. Adler felt that a clear sign of mental health was "faith in oneself." Likewise, low self-esteem has long been identified as a cause or contributing factor in many psychological diagnoses and symptoms, especially

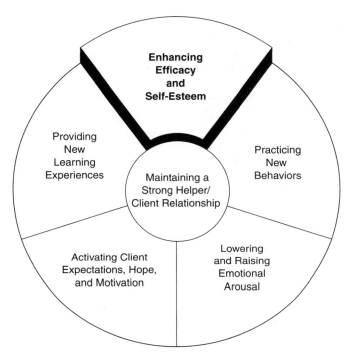

Figure 14.1
Curative Factors in the REPLAN System: Enhancing Efficacy and Self-Esteem

anxiety (Rosenberg, 1962), depression (Beck, Rush, Shaw, & Emery, 1979a; Burns, 1999; Wilson & Krane, 1980), stress, dependency, pathological guilt, borderline personality (Ingham, Kreitman, Miller, & Sasidharan, 1986), and substance abuse (Brehm & Back, 1968).

Still, self-esteem has been attacked as too vague, overpopularized, and a cure-all for problems ranging from addictions to misbehavior (Kaplan, 1995). One way of clarifying the concept is to recognize that self-esteem has two aspects: efficacy (competence) and self-worth (Branden, 1969, 1971; Witmer, 1985). Efficacy is an expectation that one can perform a specific task (Bandura, 1982, 1997). For example, when an experienced driver sits behind the wheel of a car, he or she feels a sense of confidence or expectation that driving a car is a manageable task. Efficacy is tied to specific activities, though it may generalize to similar situations. It is also subject to modification by experience. Having an auto accident could undermine one's sense of efficacy as a driver. Many clients are afraid to try new activities because of past failures. In addition, individuals with low self-esteem often do not pay sufficient attention to successes and improvements, tending to focus on their losses and failures. They may possess needed skills but do not recognize these abilities and strengths. The helper, by focusing on strengths and competencies, enhances the possibilities for success and improved self-esteem (Thompson, 1991).

In contrast to efficacy, self-worth is a global feeling that one has the right to exist, that one is basically good and is worthy to live. In short, it is self-approval. It is the sum total of one's attitudes about the self: the fundamental belief that one is "okay" or "not okay" (Berne, 1972). It is possible to feel competent or efficacious at a number of tasks and skills and still experience low self-worth. As helpers, we often meet intelligent, attractive, and talented individuals whose major problems are deeply held negative beliefs about themselves, despite their obvious competence.

Stop and Reflect

Ten Things I Can't Do

Self-esteem can be improved by increasing client self-efficacy. Efficacy is increased when clients recognize their current abilities or learn new skills. The chances that a client will attempt a new activity are increased if he or she engages in warm-up activities, including thinking about, talking about, and visualizing the new behavior. To become more familiar with this process, try the following:

1. Make a list of 10 things you cannot do at the present time but would like to be able to do. For example, your list might include:

   "I would like to learn to swim."
   "I would like to ask someone out on a date."
   "I would like to be able to use a spreadsheet on the computer."
   "I would like to be able to learn ballroom dancing."

   For this exercise, do not include personal qualities that you would like to develop or global statements about self-worth such as "I would like to be more patient" or "I would like to be a better person."
2. Once you have developed a list of 10 items, place the letter T next to each item if you have talked to a friend or family member about engaging in this activity. Place the letter V if you have ever visualized or daydreamed about yourself performing this task. Place the letter M for "models" if you have seen other people perform this task on several occasions. Place the letter A next to each task that you have attempted to perform in the last year.
3. It is thought that a person is more likely to engage in a new behavior if he or she gets ready by talking about it, visualizing it, and watching others. Conversely, when we have not readied ourselves through these activities, we are farther away from actually attempting the behavior. Look at your list and decide if your answers confirm this "readiness hypothesis." Identify one or two behaviors that have the fewest letters next to them. Which letters are missing? The missing letters should indicate which activities you can initiate if you wish to increase your readiness.
4. Do you think you might experience any change in your self-esteem if you were able to engage in all the activities on your list?
5. Compare your answers and your reactions with those of others in your training group.

Sources of Low Self-Esteem

Irrational Beliefs

Irrational beliefs are self-destructive ideas that lead to low self-esteem (Daly & Burton, 1983). They cause us to suffer emotionally, but they are so firmly entrenched that they are difficult to challenge and expunge. Albert Ellis (1973) ascribes low self-esteem to a set of "nutty beliefs" about the self and the world. It is not our experiences that keep us in a state of low self-esteem, but our ideas that hold us there. For example, Ellis asserts that it is not a black cat that makes us afraid but the belief that a black cat causes bad luck. The idea is that if we rid ourselves of irrational beliefs and develop more realistic ones, we relieve ourselves of emotional turmoil.

Although we each probably have something unique about our belief systems, Ellis found that most people's irrational ideas fall into some broad categories, and he has identified seven of the most common:

1. The idea that it is a dire necessity for an adult human to be loved or approved of by virtually every significant other person in his or her life
2. The idea that one should be thoroughly competent, adequate, and achieving in all possible respects to consider oneself worthwhile
3. The idea that certain people are bad, wicked, or villainous and that they should be severely blamed or punished for their villainy
4. The idea that it is awful and catastrophic when things are not the way one would like them to be
5. The idea that human unhappiness is externally caused and that people have little or no ability to control their terrors and disturbances
6. The idea that it is easier to avoid life's difficulties and self-responsibilities than to face them
7. The idea that one's past history is an all-important determinant of one's present behavior and that, because something once strongly affected one's life, it should definitely continue to do so (Ellis, 1973, p. 37)

Body Image

Psychological literature tells us that attractiveness is a valuable social asset (Adams, 1977) and that feeling unattractive is often equated with low self-esteem (Greenspan, 1983). Those with high self-worth generally feel good about their bodies. Those who do not like their bodies tend to be negative about themselves as a whole. An individual may have a negative body image because of a physical disability, a difference, or a lack of attractiveness by media standards. Although, in the past, low self-esteem associated with body image may have been mainly the province of women, men's magazines now reflect that society has chosen some male ideals as well. Today men are expected to have "washboard abs" and other perfect features that provide a negative comparison for the average person.

Helpers must also become aware of their evaluations of individuals who are unattractive. Helpers like attractive clients and feel less hopeful about those who are overweight and unattractive. We are all products of our culture and cultural ideas about mental health. Frequently, beginning helpers are unforgiving of clients who do not want to lose weight or who dress unattractively. In a client with a distorted body image, that body image might be a symptom of more serious psychological syndromes, especially eating disorders, resulting in the evaluation that one is fat or unattractive despite evidence to the contrary (Baird & Sights, 1986). The belief that one must be perfect is probably behind this powerful dissatisfaction that propels starvation, causes self-induced vomiting in extreme cases, and engenders low self-esteem, anger, and distress even in those without major emotional problems (Thompson & Thompson, 1986).

Stop and Reflect

One way to increase self-esteem is to ask clients to pay more attention to their strengths and abilities. Because helping is a profession where results are not often immediate, even helpers need to pause and reflect on their accomplishments from time to time. Take this moment to reflect on your own personal assets.

A Self-Esteem Personal Inventory

1. Write down eight personal characteristics that you are proud of. For example, you may be creative, organized, humorous, goal oriented, and so on.
2. List eight things that you do well.
3. Write down a few compliments about yourself that you hear from friends and family. What are the good things people say about you?
4. List three occasions when you feel that you have truly helped another person.
5. List the top three accomplishments of your life so far.
6. Write down three things that you like about your body.

Keep your answers in mind when you answer this next set of questions:

- Now that you have completed this exercise, conduct a brief scan of your emotional state. Do you notice any difference in the way you feel?
- Were there any answers you felt reluctant to write down? Were you apprehensive about "bragging"? What are the rules in your own family or culture governing when it is all right to give yourself a compliment?
- If you were given this assignment as a client, how do you think you might react to it?
- Which question was the most difficult to answer? Why? If you had been asked to list your negative qualities, would it have been easier or more difficult?

Silencing the Internal Critic: The Technique of Countering

In this section, we will learn one key method for increasing client self-esteem, *countering*, a cognitive behavioral method for decreasing the internal, negative voices that depress performance and focus on failure. Certainly many clients will also benefit from assertiveness training and other behaviors that silence external critics, but the first step is to decrease the disapproval that is coming from our own mental activity. Countering means learning to argue with this self-disapproval.

Before one can experience self-worth, it is often necessary to silence the internal critic, the "voice in the head" that reproaches and finds fault. This critic is probably created early in life through the learning of irrational beliefs that comes from family members (McKay & Fanning, 1987). These irrational beliefs and drivers persist later in life as silent sentences that the individual repeats in the mind and sometimes even aloud. Characteristically, these thoughts tend to occur automatically. For example, before giving a speech, the following thought might occur: "I am going to get up and make a fool of myself." The negative thought leads to negative emotions of anger, depression, and lowered expectations of the self. Thus, before self-esteem can be built, it is often necessary to reduce the power of the internal critic and to modify these self-statements (Dowd, 1985).

How to Counter

Countering is a term coined by McMullin (2000) to describe the production of a self-statement that is incompatible with the critical thought. Countering consists of identifying the discouraging or self-downing statements a person says to himself or herself and replacing them with equally powerful affirmations. The countering method has several steps:

Step 1: Do a brief assessment.   Once helper and client have agreed that negative self-talk is a problem, it is critical to determine the frequency of the negative self-statements and their effects on the client. For this purpose, ask the client to engage in self-assessment or self-monitoring activities to determine the frequency and types of self-downing behavior. Typically, the client carries an index card in a pocket, wallet, or purse and notes each time a self-criticism occurs. The client writes down the exact words of each self-criticism and the associated negative emotions. The client brings the card back to the next session and discusses the thoughts he or she has noticed. The self-criticism card serves two functions: It gives client and helper more data about the problem, and it helps the client make the connection between negative self-statements and the feeling states they produce. The client can begin to see that instead of providing valid criticisms, the internal monologue is producing negative emotions.

Step 2: Identify the negative thought patterns and core beliefs.   Once the client has completed at least a week's worth of self-monitoring, the major negative thought patterns and core beliefs about the self may be identified from the compiled results of the self-monitoring task. Together, helper and client look at the self-monitoring material and choose a few negative patterns to focus on. Often three or four general ideas (or core beliefs) about oneself come to the surface—for example:

"I am not disciplined and never get anything accomplished."
"I am disorganized."
"I'll never be able to reach my goals."

Step 3: Identify effective counters.   The counter can be a phrase, a sentence, or a single word such as "nonsense." The counter is a way of talking back to oneself and disputing the self-criticism. The best counters are those that are not too disturbing to the client's values and philosophy and that are the most powerful in neutralizing the client's negative thoughts.

Together, client and helper brainstorm a number of possible counters, and the client selects several with which to experiment. Here is an example of a self-criticism and a list of counters generated by client and helper:

Self-Criticism	Counters
"I am stupid."	1. "I have always performed well in school; there's no evidence for this."
	2. "Feeling stupid doesn't mean I am stupid."
	3. "That's something my dad always told me. But it's not true!"
	4. "Not true!"

Step 4: Test counters and modify them. The final stage in the process of eliminating self-criticism is to evaluate the effectiveness of the counters that the individual has practiced since the last helping session. The client will likely need more than 1 week to experience much success in neutralizing negative thoughts. Negative thoughts are automatic, and it takes time before clients can learn to "catch themselves" thinking negatively.

One method for evaluating the effectiveness of a counter ahead of time is for the helper to practice the countering technique with the client during a session. First the client selects a statement from a list of self-criticisms and reads it aloud to the helper. After making the self-criticism, the client rates his or her emotional reaction to the criticism on a 100-point SUDS (Subjective Units of Discomfort Scale). On the SUDS, 100 equals high emotional distress and 0 equals no emotional distress. Next the client reads a counter from the list that was brainstormed earlier and again rates his or her feelings of distress. In the following example, the client learned that this self-criticism was very disturbing (80) and that the counter was very effective because it reduced the strength of the emotional reaction to about 20.

Self-Criticism	Counter
"I am stupid."	"I have always performed well in school; there's no evidence for this."
SUDS after self-criticism—80	SUDS after counter—20

Step 5: Practice and report. Once the client has identified some effective counters for one or two negative thoughts, the client is asked to practice countering and report at the next session. At follow-up sessions, the helper and the client gauge progress and continually seek more effective counters. The client is asked to notice if negative thoughts have become less frequent.

Problems and Precautions When Teaching the Countering Technique

Ineffective counters should be discarded, and the client should be prepared for the fact that some counters are more potent than others. The client can be asked to modify the counter slightly in any way that might refine it or make it more effective. The helper should also suggest any personal words or phrases that might produce more self-confidence. For example, one client found that introducing each counter with "Clearly . . ." gave the counter more power for her.

Counters should be realistic. They should not be simply positive thinking or "affirmations," but should actually dispute the negative ideas. A statement such as "Every day, in every way, I'm getting better and better" is a pep talk without real substance; it is not tied to any particular self-criticism. Also, some negative self-statements are quite persistent, and it may take months to eliminate insidious automatic thoughts.

McMullin (2000) suggests that the counter should be in the same mode as the thought it is disputing. Negative visual images should be countered with positive visual images. Angry thoughts should be countered with compassionate ones, and "passive thoughts with assertive ones" (p. 5). Also, shorter counters tend to be more effective than longer ones.

A Variation on Countering: Thought Stopping

Sometimes clients are troubled by unwanted thoughts and images that create anxiety and depression and damage self-esteem. Unwanted thoughts and images may be memories of failure or concern about upcoming events. We are all familiar with lying in bed at night thinking about all the upcoming responsibilities. Once such thoughts get started, they snowball, creating more and more anxiety unless we have the skills to suppress our thinking when it gets out of control.

Compared with the developing of counters, thought stopping can be considered more of an emergency measure to halt the flow of negative messages. The helper teaches the client the technique in the office, and the client practices it whenever a severely disturbing thought arises. Three steps in the thought-stopping technique have been identified (Davis, Eshelman, & McKay, 1980; Lazarus, 1971; Witmer, 1985):

1. Stating the thought
2. Creating a startling interruption
3. Substituting a new thought

Once the troubling thought has been identified, the client is asked to label and state it either mentally or aloud—for example, "I have to get an A on this paper!" This repetition brings the thought into clearer focus. The client then creates a startling response strong enough to interrupt the negative thinking pattern. One practical method when practicing thought stopping privately is to yell "Stop!" as loudly as possible. In public, it is best to use "the tongue of thought" and say "Stop!" mentally. Some helpers suggest wearing a rubber band around the wrist and snapping it along with a mental "Stop!" to produce the startle effect.

The final step is to insert a positive thought to replace the irrational, self-downing thought. This can be either a spontaneous or a planned counter that the client produces to counteract the negative thought. In this case, the substituted thought might be something such as, "I'm not going to worry about the grade. I'll do the best that I can."

Practicing New Behaviors

The next therapeutic, or curative, factor in our list is practicing new behaviors (see Figure 14.2). Practice has always been a part of a "psychoeducational" approach to helping (Guerney, Stollack, & Guerney, 1971; Schutz, 1981; Young & Rosen, 1985). The major idea is that many client problems are due to skill deficits. Clients often

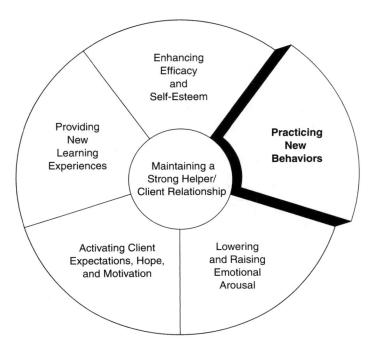

Figure 14.2
Curative Factors in the REPLAN System: Practicing New Behaviors

need to learn skills to help them become better at parenting, be more adept at communicating, face fearful situations, or develop more effective ways of thinking. As an educator, the helper cannot be content for the client to eliminate a problem behavior or merely gain insight into the fact that he or she is operating in a self-defeating manner. Clients must overcome the force of old habits by establishing a new pattern of behaviors through practice and rehearsal.

The best instruction for any skill includes the following sequence: (1) some theory is explained that provides a rationale for learning the new skill, (2) the learner is exposed to a model (therapist or group member) who correctly demonstrates the skill, and (3) the learner demonstrates the behavior in the real or simulated situation by practicing in class and completing homework assignments. For example, if you were learning to play the guitar, the instructor might explain the fingering using a chart or graph. Then the instructor would probably demonstrate how the piece is to be played, or you might listen to a recording of the selection. You would then attempt the music with the instructor present, and later you would be sent home to practice. The process of acquiring a new behavior or a new thinking pattern takes place in much the same way. Helpers use each of these steps when teaching a new skill: explanation of theory, modeling, and in-session practice and homework. In this chapter, we will focus on two specific methods used to aid clients in practicing new skills: role-playing and homework.

Role-Playing

Role-playing is a technique commonly used by helpers in providing social skills training and in helping clients face situations they are avoiding (Kipper, 1986). It involves practicing a behavior in a contrived situation with the helper playing an auxiliary or observer role. It may also take place in a group setting with other participants who can give valuable feedback and act as auxiliaries. Role-playing was introduced by the creative genius J. L. Moreno, a Viennese psychiatrist who formulated the psychodramatic method. On one occasion, following a lecture by Freud, Moreno is said to have responded, "Well, Dr. Freud, I start where you leave off. You meet people in the artificial setting of your office. I meet them on the street and in their home, in their natural surroundings. You analyze their dreams. I try to give them the courage to dream again . . ." (Moreno, 1964, pp. 5–6). Moreno's response reflects his belief that helping should involve learning in as naturalistic a setting as possible. Part of what Moreno objected to in traditional therapies was the separation of a client's problems from the natural environment, just as a religious sculpture or painting cannot be fully appreciated in a museum but must be seen in a church or temple. Since it is not always possible to see individuals in their natural contexts, the psychodramatic method proposes to re-create an individual's joys and sorrows on the psychodramatic stage (Starr, 1977). Moreno's famous dictum was, "Show me, don't tell me!" He felt that most "talk therapies" relied on the client's descriptions of problems. Since we cannot reach into the subjective experience of the person through words, we should transfer the mind onto the stage where the person's total behavior, including thoughts, feelings, and intuitions, are observable and changeable. Those who want to learn more about psychodrama should consult Adam Blatner's book, *Acting-In: Practical Applications of Psychodramatic Methods* (1998). Research on the effectiveness of psychodramatic techniques is summarized in an article by Kipper and Ritchie (2003).

Elements of Role-Playing

The technique of role-playing is a limited form of psychodrama and usually involves an encounter between two individuals or two or more different parts of the self (monodrama). Role-playing can be performed by a single individual (the protagonist), who plays all the roles in the drama, or with the help of other individuals called auxiliaries. Psychodramatic role-playing has always been conceived of as having three phases: warm-up, action, and sharing and analysis (Yablonsky, 1976).

Three Phases of Psychodramatic Role-Playing

Warm-up

The warm-up is any activity that helps the client get in touch emotionally with the experience he or she is trying to express. The warm-up decreases stage fright and allows the protagonist to develop readiness and involvement in the process. Most of us have warm-ups, or rituals, we use to prepare us for action. For example, the runner does stretching exercises, and the actor rehearses lines. In role-playing, proper warm-up is crucial to the success of the technique. Warm-up might include asking the protagonist to discuss the situation or introducing a physical activity, such as pacing back and forth.

The helper may also use role reversal to allow the client to experience the other person's viewpoint. In role reversal, the helper instructs the client to pretend to be the other person and respond as he or she might. For example, the client changes places and sits on the chair that previously represented his mother. He responds as his mother might respond in a similar circumstance. Role reversal is one of the most effective ways of getting the client involved in the role play. Besides, role reversal makes the situation more real. The client is able to anticipate the responses of a significant other, and strategies can be devised to cope with them.

The phrase "moving from the periphery to the center" is connected to the notion of a warm-up. It is a rule of thumb or a reminder to the helper to begin with tangential events before moving to more significant or central issues. For example, if the role play involves returning home to see a dying grandfather, the helper would not begin with the deathbed confrontation, but would move the client through several less potent scenes. In this case, these scenes might include driving to the house while reminiscing about the relationship or replaying previous encounters between the two. This method also gives the helper more information about the client and the client's relationships and life circumstances. With sufficient warm-up, the client overcomes stage fright and is more in tune with the actual role play when it takes place.

Action

After the warm-up, the helper asks the client to take on his or her own role and enact the situation. Scene setting is the preliminary step of this action phase. It involves asking the protagonist to set up the stage to resemble the actual setting where the incident took place or where the behavior will possibly occur in the future. The client is given free rein to use available props and to orient the stage in whatever way feels comfortable. The helper assists the client in defining the stage, designating the time of day and date, describing the situation verbally, using props, and identifying important people to be portrayed.

Sharing and Analysis

In group therapy, the sharing phase of role-playing allows the individual to reenter the group situation, that is, to get out of the spotlight. The other group members use this opportunity to relate personal experiences evoked by the client's role play. This technique reinvolves the audience and helps the client feel less alone and exposed. At some later time, a feedback or analysis session is held, during which members give feedback to the client and the role play is discussed. In an individual session, the helper normally gives the client feedback immediately after each role play.

How to Conduct Role-Playing

Role-playing is one of the most effective ways of practicing a new behavior. The immediate observation and feedback allow for actual practice, not simply talking about problems. At a deeper level, role-playing and role reversal can help the individual to become more fully aware of feelings and to explore the phenomenological worlds of the significant people in his or her life. The method described here is a generic role-playing technique for practicing new behavior. To make the method easier to understand, a hypothetical example unfolds throughout the explanation. The client, Martin, is anxious because he has to give a presentation to his board of directors concerning progress on his yearly goals. The helper, Andrea, suggests that they role-play the situation to rehearse his talk.

Step 1: Warm-up. In the warm-up, Andrea previews and explains the purpose and the elements of role-playing. Using the principle of proceeding from the periphery to the center, Andrea begins the warm-up by asking Martin to discuss aspects of his job that he will be presenting, details of the workplace, and other tangential topics. The most important aspect of this step is for Andrea to get Martin to describe the target behaviors very specifically. In this case, he wants to:

1. Maintain eye contact with his audience
2. Speak from notes in a loud, clear voice
3. Smile when questions are asked
4. End the session by thanking the audience

Step 2: Scene setting. After Martin has discussed the situation, he appears more relaxed. Andrea then invites him to describe his own office (peripheral) and later the board meeting room (central). Andrea lets Martin set the scene, rearranging Andrea's office furnishings to approximate the setup of the boardroom. Andrea encourages Martin to point out various features, such as the color of the walls and the furniture, to establish the scene.

Step 3: Selecting roles and role reversal. In this step, the client identifies important people in the scene and briefly describes them. In a group setting, other members of the group would be assigned to these roles. In an individual session, empty chairs represent these significant persons. For example, Andrea asks Martin to reverse roles and pretend to be his boss to get a sense of his demeanor and attitude. She also asks him to point out the chairs of some of the other board members and briefly describe them.

Step 4: Enactment. At this point, the helper asks the client to briefly portray the target behaviors as described during the warm-up. In Martin's case, the scene begins in his office and culminates with his entrance into the "boardroom." Andrea acts as a coach during the first run-through, prompting Martin to display each identified behavior. The helper is dissatisfied with Martin's portrayal of the final behavior, thanking the audience. Andrea stops the action and takes on Martin's role to model an effective closing statement. Following the modeling, Andrea asks Martin to try the closing a second time in his own way using whatever parts of Andrea's closing he liked.

Step 5: Sharing and feedback. In this step, the helper shares feedback with the client. The feedback should be specific, simple, observable, and understandable to the client. It should mainly reinforce positive aspects of the behavior. In our example, Andrea tells Martin, "Your voice was very strong and clear. I think you got your points across very well. I would like to see even more eye contact with the board members during the next run-through."

Step 6: Reenactment. Reenactment is a repetition of the target behavior from entrance to exit. The sequence is repeated until the client is confident that each of the behaviors in the target list has been mastered.

Step 7: Homework and follow-up. At the next session, the client is asked to report practice results. Martin has practiced the behavior by giving the presentation to some family members, and he describes this to Andrea. Further role-playing practice may be given during the session, if necessary. When the helper feels that the client has consistently demonstrated the target behaviors, the helper urges the client to attempt the behaviors in a real situation.

Problems and Precautions with Role-Playing

1. The most frequently encountered difficulty with the role-playing technique is stage fright. Resistance to the technique is ordinarily the result of insufficient warm-up, inadequate preparation time, the client's lack of confidence, or inadequate reassurance by the helper.
2. Because of the power of the technique, both the helper and the client may be unprepared for the strength of the emotion that is sometimes evoked. This is unlikely when using role-playing for practicing a new behavior. Beginning helpers should not attempt to reenact traumatic scenes from the past.
3. Because most helpers focus on the client's thoughts and feelings, we sometimes have trouble thinking in dramatic terms. In the usual session, the client is encouraged to describe an encounter with another person by saying, "I am angry because she neglected me." In a role-playing session, the client would be instructed, "Show me how you expressed your anger to her." By creating a dramatic situation, the helper learns a great deal about the quality and context of the behavior, rather than just the client's description of it.

Homework

Homework has been identified as a crucial tool in effective helping (Beck, Rush, Shaw, & Emery, 1979b; Shelton & Ackerman, 1974). Homework refers to any tasks or assignments given to clients to be completed between sessions (Last, 1985). Some tasks are used for assessment purposes; others are used to increase client awareness of the behavior (Martin & Worthington, 1982); still other homework assignments are designed as independent practice sessions. In this section, the main emphasis will be on homework that is used to practice new behaviors. These new behaviors are normally learned during the therapeutic session and may be modeled or rehearsed in the office before they are assigned as homework. Review of homework provides a starting point for each new session with a review of progress made and problems encountered in the assignment.

Reasons for Using Homework

A major advantage of using homework assignments is that they provide follow-up or treatment continuance between sessions. When one realizes that a client spends 1 hour out of 112 waking hours per week in counseling, it is easy to see how helping can be diluted by other activities. Homework assignments, especially if they require some daily work, can enhance treatment considerably (Shelton & Ackerman, 1974; Shelton & Levy, 1981).

In addition, homework assignments turn insights and awareness into tangible behaviors and prevent helping from being only a place to unload one's feelings. Transfer of training or generalization of learning is facilitated by applying descriptions and models of behavior to real-life situations as soon as possible.

Homework practice also begins the shift of control from the helper to the client. If the client attributes progress to his or her own effort in outside assignments, greater efficacy and self-esteem will result.

Examples of Homework Assignments

Bibliotherapy

Bibliotherapy means assigning readings to clients to help them achieve their goals. The plethora of self-help books now on the market is evidence of a growing awareness that psychological literature can bring about change; however, much of the offerings in trade books are oversimplified, based on opinion or a few anecdotes. Before recommending a book to a client, the helper should have read the book and should carefully think about whether the book will be acceptable to the client's present frame of reference and assist with the client's goals. At each session, the helper should discuss the client's reading and go over important points, perhaps even asking a few relevant questions about how the assignment fits the client's current dilemma.

Although it is not possible to provide an exhaustive list of good bibliographic materials here, resources for selecting books and manuals are available (cf. Gladding & Gladding, 1991; Jackson, 2001). A very good stress management workbook-and-tape set, *Kicking Your Stress Habits* (Tubesing, 1981), is available. Many clients with marital problems have benefited from Michele Weiner-Davis's (1992) *Divorce Busting*, while David Burns's (1999) *Feeling Good* contains an excellent cognitive approach to depression that the average person can easily grasp. A number of other books, such as Arnold Lazarus's (1982) *Personal Enrichment Through Imagery*, are now available on audiotape and can be listened to while driving or relaxing.

Besides informing the client, bibliotherapy can provide covert practice by exposing the client to a fictional or historical model of a desired behavior. Clients may identify with case studies or with fictional characters who face similar problems. The "Big Book" of Alcoholics Anonymous contains a number of true accounts of individuals who have successfully overcome drinking problems.

Aides

One way to increase the efficacy of homework practice is to enlist the help of a client's friend, spouse, or family member as an aide who provides either feedback or support for completing assignments. Generally, an aide comes to sessions with the client. The helper specifically identifies the aide's role as either support or feedback. Let us say that the client is attempting to become more assertive. The aide would be given specific verbal and nonverabal behaviors to observe and would report observations to the client. Alternatively, the aide might simply be enlisted to provide support or to accompany the client while he or she completes assignments. The client who is attempting to exercise regularly may use an aide as a regular walking partner. The aide would help the client increase regularity and provide encouragement from session to session. The major pitfall of using aides is that they must be supervised by the helper. Sometimes aides are too helpful and wish to take excessive responsibility for the client. If this behavior cannot be modified, the client should proceed alone.

Journaling and Record Keeping

Journaling is a daily writing assignment given to the client by the helper. Ordinarily, the client brings the journal to the next session for the helper's reaction. Journals usually serve one of two purposes. Sometimes journals are assigned as an open-ended writing assignment to help the client do more in-depth examination of his or her thoughts, feelings, and behaviors. Alternatively, the helper may use journaling to record practice sessions. These might include keeping track of countering skills (cognitive), recording the amount of emotional discomfort (affective), or noting the number of times a new behavior was actually practiced (behavioral).

Consider the following case study of Joe, a 29-year-old administrator for an insurance company who has come for help to deal with problems associated with "stress." He has borderline high blood pressure, is often tense and angry after work and, as a result, sometimes becomes rude to his fiancée, alienating her. He plays racquetball competitively, and last week he purposely broke an expensive recquet after a bad shot. He wishes to control his anger and feel less "stressed" at work. During the assessment, the counselor identified negative self-statements as a major cause of the client's stress and felt that, in general, the most useful path for Joe was to increase self-esteem. Joe agreed, but also felt he needed better organizational skills. The initial plan was negotiated as a two-pronged attack: to decrease self-criticism and to develop better time management and organizational skills. Joe enrolled in a 3-day time management workshop sponsored by his company and, at the same time, began keeping a journal, as shown in Table 14.1. Figure 14.3 is a graph of Joe's SUDS levels and negative self-statements over the first 10 days. (As noted earlier, SUDS is an acronym for the Subjective Units of Discomfort Scale). In this case, 0 represents no discomfort and 100 represents extreme distress. Using a homework card, Joe found that he was producing anger by his self-statements, which were first aimed at himself and sometimes directed at innocent bystanders. Joe agreed to continue to monitor his self-statements for two more weeks and noticed a marked diminishing of his self-criticism. In Joe's case, there seemed to be a correspondence between his self-criticism and his emotional discomfort. Although the major purpose of keeping this journal was to encourage practice, the client also developed insight into the way he maintained his anger.

Table 14.1

Self-Criticism Homework Card for Joe

No.	Time	Self-Statement	Feeling	SUDS
1.	8:15	I'll never get all this work done.	Discouraged	85
2.	9:00	I didn't do a good job on that report.	Disgust	50
3.	10:00	I'll never be good at this job. I'm just average and that's all.	Self-pity	60
4.	10:35	I'm daydreaming again. Why am I so lazy?	Anger	35
5.	12:00	I offended the secretary again. Why can't I just keep my mouth shut?	Anger	45
6.	1:00	I feel fat after eating so much. I'm turning into a blimp.	Disgust	35
7.	2:40	Another day almost done, and I've completed nothing.	Anger	40
8.	3:30	My desk is a mess. What a slob!	Discouraged	50
9.	5:15	Even my car is full of trash. I wish I were more organized.	Anger	25

SUDS = Subjective Units of Distress Scale

0. 100

No emotional distress   Extreme emotional distress

Emotions = fear, anger, sadness, guilt, interest-excitement/(boredom), joy, disgust, surprise

Summary

9 = negative self-statements; average SUDS = 47 (approx.)

Most prevalent emotion = self-anger/disgust

Problems and Precautions with Homework

1. Homework assignments that have a high probability of success should be chosen (Dyer & Vriend, 1977). This is true especially early in the helping relationship in order to keep the client's hope alive. Also, by promoting small, easily completed goals, the client begins to learn that most change is gradual, not an overnight phenomenon.
2. Homework strategies should be individually tailored for each client (Haley, 1978, 1989). Too often, the helper uses a standard homework assignment that, to the discouraged client, may feel impersonal. By stretching one's creativity, some assignments can incorporate more than one of the client's goals. If the client likes to read, recommending self-help books as homework might work well. If the client enjoys writing, assign a journal.
3. Practicing regularly is important. It would be better, for example, if the client performs a rehearsal for 10 minutes once per day, rather than practicing for an hour one time per week.
4. Homework should be simple and fit easily into the lifestyle of the client. Complicated homework involving extensive record keeping may not be completed.
5. As the client progresses, homework should increase in difficulty or discomfort. Clients usually have a feel for when they are ready for more challenging tasks and for tasks that are presently beyond them.

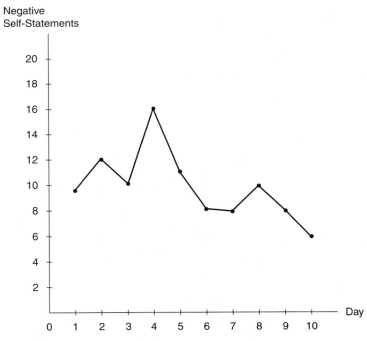

Figure 14.3
Graph of Daily SUDS Levels and Critical Self-Statements for Joe

Summary

In this chapter, you were introduced to the idea of using curative factors as a method for understanding the reasons for the effectiveness of various therapeutic techniques, and we describe a method of treatment planning called the REPLAN model that utilizes six curative factors to organize our therapeutic efforts. Next we examined two of these factors more closely: (1) enhancing efficacy and self-esteem and (2) practicing new behaviors. Self-esteem has two components: self-worth and efficacy. Enhancing both is critical for boosting self-esteem. Client's with better self-esteem are more likely to succeed in accomplishing other goals. Clients can learn to enhance efficacy by attempting new behaviors and by paying attention to their present strengths and skills. Low self-worth is a general attitude that the self is "not okay," worthless, or ineffective. Low self-worth is responsible for a number of serious psychological conditions, negative emotions, and a demoralized attitude toward life. We have explored causes of low self-worth and identified injunctions learned early in life, including irrational ideas and negative body image. We also looked at one method for enhancing self-esteem called countering. Countering is aimed at reducing negative self-talk.

Practice is a method that helpers promote to help clients put insights into action and try out new behaviors in a protected environment. In this chapter we looked at two techniques for practice: role-playing and homework. Role-playing is a practice technique that involves re-creating the context of a desired behavior right in the helper's office. Major contributions to this technique have come from psychodrama and the behaviorists (Lazarus, 1985). This technique allows the helper to obtain firsthand knowledge about the client's behavioral style, while the client benefits from rehearsal and feedback. Homework assignments are given to clients to prolong treatment between sessions as well as to establish the new behavior as a habit. Assignments should be individually tailored to the client and may involve journaling activities, lay helpers as aides, and bibliotherapy. Helpers who regularly utilize practice in the office or as homework are more likely to increase the transfer of training to real-life situations.

Exercises

Group Exercise 1: Identifying Irrational Beliefs

Part I First, form groups of four, with each student, in turn, taking on the roles of client, helper, and observers. The client discusses one of the following topics with the helper:

- A time when the client was very angry at someone
- A time when the client was very angry at himself or herself
- A time when someone disappointed the client
- Something the client has a difficult time forgiving

The helper's job is to listen, using all the skills in the nonjudgmental listening sequence, for 5–10 minutes. He or she is not to make an effort to challenge the client's beliefs, but simply to draw them out.

Observer 1 writes down all the helper's interventions verbatim. Observer 2 reviews the list of Ellis's seven irrational beliefs described earlier in the chapter. Then, during the session, observer 2 listens carefully to the client's statements and records the gist of those that seem to indicate an underlying irrational belief.

Part II: Debriefing

1. Take a couple of minutes to allow client, helper, and observers to share their thoughts about this exercise.

2. Then observer 1 gives the helper the list of interventions and feedback about his or her performance on the nonjudgmental listening sequence. The helper can keep the list of interventions and review them later. At this point, the list of interventions should include several paraphrases, reflections of feeling, and perhaps a reflection of meaning or two, depending on the depth of the client's story. If questions predominate, the helper should return to previous chapters for review and should schedule additional practice sessions with classmates.

3. Observer 2 indicates any irrational ideas that he or she identified in the client's statements. As a group, the helper and the two observers can identify some counters that might be used by the client as an antidote to these beliefs. The client either confirms or disagrees with the observer's ideas and then indicates which he or she feels might be the most effective.

Group Exercise 2: Role-Playing

Role-playing as a rehearsal technique sometimes focuses on situations in the past that clients would like to resolve. By attempting to bring them to closure in a role-play situation, the client is rehearsing for a later time when the issues can be addressed in real life.

The exercise begins with the client, who identifies an individual in the past or present with whom he or she has "unfinished business." Unfinished business refers to a relationship or an issue that he or she was unable to adequately resolve in the past, but would like to bring to a positive conclusion. It is recommended that participants choose minor situations such as:

"My friend did not invite me to her wedding."
"My boyfriend criticized me in front of his mother, but I did not mention it."
"A teacher treated me unfairly, and I was never able to explain."
"I was attracted to someone in the past, but I never told her."

For this exercise, students form groups of four with roles of helper, client, observer 1, and observer 2. Observer 1 gives the client feedback, and observer 2 gives the helper feedback on his or her ability to demonstrate the skill of role-playing.

Briefly, this exercise has the following phases:

1. The roles of helper, client, observer 1, and observer 2 are assigned.
2. The client thinks of a situation involving unfinished business.
3. The helper directs the client through the first five steps of role-playing.
4. Observer 1 and the helper give the client feedback; the client reenacts the role-play if more practice seems advisable.
5. Observer 2 gives the helper feedback and discusses the exercise.

Step 1: Warm-up. As a warm-up, the helper invites the client to explain the situation and uses the nonjudgmental listening cycle to get a clear understanding of the situation.

Step 2: Scene setting. The helper asks the client to briefly describe where and when a meeting with the affected individual might take place. The client sits in one chair, and the other chair is left empty for the person with whom the client has unfinished business.

Step 3: Selecting roles and role reversal. In this exercise, the client will play both himself or herself and the other person with whom the client has unfinished business. To begin, the helper asks the client to reverse roles and sit in the empty chair while completely taking on the identity of the other person. The helper asks this significant other to describe himself or herself and to give a little bit of background about the situation from that person's perspective.

Step 4: Enactment. Once the client has presented the other person, the helper asks him or her to return to the original chair and resume his or her natural identity. Now the client expresses some of the thoughts and feelings that he or she has wanted to get out into the open. The helper facilitates the client to express this in any way the client wishes. The client speaks these thoughts and feelings to the empty chair as if the other person were actually present.

Once the client has had the opportunity to express his or her thoughts and feelings, the client reverses roles again and becomes the other person, responding to the charges leveled against him or her. The enactment ends when the client returns to his or her natural role and original seat and responds to the other person's reaction.

Step 5: Sharing and feedback. In this step, the helper and observer 1 give the client feedback on how well the client was able to finish the unfinished business. For example, was the client able to express everything he or she intended in an assertive and straightforward way? Was the client overly aggressive or too tentative and passive?

Step 6: Reenactment. Reenactment follows sharing and feedback if the client needs to make improvements. In reenactment, the client stays in the client chair and has another opportunity to

clearly and assertively make complaints and requests. Following this, the helper and observer 1 give the client feedback.

Step 7: Homework and follow-up. Group members discuss what possible homework and follow-up procedures they might employ had this been a real client problem.

The final phase of this group exercise is for observer 2 to give feedback to the helper on how well he or she was able to assist the client in practicing the new behavior. Observer 2 should have notes on each of the steps of role-playing and give specific feedback. Both client and observer 1 may also have feedback to share.

Quick Tips: Role-Playing

- Help the client overcome stage fright and initial discomfort by using a warm-up process such as a discussion of the situation before the role play begins.
- Getting the client to physically move around, arrange chairs, and set the scene helps to warm up the client.
- If clients resist the role-play technique, you may have to abandon it until trust is better developed. On the other hand, your confidence in the procedure will encourage them, and reassurance that "you'll get into it" may help them to get over their initial reluctance.
- If clients experience emotional arousal as a result of the role play, the helper may find it necessary to implement the non-judgmental listening cycle rather than continuing with the role-play.

Group Exercise 3

Consider the following case studies in a small group of fellow students. What does each client need to practice? Which issues would you address first? What kind of rehearsal seems best suited to each of these client's problems? In a

small group, brainstorm two or three creative homework assignments for each client. Role-play one of these situations, with one student playing the client and the other, the helper, making a homework assignment.

a. Carol is a 37-year-old married woman with one child. She and her counselor agree to work on her extreme reluctance to leave home even for a few hours to go to the grocery store. She experiences fear and panic attacks in public situations. She has not been shopping in 2 years and has lost respect for herself as a contributing member of her family. Following two sessions of history taking and a medical evaluation (the client incorrectly believes she has a heart condition), the counselor and client, following a complete assessment, agree that she needs assistance in dealing with low self-esteem and that she needs to practice going out in public. The client has a number of dysfunctional beliefs, including "I am weak," that seem to contribute to her inability to attempt new behaviors.

b. Maureen is a 20-year-old college student, the only child of parents who appear to be on the verge of divorce. She comes to the college counseling center complaining that she is always in the middle of her parents' quarrels and that each parent calls to tell her about the other's failings. In her attempts to placate both sides, Maureen has become anxious and depressed and has trouble studying. She experiences periods of crying and expresses sympathy for both parents. Maureen initially frames her problem as "how to help my parents cope with their divorce." In the second session, Maureen agrees that what she wants is to maintain a relationship with both parents, to be supportive of both, and not to listen to their complaints about each other.

Homework

Homework 1: Diary

Select a personal growth goal for yourself that involves practicing a new behavior. For example:

"I would like to play my guitar every day."

"I would like to cook regular meals to combat my tendency to snack throughout the day."

"I would like to take time every day to improve my relationship with people at work."

- At the end of each day, for 1 week, write down the number of times you engaged in the behavior, or indicate if you did not practice during the day. Write down any ideas you have about why you did or did not practice the behavior during the day.
- At the end of a week, summarize your conclusions in a half-page reaction. Do you think that self-monitoring by keeping a journal was helpful to you? What kinds of clients might benefit from this approach? What kinds of problems are best suited to keeping a diary such as this?

Homework 2: Practicing a Skill

Select a building block skill from this book that you would like to improve.

a. Write down the name of the skill:

_____

b. Does the skill need to be broken down into small components? If so, list them here:

_____

_____

c. Spend 5 minutes imagining yourself successfully demonstrating each part of the skill. (This could be called "imaginal rehearsal.")

d. Ask a fellow student who is proficient in the skill to model it for you.

e. Ask a student partner to act as an observer and practice the skill with a third student, who will serve as the client.

f. Get feedback and rehearse again, incorporating the suggestions you received.

g. With help from your training group, select several situations in real life where you might practice this skill.

h. Make an appointment with a fellow student to call him or her and report on your progress in a week.

Homework 3: Personal Experiments

Think about something that you don't do very well, or think about a part of your body that you do not feel is very attractive. Get opinions from eight friends or family members. How accurate is your self-concept? If they do not agree, why do you cling to this belief? In what ways have you distorted your view of the self? Write a half-page reaction to this exercise.

Journal Starters

1. Sometimes helpers ask clients to consider incidents in their lives in which low self-esteem might have originated. For example, was the client affected by excessive criticism or perfectionistic expectations? Some authors have even said that self-concept is "the reflected appraisals of others." On the other hand, Eleanor Roosevelt believed that no one can make you feel bad about yourself without your permission. Think about your own life experiences and decide which view is closest to your opinion on the subject? Are both true for you?

2. The curative factor of practicing new behaviors implies that the helper should encourage the client to act. It is assumed that practice leads to change even if the change did not start within. What is your reaction to these ideas? What have been the most significant catalysts for change in your own life? Can you identify any times in your own life when you have tried to face fears or have used action to produce a change?

References

Adams, G. R. (1977). Physical attractiveness research: Toward a developmental social psychology of beauty. *Human Development, 20,* 217–239.

Antony, M. M., & Barlow, D. H. (Eds.). (2002). *Handbook of assessment and treatment planning for psychological disorders.* New York: Guilford.

Baird, P., & Sights, J. R. (1986). Low self-esteem as a treatment issue in the psychology of anorexia and bulimia. *Journal of Counseling and Development, 64,* 449–451.

Bandura, A. (1982). Self-efficacy mechanism in human agency. *American Psychologist, 37,* 122–147.

Bandura, A. (1997). *Self-efficacy: The exercise of control.* New York: Freeman.

Beck, A. T., Rush, A. J., Shaw, B. F., & Emery, G. (1979a). *Cognitive therapy of depression.* New York: Guilford.

Beck, A. T., Rush, A. J., Shaw, B. F., & Emery, G. (1979b). Integration of homework into therapy. In A. T. Beck, A. J. Rush, B. F. Shaw, & G. Emery (Eds.), *Cognitive therapy of depression* (pp. 272–294). New York: Guilford.

Bednar, R. L., & Peterson, S. R. (1995). *Self-esteem: Paradoxes and innovations in clinical theory and practice.* Washington, DC: American Psychological Association.

Berne, E. (1972). *What do you say after you say hello?* New York: Grove Press.

Blatner, A. (1998). *Acting-in: Practical applications of psychodramatic methods.* New York: Springer.

Branden, N. (1969). *The psychology of self esteem.* Los Angeles: Nash.

Branden, N. (1971). *The disowned self.* New York: Bantam.

Brehm, M., & Back, W. (1968). Self image and attitude towards drugs. *Journal of Personality, 36,* 299–314.

Burns, D. (1999) *Feeling good.* New York: William Morrow.

Burns, D. D. (1999). *Ten days to self-esteem.* New York: Quill.

Carlock, C. J. (1998). *Enhancing self-esteem* (3rd ed.). Muncie, IN: Accelerated Development.

Daly, M. J., & Burton, R. L. (1983). Self-esteem and irrational beliefs: An exploratory investigation with implications for counseling. *Journal of Counseling Psychology, 30,* 361–366.

Davis, M., Eshelman, E. R., & McKay, M. (1980). *The relaxation and stress reduction workbook.* Richmond, CA: New Harbinger.

Dowd, E. T. (1985). Self statement modification. In A. S. Bellack & M. Hersen (Eds.), *Dictionary of behavior therapy techniques* (p. 200). New York: Pergamon.

Dyer, W., & Vriend, J. (1977). *Counseling techniques that work.* New York: Funk & Wagnall.

Ellis, A. (1973). *Humanistic psychotherapy.* New York: McGraw-Hill.

Gladding, S. T. & Gladding, C. (1991). The ABCs of bibliotherapy for school counselors. *School Counselor, 39*(1), 7–13.

Greenspan, M. (1983). *A new approach to women and therapy.* New York: McGraw-Hill.

Guerney, B., Stollack, G., & Guerney, L. (1971). The practicing psychologist as educator: An alternative to the medical practitioner's model. *Professional Psychology, 11,* 276–282.

Haley, J. (1978). Ideas which handicap therapists. In M. Berger (Ed.), *Beyond the double blind: Communication and family systems, theories, techniques with schizophrenics* (pp. 24–36). New York: Brunner/Mazel.

Haley, J. (1989, April). Strategic family therapy. Symposium conducted at Stetson University, DeLand, FL.

Ingham, J. G., Kreitman, N. B., Miller, P. M., & Sasidharan, S. P. (1986). Self-esteem, vulnerability and psychiatric disorder in the community. *British Journal of Psychiatry, 148,* 373–385.

Jackson, S. A. (2001). Using bibliotherapy with clients. *Journal of Individual Psychology, 57,* 289–297.

Kaplan, L. (1995). Self-esteem is not our national wonder drug. *School Counselor, 42,* 341–345.

Kipper, D. A. (1986). *Psychotherapy through clinical role-playing.* New York: Brunner/Mazel.

Kipper, D. A., & Ritchie, T. D. (2003). The effectiveness of psychodramatic techniques: A meta-analysis. *Group Dynamics: Theory, Research and Practice, 7*(1), 13–25.

Kurpius, D., Rockwood, G. F., & Corbett, M. O. (1989). Attributional styles and self-esteem: Implications for counseling. *Counseling and Human Development, 21*(8), 1–12.

Last, C. G. (1985). Homework. In A. S. Bellack & M. Hersen (Eds.), *Dictionary of behavior therapy techniques* (pp. 140–141). New York: Pergamon.

Lazarus, A. A. (1971). *Behavior therapy and beyond.* New York: McGraw Hill.

Lazarus, A. A. (1982). *Personal enrichment through imagery* (Cassette Recording). New York: BMA Audio Cassettes/Guilford.

Lazarus, A. A. (1985). Behavior rehearsal. In A. S. Bellack & M. Hersen (Eds.), *Dictionary of behavior therapy techniques* (p. 22). New York: Pergamon.

Martin, G. A., & Worthington, E. L. (1982). Behavioral homework. In M. Hersen, R. Eisler, & P. M. Miller (Eds.), *Progress in behavior modification* (Vol. 13, pp. 197–226). New York: Academic Press.

McKay, M., & Fanning, P. (1987). *Self-esteem.* Oakland, CA: New Harbinger.

McMullin, R. E. (2000). *The new handbook of cognitive therapy techniques.* New York: Norton.

Moreno, J. L. (1964). *Psychodrama* (Vol. 1, 3rd ed.). New York: Beacon House.

Rosenberg, M. (1962). The association between self-esteem and anxiety. *Journal of Psychiatric Research, 1,* 135–152.

Schutz, W. (1981). *Holistic education.* In I. R. Corsini (Ed.), *Handbook of innovative psychotherapies* (pp. 378–388). New York: Wiley.

Shelton, J. L., & Ackerman, J. M. (1974). *Homework in counseling and psychotherapy.* Springfield, IL: Thomas.

Shelton, J. L., & Levy, R. L. (1981). *Behavioral assignments and treatment compliance.* Champaign, IL: Research Press.

Starr, A. (1977). *Psychodrama: Rehearsal for living.* Chicago: Nelson Hall.

Thompson, J. K., & Thompson, C. M. (1986). Body size distortion and self-esteem in asymptomatic, normal weight males and females. *International Journal of Eating Disorders, 5,* 1061–1068.

Thompson, S. C. (1991). Intervening to enhance perceptions of control. In C. R. Snyder & D. R. Forsyth (Eds.), *Handbook of social and clinical psychology* (pp. 607–623). New York: Simon & Schuster.

Tubesing, D. (1981). *Kicking your stress habits.* Duluth, MN: Whole Person Press.

Walz, G. (1990). *Counseling for self esteem.* Alexandria, VA: American Association for Counseling and Development.

Weiner-Davis, M. (1992). *Divorce busting.* New York: Summit Books.

Wilson, A., & Krane, R. (1980). Change in self esteem and its effect on symptoms of depression. *Cognitive Therapy and Research, 4,* 419–421.

Witmer, J. M. (1985). *Pathways to personal growth: Developing a sense of worth and competence.* Muncie, IN: Accelerated Development.

Woody, S. R., Detweiler-Bedell, J., Teachman, B. A., & O'Hearn, T. (2003). *Treatment planning in psychotherapy: Taking the guesswork out of clinical care.* New York: Guilford.

Yablonsky, L. (1976). *Psychodrama: Resolving emotional problems through role-playing.* New York: Basic Books.

Young, M. E., & Rosen, L. S. (1985). The retreat: An educational growth group. *Journal for Specialists in Group Work, 10,* 157–163.

Curative Factors and Advanced Skills: Part II

15

This chapter is devoted to finishing our look at the REPLAN model by describing the final three curative factors: lowering and raising emotional arousal (L), activating expectations, hope, and motivation (A), and providing new learning experiences (N). The curative factors in the REPLAN model provide a basis for understanding the therapeutic commonalities at the roots of the various theoretical

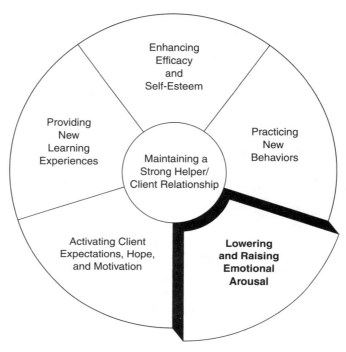

Figure 15.1
Curative Factors in the REPLAN System: Lowering and Raising Emotional Arousal

systems and the new techniques that arise independently of a theory. As we saw in Chapter 14, the curative factors also provide one way to plan treatment by considering which factors are most likely to be helpful in helping the client reach his or her goals.

In Chapter 3, we discussed the central therapeutic factor, the relationship or therapeutic alliance. In the last chapter, we talked about the factors of enhancing efficacy and self-esteem and practicing new behaviors. Figure 15.1 again shows these therapeutic factors and emphasizes the next factor we will take up: lowering and raising emotional arousal.

Lowering and Raising Emotional Arousal

The fourth curative factor in the REPLAN system is lowering and raising emotional arousal. At times, helpers are called upon to help clients deal with overpowering feelings of anger, stress, and fear, primarily through methods of relaxation and mental quieting. At other times, helpers arouse emotions to act as catalysts for change and to encourage clients to express deep feelings within the therapeutic relationship. These two methodologies, quieting and arousing, are at each end of a continuum, and the client's problem and needs determine which should be employed.

Many clients benefit from relaxation training, meditation, and other quieting techniques. "Hurry sickness," or a high level of stress, is a common symptom in this increasingly hectic world. On the other hand, methods that encourage clients to experience and then express deeply held feelings are helpful for clients who have not dealt with painful or traumatic events, who are underexpressive, or who are using defense mechanisms rather than dealing with important emotional problems.

Although quieting methods are safe and quickly lead to positive experiences by clients, arousing emotions in clients is risky without a long period of training and close supervision. Most of these methods, such as the "empty-chair" technique of Gestalt therapy and several psychodramatic tools, are too advanced for the scope of this book. This does not mean, however, that the beginning helper must shy away from exploring unexpressed emotions. For one thing, you have already learned methods for reflecting emotions and personal meanings through the nonjudgmental listening cycle.

Reducing Emotional Arousal

While a little anxiety may actually enhance performance at times and anger may motivate us to act assertively, these emotions can easily run out of control, causing distress and interfering with relationships and job performance. Modern life, with more crowding, more work pressure, and more choices, has led to greater stress levels in just about everyone. The emotional arousal associated with anger and fear (fight or flight) may have been useful in more primitive times. What once may have increased the chances for survival now threatens our health, because the physiological by-products of stress cannot be easily dissipated in a sedentary lifestyle. Today's helper is frequently called upon to help clients learn to reduce the causes of stress by acquiring time management skills; developing a capacity for self-care, including exercise and good nutrition; and gaining a more healthy outlook on life. In addition, helpers assist clients to lower stress by reducing emotional arousal through quieting techniques.

Some of the better known methods for reducing emotional arousal are systematic desensitization for phobic anxiety (Wolpe, 1958), progressive relaxation (Jacobson, 1938), coping skills training (Tubesing, 1981), guided imagery (Overholser, 1991; Witmer & Young, 1985, 1987), confession/ventilation (Menninger, 1958), emotional support (Gilliland, James, & Bowman, 1989), stress inoculation (Novaco, 1977, 1983), biofeedback training (Fair, 1989), and meditation (Bogart, 1991; Carrington, 1998; Shapiro, 1994; Shapiro & Walsh, 1984; Singh, 2003a, 2003b). These techniques are frequently combined and offered in a psychoeducational format as stress reduction or coping skills training courses. In a group setting, participants can also benefit from the support of fellow participants, which also helps to reduce stress.

The most fundamental method for helping clients reduce arousal is muscle relaxation. Muscle relaxation training brings about relief from troubling symptoms of anxiety immediately and lets clients experience the positive sensations associated with lowered muscle tension. This technique is explained in detail here since it is part of most stress reduction courses and forms the basis of systematic desensitization and biofeedback training.

Relaxation Training

Edmund Jacobson's progressive relaxation technique (1938) was, for many years, the favored method for teaching clients deep muscle relaxation. Muscle relaxation had been found to reduce emotional arousal in fearful clients. Jacobson's method, if faithfully followed, enables the client to identify and relax every major muscle group in the body. The traditional training process may actually take several months in weekly sessions, although abbreviated versions have been used successfully (Gatchel & Baum, 1983). Following is a simple and even quicker format developed by Witmer (1985), which can be learned in three or four sessions, each lasting about 20 minutes. Every session is identical and provides a complete tensing and then relaxing of all the major muscle groups (see Table 15.1). Please note that relaxation alone is not as effective as a treatment program that also includes mental or cognitive control of anxious thoughts (Hazaleus & Deffenbacher, 1986).

The Technique of Deep Muscle Relaxation

Step 1: Preparation.   Ask the client to find the most comfortable position with eyes closed. This may be sitting or lying down, but in either case, there should be support for the head. The legs and arms should not be crossed. The procedure is best practiced without the distractions of noise or glaring lights. Instruct the client to speak as little as possible and to avoid moving except as necessary to achieve a more comfortable position. The client may be instructed to raise one finger to indicate when an instruction has been understood or completed.

Step 2: Tighten and relax.   Ask the client to progressively tighten and then relax each muscle group, using the instructions in Table 15.1. Encourage the client to hold each tensed muscle about 6 or 7 seconds until the experience of tightness is fully felt. If the posture is held too long, cramps and spasms may result. While a muscle group is tensed, ask the client to focus attention on that area, simultaneously relaxing other parts of the body and holding the breath.

Step 3: Relax fully and breathe.   Following the tensing of a muscle group, instruct the client to exhale and relax fully and completely. This relaxation is to be accompanied by slow, deep, diaphragmatic breathing and should last 20 seconds or so. The tension and relaxation of the same muscle group is then repeated before moving on.

Diaphragmatic breathing consists of inhaling and exhaling below the ribs rather than in the upper chest. It is the relaxed breathing demonstrated by sleeping babies and practiced by singers. Help clients learn diaphragmatic breathing by placing one hand on the chest and the other on the diaphragm/stomach area. Diaphragmatic breathing occurs when the stomach hand goes up and down but the chest hand remains relatively immobile.

Step 4: The body scan.   The most important phase of the lesson is the body review, or *body scan*. This phase is critical because the client is asked to return to specific, discrete areas of tension during the relaxation procedure and to relax them. This allows the helper to individualize the relaxation so that the client can spend time on the areas that he or she tends to tighten. Tell clients that a body scan can be used on their own, at any time during the day, to check bodily tension.

Table 15.1
Instructions to the Client for Tensing and Relaxing Muscle Groups

Major Muscle Group and Area of Tension	Tensing and Relaxing Instructions
1. Hands and Arms	
Hand: The back of your hand, fingers, and the wrist	Tense the muscles in the right hand and lower right arm by making a tight fist. Hold for at least five seconds. Feel the tension. Now relax. Notice the difference between the tensing and relaxing. Repeat the same procedure. Now do the same thing with your left hand. Finish by tensing and relaxing both hands together.
Lower Arm: The forearm and the wrist	Hold both arms out in front of you with palms up, bend the hands down. Feel the tension in the hand, wrist, and forearm. Then relax. Repeat the same procedure. Now extend your arms out in front of you but with palms down. Bend your hands up. Feel the tension. Relax. Repeat the same procedure. Now let both arms hang loosely at your side.
Upper Arm: The bicep muscles	Start with your right arm. Bend the elbow, touch your shoulder with your fingers, and tense the bicep just like you want to show off your muscles. Feel the tension, then relax and notice the contrast. Repeat the same procedure. Now do the same thing with your left arm. Finish by tensing, then relaxing both arms together. Now let both arms hang loosely at your side.
2. Head, Face, and Throat	
Forehead and Scalp: The entire forehead and scalp area	Wrinkle your forehead by raising your eyebrows as high as you can. Feel the tension in the forehead and scalp area. Now relax, notice the difference between tension and relaxation. Repeat the procedure. Next frown by pulling your eyebrows down as far as you can. Feel the tension, then relax. Repeat the same procedure. Let go of all tension, then relax. Repeat the same procedure. Let go of all tension in the forehead and scalp area. Feel the smoothness of the muscles.
Eyes and Nose: The eyelids and muscles around the eyes, nose, and upper cheeks	Squeeze your eyes shut and at the same time wrinkle up your nose. Feel the tension, then relax. Repeat the procedure. Next roll your eyes left and right, up and down or rotate them in both directions. Finish by opening your eyes as widely as you can, then relaxing them. Now feel the relaxation of muscles around your eyes.
Mouth and Jaw: The area around the mouth and the lower face	Bite your teeth together and pull the corners of your mouth back. Feel the tension, then let go. Now press your lips tightly together and extend them as though you are sucking a straw. Feel the tension

Throat and Jaw: Muscles inside the mouth and throat

Entire Head and Facial Area

and relax. Next open your mouth widely, then relax. Now pull your mouth to the left side of your face, then to the right. Repeat any of the above exercises until this part of your face is deeply relaxed.

Push your tongue against the roof of your mouth. Feel the tension, then relax. Clench your jaw tightly, then relax.

Try a final tensing and relaxing by making a face. Scrunch up your face so your eyes squint, your nose is wrinkled up and your mouth is pulled back. Now your face feels smooth and relaxed as you let go of any tension left over.

3. Neck and Shoulders

Neck: The muscles in the back of the neck, at the base of the scalp, and across the shoulders

Drop your chin down against your chest. Press down hard enough so you feel tension under your chin and at the back of your neck. Now lift your head and press it backward. Roll your head to the right, then forward to your chest, then to the left and back to where you started. Go slowly and gently. Repeat this at least twice in the same direction. Next, do the same exercise in the other direction. Relax with your head in a normal position, stretching it in whatever way you need for working out remaining tension spots.

4. Chest, Shoulders, and Upper Back

Muscles in the Chest, Shoulders, and Upper Back Area

Take a deep breath, hold it and at the same time pull the shoulders back, trying to make the shoulder blades touch. Feel the tension around your ribs, shoulders, and the upper back. Exhale slowly and feel the relaxation as you return to a natural position. Now pull your shoulders as far up as you can, then as far up, as far back, and as far down as you can, making a kind of circular motion. Repeat this at least twice. Feel the tension and relaxation. Next go in the opposite direction in your rotation of the shoulders. Sense the looseness and relaxed feeling in this part of your body.

5. Lower Back, Stomach, and Hips

Lower Back: The muscles across the lower back area

Begin by taking a deep breath and sitting up straight. Pull the shoulders back and arch your back so your stomach sticks out. Exhale and let all the air and tension flow out. Repeat this procedure. Next bend forward arching your back the other way with your head down to your knees and your hands touching the floor. Feel the muscles stretching. Return to a normal sitting position and feel the relaxation. Repeat the procedure.

Table 15.1

Instructions to the Client for Tensing and Relaxing Muscle Groups *(Continued)*

Stomach and Hips: The muscles in the abdominal area and hips	Take a deep breath and hold it as you make your stomach muscles hard. Just tighten them up as though you were going to hit yourself in the stomach. You should feel a good deal of tightness in the stomach area. Breathe out and feel the relaxation as you do. Let go of this tension. Repeat the procedure. Next breathe out as far as you can, feeling the tension in your stomach area as you hold your breath. Now let go and allow yourself to breathe naturally, noticing the difference between tension and relaxation.
6. Hips, Legs, and Feet	
Hips and Upper Legs: The muscles in the upper and lower parts of the thighs	Gently hold fast to the bottom of your chair. Press your heels down hard on the floor. Feel the tension around your hips and the hardness of the large upper leg muscles. Relax and notice the difference between tension and relaxation. Repeat the procedure.
Lower Legs: The muscles from the knees to the ankes	Hold both legs straight out in front of you. Point your feet and toes away from your head. Feel the tension in your legs and on top of your feet. Relax and drop both feet on the floor. Now extend your legs again, but point your feet and toes toward your head. Feel the tension in the calf muscles and around your ankles. Relax and drop both feet. Notice the relaxed feeling.
Feet: The muscles around the ankles, over the top of the feet, the arch and ball of the feet, and the toes	Extend both toes pointed away from you. Then turn both feet inward and at the same time curl your toes. Gently tense the muscles just enough to feel the tension and relax. Now try moving each foot in a circulation motion, feeling the stretching and tensing. Relax. Repeat but reverse the direction and relax! Try spreading your toes, then relaxing, letting all the tension go out of your feet. Now put both feet flat on the floor, take a deep breath and relax.
7. Body Review	Scan your whole body and recognize how it now feels more relaxed. Let the muscles of your body relax even more as you do a body scan from head to toe. Muscles that still feel a bit tight can be tensed, then relaxed.
	Next, try tensing your whole body at one time. Take a deep breath and feel the tension all over your body. Hold for several seconds, then let go. Let all the air out and feel the deep relaxation coming over your entire body. The tension is flowing out like the air escaping from a balloon. Enjoy the relaxed feeling.

Source: Witmer, J. M. (1985). Pathways to Personal Growth, Muncie, IN. Accelerated Development. Copyright J. M. Witmer. Reprinted with permission.

Step 5: Assign practice. The first administration of the relaxation technique should be recorded on audiocassette for the client, or a standardized commercially available version of the technique should be provided. Ask the client to practice the relaxation technique twice daily, usually once upon arising and once in bed before falling asleep. Have the client note which of the six bodily areas show the greatest sources of tension during the day, and ask the client to report this information at the next session.

Meditation

Meditation may be one of the most effective means for decreasing anxiety, panic, and persistent anger (Brooks & Scarano, 1985; Kabat-Zinn, Massion, Kristeller, Peterson, Fletcher, Pbert, Lenderking, & Santorelli, 1992; Smith, 1975). Moreover, meditation is not merely a method for reducing tension; it actually produces positive states of alertness, improved concentration, fearlessness, optimism, joy, and feelings of well-being (Chandler, Holden, & Kolander, 1992; Singh, 2003a). Meditation has been used to treat and prevent substance abuse (Shafii, 1974, 1975).

An immediate benefit of meditation is that it stops the constant chattering of the mind and eliminates the mental images that produce anxiety. For example, have you ever tried to sleep and found plans for the next day going around in your head? Meditation is a means of putting such thoughts to rest for a while. Unlike relaxation techniques, meditation has the effect of producing mental quietude, not just physical rest, and is, therefore, for some, a good alternative to tranquilizers.

Like relaxation, meditation must be practiced on a regular basis for at least 15 minutes per day for several weeks, before real benefits can be realized (Benson, 1984). After that, at least 30 minutes a day should be devoted to meditating. Regular, longer meditations are considered to be more beneficial than several short meditations. Like any skill, a teacher is helpful at all stages of training (Singh, 2003b).

To keep the mind occupied, meditation practitioners have found that a "mental device" (Benson, 1984), or *mantra*, is an effective way of reducing the stressful thoughts coming from the mind. A mantra gives your mind something with which to occupy itself while you are concentrating. A word or phrase is repeated slowly and at intervals, mentally, not aloud but with the "tongue of thought" (Singh, 2003b). For those who are spiritually inclined, any name of God can be used. Others have found it effective to repeat a word such as "one" or "calm." Learning to quiet the mind is a challenge, but the benefits make the investment of time worth the effort. If you are interested in learning more about meditation, read Rajinder Singh's book *Inner and Outer Peace through Meditation*. It contains complete and simple instructions for nondenominational spiritual meditation and exercises for getting started. For those who are not attracted to a spiritual meditation procedure, Patricia Carrington's *The Book of Meditation* (1998) may be of interest.

Raising Emotional Arousal

The patient only gets free from the hysterical symptom by reproducing the pathogenic impressions that caused it and by giving utterance to them with the expression of affect and thus the therapeutic task consists solely in inducing him to do so.

Breuer and Freud, 1895/1955, p. 283

The earliest records of cathartic methods are found in ancient Greek drama. The word *katharsis* indicates a purging or purification experienced after the expression of emotions. The effectiveness of traditional uses of cathartic methods is documented in the history of religious rituals, confession of sins, mesmerism, drug-induced emotional states, and rituals of mourning. Today helpers use cathartic techniques to encourage clients to open up verbally and emotionally.

The basis for the modern approach is found in the very roots of psychoanalysis (Bemak & Young, 1998; Young & Bemak, 1996). The quotation that opens this section is from the classic book *Studies on Hysteria*. It was in this publication that Breuer and Freud (1895/1955) presented their discovery that reliving past traumas by provoking emotional reactions and getting clients to express their feelings had healing power. Freud's idea was that relief from emotional suffering can be obtained by releasing pools of stored emotions that are held in the unconscious. When freed, these stored emotions dissipate like water running down a drain. In all fairness to Freud, he modified his ideas about emotions later in his life, but this idea of releasing stockpiled emotions became popular and took root in many other therapeutic systems. Since Freud's time, the terms *catharsis*, *abreaction*, *emotional insight*, *corrective emotional experience*, *releasing blocked emotion*, and *experiencing* have been used to describe the release of emotions in the helping relationship (Nichols & Efran, 1985; Nichols & Zax, 1977).

Most helping professionals do not subscribe to Freudian principles today (Young & Feiler, 1993). Although they may not accept this "hydraulic" metaphor, many still embrace arousal and expression of emotions as a major technique. This group includes practitioners of Gestalt therapy (Perls, 1977; Prochaska & Norcross, 2003), psychodrama (Moreno, 1958), and a number of group approaches, including encounter and marathon groups. Emotional arousal has been activated through hypnosis and drugs (Wolberg, 1977), psychodramatic methods (Moreno, 1958), guided imagery (Witmer & Young, 1985), reflective listening in client-centered therapy, confrontation, depreciating and devaluating feedback in Synanon groups, free association in psychoanalysis, the empty-chair technique of Gestalt therapy (Polster & Polster, 1973), focusing (Gendlin, 1969, 1978), flooding, implosive therapy (Stampfl & Levis, 1967), bioenergetics (Lowen, 1967), primal therapy (Janov, 1970), reevaluation counseling (Jackins, 1962), provocative therapy (Farelly & Brandsma, 1974), and many others.

Arousal and Expression

The term *catharsis* is the most commonly used term in the context of arousal and expression, but it has become a catchall that actually encompasses two separate activities: (1) stimulating emotional arousal of the client and (2) encouraging emotional expression by the client (Young & Bemak, 1996). Arousing techniques frustrate, shock, anger, or evoke some other state of emotional arousal for the purpose of motivating change. Expressive techniques, on the other hand, help clients fully experience their feelings and allow them to communicate these emotions to the helper. Clients report "cathartic events" as extremely significant; however, several studies indicate that emotional arousal should be accompanied by a cognitive change or perspective shift to achieve maximum effectiveness. Furthermore, there is some indication that individuals who are underexpressive will benefit most from highly arousing and expressive techniques (Young & Bemak, 1996).

Be aware that methods that arouse emotions can be traumatic and potentially harmful to clients. Arousing techniques, in their simplest and most benign form, include helpers encouraging clients to talk about troubling experiences and feelings rather than avoiding them. At the most harmful level, helpers may force clients to face powerful emotions that make the client feel out of control. Because some arousing techniques can produce harmful reactions, we will discuss methods that encourage clients to focus on their emotions but do not pressure them to do so. The more confrontional and cathartic methods are very advanced skills to be used only by experienced practitioners within strict ethical guidelines and in conjunction with close supervision (Young & Bemak, 1996). They are mentioned here because, sooner or later, every helper will see these methods on films or at conference workshops. Like a knife that cuts both ways, it is important to keep in mind that while these methods can produce strong reactions, the risks are substantial.

Besides the risks associated with arousing and expressive techniques, there is what Goleman (1995) calls a "ventilation fallacy." Because expressing anger feels so good immediately, we are seduced into thinking that we have dispelled it. In fact, the opposite may be true (see Tavris, 1989). Expressing anger tends to arouse a person more, making him or her more likely to feel anger later. Thus, there are very good reasons to consider arousing techniques as highly advanced, requiring training, supervision, and caution.

Techniques That Stimulate Emotional Arousal and Expression

Stimulus Techniques

Several methods for emotional arousal and expression can be grouped together as *stimulus techniques*. Helpers supply clients with media such as music, films, or books that relate to their personal problems. The ability of the client to identify with the protagonist of the story enhances the emotional arousal and subsequent expression. For example, a helper might suggest the movie *The Great Santini* to a client from a military family. Later, helper and client discuss the film in terms of what feelings and thoughts were aroused.

Creative Arts

A second set of techniques is associated with the use of the creative arts in counseling (Gladding, 1998). Helpers encourage clients to express themselves through artistic media. Arts as emotional catalysts differ from stimulus methods in that clients are not passive, but actively create an artistic work that reflects an inner state. These media may include dance and movement, music performance, expressive writing of poetry, journaling, painting, drawing, sculpting, construction of collages, and sand tray work, and dramatic use of puppets and dolls. For example, a client who has trouble understanding his feelings about a past relationship could be asked to paint a picture or write a poem about the experience and share it during the next session.

Stop and Reflect

Journal writing is an activity that can be used in the helping relationship for the expression and release of emotions. Writing down our inner thoughts is a different activity from merely thinking about them or talking about them. In writing, we have the opportunity to really examine thoughts in detail, and to challenge them. We may record dreams, daily feelings, reflections on self-concept, or spiritual progress, or we may write about particularly troubling or significant periods of change in our lives. All these activities may help us become more deeply aware of emotional issues behind these events.

In this activity, called a "period log" (Gladding, 1998), you are asked (1) to indicate a particular interval of your life during which you experienced a number of changes or personal growth and (2) to reflect on your experiences at that time. Once you have identified a particular time period, begin writing and do not stop to edit your thoughts. Because you need not show this work to anyone, turn off the internal censor and try and write whatever comes up or emerges without stifling your thoughts or feelings. This is a free association, or stream-of-consciousness, method that psychodynamic therapists have found to be effective for uncovering underlying issues. Some practice is required before one can really let go and let thoughts and feelings flow. One way of doing this is to place your pen on a blank sheet of paper with a headline indicating the particular time period and write without picking up the pen for about 5 minutes. Start with the words "I felt . . ." and continue writing for the allotted time. When you have finished, answer the following questions.

- What were the major feelings you experienced during this period in your life? Did you reexperience any of them while writing?
- Did you find it hard to write in a stream-of-consciousness style?
- How did you block yourself from letting the ideas flow out?
- Do you think clients censor their true feelings about issues or a particular period in their lives?
- Did you encounter any personal reluctance to look at this period in your life?
- Do you see any value in reviewing the past, or would it be best to let these issues lie?
- What does your writing indicate about how comfortable you are now with this important period in your life?
- What other artistic media would you personally be most likely to use if it were suggested by a helper?
- How could you determine which methods would be best for a specific client?

Activating Client Expectations, Hope, and Motivation

Next we will take a closer look at the curative factor involved in instilling hope and increasing expectations. Figure 15.2 shows this factor highlighted among the six curative factors. Before learning the techniques for increasing hope, expectations, and motivation, it is important first to recognize the discouragement, lack of confidence, and demoralization that most clients are experiencing when they first come

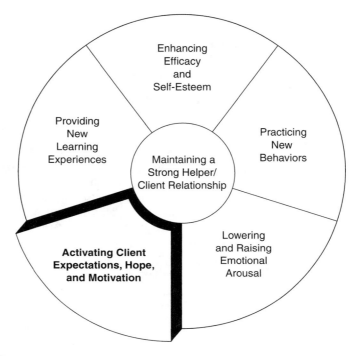

Figure 15.2
Curative Factors in the REPLAN System: Activating Client Expectations, Hope, and Motivation

for help. Beginning helpers are often surprised when clients fail to follow through with plans or seem unwilling to try anything new. Remember that seeking professional help is often a last resort. The clients have already tried several ways to solve their problems before coming to the helper, even seeking help from family and friends. They have come to believe that there is no way out of their difficulties. Therefore, before the clients can attack problems, they must first overcome the conviction that their situation is hopeless.

The Demoralization Hypothesis

According to Jerome Frank (Frank & Frank, 1991), those who seek counseling are demoralized. *Demoralization* is described by Frank as a "state of mind characterized by one or more of the following: subjective incompetence, loss of self-esteem, alienation, hopelessness (feeling that no one can help), or helplessness (feeling that other people could help but will not)" (p. 56). Demoralization is known by many different names in various theories, but the concept was best developed by Adler (1954).

Seligman (1975) experimentally discovered an aspect of demoralization called *learned helplessness*, which is a state analogous to depression. It was discovered in animal research and later in humans. Seligman found that persons exposed to unsolvable problems became so discouraged that their later performance on solvable problems was negatively affected. Frank believes that anxiety, depression, and loss of self-esteem (the most common presenting symptoms) are due primarily to demoralization. Frank also proposes that symptoms and mental demoralization interact. In other words, client problems and symptoms are worsened by the sense of discouragement and isolation. For example, a physical problem may be seen as a minor annoyance by one person, whereas the demoralized individual sees it as another sign of the hopelessness of the situation.

Increasing Expectations

Many clients improve radically early in the helping process. Even those on waiting lists show improvement! This has been attributed to the *placebo effect*, a medical analogy that has been unfortunately applied to the psychological realm. The placebo effect implies that the helper is fooling the client with an imaginary treatment. In actuality, the placebo effect, or expectancy effect, is tapping well-established factors in social influence, especially the attractiveness and trustworthiness of the helper as well as high expectations for treatment (Frank, Nash, Stone, & Imber, 1963; Patterson, 1973). It is the expectation itself that is healing. Faith is powerful medicine (Siegel, 1986).

Encouragement

As we discuss demoralization, our thoughts naturally turn to its interpersonal antidote, encouragement. Encouragement is a concept and a technique that is closely aligned with Alfred Adler's theory of individual psychology. Yet encouragement is not limited to Adlerians. In a national survey conducted by the author (Young & Feiler, 1993), encouragement was the second most frequently used counseling technique. It was utilized by 90 percent of the mental health counselors and counselor educators surveyed. We cannot be certain from these data that all respondents were operating under the same definition of encouragement; however, the survey is supportive of the notion that encouragement is an essential therapeutic ingredient for most helpers.

Encouragement Versus Praise

Earlier we indicated that praise can be a roadblock in the helping process. This idea goes against the grain for many beginning helpers, especially those who work with children. We sincerely want to uplift the client's spirits, and we want them to pay attention to their positive attributes. There are times when praise is useful. However, praise definitely puts the helper in the role of a judging parent and the client in the role of the child. Most adults do not need a cheerleader; instead they need to develop faith in themselves. This is where encouragement comes in. Through encouragement, the helper focuses on respectfully pushing the client to develop a more positive view of life rather than merely giving the client approval.

To get a clearer idea about encouragement, look at Table 15.2, which compares the concepts of reinforcement from the behavioral tradition and the Adlerian concept of encouragement. The table shows that praise (positive reinforcement) and encouragement each have important but distinct uses. In general, encouragement is designed to inspire, to foster hope, to stimulate, and to support (Pitsounis & Dixon, 1988), whereas praise is designed to increase the likelihood that a specific behavior

Table 15.2
Comparison of Encouragement and Praise/Reinforcement

Dimension	Encouragement	Praise Reinforcement
Purpose	To motivate, inspire, hearten, instill confidence	To maintain or strengthen a specific behavior
Nature	Focuses on inner direction and internal control; emphasizes personal appreciation and effort more than outcome	Focuses on outer direction and external control; tends to emphasize material appreciation; emphasizes outcome
Population	All ages and groups	Seems most appropriate for children, situations with limited self-control and development, and conditions of specific problem behavior
Thoughts/ Feelings/ Actions	A balance of thinking, feeling, and actions with feeling underlying the responses; i.e., satisfaction, enjoyment, challenge	Attending primarily to an action (behavioral) response that is observable
Creativeness	Spontaneity and variation in how encourager responds; encouragee has freedom to respond in spontaneous and creative ways; however, it may be difficult to understand the expectations of the encourager	Reinforcer responds to very specific behavior in a specific way; reinforcee is expected to respond in a specific and prescribed way; little doubt about the expectations of the reinforcer; helpful in establishing goals
Autonomy	Promotes independence, less likelihood of dependency on a specific person or thing; more likely to generalize to other life situations	Tends to develop a strong association, perhaps dependence, between a specific reinforcer and a behavior; less likely to generalize to other life situations

Source: Witmer, J. M. (1985). *Pathways to personal growth.* Muncie, IN: Accelerated Development. Reprinted with permission.

will be repeated. Encouragement focuses on developing autonomy, self-reliance, cooperation rather than competition (it avoids comparisons), and an internal locus of control (Hitz & Driscoll, 1988). Praise is a reward that strengthens a behavior when it occurs. In summary, praise has several drawbacks in the helping relationship since it only recognizes success, not intentions, and it places the helper in a position of superiority.

Who Benefits Most from Encouragement?

According to Losoncy (1977), persons who are dependent, depressed, cut off from social support systems, or suffering from low self-esteem respond to encouragement. Encouragement also helps clients who show an excessive need for attention, for power, for control of situations and people, and for revenge. It is useful as well with clients who avoid participation and responsibility, who are perfectionistic, or who tend to be close-minded.

Types of Encouraging Responses

Some of the major writers in the area of encouragement are Dinkmeyer and Losoncy (1980, 1995), Losoncy (1977), Sweeney (1998), and Witmer (1985). They identify 14 types of effective encouraging behaviors:

1. Acknowledging the client's efforts and improvement
2. Concentrating on the client's present capacities, possibilities, and conditions rather than on past failures
3. Focusing on the client's strengths
4. Showing faith in the client's competency and capabilities
5. Showing an interest in the progress and welfare of the client
6. Focusing on those things that interest or excite the client
7. Asking the client to evaluate his or her own performance rather than comparing it with another standard
8. Showing respect for the client and the client's individuality and uniqueness
9. Becoming involved with the client through honest self-disclosure
10. Offering assistance as an equal partner in the counseling process
11. Using humor
12. Providing accurate feedback on deeds rather than on personality
13. Confronting discouraging beliefs
14. Lending enthusiasm and asking for commitment toward goals

Summarizing these 14 interventions may oversimplify the Adlerian concept, but it may also give some general direction to helpers and improve the understanding of the method. I have divided these interventions into three major helper activities: focusing on the positive and the changeable, emphasizing equality and individuality, and pushing with enthusiasm.

Focusing on the positive and the changeable. Optimism is the tendency to view the world as a benign, friendly source of support. Not everyone shares this view of life, but optimism can be learned (Seligman, 1998). The work of Simonton and Mathews-Simonton (1978) with cancer patients has pointed to the potential health benefits of optimism. More recently, the work of Bernard Siegel (1986) has interested millions in the power of optimistic attitudes in dealing with medical crises. An optimistic point of view is also associated with good mental health and freedom from stress (Seligman, 1998; Witmer, 1985). On the other hand, research indicates that pessimism correlates with depression, lowered achievement, and health problems (Seligman, 1998).

In the preceding list, interventions 1 through 4 are grouped together into the encouraging helper behavior of focusing on *the positive and the changeable*. All foster development of an optimistic attitude by helping to shift the client's attention from the deficits to the strengths in his or her life. Such encouragement entails noticing the client's success as well as showing faith in the client's ability to succeed. Focusing on the positive and the changeable also includes redirecting the client's discussions from the past to the present. Interventions of this nature are apparent in the following client/helper dialogue:

Client: "I feel like I've totally messed up my future."

Helper: "Tell me what you really enjoy doing." (focusing on the positive)

Client: "What? . . . Oh, well, I really enjoy working in the garden." (The client goes on to describe the feelings he enjoys, and the helper encourages him.)

Helper: "How do you feel now?"

Client: "Better. But I always feel better when I think about good things like that."

Helper: "Yes, so do I. I prefer to feel good."

Client (laughing): "So do I. But it isn't always easy."

Encouragement should not be seen as trying to get the client to ignore difficult issues; instead it asks the client to develop a balanced view that includes the positive aspects of life. In addition, it helps to focus the client on the parts of the problem that can be changed, rather than ruminating over the unchangeable. Here is an example:

Client: "We went to the picnic, and it was a total disaster just like I said it would be. Her mom started criticizing us again, so my wife and I ended up spending most of the time playing with the kids and talking to each other."

Helper: "It sounds like there were some uncomfortable moments, but it also sounds like you did something positive to deal with her mother's criticism."

Client: "What?"

Helper: "Well, instead of getting involved in the argument, you got away from it and spent some time with each other and with some of the kids. It sounds like you hit on a good strategy. Do you agree?"

Emphasizing equality and individuality of the client The essence of interventions 5 through 10 on the list of encouraging responses is to communicate to the client that the helper and client are on equal footing and that each is unique. By self-disclosing, the helper takes away some of the artificiality of the helper role and connects with the client in a more genuine way. Finally, the helper teaches the client to challenge the idea that the worth of a person is judged by external standards. The client must come to evaluate performance against internal standards and to appreciate his or her personal strengths and unique approach to life, as in the following client/helper exchange:

Client: "I finally got off drugs, got a job and an apartment. My life is back on track, but it's still not good enough."

Helper: "What do you mean?"

Client: "My mom won't let up about how I disappointed her, how I was supposed to finish college 2 years ago. Even though I'm back in school in the fall, all she can say is, 'Two years too late.' "

Helper: "What about you—how do you look at it? Are you proud of what you've accomplished in the last 8 months?"

Client: "Well, don't you think I've done a lot?"

Helper: "You tell me." (asking the client to self-evaluate)

Client: "I have. I have come a long way. It was hard, too."

Pushing with enthusiasm Interventions 11 through 14 demonstrate that encouragement is not merely support; it does not mean accepting the status quo.

There is an element of confrontation and a sincere effort to produce movement in the client. Discouragement is actually a defensive maneuver that seeks to maintain the status quo through inaction. Encouragement pushes the client by giving feedback, confronting the private logic of the client, asking for a commitment, and using humor to turn the client around (Mosak, 1987). The following example continues the client/helper dialogue from the previous section. Notice the confrontation and the helper pushing the client to make a commitment:

Helper: "So although you know you've overcome a lot, sometimes you still use your mother's yardstick on your life rather than your own. Would you agree?"

Client: "That's when I get depressed. I'm not sure I can ever please her, but that's not going to stop my recovery."

Helper: "So how are you going to stop doing that?"

Client: "Well, first of all, I will try to let it go in one ear and out the other. But really, I think I'll just spend less time over there."

Helper: "That sounds like a good start. Let's consider that as a plan for this week, and when we get back together, you'll let me know, right?"

Client: "Right."

How to Encourage

Following are general guidelines that can assist the helper in dealing with discouragement. The steps to take in encouraging a client are shown in conjunction with a case example that includes client statements and helper responses. This example shows that the technique of encouragement consists of giving the client directives to pay attention to his or her own strengths and to focus on what can be changed. Notice that the nonjudgmental listening cycle forms the foundation for the encouraging remarks of the helper.

Step 1: The helper uses the nonjudgmental listening cycle to gain rapport and understand the problem. Encouraging responses will not be appropriate if the helper does not fully understand the client's problem. The nonjudgmental listening cycle is encouraging in and of itself because it promotes a relationship based on equality and respect, one of the hallmarks of encouragement.

Herb was a furniture salesman out of a job. He was very pessimistic about getting hired again after being out of work for 4 months. Although he had initially been rather active, recently he had spent more time driving around in his car than actually looking for a position. His wife accompanied him to the first session, but she refused to return for later appointments. During the first session, she strongly expressed her worry, anger, and frustration. According to Herb, he had lost all ambition, he was embarrassed, and he feared he would never be able to locate a new job.

Helper: "So tell me, what it is like to be out of a job?"

Herb: "It is hell! Everyone blames me. I get depressed and resentful, but mostly I am angry."

Helper: "You're mad at yourself for being in this situation."

Herb: "Exactly. What kind of a man am I? My father never lost a job. Neither did my father-in-law."

Helper: "You mention your father and father-in-law. You seem to be saying that working is an important part of being a man."

Herb: "Of course, I am supposed to be the provider. Now my wife is taking care of me."

In this part of the dialogue, the helper begins with an open question, reflects feelings, and finally reflects meaning. These responses convince the client that the helper understands the situation at a fairly deep level.

Step 2: The helper offers to be an ally.

Helper: "Herb, my feeling is that what you really need right now is a coach. You seem to have job-seeking skills, a good work history, and a positive attitude about your chosen profession. You've shown a lot of success in sales previously. Perhaps together we can help you find your enthusiasm again."

Herb: "I guess you're right that I have had success in the past, but I am at a dead end now. Sometimes I think it is hopeless."

Helper: "My thought is that we begin to look at this thing from a different angle. Perhaps if we put our heads together, we might be able to find a solution."

Step 3: The helper focuses on the positive and notes client attempts, however small, to accomplish the goal.

Client: "I still get up at 6:30 a.m. like I did when I was working. I get dressed and start out all right. First, I read the paper and start to make a call or two. That's when I start getting down. I end up driving around town, killing time until dinner, making my wife think that I am out looking for a job. Why am I doing this?"

Helper: "Well, one of the things I notice is that the rhythm is still there. You are set to get back into a work routine, and you seem to like that. Even though you are not making the contacts, you are practicing, rehearsing for that day when you are back to work. That is a good sign and something we can build on."

Step 4: The helper offers feedback or confrontation and asks for commitment.

Helper: "I've got some feedback for you if you want it."

Herb: "Okay."

Helper: "It seems like one of the problems is that you are not being honest with yourself or your wife about what you do all day. I would like you to keep track of your activities a little better. I think this would help you feel better about yourself, and it might help the relationship, too."

Herb: "It is hard to do when I get nothing back."

Helper: "I agree. It is difficult. But I am only asking that you begin to keep a log of what you're doing toward finding a job each day, and we will see if we can increase that or make some changes in the direction of your search."

Herb: "All right. I can do that."

Step 5: The helper shows continued enthusiasm for the client's goals and interest in the client's feelings and progress.

Herb (one week later): "Since the last time we talked, I didn't do what we decided. I didn't make two calls per day looking for a job. I guess I averaged about one call per day. The first day I did three, then one, then one again, and I took the week-end off. I got no response."

Helper: "I am very glad to hear about this. That kind of progress is what we've been looking for. It seems that getting off dead center is the hardest part, and you've gotten through that. Besides, by being honest about it, you've now included me in what's going on. Now what is needed is keeping up your efforts. Right?"

Client: "I guess so. I'm afraid that this won't work, that it will be just like last time and fizzle out."

Helper: "Yes, it can be scary, but let's try to focus on the present if we can, rather than look back. I have been hoping that you'd make this beginning and then hang in there until something breaks. Let's continue with this plan. I'll call you about Wednesday to see how things are going. Again, I feel good about these first steps."

Identifying Levels of Motivation

Clients vary in their motivation for change. Some are merely considering change, while others are ready to act. Two different groups of writers have begun to classify clients based on their levels of motivation so that specific treatments can be matched with the client's state of readiness. One view is promoted by the eclectic thinkers Norcross, Prochaska, and DiClemente (Prochaska & DiClemente, 1983, 1986; Prochaska & Norcross, 2003; Prochaska, Norcross, & DiClemente, 1994). Another comes from the Brief Family Therapy Training Center (de Shazer, 1988). Both groups see the client's level of readiness for the helping process as an important aspect of planning treatment.

Prochaska and DiClemente's Stages of Change

Prochaska and DiClemente's model (1983, 1986) proposes that clients move through a series of six stages in the process of change. Each stage represents a period of time and a set of tasks needed for movement to the next stage. This model is particularly applicable to the addictions field, since it mirrors the process that individuals undergo in the decision to receive treatment and in their relapse or recovery (Marlatt, 1988). The model also indicates that a helper can select the most effective interventions depending on the client's level of motivation (see Table 15.3).

Clients who are unaware of a problem are in the stage of *precontemplation.* At this point, they are not considering a change and are surprised when friends and family suggest that they have a problem. Courts and significant others refer many such people for help each year. The best treatments for clients at this level are primarily educational. The helper avoids moralizing and instead invites the client to think more and more about the problem.

When a person becomes aware that a problem might exist, he or she has entered the stage of *contemplation.* A client at this stage may admit that a problem exists, but he or she denies that it is a serious problem or that professional help is needed. Many who suffer from alcoholism cannot cross the threshold of the Alcoholics

Table 15.3

Prochaska and DiClemente's Stages of Change Model

Stage of Change	Client Characteristics	Appropriate Techniques
Precontemplation de Shazer calls these clients "Visitors"	Not even thinking about changing	Validate that the client does not feel ready to change Validate that the decision to change is up to them Encourage self-exploration, reading, and gaining information
Contemplation de Shazer calls these clients "Complainants"	The client is ambivalent about changing. The client is not considering changing within the next month	Encourage clients to weigh the pros and cons Help the client think about positive aspects of change and increase expectations
Preparation	The client is testing the waters and is trying to make changes. Client seems to be planning to act within one month	Help client identify obstacles to change and help them reduce these obstacles Help client recognize sources of social support Assess client to see if they need to learn new skills in order to change Help client make small beginning steps
Action de Shazer calls these clients "Customers"	Client has made initial steps towards change, has entered a treatment program, and has probably been practicing new behaviors for 3–6 months	Help client recognize times when they are being effective in dealing with obstacles Help client avoid environmental issues that will trigger relapse and assist them in dealing with changes in social support group. Help client reduce feelings of loss associated with change
Maintenance	Client has made a commitment to sustaining new behavior and has been practicing new behavior for six months to five years	Plan for follow-up support Helpers assist clients in identifying support following treatment and also help them recognize the ways they can reward themselves for maintaining change. At the same time, helpers need to bring up the topic of relapse as a normal part of the process

Table 15.3
Prochaska and DiClemente's Stages of Change Model *(Continued)*

Relapse	A relapse is a return to old behaviors. For example, a client begins smoking after a period of five years without tobacco	Help clients recognize triggers that caused relapse and plan to deal with them Help clients become aware of the motivation they possess for change, their present level of motivation, and issues that block them Help them develop more effective coping strategies

Anonymous 12-step program because the first step begins with the admission that one's life has become unmanageable because of alcohol. People may remain in this "I'll quit tomorrow" stage for years until they experience enough pain to motivate further movement.

In the *preparation* stage, clients are planning to act but are still going back and forth. They may try a few tentative steps towards change. The helper can assist the client by considering whether the client has the requisite skills to change. For example, if someone wants to change their status from uninvolved to involved parent, he or she may need some parenting skills which could serve as a valuable preparation.

Action, or *determination*, is the phase of treatment in which the individual is ready to change behavior patterns or begins to seek outside help. The balance may shift suddenly toward the action phase or it may be a gradual process. Normally, the decision to take action is made when the client experiences so much discomfort that "something has to change." Clients at this stage benefit from directives, treatment programs, and homework assignments that involve experimenting with different behaviors.

Once a client seeks help and receives treatment, the *maintenance* stage begins. When the problem has come under control, the client attempts to change his or her lifestyle to accommodate the changes made. This is a crucial period in the process of change and one that is often neglected in treatment programs. The maintenance stage may lead to stable change or relapse depending on how well the helper is able to extend treatment through follow-up and the degree to which the client can develop personal and environmental supports for new behaviors. Clients at the maintenance stage need continuing support from peers and family and need to practice self-care and self-control strategies.

The *relapse* phase is not inevitable, but it is typical to regress. Most babies do not get up and walk one day. They take a few steps, then fall. Relapse means returning to one's old ways. This can be temporary or permanent. The helper can intervene best here by helping clients regain motivation, not overemphasize the loss, and develop better methods for dealing with triggers that precipitate a return to old behavior.

de Shazer's Model

Another way of looking at levels of motivation is presented in a model suggested by Steve de Shazer (1989). His model divides clients into three categories: visitors, complainants, and customers. At the lowest level of motivating, *visitors* are individuals who seemingly have no complaints. They may be forced or coerced into the helping process by some third party who does have a complaint. Visitors can be helped by giving them information, suggesting educational programs, and getting them to think about their problems. The helper may be able to help the client recognize that a problem exists or at least prepare the client to get help later by helping the client become aware of available resources when help is needed.

Complainants are those clients who are uncomfortable and are seeking solutions. They clearly wish to consider a change of some kind, but they may not be ready to do much about it. On the other hand, clients who are ready, willing, and able to take action are labeled *customers*. Helpers frequently become frustrated because they confuse complainants with customers. With complainants, the helper's job is to try and tip the balance and make the client aware of the need to change. Complainants will not follow through with action-oriented directives or homework, and so it is best to avoid these. Only customers should be given homework or other behavioral tasks. Table 15.3 shows Prochaska & DiClemente's Model of Stages of Change. The table also shows where de Shazer's client types, visitors, complainants, and customers might fit in this scheme. A helper can refer to this table to think about possible interventions based on the client's motivational level. Thinking about motivation in its various levels can stimulate us to devise appropriate interventions and accept the client's current state of readiness without getting frustrated.

Providing New Learning Experiences

Education is not the filling of a pail, but the lighting of a fire.
William Butler Yeats

In this section, we want to explore the techniques included under the final therapeutic factor—the new learning experiences (Figure 15.3). We begin by looking at how helpers educate clients and encourage them to see the world in a slightly more constructive way. As the quote from Yeats suggests, though, teaching is not necessarily a classroom activity. New learning can be sparked through instruction or modeling, but it can also be stimulated indirectly through techniques such as humor, stories, metaphors, interpretation, and reframing.

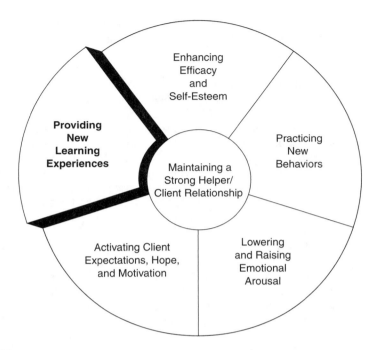

Figure 15.3
Curative Factors in the REPLAN System: Providing New Learning Experiences

According to research, gaining a new perspective is one of the most frequently mentioned therapeutic experiences cited by therapy clients (Elliott, 1985). Clients have been able to recall insights and learning up to 6 months following therapy (Martin & Stelmaczonek, 1988). Yalom (1995) also found that group therapy participants identified interpersonal learning as one of the most important curative factors. They learn from listening to each other, through modeling, and by paying attention to their own words and feelings.

Definitions of New Learning

A number of terms have been used to describe this therapeutic factor, such as *changing the worldview, redefining personal mythology, developing insight, developing outlook skills, perception transformation, cognitive restructuring, reframing, meaning attribution, perception shifts, the "aha!" experience, relabeling,* and *redecision.* All these terms seem to involve two basic helping techniques: (1) imparting to clients new information or skills and (2) persuading clients to change inappropriate beliefs, perceptions, and outlooks. Let us look at a couple of client stories in order to demonstrate how these two types of new learning experiences are commonly embedded in a treatment plan.

- Rhonda is a 23-year-old woman who was admitted for substance abuse problems following her arrest on a charge of driving while intoxicated. On the first day, the goal of the staff is to introduce clients to a "disease concept" model of alcoholism. Rhonda attends a class where she learns that she is genetically predisposed to addiction based on her family history and that she cannot help the effect alcohol has on her. The result of this information is that Rhonda begins to stop thinking of herself as "weak" or as morally unworthy. Instead, she starts to realize that she has a biological weakness. This new perspective has been stimulated by learning. It changes her attitude about herself and increases her hope for recovery.
- Dujuan is a 30-year-old man referred for help with panic attacks. During moments of high anxiety, he has been experiencing shortness of breath, rapid heart rate, and intense fear. At their first session, the helper identifies a core belief that seems to increase his anxiety, "I could lose control over myself and go crazy." During the next 3 weeks, the helper encourages Dujuan to examine and modify this core belief. The goal is to help him to focus on the evidence for and against this belief and to develop a more reasonable point of view. After a month, Dujuan is able to say, "Watching for danger actually increases my fear rather than reducing it. It is better to have a panic attack once a month than to spend every day worrying about it." Six months later Dujuan claims that he rarely finds himself falling into his old way of thinking. He feels that he has modified a core belief.

What Client Problems Are Helped Through New Learning?

A number of client problems are the result of inadequate training or lack of knowledge. In seminars and workshops, one can learn to cope with stress, learn alternatives to addictive behavior, and develop better interpersonal, marital communication, and parenting skills. Through new learning and by adopting new perspectives, clients can change their thinking about painful remembered events and rethink their sense of guilt and failure. They can see themselves and others in a new light, and they can discover that many situations that they have feared and avoided are not really harmful.

Resistance to New Learning

"The truth will set you free, but *first*, it will make you miserable." This saying from a humorous poster summarizes the experience of a person who is undergoing a significant change. Change brought about by new information may ultimately bring about enlightenment, but it can be extremely unsettling at first. Change is disquieting not only to the changing individual, but also to those in the client's sphere of influence. The story of Copernicus is a good example. He taught that the earth revolved around the sun and not the other way around. This upset the existing worldview so much that he was forced to recant, and his student Bruno was put to death 50 years later for spreading the news (Bernard & Young, 1996). On a much smaller scale, a helper tries to persuade a client to leave behind self-defeating ideas and teaches the client new skills and a way to construct a slightly different worldview. The result is that both the client and those close to the client experience discomfort and may actually try to resist or slow down change. For example, a social worker was seeing a client, a 65-year-old Italian woman whose husband had died a year ago. The client was lonely and depressed but refused to go to social functions in her retirement community because going unaccompanied to such an event was, in her view, undignified and a sign to the world that she was looking for a new partner. She had grown up in a strictly religious, Italian community where such behavior was frowned upon. No external force prevented her from enjoying the company and support of others, only her outdated ideas of propriety. The social worker's attempts to get this client to change her bahavior or think about this in a different way met stiff resistance bolstered by years of experience and cultural reinforcement. The flip side of the coin is that when clients can change their outmoded concepts and self-imprisoning ideas, enormous growth occurs. This chapter examines a few of the many tools helpers use to assist clients in seeing things in a different way and creating new visions of the future.

Common Methods Helpers Use to Provide New Learning Experiences for Clients

Interpretation

Interpretation is one of the oldest therapeutic techniques (Clark, 1995). Interpretation consists of encouraging the client to look at the problem in the context of the theoretical orientation of the practitioner. Once the helper explains the reason for the problem, a client develops insight and is then presumably better able to change. For example, from a psychodynamic perspective, a client's reaction to his boss may be a carryover from his lifelong issues with his own father. Once this reaction is interpreted, confronted, and clarified, the client may start to see the unconscious motives behind his actions. Insight may occur, ("aha!), or it may dawn gradually. Once insight occurs, that learning may be applied to other situations. In this example, the client may become aware of similar tendencies in his relationships with other authority figures. The psychodynamic technique of interpretation is an advanced method that cannot be grasped in a few paragraphs and must be learned in an extended training program.

Today interpretation is a controversial technique because it firmly places the helper in the role of expert; thus it is not entirely compatible with the current emphasis on collaboration and a focus on shifting the client's interpretive system rather than forcing him or her to accept the therapist's worldview.

Modeling as New Learning

Another way that we acquire new learning is by copying the behavior of others. Bandura (1971) is responsible for recognizing the potential power of modeling in the helping process. Modeling has been used extensively to help children learn prosocial behaviors, to assist developmentally delayed adults in skill development, to teach alcoholics methods of relapse prevention, to train helpers, to instruct parents, and to help clients deal with fearful situations (Perry & Furukawa, 1986).

In group therapy, it is common for members to copy the helper or other group members who are functioning more effectively. Clients learn to be more self-disclosing, assertive, and spontaneous by seeing examples of these behaviors and trying them in the safe environment of the group.

Modeling can take place in the helping arena, either as an intentional process or as an unexpected by-product. An example of the latter occurs when clients take on the mannerisms or copy the clothing of the helper. Intentional modeling is exemplified by a helper's use of role-playing a specific behavior while the client watches or by exposing clients to symbolic, biographical, or fictional models in books, tapes, and films (Milan, 1985). Through modeling, clients are able to see a successful performance of a skill. The client then attempts to reproduce the skill, getting feedback from the helper (Mitchell & Milan, 1983).

Stop and Reflect

Think about three of your favorite teachers. Write their names in the following chart and describe them as best you can in the space provided:

Name	Personal Trait You Most Admired	Subject Taught	Values Held by Teacher	Most Important Thing You Learned	How Did Teacher Influence You?

- As you look over your answers, how do you think the teacher influenced or changed you? Was it primarily through modeling, or was it through the subject matter that he or she taught?
- Look over the list of personal traits. Are these traits you have tried to develop in yourself?
- Which traits of your favorite teachers would you consider to be therapeutic? Why?

Using Metaphors and Stories

Metaphors, stories, parables, and tales are common means for stimulating new learning in clients (Barker, 1985; Gordon, 1978). For example, a helper once came up with this little aphorism for a client who was stewing about a situation over which he had no control: "You know, worry is like a rocking chair. It doesn't get you anywhere, but it's something to do." A thought like this can gently suggest that the client think about his or her behavior.

Metaphors and stories engage the listener with imagery, suspense, and humor. Consequently, the client is not fully aware that he or she is learning something. A story bypasses some of a client's resistance to new ideas; the client is too engaged to fight. This was true in the case of Judie, a 35-year-old woman living in New York City who had grown up on a farm.

> Judie had considered marriage to several different men while in her twenties. Each time she had ended the relationship when marriage seemed to be the next step. Judie was an only child and was close to her parents, whose marital relationship was quite poor. They had fought bitterly for years, and she believed that they had stayed together for her sake. She admitted that she saw love as "chains." Judie came for help because she had finally met a man whom she wanted to marry. She was filled with confusion and had changed the date of the wedding twice. In the first few counseling sessions, reflective listening uncovered her fears about marriage and relationships. She felt better about her decision to get married after these sessions, but one night (a week before the wedding), she telephoned the helper in a crisis of doubt about whether to go through with the ceremony. On the telephone, her helper told her the following story:

> When I was a boy, we lived on a farm, and we had a very healthy and strong mare. She was high spirited, but gentle. She also had one peculiarity. She hated it when we closed the gate of the corral. In fact, she would run around in circles, rearing up, sometimes even hurting herself on the wooden fence. One day, we discovered by accident that if we left the gate open, she calmed down. And she never ran away. She didn't mind being in the corral. She just wanted to make sure that she could leave at any time.

The helper credited this story as the turning point in Judie's treatment and in restoring her sense of control. Although no interpretation was made, she apparently grasped that she did not have to feel imprisoned by marriage, that she could retain a sense of freedom. The helper used the farm story because of his knowledge about Judie's background. He used the metaphor of the corral because she saw marriage as a form of prison. Through the image of the open gate, he was telling her that she could retain the option of leaving. Knowing that she had this option would help her stop worrying about being trapped and let her enjoy her marriage. The story seemed to be much more effective than giving advice because it allowed her to decide for herself how to act. Stories such as these sometimes work like magic to help a client reconsider the problem situation. Of course, there is danger in overuse and in telling stories that do not fit the client's worldview.

Exposure to Avoided Stimuli

There is a story about a woman who sees a man rubbing a rabbit's foot furiously and asks what he is doing. "I am keeping the tigers away," he replies.

"But there aren't any tigers around here," she argues.

"See," he says, "it's working."

Many clients come for help because of avoidance of social situations, fear of dogs, fear of airplanes, or a feeling of discomfort at being far from home. Like the man in the story, they are not willing to give up avoidance behaviors even when those behaviors are superstitious or ineffective. Because a client has learned to reduce anxiety by avoidance, he or she must be taught that the feared object or situation is not really harmful.

Exposure is the technique of helping clients to gradually face feared stimuli (Emmelkamp, 1982; Foa & Goldstein, 1978). Exposure is an important treatment for all sorts of fears and phobias. Helpers set up hierarchies of feared situations and, step-by-step, encourage clients to face more and more difficult scenarios. Clients learn important lessons from facing rather than avoiding. They learn that many of their fears are groundless and that their perception of how people will react to them may be erroneous. For example, many people fear that being more assertive will create worse relationships in their families. As they become more assertive, they learn that most of the feared consequences of assertiveness never occur and that their relationships actually improve.

Humor

We know that learning is facilitated in a light atmosphere (Gardner, 1971). Humor also offers a subtle way to shift a client's viewpoint (Ansbacher & Ansbacher, 1956; Mosak, 1987). Like a metaphor, a joke tells a story and sometimes contains a philosophical shift, interpretation, or message. One of the most common ways that helpers use humor to get clients to think about a situation in a different way is to use exaggeration. By exaggerating a client's situation, sometimes it helps to put it into perspective. Once, when a client was stewing about the fact that her divorce would become public, it was clear that she was making a mountain out of a molehill. The helper made the following comments, "Yes, undoubtedly this will make the front page with a big headline: 'Woman gets divorce—friends abandon her.' Perhaps it will make the television news." The client laughed and was able to recognize her tendency to catastrophize.

Linguistic Changes

Linguistic changes are helper suggestions that the client use different language in talking about the problem. Since language mirrors thought, what we say is a reflection of our worldview. Helpers often suggest that clients use new jargon or use specific words that promote the ideas that the client is responsible for his or her own life, thoughts, and feelings. For example, when a client says, "I can't seem to get to work on time," the helper challenges the client's lack of responsibility by suggesting that the client rephrase as follows: "I won't go to work on time." Helpers also challenge clients when they engage in black-and-white thinking by using such terms as *always* and *never.*

Direct Instruction

Direct instruction is one of the most often used methods in helping. Direct instruction involves lecturing, discussion groups, modeling, and the use of films and demonstrations to provide new information to clients. Psychoeducational seminars that utilize direct instruction are the stock-in-trade of parent education programs, stress reduction groups, anxiety management training, cognitive therapy for depression, marriage enrichment seminars, substance abuse education, and a myriad of other programs. Besides the educational material that is presented, clients benefit from the support of others who are experiencing the problem, and they learn vicariously from the experiences of fellow learners.

Direct instruction can just as easily take place in the helper's office. Marriage counseling may involve training in good communication skills, and helpers often assign books and other reading material to educate clients about specific topics such as stress, substance abuse, anxiety or depression, proper parenting procedures, and particular social skills that a client needs to acquire.

The Technique of Reframing

There was an advertisement for the Peace Corps that ran on television during the 1960s. It challenged viewers to determine whether they saw a glass as half empty or half full. This commercial points out that there are two ways of looking at a situation: in terms of its assets or in terms of its deficits. When a helper asks a client to see the problem situation in a new, more solvable or positive way, he or she is using the technique of *reframing*. An even better example of reframing comes from Mark Twain's story of Tom Sawyer, who convinces his friends that painting a fence is fun and a privilege, not work.

One other illustration, a more contemporary one, comes from the movie *Moonstruck*. The hero of the story is rejected by his fiancée when his hand is severed by a bread slicer. The hero had always blamed his brother for distracting him at the crucial moment when the accident occurred. The reframing takes place when his new girlfriend convinces him that the real reason for the accident was his unconscious wish to stay single. She elegantly uses the metaphor of a lone wolf and accuses the hero of gnawing off his own leg to avoid the trap of marriage. Helpers use reframes like this to help the client see the problem in a more constructive and responsible way. They move clients from blaming to taking responsibility, from the victim's role to the survivor's role, by gently urging them to look at the world through a different lens.

Stop and Reflect

The technique of reframing is based on the assumption that there are many different ways to understand a problem—there is not just one correct viewpoint. One easy way of understanding the idea of multiple viewpoints is a technique called *relabeling*. We use relabeling in career counseling to help clients recognize their personal strengths. Have you ever noticed it is easier to get people to identify their weaknesses than their positive qualities? In this exercise, clients make a list of their own undesirable traits and a list of some undesirable traits of someone else they know. Then they try to think of another descriptor that puts a positive spin on the very same trait.

Take a look at these examples that have been "spun" positive:

Negative Viewpoint	*Positive Viewpoint*
Compulsive	Organized
Sloppy	Casual, relaxed
Loud	Enthusiastic

Now make a list of your own negative traits and another list for someone you know. Relabel each trait in a more positive way as shown above. Then consider the following questions:

- Is reframing like this just putting a coat of paint on a negative trait, or does it really uncover something positive about the tendency?
- As you look over your own list, would you really want to lose this quality? What would you be giving up?
- Does your relabeling another person's traits help you to see that person differently?

Discuss some of these issues and your own reactions with your classmates.

How to Reframe

According to Watzlawick, Weakland, and Fisch (1974), reframing means coming up with a new, more constructive definition of the problem that fits the facts just as accurately as the old definition. To reframe a client's problem, the helper must appreciate the client's worldview and then replace it with an acceptable alternative. Reframing fails when helpers do not take the time to make sure that the new viewpoint is accurate and that it does not clash with the client's perspective. For these reasons, it is best to proceed as follows:

Step 1: Use the nonjudgmental listening cycle to fully understand the problem. The nonjudgmental listening cycle gives the helper a firm grasp of the details of the problem, including the people involved, their relationships, and the environment where the problem exists. Before reframing, it is especially helpful to reflect meaning to get a grasp of the client's worldview and values. In the following example, the helper summarizes a number of the feelings and meanings the client, Marlene, has expressed during the session.

Marlene: "So that's the story. I have to move whether I like it or not. It's like being fired and I have no control over it. Either I move or I am out of work. I've never lost a job before. Sometimes I think it's their way of telling me they want me to quit."

Helper: "From what I have heard so far, what bothers you the most is the lack of control over the decision. That makes you mad. But sometimes you see this situation as your failure and, at the same time, a personal rejection."

Step 2: Build a bridge from the client's viewpoint to a new way of looking at the problem. Develop a reframe that bridges the client's old view of the problem with a new viewpoint that stresses the positive aspects of the problem or presents it as solvable. The important point is to acknowledge some aspect of the client's viewpoint while, at the same time, suggesting another way of looking at it.

Helper: "I wonder if you could start thinking about this move in a different way? You have always wanted to travel. A few months ago, you were even considering a new job or moving to another state. Although you feel uneasy about this because you don't like it when the decision is made for you, I wonder if this may not be a blessing in disguise. How might this job actually give you a little more freedom?"

Step 3: Reinforcing the bridge. A shift in perspective is often something that develops slowly. One way of sustaining the shift is to assign homework that forces the client to see the problem in a new light. Marlene, for example, might be given a homework assignment to do more research on the positive aspects of the move.

Problems and Precautions of Reframing

Reframing is most likely to be successful if the client is able to relate the significant aspects of the new frame of reference to corresponding features in the old frame of reference. For example, an algebra teacher used to try to reframe her examinations as "sharing experiences." The analogy was not successful, and everyone groaned because "sharing" is not a graded activity (an important feature). Unfortunately, it may be impossible to identify all aspects of a problem that might be important to the client; however, every effort should be made to imagine those that could be crucial. In a metaphor or story told by the helper, the basic elements of the tale must conform to the client's situation, or else the reframe may be rejected.

Poorly timed reframing can sometimes be worse than none at all. One example that comes to mind concerns the reframes often extended to persons grieving over the death of a family member. Well-meaning friends are apt to say such things as, "It is God's will," or, "She's gone to a better place." Because a person is dealing with strong emotions, these kindly offered phrases are perceived as platitudes. Later, such words may be comforting when emotions have subsided and the person tries to place the experience into perspective.

Summary

In this chapter, we looked at three curative factors in the REPLAN Model: lowering and raising emotional arousal (L); activating client expectations, hope, and motivation (A); and providing new learning experiences (N). In so doing, we looked at the rationale for addressing each of these factors and examined the techniques of relaxation, encouragement, and reframing. Some time was spent on the issue of understanding and enhancing client motivation. The primary technique that we examined was Prochaska and DiClemente's model of stages of change. By identifying the client's readiness for treatment, we can select the best methods that correspond with the level of motivation.

We also discussed in less detail the methods of meditation and ways to stimulate emotional expression. Finally, we touched on interpretation, modeling, use of metaphors and stories, exposure to avoided stimuli, humor, linguistic changes, and direct instruction as ways of providing new learning experiences.

As we bring this book to a close, it is apparent that we have only scratched the surface and that there are many more techniques to be learned on the journey. You will encounter many books, articles, and conferences where some system or technique will be touted as the previously undiscovered panacea. I believe that recognizing the uniqueness of individuals implies that there will never be a perfect technique or a perfect theory. Instead I encourage you to rely on the therapeutic relationship as your fundamental technique and to make your choice of tools based on what is respectful and what is likely to be effective for your client.

Exercises

Group Exercise 1: Relaxation Training

For this exercise, the training group divides into dyads. Each person has a turn as either client or helper. Each dyad finds as quiet a spot as possible to practice the training. The helper takes the client through an abbreviated version of deep muscle relaxation given in Table 15.1. In this shorter variant, steps 2 and 5 are eliminated and the helper reads the instructions for steps 1, 3, 4, 6, and 7 only. For time considerations, each muscle group is to be tightened and relaxed only once rather than twice, as one would do in normal practice.

Following the relaxation sequence, take 5 minutes to discuss the effectiveness of the procedure. The client should answer the following questions:

- Using a 100-point scale (0, most relaxed you've ever been; 100, very tense), how deeply were you able to relax in this exercise?
- Were the helper's instructions presented in a calm and methodical way?
- Did the helper allow sufficient time for relaxation before proceeding to a new muscle group?

- What might the helper have done to deepen your relaxation?

After this feedback, client and helper switch roles and repeat the exercise.

Quick Tips: Relaxation Training

- Ask the client to move around slightly and find the most comfortable seating position before you begin the relaxation instructions.
- Keep your voice tone modulated and soothing.
- Watch the client for signs of tension or discomfort. When the procedure is complete, do a body scan by returning to those areas where the client has difficulty relaxing, and ask the client to tense and relax those areas again.
- Make sure that you suggest deep diaphragmatic breathing as a transition between tensing and relaxing muscle groups.

Group Exercise 2: Practicing Encouragement

Below are a number of client responses that suggest pessimism and discouragement. Review the list of encouraging responses and make a statement that reflects feelings or meanings. Then write down one or more encouraging responses that (1) focus on the positive and the changeable, (2) communicate equality in the helping relationship and respect the individuality of the client, or (3) push or confront the client, adding energy and enthusiasm for the goal.

Example

Client: "Our marriage is on the rocks. We just can't talk anymore. Anytime I try, she just starts an argument. I need some freedom to be alone once in a while, to work in my shop or on the computer, to read, or to go over to Jeff's house and watch the game. It wasn't like this when we were living together, but now she thinks she owns my time. Before, she would have her interests, I would have mine, and then we would spend some time together. I wish she had some hobbies or something. It's just too much pressure."

Helper, reflecting: "You feel trapped, and you don't know how to improve the situation."

Helper, encouraging (focusing on the positive and the changeable): "You say that you used to manage this issue pretty well before you were married. You were able to balance alone time and together time. It sounds like you two have the ability to communicate well at times. Is that something you might be able to do again?"

Now give both a reflecting and an encouraging response to the following client statements:

a. "I don't like talking about myself very much. For one thing, how will it really help? You just throw things out. That doesn't change them, and, besides, I was taught never to air dirty laundry in public."

b. "My wife feels I have problems with drinking. But I don't. She says she's at the end of her rope and is going to leave me unless I get help. I'm working every day. I bring home my paycheck. Lots of people drink more than I do."

c. "I've tried everything to quit smoking in the past. Why, 2 years ago, I went to hypnosis. Once when I was younger, I went to a seminar. Somebody said I should try nicotine gum or patches. But I've tried before. I know it's bad for my health and the kids are always nagging me, but some people just can't quit."

d. "I'm in a dead-end job. I know I should look for a new job. But maybe I'm too old to go back to school, learn a whole new way of doing things. When I see these young people on computers, they already know so much. Could I really keep up?"

In a small group, discuss your answers to these exercises. Note that these helping responses are designed to increase the client's sense of optimism and hope, not to solve the client's problem for him or her. Evaluate both your reflecting and your encouraging responses. When looking at your encouraging responses, think about whether the client might perceive these as patronizing, or not genuine, or whether the client might get the impression that you are ignoring the seriousness of the problem.

Group Exercise 3

Reframing with a Reflecting Team

A recent innovation in family therapy is the reflecting team. A family therapist meets with a family and gets their perspective on the problem facing them. Midway through the session, the therapist stops and consults with a group of observers who have been watching through a one-way mirror or on a monitor. The observers suggest alternative ways of looking at the family's problem. The therapist then returns to the family and presents a reframe of their problem based on the suggestions he or she has heard.

In the following exercise, a small group of learners form a reflecting team as a way to practice reframing. Form groups of six or eight students. One person is designated as the helper, one acts as the client, and the remaining members form the team.

Step 1: The client discusses a real or role-play situation with the helper, who uses the nonjudgmental listening cycle to understand the problem as completely as possible in the 5 to 10 minutes allotted for this activity.

Step 2: Once the helper feels that he or she has a good grasp of the client's viewpoint and has summarized the client's situation, the client is asked to move out of earshot or leave the room for approximately 5 minutes. During this time, the team conducts a group discussion about alternative ways in which the client's problem might be viewed. The team is encouraged to identify viewpoints that are consistent with the client's worldview and values, but that are more positive and change-oriented than the client's current way of looking at the problem.

Step 3: The helper brings the client back into the presence of the reflecting team and delivers a reframe to the client. The helper chooses the best reframe for the client based on his or her own thinking and the thoughts of the reflecting team. The client is encouraged to respond to the reframe. When this has been completed, the role play is over.

Step 4: The client gives written feedback regarding the reframe that was presented by the helper and team using a 5-point scale, as shown in the Feedback Checklist.

Feedback Checklist: Reframing

Client Name: _____ Helper Name: _____

1. Disagree
2. Slightly disagree
3. Neutral
4. Agree
5. Strongly agree

_____ 1. The helper understood my problem completely.

_____ 2. The reframe was a more positive viewpoint than the original statement of the problem.

_____ 3. The reframe was a more constructive way of looking at the problem.

_____ 4. The reframe fit with my own personal outlook and values.

The exercise continues in order to allow several team members to have the opportunity to play the role of helper as time allows.

Homework

Homework 1: Collage as a Stimulus for Emotional Expression

Make two separate collages using photos, drawings, and words from newspapers, magazines, and other print media. The first collage should represent a time in your life when you were experiencing troubling or conflicting emotions. Prepare a second collage that represents your feelings and experiences during one of the best times of your life. Identify these feelings in writing beneath each picture. As you look back at each period of your life, does it reawaken any of these feelings in you? Which of these periods do you think about the most in your daily life? How might a collage such as this be useful for a client who is trying to deal with conflicting emotions from the past? Collages have been successfully used with adolescent clients. How would you develop a conversation with adolescent clients. How would you develop a conversation with an adolescent client using the college as a stimulus?

Homework 2: Relaxation Techniques

The skill of relaxation requires the therapeutic factor of practice to make it a part of one's life. Find a way of building relaxation practice into your daily routine. Consider the following suggestions and then implement one in your own life. Report on your attempts in a paragraph or two.

- Every time you stop at a traffic light, do deep diaphragmatic breathing to lower your tension.

- Use small colored dots, available in office supply stores, to remind you to do a body scan. Place these dots on your computer screen, watch, or appointment book. Whenever you see one, tense and relax those muscles that seem the most tense.

- Before going to sleep each night, do a complete body scan and note the areas where the most tension resides. Keep a diary for a week and see if the same areas tend to hold much of your tension.

- Meditate for 10 to 15 minutes each morning. What effects does it have on your level of tension and your mental attitude?

Homework 3: Reframing a Problem Situation

Think of a problem situation in your own life. Suppose that you decided that drastic action on your part was unreasonable and you only wanted to change your outlook or attitude about it. When you have settled on a particular problem, answer the following questions:

- What are the things about the situation that make you feel uncomfortable?

- What other things about the situation are positive (not just bearable)?

- What keeps you focused on the negative aspects of the problem?

- Can you see this situation as an opportunity rather than as a problem?

- What points would you need to focus on to keep your view of the situation positive?

- When would it not be a good idea to encourage a client to change his or her perspective on a problem?

Journal Starters

1. Motivation is a knotty issue in helping. There are important ethical issues concerning treating clients who are unwilling or unmotivated to change. How would you feel about having a client who was forced to come to counseling but was unmotivated? What do you think about the whole issue of requiring counseling? Should children be forced to receive help by schools or by their parents?
2. Reread one of your journal entries from the beginning and another from the middle of training. What do you notice about your development? Look again at Perry's stages

in Chapter 1. They are dualistic, multiplistic, and relativistic. Have you noticed any changes in your thinking during training? Review Table 1.1, which shows the levels of expertise, beginning with naivette and ending with master. Where do you place yourself on this chart? What training experiences will help you develop to the next level?

For more journal ideas, as well as more practice with providing new learning experiences and evaluating the effectiveness of helping, see Chapter 15 in *Exercises in the Art of Helping*.

References

Adler, A. (1954). *Understanding human nature*. New York: Fawcett Premier.

Ansbacher, H. L., & Ansbacher, R. R. (Eds.). (1956). *The individual psychology of Alfred Adler*. New York: Basic Books.

Bandura, A. (1971). Psychotherapy based on modeling principles. In A. E. Bergin & S. L. Garfield (Eds.), *Handbook of psychotherapy and behavior*

change: An empirical analysis (pp. 653–708). New York: Wiley.

Barker, P. (1985). *Using metaphors in psychotherapy*. New York: Brunner/Mazel.

Bemak, F., & Young, M. E. (1998). Catharsis in group psychotherapy. *International Journal of Action Methods, 50,* 166–184.

Benson, H. (1984). *Beyond the relaxation response.* New York: Berkley.

Bernard, T., & Young, J. M. (1996). *The ecology of hope.* Easthaven, CT: New Society Press.

Bogart, G. (1991). The use of meditation in psychotherapy: A review of the literature. *American Journal of Psychotherapy, 45*, 383–412.

Breuer, J., & Freud, S. (1895/1955). *Studies on hysteria.* In J. Strachey (Ed.), *The complete works of Sigmund Freud*, Standard Edition (Vol. 2). London: Hogarth.

Brooks, J. S., & Scarano, T. (1985). Transcendental meditation in the treatment of post-Vietnam adjustment. *Journal of Counseling & Development, 64*, 212–215.

Carrington, P. (1998). *The book of meditation: The complete guide to modern meditation.* Boston: Element Books.

Chandler, C. K., Holden, J. M., & Kolander, C. A. (1992). Counseling for spiritual wellness: Theory and practice. *Journal of Counseling & Development, 71*, 168–175.

Clark, A. J. (1995). An examination of the technique of interpretation in counseling. *Journal of Counseling and Development, 73*, 483–490.

de Shazer, S. (1988). *Clues: Investigating solutions in brief therapy.* New York: Norton.

de Shazer, S. (1989, October). Brief therapy. Symposium conducted at Stetson University, Deland, FL.

Dinkmeyer, D., & Losoncy, L. E. (1980). *The encouragement book.* Upper Saddle River, NJ: Prentice Hall.

Dinkmeyer, D., Sr., & Losoncy, L. E. (1995). *The skills of encouragement: Bringing out the best in yourself and others.* Boca Raton, FL: St. Lucie Press.

Elliott, R. (1985). Helpful and nonhelpful events in brief counseling interviews: An empirical taxonomy. *Journal of Counseling Psychology, 32*, 307–322.

Emmelkamp, P. M. G. (1982). Exposure in vivo treatments. In A. Goldstein & D. Chambless (Eds.), *Agoraphobia: Multiple perspectives on theory and treatment.* New York: Wiley.

Fair, P. L. (1989). Biofeedback-assisted relaxation strategies in psychotherapy. In J. V. Basmajian (Ed.), *Biofeedback: Principles and practice for clinicians* (3rd ed., pp. 187–196). Baltimore: Williams & Wilkins.

Farelly, F., & Brandsma, J. (1974). *Provocative therapy.* Cupertino, CA: Meta Publications.

Foa, E. B., & Goldstein, A. (1978). Continuous exposure and complete response prevention in the treatment of obsessive compulsive neurosis. *Behavior Therapy, 9*, 821–829.

Frank, J. D., & Frank, J. B. (1991). *Persuasion and healing.* Baltimore: Johns Hopkins University Press.

Frank, J. D., Nash, E. H., Stone, A. R., & Imber, S. D. (1963). Immediate and long-term symptomatic course of psychiatric outpatients. *American Journal of Psychiatry, 120*, 429–439.

Gardner, R. A. (1971). *Therapeutic communication with children: Mutual story-telling technique.* New York: Science House.

Gatchel, R. J., & Baum, A. (1983). *An introduction to health psychology.* Reading, MA: Addison-Wesley.

Gendlin, E. T. (1969). Focusing. *Psychotherapy: Theory, Research and Practice, 6*, 4–15.

Gendlin, E. T. (1978). *Focusing.* New York: Everest House.

Gilliland, B. E., James, R. K., & Bowman, J. T. (1989). *Theories and strategies in counseling and psychotherapy.* Upper Saddle River, NJ: Prentice Hall.

Gladding, S. T. (1998). *Counseling as an art: The creative arts in counseling* (2nd ed.). Alexandria, VA: American Counseling Association.

Goleman, D. (1995). *Emotional intelligence: Why it can matter more than IQ.* New York: Bantam.

Gordon, D. (1978). *Therapeutic metaphors.* Cupertino, CA: Meta Publications.

Hazaleus, S. L., & Deffenbacher, J. L. (1986). Relaxation and cognitive treatments of anger. *Journal of Consulting and Clinical Psychology, 54*, 222–226.

Hitz, R., & Driscoll, A. (1988). Praise or encouragement? New insights into praise: Implications for early childhood teachers. *Individual Psychology: Journal of Adlerian Theory, Research and Practice, 43*, 138–141.

Jackins, H. (1962). *Elementary counselor's manual.* Seattle: Rational Island.

Jacobson, E. (1938). *Progressive relaxation.* Chicago: University of Chicago Press.

Janov, A. (1970). *The primal scream.* New York: Dell.

Kabat-Zinn, J., Massion, A. O., Kristeller, J., Peterson, L., Fletcher, K. E., Pbert, L., Lenderking, W. R., &

Santorelli, S. F. (1992). Effectiveness of a meditation-based stress reduction program in the treatment of anxiety disorders. *American Journal of Psychiatry, 149*, 936–943.

Losoncy, L. E. (1977). *Turning people on: How to be an encouraging person.* Upper Saddle River, NJ: Prentice Hall.

Lowen, A. (1967). *The betrayal of the body.* New York: Collier.

Marlatt, G. A. (1988). Matching clients to treatment: Treatment models and stages of change. In D. M. Donovan & G. A. Marlatt (Eds.), *Assessment of addictive behaviors* (pp. 474–483). New York: Guilford.

Martin, J., & Stelmaczonek, K. (1988). Participants' identification and recall of important events in counseling. *Journal of Counseling Psychology, 35*, 385–390.

Menninger, K. (1958). *Theory of psychoanalytic technique.* New York: Harper & Row.

Milan, M. (1985). Symbolic modeling. In M. Hersen & A. S. Bellack (Eds.), *Dictionary of behavior therapy techniques* (pp. 212–215). New York: Pergamon.

Mitchell, Z. P., & Milan, M. (1983). Imitation of high-interest comic strip models' appropriate classroom behavior: Acquisition and generalization. *Child and Family Behavior Therapy, 5*, 25–30.

Moreno, J. L. (1958). *Psychodrama* (Vol. 2). New York: Beacon House.

Mosak, H. H. (1987). *Ha ha and aha.* Muncie, IN: Accelerated Development.

Nichols, M. P., & Efran, J. S. (1985). Catharsis in psychotherapy: A new perspective. *Psychotherapy, 22*, 46–58.

Nichols, M. P., & Zax, M. (1977). *Catharsis in psychotherapy.* New York: Gardener Press.

Novaco, R. W. (1977). Stress inoculation: A cognitive therapy for anger and its application to a case of depression. *Journal of Consulting and Clinical Psychology, 45*, 600–608.

Novaco, R. W. (1983). Stress inoculation therapy for anger control. In P. A. Keeler & L. G. Rift (Eds.), *Innovations in clinical practice: A source book* (Vol. 2, pp. 181–201). Sarasota, FL: Professional Resource Exchange.

Overholser, J. C. (1991). The use of guided imagery in psychotherapy: Modules for use with passive relaxation training. *Journal of Contemporary Psychotherapy, 21*, 159–172.

Patterson, C. H. (1973). *Theories of counseling and psychotherapy* (2nd ed.). New York: Harper & Row.

Perls, F. S. (1977). *The Gestalt approach: An eye witness to therapy.* Palo Alto, CA: Science and Behavior Books.

Perry, M. A., & Furukawa, M. J. (1986). Modeling methods. In F. H. Kanfer & A. P. Goldstein (Eds.), *Helping people change* (pp. 66–110). New York: Pergamon.

Pitsounis, N. D., & Dixon, P. N. (1988). Encouragement versus praise: Improving productivity of the mentally retarded. *Individual Psychology: Journal of Adlerian Theory, Research and Practice, 44*, 507–512.

Polster, E., & Polster, M. (1973). *Gestalt therapy integrated.* New York: Brunner/Mazel.

Prochaska, J. O., & DiClemente, C. C. (1983). Stages and processes of self-change in smoking: Toward an integrative model of change. *Journal of Consulting and Clinical Psychology, 51*, 390–395.

Prochaska, J. O., & DiClemente, C. C. (1986). The transtheoretical approach. In J. C. Norcross (Ed.), *Handbook of eclectic psychotherapy* (pp. 163–200). New York: Brunner/Mazel.

Prochaska, J. O., & Norcross, J. C. (2003). *Systems of psychotherapy* (5th ed.). Pacific Grove, CA: Brooks/Cole.

Prochaska, J. O., Norcross, J. C., & DiClemente, C. C. (1994). *Changing for good.* New York: William Morrow.

Seligman, M. E. P. (1975). *Helplessness.* San Francisco: Freeman.

Seligman, M. E. P. (1998). *Learned optimism.* New York: Simon & Schuster.

Shafii, M. (1974). Meditation and marijuana. *American Journal of Psychiatry, 131*, 60–63.

Shafii, M. (1975). Meditation and the prevention of alcohol abuse. *American Journal of Psychiatry, 132*, 942–945.

Shapiro, D. H. (1994). Examining the content and context of meditation: A challenge for psychology in the areas of stress management, psychotherapy and religion/values. *Journal of Humanistic Psychology, 34*, 101–135.

Shapiro, D., & Walsh, R. (Eds.). (1984). *Meditation: Classic and contemporary perspectives.* New York: Aldine.

Siegel, B. S. (1986). *Love, medicine and miracles.* New York: Harper & Row.

Simonton, O. C., & Mathews-Simonton, S. (1978). *Getting well again*. Los Angeles: Tarcher.

Singh, R. (2003a). *Empowering your soul through meditation*. London: HarperCollins

Singh, R. (2003b). *Inner and outer peace through meditation*. London: HarperCollins.

Smith, J. C. (1975). Meditation as psychotherapy: A review of the literature. *Psychological Bulletin, 82*, 558–564.

Stampfl, T. G., & Levis, D. J. (1967). Essentials of implosive therapy: A learning-theory-based psychodynamic behavioral therapy. *Journal of Abnormal Psychology, 72*, 496–503.

Sweeney, T. J. (1998). *Adlerian counseling* (4th ed.). Muncie, IN: Accelerated Development.

Tavris, C. (1989). *Anger: The misunderstood emotion*. New York: Touchstone.

Tubesing, D. (1981). *Kicking your stress habits*. Duluth, MN: Whole Person Press.

Watzlawick, P., Weakland, J., & Fisch, R. (1974). *Change: Principles of problem formation and problem resolution*. New York: Norton.

Witmer, J. M. (1985). *Pathways to personal growth*. Muncie, IN: Accelerated Development.

Witmer, J. M., & Young, M. E. (1985). The silent partner: Uses of imagery in counseling. *Journal of Counseling and Development, 64*, 187–189.

Witmer, J. M., & Young, M. E. (1987). Imagery in counseling. *Elementary School Guidance and Counseling, 22*, 5–16.

Wolberg, L. B. (1977). *The technique of psychotherapy*. New York: Grune & Stratton.

Wolpe, J. (1958). *Psychotherapy by reciprocal inhibition*. Stanford, CA: Stanford University Press.

Yalom, I. R. (1995). *Theory and practice of group psychotherapy* (4th ed.). New York: Basic Books.

Young, M. E., & Bemak, F. (1996). Emotional arousal and expression in mental health counseling. *Journal of Mental Health Counseling, 18*, 316–332.

Young, M. E., & Feiler, F. (1993). Trends in counseling: A national survey. *Guidance and Counselling, 9*, 4–11.

Index